D1566497

The Collapse of the German War Economy, 1944–1945

Jeder Wagen mehr –

EIN PANZER MEHR

gegen den Feind!

D R

Helft mit! Spart Wagenraum!

Räder müssen rollen für den Sieg!

"Wheels Must Roll for Victory!" (*Völkischer Beobachter*, 1 July 1942)

The

Collapse of

the German

War Economy,

1944–1945

Allied Air Power and the

German National Railway

Alfred C. Mierzejewski

The University of North Carolina Press

Chapel Hill & London

©1988 The University of North Carolina Press
All rights reserved
Manufactured in the United States of America

The paper in this book meets the guidelines
for permanence and durability of the Committee on
Production Guidelines for Book Longevity
of the Council on Library Resources.

95 94 93   5 4 3 2

Library of Congress Cataloging-in-Publication Data

Mierzejewski, Alfred C.
    The collapse of the German war economy, 1944–1945: Allied air
power and the German national railway / by Alfred C. Mierzejewski.
        p. cm.
    Bibliography: p.
    Includes index.
    ISBN 0-8078-1792-9 (alk. paper)
    1. Germany—Economic conditions—1918–1945. 2. Bombing, Aerial—
Germany—History. 3. Transportation—Germany—History—20th
century. 4: Deutsche Reichsbahn (Germany)—History—20th century.
5. Railroad and state—Germany—History—20th century. 6. Germany—
Strategic aspects. I. Title.
HC286.4.M45   1988   88-4777
330.943'087—dc19   CIP

Contents

Tables

Figures and Maps

Figures

Maps

Preface

The following work is an account of the collapse of the German economy in 1944–1945. It examines how the intricate economic system created by the Germans after the mid-nineteenth century and refined for war purposes by Albert Speer crumbled due to the paralysis of its transportation system. The German transportation net and especially the German National Railway, the Deutsche Reichsbahn, was subjected to a violent bombing campaign by the American and British strategic air forces beginning in September 1944. Within four months the exchange of vital commodities in the Reich economy, especially coal, had broken down and every form of industrial production was in decline or had ground to a halt. How this happened, and how the Allies came to conduct this devastating campaign is portrayed in detail.

Until recently the economic history of the Third Reich has been comparatively neglected. Among the works that have appeared during the last few years none has focused on the operation of the German economy during World War II.[1] Moreover, only one study deals with the Deutsche Reichsbahn.[2] At the same time, there is a dearth of serious works that examine the impact of strategic bombing on the Nazi economy. Most focus on the struggle for air supremacy which was only a preliminary to the actual offensive. No attempt will be made to list the superfluity of works on the subject.[3] The ultimate purpose of the strategic bombing offensive was to weaken or destroy Germany's war machine: its administrative apparatus, its industry, and its military forces. Only a few studies have examined this aspect of the air war though none recently and none using the full range of German, American, and British archival sources. Most notable are the British and American official histories and the reports of the United States Strategic Bombing Survey.[4] A few other works have examined the fate of certain industries under the bombing.[5] To help fill this gap, new documentary sources obtained in German, American, and British archives are used in this book, combined with a fresh perspective from one who has no institutional ties past or present to any of the actors. Considerable detail relating to developments throughout the Reich economy and to policy decisions on both sides has been included because it is indispensable to untangling the confusion and misconceptions that arose at the time and have persisted to the present concerning the nature of the German war effort and how the disruption of its transportation sector by bombing contributed to its collapse.[6] A chronological account is given because no thematic rendering can fully portray the sequence of events and the chaos that swept Germany beginning in September 1944 and the interaction between the leaders of the German economy and their assailants. It is hoped that an anatomy of the collapse of a highly developed industrial economy is the result. This may illuminate how complex organizations, in this case the Deutsche Reichsbahn and the Speer ministry, attempted to cope with massive external challenges. It should also provide a warning to those who, even in this nuclear age, lightly contemplate future conventional air offensives.

Three analytical themes shape the present work. Because of their importance and the novelty of their application they bear elucidation at the outset.

The first crucial consideration holds that the German industrial economy had been shaped decades before the Nazi seizure of power by a geographical and functional division of labor based on proximity to and exploitation of the nation's coal supplies. A large and highly ramified transportation system enabled the division of labor to function effectively, permitting coal to flow to consumers far removed from the mines and manufactured goods and food to be exchanged among economic regions. The transportation system itself relied on coal for energy, and the prime mover of coal was the system's largest component, the national railroad, the Deutsche Reichsbahn. The Reichsbahn was an extensive network that connected the raw material base of the German industrial pyramid to the administrative pinnacle, the military consumer of armaments, and every intermediary level. The marshalling yard was its heart. Here the division of labor found physical expression. Here the Reichsbahn gathered its strength. Here movement on the entire rail net was controlled. But the marshalling yard was also its Achilles heel. These yards were vulnerable to a host of forms of delay and disruption, which would rapidly reverberate throughout the railroad and the economy if unchecked. Moreover, a few marshalling yards closely associated with the division of labor set the pace for the entire mechanism. They were of overriding importance and the

Reichsbahn made extensive provision to shield them from the vicissitudes of war.

The second leading idea is that working within the constraints set by the division of labor and Nazi economic ideas, Albert Speer imposed a system of industrial efficiency that enabled Germany vastly to increase its armaments production after February 1942. The ideological and political obstacles confronting Speer were more complex than has frequently been recognized. They did not consist of a set of coherent plans characterized as "Blitzkrieg economics," as has recently been made clear.[7] The Nazis did indeed divert a considerable proportion of national resources to rearmament. But two crucial factors prevented them from reaping the full return on their investment. First, their efforts were hamstrung by their own gross inefficiency born of haste and internally contradictory ideological imperatives. Secondly, their buildup did not correspond with the foreseeable ultimate proportions of the war that they hoped to ignite. There can be no doubt that the Nazis sought to adapt then current ideas of mechanized warfare to the Moltkean strategic tradition of quick victory. They hoped to avoid another prolonged attritional contest similar to World War I. They sought short though not necessarily small wars. This is an important consideration when weighing Nazi economic mobilization and the Reichsbahn's place in it. The scale of measurement must be the effort made by Germany during World War I, not current standards. Speer and his cohorts in his ministry and the Reichsbahn worked in that intellectual environment, not our late twentieth-century one. He articulated a response that was uniquely suited to it. The keys to Speer's reforms were the improvement of production practices through his revitalization of the network of rings and committees, his careful effort to obtain and preserve the explicit support of Hitler for his policies, and his creation of a centralized apparatus for the establishment of priorities and the evaluation of economic data that allowed him to orchestrate the whole as a system. Speer's edifice was very carefully balanced and its emphasis on the highest efficiency placed a great burden on the Reichsbahn.

Finally, constantly operating unseen, and in the end explicitly called upon by Speer to help Germany overcome the transportation crisis of 1944, was the phenomenon of elasticity of supply. Briefly explained, under normal circumstances the production of any good involves the use of a certain amount of materials. If the supply of materials is reduced or halted, production can continue at or near normal levels by using stocks, and by making emergency savings in their use on the factory floor. The length of time during which elasticity can be invoked varies among industries. But when it is exhausted, the resultant fall in production exceeds that which would have come about if output had been reduced immediately, commensurate with the decline in available resources. The critical realization from this is that the denial of materials through the disruption of transportation cannot result in an immediate, comparable drop in production. Instead the fall in output is delayed, necessitating a more prolonged interruption of transport. However if transportation disruption can be maintained long enough it promises rich dividends. This raises a subsidiary consideration—the time element. It appeared in the strategic bombing offensive in 1944 in two ways. It constituted a race between, on the one hand, the bomber's ability to destroy transportation facilities and thus to continue the disruption of traffic, and on the other, the Reichsbahn's ability to repair them. In the second instance, it pitted German doggedness and inventiveness in exploiting elasticity against Allied intelligence's perception of the state of German industry and the bomber commanders' persistence in striking marshalling yards. Both sides set these considerations against their estimates of the general war situation. The Germans hoped to prolong the war, the Allies to end it as soon as possible.

The combination of these considerations results in a study that focuses on the decisive components of the German economy and the most important activities of the transportation system. It ignores functionally marginal forms of production and low-volume traffic because they did not exert a decisive influence on war production. One of these was the transport of Jews to their deaths.[8]

No work of this nature can be completed without extensive help. I have benefited throughout from the advice and unstinting support of Dr. Gerhard L. Weinberg and Dr. Samuel R. Williamson. The criticisms of Dr. Josef Anderle, Dr. Michael H. Hunt, Dr. James R. Leutze, and Dr. George V. Taylor were also of inestimable value. The comments of Lord Zuckerman were most enlightening. Without the financial assistance of the Office of Air Force History, the Air Force Historical Foundation, the German Academic Exchange Service, and the Smith Fund I could not have performed the research that is the basis of the work. Archivists are the crucial intermediaries between historians and the documents that are the substance of their accounts. For their assistance in this regard I am indebted to Mr. John E. Taylor and Ms. Teresa E. Hammett of the Modern Military Headquarters Branch of the National Archives in Washington, D.C. Work at the Office of Air Force History was made easy by Lt. Col. Elliott Converse III and Msgt. Jernigan. Mrs. Judy E. Endicott of the USAF Historical Research Center at Maxwell Air Force Base assisted mc in obtaining microfilms of Allied intelligence documents. No researcher using the Reichsbahn's and the Speer ministry's records at the Bundesarchiv in Koblenz can fail to be impressed by the sunny countenance and constant readiness to help of Frau Meiburg. To her and her colleagues go my most sincere thanks. I am also indebted to the very competent staff of the Bundesarchiv-Militärarchiv at Freiburg-im-Breisgau. Frau Renate Rimbach and her assistants at BEWAG were most cordial and generous of their time during my stay in Berlin. Frau Dr. Evelyn Kroker and her efficient team at the Deutsches Bergbau-Archiv in Bochum operate a model private archive where I was accorded every form of assistance. I also profited greatly from the enthusiasm and help of Herr Jürgen Weise and his colleagues at the Rheinisch-Westfälisches Wirtschaftsarchiv zu Köln in Cologne. To the staff of the Public Record Office, Kew, go my thanks for their help. I am also grateful for the provision of literature by the Gesamtverband des deutschen Steinkohlenbergbaus. My thanks go to all of those in municipal and company archives in Germany who answered my queries for material. I would also like to express my gratitude to Mrs. Carolyn Ocell and Dr. Richard J. Kopec of the Geography Department of the University of North Carolina at Chapel Hill who are responsible for the maps. Finally I would like to thank those who typed the various permutations of this study during its years of gestation. They include Ms. Gail Urbanek, Ms. Kathy Woods, Ms. Shelly Ackerman, and Mr. Paul Sherer. My special thanks go to Mrs. Sarah Sherer. Her wizardry with the word processor and intervention at a crucial moment are beyond all praise. I would like to thank Nancy Brown Brewer for her help. The errors that remain are the sole responsibility of the author.

Abbreviations

The following abbreviations are used in the text. For abbreviations used in the notes, see pages 199–200.

A-2	Intelligence Section on USAAF staffs
ACIU	Allied Central Interpretation Unit
AEAF	Allied Expeditionary Air Force
AWPD	Air War Plans Division
Basa	Bahnselbstanschlussanlage (railway automatic communications equipment)
BBC	Brown, Boveri et Cie.
BEWAG	Berliner Kraft- und Licht (Berlin Power and Light)
Bf	Bahnhof (railway station)
BVL	Bezirksverkehrsleitung (Regional Traffic Office)
Bw	Bahnbetriebswerk (Operating Works)
CCS	Combined Chiefs of Staff
COA	Committee of Operations Analysts
CSTC	Combined Strategic Targets Committee
DEK	Dortmund-Ems-Kanal
DR	Deutsche Reichsbahn (German National Railway)
DRB	Deutsche Reichsbahn (German National Railway)
EOU	Enemy Objectives Unit
Ganzzug	Unit train
GBAG	Gelsenkirchener Bergwerks AG (Gelsenkirchen Mining Company)

GBL	Generalbetriebsleitung (General Operating Office)
GVL	Generalverkehrsleitung (General Transportation Office)
G-Wagen	Gedeckter Güterwagen (box car)
Hwa	Hauptwagenamt (Main Car Office)
IS	Instandsetzungsdienst des Sicherheits- und Hilfsdienstes (Repair Service of the Security and Emergency Service)
JIC	Joint Intelligence Sub-Committee
KWJ	Kohlenwirtschaftsjahr (coal economy year; heating year, April to March)
LWA	Landeswirtschaftsamt (State Economics Office of the RWM)
MAAF	Mediterranean Allied Air Force
MEW	Ministry of Economic Warfare
MLK	Mittelland-Kanal
NSDAP	Nationalsozialistische Deutsche Arbeiterpartei (National Socialist German Workers' Party)
OKL	Oberkommando der Luftwaffe (High Command of the Air Force)
OKW	Oberkommando der Wehrmacht (Armed Forces High Command)
OSS	Oberschlesiches Steinkohlensyndikat (Upper Silesian Hard Coal Syndicate)
OSS	Office of Strategic Services
OT	Organisation Todt
O-Wagen	Offener Güterwagen (open freight car)
Ozl	Oberzugleitung (Train Operating Headquarters)
R&A	Research and Analysis Branch of Office of Strategic Services

RAW	Reichsbahn Ausbesserungswerk (Reichsbahn Repair Works)
RBD	Reichsbahndirektion (Reichsbahn directorate)
Rbf	Rangierbahnhof (marshalling yard)
RBS	Rheinisches Braunkohlensyndikat (Rhenish Brown Coal Syndicate)
RHK	Rhein-Herne-Kanal
RLV	Reichslastverteiler (Reich Load Distributor)
RMfRuK	Reichsministerium für Rüstungs- und Kriegsproduktion (Reich Ministry for Armaments and War Production)
RRS	Railway Research Service
RVE	Reichsvereinigung Eisen (Reich Iron Association)
RVK	Reichsvereinigung Kohle (Reich Coal Association)
RVM	Reichsverkehrsministerium (Reich Ministry of Transportation)
RWE	Rheinisch-Westfälisches Elektrizitätswerk (Rhenish-Westphalian Electricity Works)
RWHG	Reichswerke Hermann Göring
RWKS	Rheinisch-Westfälisches Kohlen-Syndikat (Rhenish-Westphalian Coal Syndicate)
RWM	Reichswirtschaftsministerium (Reich Ministry of Economics)
RZA	Reichsbahn-Zentralamt (Reichsbahn Central Office)
SHAEF	Supreme Headquarters Allied Expeditionary Forces
SHG	Syndikatshandelsgesellschaft (Syndicate Trading Company)
SIGINT	Signal Intelligence

SNCF	Société Nationale des Chemins de Fer Français (French National Railways)
USAAF	United States Army Air Forces
USSBS	United States Strategic Bombing Survey
USSTAF	United States Strategic Air Force
Vbf	Verschiebebahnhof (marshalling yard)
VSt	Vereinigte Stahlwerke A.G. (United Steel Company)
Wi-Rü Amt	Wehrwirtschafts- und Rüstungsamt (Military Economics and Armaments Office in OKW)
ZVL	Zentralverkehrsleitstelle (Central Transportation Directorate)

The
Collapse of
the German
War Economy,
1944–1945

1 Albert Speer's System of Industrial Efficiency

On New Year's Day 1945, Albert Ganzenmüller, the young, dynamic head of the German National Railway, the Deutsche Reichsbahn (DR), addressed an inspirational message to his subordinates.[1] He praised their efforts during the preceding twelve months and promised them that they would be rewarded with success for German arms during the coming year. But nothing that Ganzenmüller could write could conceal the rapid decline that his railway had suffered during the preceding three and a half months. Because of merciless Allied air attacks, the Reichsbahn was reeling and could no longer perform its economic role. The Reich economy was spiralling downward toward the abyss in spite of Ganzenmüller's and his friend Albert Speer's efforts. Ganzenmüller and Speer had assumed office during a similar though less severe emergency three years before. Speer had instituted a series of economic reforms that encompassed the Reichsbahn and enabled Germany to increase its armaments output spectacularly. To understand the crisis facing Ganzenmüller and the Reichsbahn in January 1945, we must trace the course of Speer's reforms and see how they fit into the history of the German economy under Hitler.

The economic history of Germany during Nazi rule may be divided into three periods. The first stretched from the seizure of power in January 1933 to September 1936. A dual policy of labor creation and expansion of armaments production was followed. It was predicated on Hitler's fears of domestic political unrest stemming from high unemployment and from his need for a measure of military power to back his diplomatic intentions. Unemployment was reduced to pre-Depression levels, the GNP neared that of 1929, and government expenditure was shifted decisively toward armaments.[2]

The second period began in September 1936. In response to a foreign exchange shortage and the opposition of the minister of economics, Hjalmar Schacht, Hitler modified his economic policy by enunciating the second Four Year Plan under Hermann Göring. He called upon industry to make Germany ready for war within four years. To this end the government would sponsor the expansion of the synthetic fuel industry and promote the greater use of low-grade domestic iron ore. For some years the Air Ministry, moving independently, had been expanding the capacity of the aviation industry.[3]

Due to the technical immaturity of the hydrogenation and Fischer-Tropsch processes and shortages of certain components made from steel, synthetic fuel production lagged badly behind expectations.[4] Resistance by heavy industry centered in the Ruhr stymied progress in exploiting domestic iron ore. In response, the government sharpened its intervention in economic affairs. On 15 July 1937 Göring decreed the formation of the gigantic Reichswerke Hermann Göring AG (RWHG), using forced loans and drafts of engineers from existing iron and steel companies to create a management staff overnight.[5] The complex would exploit the low-quality iron ores located near Salzgitter in central Germany.[6] Named to lead the new combine was Paul Pleiger, an energetic manager cum technocrat from the Ruhr and a member of the Nazi Party.[7]

A further acceleration of rearmament followed in 1938. Production of most armaments had risen but nevertheless failed to meet Hitler's ambitious demands, primarily due to the inefficiency of Göring's organization.[8] The synthetic fuel program had yet to yield appreciable results and the RWHG was still almost two years away from smelting its first ton of iron.[9] Schacht resigned as minister of economics and plenipotentiary for the war economy in November 1937. He was replaced by the political nonentity Walther Funk on 7 February 1938.[10] Göring was given control over the Ministry of Economics in the interim. He used this opportunity to merge his diffuse Four Year Plan organization with the ministry and to cut back on projects, including a few in the synthetic fuel sector that promised only long-term benefits. He also set a drastically shortened timetable for the first appearance of significant quantities of synthetic gasoline.[11] The whole scheme worked toward the realization of gains that would enable Germany to embark upon the first stage of a career of military conquest in the near future. By the outbreak of hostilities, then, the German economy as a whole had not been prepared for a prolonged war. But significant changes had been made in the allocation of resources. Private consumption had fallen from 78 percent of the GNP in 1933 to 52 percent in 1938.[12] Armaments spending rose from 4 to 22 percent of GNP which itself had risen by 16 percent compared to 1928.[13] A significant increase in the size in arms spending had occurred, but the economy had not been prepared for "total war" on the model of the First World War.[14] Twenty-nine percent of total industrial output still served consumer needs.[15] The increase in military strength had been won primarily by exploiting capacity idled by the Great Depression, and by concentrating on producing finished armaments. It was complemented by a hurried effort to build new capital facilities that would render Germany temporarily less dependent on imports of militarily important raw materials in selected industries and would be located in areas less vulnerable to air attack.[16] The largest prewar increase in the share of national income devoted to the military buildup occurred only in 1938 and 1939, too late to create significant reserves of armaments.[17] The basic structure of German industry was not altered.[18] Advanced production methods were not employed and the demands made on both capital and labor, with a few critical exceptions, were modest compared to Hitler's ambitions.

The Reich's economic preparations for war bore the imprint of Nazi ideology and the corrosive internal bureaucratic competition fostered by Hitler. Five groups emerged hoping to shape Germany's economic destiny. One, the weakest, was centered in the Nazi Party. It sought to restructure German society on corporatist lines deemphasizing urbanization and industrialization. But it was abandoned early by Hitler since it opposed his rearmament goals and the concomitant alliance with industry.[19] However it did not disappear. It simply bided its time secure in its own power base in the Party's regional Gau structure.

A second group, the military, was weakened by internal divisions. Each branch of the three services had its own weapons procurement office which set production targets and raw material requirements without reference to either of the others. Nominally above these bodies was the War Economics and Armaments Office (Wi-Rü Amt) of the Armed Forces High Command (Oberkommando der Wehrmacht, OKW) commanded by General Georg Thomas. Hitler's policy of rapid rearmament, which eschewed the creation of reserves and avoided major reshaping of the economy, found no favor with Thomas.[20] During the 1930s his shrill calls for thorough industrial preparations not only went unheeded but cost him political influence. In spite of his political isolation he did possess an asset of inestimable importance. Thomas had laboriously fashioned a local reporting organization consisting of military economics officers (Wehrwirtschaftsoffiziere) and armaments officers (Rüstungsoffiziere). Germany was divided into fifteen military regions (Wehrkreise) each of which was also subdivided into commands. A defense economics or armaments officer or both were assigned to all of these areas.[21] They were responsible for the allocation of contracts and raw materials, and for preparing quarterly reports that were submitted to headquarters in Berlin.[22] Thomas, therefore, possessed the most comprehensive economic control and reporting network in the Reich. He simply lacked sufficient bureaucratic power to use it effectively.

Approaching the Wi-Rü Amt in organizational development and matching it in political impotence after 1937 was the Reich Ministry of Economics (Reichswirtschaftsministerium, RWM). The RWM attempted to influence economic affairs through its ministerial offices and a complicated series of compulsory organizations that grouped all economic activities geographically and functionally. The ministerial apparatus was the simplest. It consisted of seven main sections in Berlin supported by regional State Economic Offices (Landeswirtschaftsämter). In addition, the ministry also operated Reich Offices (Reichsstellen) that attempted to ration selected raw materials. Atop the geographical organization was the Reich Economic Chamber (Reichswirtschaftskammer). Its subordinate branches were composed of regional Economic Chambers (Wirtschaftskammern) and local Chambers of Industry and Commerce (Industrie- und Handelskammern). The functional structure was composed of National Groups (Reichsgruppen), of which there were seven in 1938, regional Economic Groups (Wirtschaftsgruppen), and the Specialty Groups (Fachgruppen).[23] The middle and lower levels of the functional structure as well as the entire geographical edifice had been co-opted by big business, especially heavy industry, to serve its own purposes. The interest groups and cartels simply used the chambers and groups as cloaks behind which they pursued their customary goals. Industry, the fourth entity, therefore played a de facto independent role.

In 1936 the poorly managed Four Year Plan organization was created to focus the energies of these groups on the expansionist aims laid down by Hitler. Göring hoped to use segments of existing bureaucracies to serve his purposes and so began by creating only a very small office. But over the months it mushroomed until finally, in 1938, he meshed it with the RWM. Subsequently, both for this reason and because Göring began to turn his attentions elsewhere, the Four Year Plan faded into virtual insignificance.[24]

When the war began, these power centers were competing with each other causing the utmost confusion in the management of the economy. While many proposals had been made to name an economic dictator to impose order, nothing had been done. No tightly organized economic control structure had been created and no effort to prepare the economy for a long war had been made because Nazi ideology either dismissed these things as unnecessary or forbade them as harmful.

Nazi ideology was the product of tensions that grew out of the peculiar political and economic development of Germany during the preceding sixty years. It crystallized after defeat in 1918, which it attributed to the collapse of popular morale due to economic hardship, and gained political strength and broad popular acceptance thereafter. It advocated the rejection of industrialization and liberalism and a flight to folkish forms of romanticism.[25] The concomitant was the denigration of bureaucratic organization and the discounting of the role of the state.[26] From this flowed an irrational conception of social mobilization as a fanatical burst of national emotional energy. Hitler visualized it as an imperialist war that would either conquer the territory needed for Germany's survival or lead to the Volk's utter ruin.[27] Economic reality would be compelled to serve the adventure by the force of indomitable will.[28] Hitler expressed the latter idea when he asserted that, "The state orders and the economy meets the requirements of the state."[29] The state, in this formulation, was seen as the tool of the Nazi Party.

The specific form of economic organization that issued from this conception was the "Leadership Principle."[30] Dynamic individuals would master problems through the application of energy and resourcefulness. Bureaucracy would be kept to a minimum by means of "industrial self-responsibility," the voluntary management of the economy by businessmen to serve folkish needs.[31]

These economic ideas were intertwined with similar military and political notions. Concepts of mobile warfare stressing speed and the innovative use of combined arms were developed by others and were adopted by the Nazis. Hitler applied them to his imperialist dreams by conceiving of a series of short, sharp wars of territorial conquest culminating in the final titanic confrontation with the Soviet Union.[32] At the outset, the economy would generate only the military power necessary to defeat Germany's initial opponents, who would be weak and isolated. The preliminary conquests would not only clear Germany's strategic rear but also enhance its economic position.[33]

No formal statement was drawn up outlining this design. But each of its components—mobile warfare, conquest of territory, and economic stimulation—had long been topics of public discussion in Germany. Hitler himself spoke so often on these subjects that there can be no doubt that he was aware of them.[34] Hitler was not only the embodiment of the anxieties of the German people; he had also assimilated the historic German preference for rapid wars and combined it with new ideas for the use of technology on the battlefield. However, neither he nor Göring made a consistent effort to shape the economy during the first two periods. Instead they resorted to exhortation and compulsion.

The result was an economic system that by Western standards was chaotic and horrendously inefficient. But it suited the needs expressed by Hitler and the German people. It created jobs before 1936 and afterward built a powerful military. It was characterized by fitful but violent government intervention taken in reaction to emergencies caused by external developments. Its informality, "planlessness," and lack of centralized control and systematic growth at once limited its overall potential and conferred upon it considerable flexibility. It fostered ruthless bureaucratic competition and permitted the growth of administrative empires that did not necessarily share the general system's objectives. But it also gave scope to dynamic individuals who made indispensable contributions to the war effort.

The first such individual was Fritz Todt. He had made his reputation as head of the construction team bearing his own name which had rapidly and efficiently erected the first segments of the Autobahnen and the West Wall. He also held other governmental and professional posts. With his prestige, Todt was able to make recommendations for economic reorganization incorporating ideas of advanced control and technological rationality that promised to increase production while making few additional demands for resources. These ideas found favor with Hitler. Sensing this, Göring attempted to harness Todt's rise for his own purposes by naming him General Inspector for the Special Tasks in the Four Year Plan on 23 February 1940. Todt seized the opportunity to consolidate his position by arranging with Hitler to be named minister of armaments and munitions (Reichsminister für Bewaffnung und Munition, RMfBuM) on 17 March.[35] Todt's subsequent efforts won only a qualified success. He engineered a modest increase in arms production and enacted reforms that laid the groundwork for later improvements. But ultimately he failed because he stumbled badly in the jungle of bureaucratic politics.

The new minister's greatest error was his decision not to create a supporting bureaucracy. Instead, he established committees composed of leading manufacturers and engineers who would steer production using the concept of industrial self-responsibility. In its initial form, which combined some boards responsible for the production of certain weapons and some organized regionally, the structure was far from perfect. Todt ultimately realized that his domain was both too small and isolated. It was too small in that he could not effectively manage his own area, confined as it was to army armaments, without delving into general questions of raw materials allocations. This in turn brought him into conflict with the Luftwaffe and the navy. To overcome his second problem, isolation borne of the absence of a national information-gathering system, Todt, with Hitler's approval, moved to extend his influence over Thomas's regional reporting organization. Thomas obliged, seeing this as a means of reducing the confusion afflicting arms production.[36]

The failure to achieve a quick victory over the Red Army convinced Todt that Germany could not win the war. On 29 November 1941 he first informed Hitler of his opinion. There followed a series of indecisive conferences in which Todt failed to move the Führer to open peace negotiations and in which weak measures to raise armaments production were agreed. The first was the order entitled "Simplification and Performance Increase in Our Armaments Production" of 3 December.[37] It provided for the introduction of mass production techniques, concentration of production in the most efficient factories, and the end of development projects that would mature far in the future. These were goals that Todt had canvassed and that for months had been incorporated in orders. Hitler foresaw no fundamental reordering of economic priorities, only a brief push to overcome the immediate crisis.

The final German drive on Moscow stalled, and a new phase in the war opened with the eruption of a dangerous Soviet counteroffensive on 6 December 1941 that tumbled the Wehrmacht back over 150 kilometers. Casualties were severe, losses of weapons and materiel massive and stocks of replacements dwindled.[38] Now the failure to increase armaments production loomed large, threatening to magnify the retreat into a rout. In 1941, munitions output amounted to only 540,000 tons, 325,000 tons less than in 1940.[39] Armaments final production still accounted for only 19 percent of total industrial output.[40]

Hitler's reaction to the crisis was the Führer Order Rüstung 1942 issued on 10 January 1942. While genuflecting to his previous aim of defeating Britain, the order decisively turned the emphasis of production to the army to enable it to conclude the campaign in the East. Stock levels were to be increased to cover four months's consumption and the variety in types of weapons was to be reduced. A program would be inaugurated that would provide for increased use of synthetics, the exchange of simple for complicated components, and savings in raw material consumption. It ordered an increase in coal and oil production but gave responsibility for achieving it to the Four Year Plan Office, which had been trying to do just that for six years. Field Marshal Keitel, chief of OKW, was empowered to resolve disputes arising among the services. But the heads of the three branches of the armed forces were left responsible for the direction of their own programs.[41] Allocation of labor among industries was to be done by Keitel and Todt. No mention was made of reducing civilian production. No changes were made in the organizational structure.

It has become a commonplace to view the Führer Order Rüstung 1942 as a turning point in the economic affairs of the Third Reich.[42] But the text of the order provides no clue as to why it should have triggered a major change. Certainly it called for increased arms production and concentration both in terms of resource allocation and production effort. But that had been done before. In fact the order represented a continuation of the existing system at a higher level of intensity. While important, it presaged no fundamental change in policy. It has gained importance only because it has been associated with events that followed and were only incidentally related to it.

On 8 February 1942, under circumstances that have not been fully clarified, Todt died in an airplane crash while leaving Hitler's headquarters at Rastenburg.[43] Viewed solely in relation to the performance of preceding years, Todt's stewardship of the German economy during 1940 and 1941 was creditable. He did increase overall production. Where it fell, the cause was lack of demand by the military. Yet when set against the vast military tasks and the impending avalanche of materiel from Allied factories facing Germany, it was utterly inadequate. For years Thomas had warned Hitler of the stakes.[44] Todt had himself counselled peace negotations. But the Führer was working with another, unrealistic set of premises. Todt cannot be held responsible for the failure to change basic policy. Yet he can be criticized for not exploiting his opportunity to enact more far-reaching reforms and to press for greater increases in output. Moreover, despite Todt's efforts to streamline the management of armaments production, the overlapping of responsibilities and proliferation of organizations functioning in economic affairs had worsened. Because he was unable to gather all the threads of economic control in his hands, his committees contributed to the confusion.[45] In effect, Todt laid a foundation but he lacked the bureaucratic power to build a structure above it. His successor, Albert Speer, named almost carelessly by Hitler on 9 February, resolved to end this state of affairs.[46] This marked the beginning of the third phase of Nazi economic activity. So as not to fail where everyone else had before, he moved at the outset to implement a three-pronged bureaucratic strategy. He attempted to assure his political base, sought to monopolize economic decision making, and worked to create a centralized economic policy-making apparatus. The immediate major problem confronting him was not to increase the volume of resources allocated to arms production, but to use more effectively the sizeable resources already made available.

Speer moved first to assure himself of Hitler's support. Fending off an effort by Funk and Göring to restrict his authority, he contrived to have the Führer appear personally to endorse him at a meeting held at the Reich Chancellery on 13 February.[47] To mollify Göring, he had himself appointed as the Reich Marshal's nominal subordinate as Plenipotentiary for Armaments Tasks in the Four Year Plan.[48] He also instituted a regular series of meetings with Hitler to resolve armaments production issues. Realizing that Hitler had the dilettante's penchant for absorbing the technical details of weapons, he always brought along specialists on the subject to be discussed, confining himself to steering the meeting in the desired direction and to addressing basic policy issues.[49] Thereby he enhanced his own prestige and stayed close to the Führer, a crucial consideration in the byzantine politics of Nazi Germany.

His first attempt to broaden his domain misfired. Speer proposed his friend, Gauleiter Karl Hanke of Breslau to serve under him as special plenipotentiary for labor matters. But due to opposition from the other Gauleiters, who as Reich Defense Commissars for their regions exerted considerable influence over labor allocation and consumer goods production, his candidate was vetoed. Instead a member of the Party's old guard, Fritz Sauckel, Gauleiter of Thuringia, who enjoyed the support of Martin Bormann, was given the post. Worse yet, he was not subordinated to Speer.[50] This failure proved a constant source of difficulty in the future as Sauckel refused to coordinate his labor drives with Speer's industrial policies.

Speer's first centralization measure was realized after complicated negotiations with the formation of Central Planning (Zentrale Planung) on 22 April 1942.[51] The new control organ consisted of Speer, Paul Körner, and Erhard Milch. Körner was Göring's representative from the Four Year Plan. He was the weakest of the three in terms of both political power and strength of personality. Milch was state secretary of the Air Ministry and responsible for air armaments production (Generalluftzeugmeister). An aggressive individual, Milch worked well with Speer, and his presence assured consideration of the Luftwaffe's needs. Nominally, Central Planning was intended to set long-term priorities. But the name belied its function. It lacked a staff to prepare plans and gather information. It had no statutory power to enforce adherence to its decisions. It did no planning. Rather, it functioned as a board of appeal before which rival claimants argued their cases. This relatively unstructured format gave Speer free range for his sharp wit and ability to dominate personal encounters. Central Planning gained influence because of the bureaucratic power and dynamism of its de facto chairman. It became Speer's vehicle for imposing his priorities concerning the ordering of the economy on the other actors in the economic arena.

At the outset, Central Planning concentrated on reforming the chaotic method of steel allocation. This was perceived as a shortcut to reforming the entire war economy because steel was the basic commodity in armaments production. Controlling it would determine what weapons could be built and in what volume. It would also shape the distribution of other basic factors such as coal, iron ore, and transportation space. The old practice of parceling out steel according to demand was abandoned and replaced by distribution according to anticipated production levels on a quarterly basis.[52]

Raw materials not affected by steel allocations were apportioned by Speer's ally at the Economics Ministry, Hans Kehrl.[53] As head of Main Section II, Kehrl divided the commercial economy into "Steering Areas" (Lenkungsbereiche) corresponding to the ministry's Economic Groups. He initiated procedures for the regular collection of statistical information and obtained the very able Dr. Rolf Wagenführ of the Institute for Research into Economic Trends to oversee the effort.[54] Kehrl became a regular participant in Central Planning's meetings. The result was that Speer gained powerful influence over an area not officially within his purview and improved the coordination of economic affairs.

A weakness in both Todt's organization and the Four Year Plan had been their reliance on others to gather information and implement their plans at the local level. Speer moved to avoid this error by seizing Thomas's Wi-Rü Amt on 7 May. The War Economics Office remained with OKW while the regional officers and inspectors were transferred to the Ministry of Armaments and Munitions. By November, Thomas had been completely banished.[55]

Speer's drive to collect the strings of economic control in his hands and Central Planning's preoccupation with steel led the industry to organize a formidable self-protection agency, the Reich Iron Association. The forerunner of the new interest group was the Reichsvereinigung Kohle (Reich Coal Association, RVK) created on 3 March 1941. The RVK was a reaction to Todt's and Göring's initiatives in the energy sector. In a shrewd move, the companies obtained as the organization's head Paul Pleiger of the Reichswerke Hermann Göring. As chief of the RWHG, Pleiger had been a nettlesome opponent of the established coal interests. But he had also won their respect. The RVK was empowered to take all measures necessary to increase production, improve labor conditions for the miners, control sales and relations among the coal syndicates and their members, organize the regional distribution of coal, gather and evaluate statistics, and plan transportation measures.[56]

The Reichsvereinigung Eisen (Reich Iron Association, RVE) fol-

lowed this model. Its goal was to eliminate the confusion arising
from the competition among the twelve entities that then had a
hand in allocating iron by superseding them. It would present a
united front for both the iron and the steel industries to Central
Planning. As time would show, it would also become a serious opponent of the RVK and the Reichsbahn. To head the new organization, formed on 29 May 1942, Speer called upon the maverick Hermann Röchling, owner of the Röchling'sche Stahlwerke, Völklin-
gen, Saar.[57] As vice chairmen Speer named Alfred Krupp and, the
man who became its de facto head, Walter Rohland of United Steel
(Vereinigte Stahlwerke A.G., VSt) and leader of the Main Committee for Panzer Construction.

On 20 March, Speer created the best known of his managerial
organizations, the Committees (Ausschüsse) and Rings (Ringe).[58]
The committees were placed under Karl Saur, head of the Technical
Office in the Speer ministry while the rings were entrusted to Walter Schieber, head of the Armaments Supply Office (Rüstungslieferungsamt). The committees controlled final production of particular types of weapons while the rings organized the production
of important, widely used components. The committees and rings
possessed no executive power. They were to embody the principle
of industrial self-responsibility in hopes of unlocking the energy
and creativity of industry and harnessing it to the war effort. Along
with the ministry's offices in Berlin on the Pariserplatz, they were
the arenas where the young technicians and engineers who had
hankered for opportunities to restructure the economy worked to
realize their dreams.[59] It was for this reason that the Party objected
to them. They gave the technocrats altogether too much freedom.
Those sections of the Party that still harbored corporatist, anticapi-
talist, and antimodernist ideas, which coalesced around the Gauleiter, became tireless opponents of both Speer and his creations.
On 20 April 1942 the Committee and Ring system went into operation. Industry had largely shaken off the fetters of the Economics
Ministry and the Four Year Plan. In return for greater freedom it had
taken upon itself a share of the burden of seeing the war effort to a
successful conclusion. But as the new system began to function,
the old tendencies of bureaucratic proliferation and competition re-
emerged. As of 1 June 1942 there were 178 Special Rings and Committees subordinated to an ever-changing number of Main Rings
and Committees. Many factories were uncertain which committee

or ring they were responsible to, and many committees and rings were unclear as to the extent of their membership. The flow of production information was snarled and new rivalries and disputes over authority arose. Central Planning itself frequently became bogged down in detailed discussion and ignored the broad issues it had been created to resolve. Civilian production was not reduced, as Speer failed to overcome the opposition of the Gauleiters.[60]

The only solution that Speer could see to the problem was to press forward with his policy of expansion and centralization. First, after having sought to do so since the beginning of his tenure, he gained control of naval armaments. The obstacle had been Hitler who had prevented the navy from being represented on Central Planning when it was formed. Now his objections were removed and at Admiral Dönitz's own urging Speer assumed responsibility for naval armaments on 31 March 1943.[61]

Next, Speer stretched his grasp toward the Economics Ministry. On 10 June, after long and difficult negotiations, he and Funk initialed an agreement under which Speer would assume responsibility for all sectors of the economy except food and general civilian planning.[62] This was the precondition for the third major addition to Speer's machine—the Planning Office (Planungsamt).

On 4 September 1943 Göring signed the order authorizing the creation of the Planning Office and admitting Funk to Central Planning. The Reich Offices and Reichsvereinigungen were transferred to Speer and his ministry was renamed the Reich Ministry for Armaments and War Production (Reichsministerium für Rüstungs- und Kriegsproduktion, RMfRuK) consonant with its widened responsibilities. Ten days later the Planning Office was formed and placed immediately below Central Planning. Its head was Hans Kehrl, who brought with him the personnel of Main Section II of the Economics Ministry.[63] The Planning Office prepared statistics and agenda for Central Planning, drafted orders embodying its decisions, and monitored production programs. The committees and rings were subordinated to it. Kehrl took personal charge of one of the office's subsections, the Raw Materials Office. The vital basis for planning that had been lacking had finally been created. For the first time, rather than functioning as a referee, Central Planning was able to look into the future and take initiatives based on a sound empirical foundation.

Speer and the Planning Office now had control of all forms of armaments production except aircraft, which he heavily influenced, a considerable share of consumer goods output, and all raw materials production. But the Planning Office was not omnipotent. It was not given responsibility for iron production, resulting in competition with the Armaments Supply Office under Walther Schieber. In addition it possessed no authority in the field of labor.[64] Here Sauckel had strengthened his position. Considerable room for mischief remained because the armaments offices of the armed services still prepared production plans based on the alleged needs of their branches. These were submitted to the Planning Office, coordinated with other schemes and raw material supplies, and laid before Central Planning for approval.

Overall, the system had been greatly improved. Many abuses of the pre-February 1942 era had been eliminated. Kehrl had become one of the most powerful administrators in Germany. But the very size of the organization led to frictions within and conflicts outside. The first period of the Speer regime had resulted in substantial gains, but the task remained far from completed.

The framework of the armaments bureaucracy had assumed its definitive shape with one crucial exception, aviation. That would be absorbed not as the result of bureaucratic competition but in response to an air-raid emergency. It marked the first weakening of the system. The initial economic emergency caused by an air raid occurred in the summer and fall of 1943 as a result of the Eighth Air Force's attacks on the ball-bearing plants concentrated at Schweinfurt. The response hit upon by Speer was the appointment of Philip Kessler as Plenipotentiary for Ball-Bearings. Kessler brilliantly mastered the problem and did not disturb the regular armaments organization. Speer had been fortunate because Kessler was an unusually selfless individual. But an ominous precedent had been set.[65] He would not be so lucky in the future.

The second armaments emergency caused by air raids erupted in the week of 19 to 25 February 1944. The American Eighth and Fifteenth Air Forces, using escort fighters to protect their bombers, conducted a series of violent attacks against airframe plants in Germany and Austria. Speer, supported by Gen. Adolf Galland, Inspector of Fighters in the Luftwaffe, had long been clamoring for an increase in fighter production.[66] The incentive of the attacks, combined with a smouldering dispute between Milch and Karl Saur of Speer's Technical Office, led to the formation of the Fighter Staff

(Jägerstab) under Saur on 1 March 1944. Speer and Milch had not desired Saur's appointment, but Hitler, acting on impulse, named him during a discussion at his headquarters.[67] He immediately set to work with ruthless energy and within weeks had not only made good the losses suffered from the bombing but even doubled fighter production. He also hastily initiated a program of plant dispersal, which spread both fuselage and engine factories throughout the Reich and began ambitious projects to build underground and concrete protected plants.[68] Speer had resorted to the method used before to solve this second armaments emergency. The result was organizational chaos and the emergence of a powerful if clumsy competitor from within his own ranks. Contributing to his loss of control was his absence throughout the crisis due to illness.[69] The acquisition of control over air armaments during the spring of 1944 marked the end of the second phase of the Speer period and the beginning of Speer's loss of the initiative to the Allied bombers.

A third armaments emergency exploded in May 1944 as a consequence of a series of very heavy strikes by the Eighth Air Force on synthetic fuel plants in central Germany.[70] Speer again met the emergency by naming a plenipotentiary, Edmund Geilenberg. The Fighter Staff phenomenon recurred. Geilenberg ignored all other needs and ruthlessly requisitioned materials for his repair and concrete-shelter programs. Miracles were performed, but oil output plummeted under repeated bombings and the fragile system of economic control was further disrupted.

The period after February 1942 had witnessed substantial progress. True centralization of planning and control, with the important exception of labor affairs, had been accomplished. The most important development in this regard was the creation of the Planning Office in September 1943. For the first time Germany possessed the institutional machinery necessary for rational management of its overall war effort. A decision-making body without either direct lines of authority to the working level or support from a centralized apparatus that harnesses the information flow cannot function effectively. Todt's efforts had demonstrated this clearly. Speer initially acquired the local control mechanism but naively thought that he could do without the central bureaucracy. His experience with Central Planning meetings taught him otherwise. As a result he bowed to the need to form a bureaucracy and turned to Hans Kehrl to hammer out the specifics.

Equally important was Speer's success in playing bureaucratic politics. He had vanquished Göring, Keitel, and Funk and overwhelmed Thomas. But in the hothouse environment of government in the Third Reich, functioning without the input of public opinion, the political competition flourishing within the bureaucracy immediately spawned new enemies. Some appeared outside the RMfRuK. Until the spring of 1944 the most troublesome was Fritz Sauckel. But Sauckel's influence waned as his labor drives became less effective with the loss of the reservoir of foreign workers due to the retreats of 1943 and 1944.

The uneasy coalition consisting of the Gauleiters, led by Martin Bormann, gained power and in the spring of 1944 intensified its opposition to Speer. Sometimes a member of this clique, sometimes cooperating with Speer, was the Reich minister of propaganda and Gauleiter of Berlin, Joseph Goebbels. He had repeatedly called for total mobilization of the economy to meet the heightened demands of the war.[71] But he was reluctant to strengthen Speer's hand and sought to increase his own authority, particularly over labor.

Another competitor of as yet uncertain strength was Heinrich Himmler, commander of the SS and German police. Based on his monopoly of the use of concentration camp labor, Himmler had created a small production apparatus to supply some of the needs of the SS military formations.[72] During the spring of 1944, Himmler increased his effort to expand his empire and repeatedly collided with Speer.

Two opponents emerged during Speer's illness during the spring of 1944. Xaver Dorsch, head of the Organisation Todt construction machine within the RMfRuK, raised severe criticisms of Speer's policies and initiated a serious move to oust him. His drive was only narrowly turned aside. But the affair had poisoned the atmosphere within the ministry, and Dorsch had far from abandoned his plans.[73] Simultaneously, Saur, while not explicitly assaulting Speer's position, had increased his personal authority. His leadership of the Fighter Staff and its apparent production successes vastly enhanced his prestige. Of equal importance was the fact that during Speer's illness Saur conducted the meetings with Hitler on armaments matters. With a self-confidence born of ignorance of the complexity of the issues, Saur promised rapid and spectacular results in answer to the Führer's unrealistic demands. The upshot was that Hitler, rather than face the contingent responses and veiled criticisms expressed by Speer during the summer, increasingly turned to Saur to resolve economic and armaments problems. Just as Speer had completed construction of his economic machine it was beset by new enemies from without and began to disintegrate from within.

Despite the energy dissipated in internal political disputes, arms output rose dramatically. The overall index of armaments production, taking January/February 1942 as 100, had risen in two distinct leaps (see Figure 1.1).[74] The first increase lasted from February 1942 until May 1943, jumping from 97 to 232, and averaging 5.5 percent per month. Bearing in mind that a 5 percent annual growth rate for an economy is considered good, such a sustained performance must be judged outstanding. There followed a second period during which growth hovered at 0.9 percent per month stretching from June 1943 to February 1944. The armaments index rose during this span only from 226 to 231. Then a second armaments boom began featuring a spectacular 17 percent spurt in March 1944. Overall, then, Speer and the German economy had registered a striking production success. Precisely how this was realized is surprising.

Between Speer's assumption of his duties and the apogee of armaments production in mid-1944, Germany's gross national product had risen by only about 6 percent. The share spent on weapons output increased by only about 5 percent.[75] Production of raw materials rose by just 7 percent.[76] Moreover, civilian consumer goods output had not been drastically curtailed until after Speer wrested control of the raw materials and consumer goods industries from the Economics Ministry in September 1943.[77] So even under Speer there was no major restructuring of the German economy. Increases in armaments output had been won with other more subtle methods.

One means used by Speer was the reallocation of resources within industry. Changes in the distribution of labor provide an insight into this. The overall size of the labor force hardly changed throughout the war.[78] But employment in armaments factories increased by 30.7 percent between 30 June 1941 and 31 March 1944.[79] Measured in terms of value of output, the share of armaments final production in overall industrial output rose from 19 percent in 1941 to approximately 50 percent in 1944.[80] But neither the increase in GNP nor the transfer of factors of production to military purposes was sufficient to propel the massive and sustained growth

Figure 1.1 *Percentage Change in the Index of Armaments Production, 1942–1945*

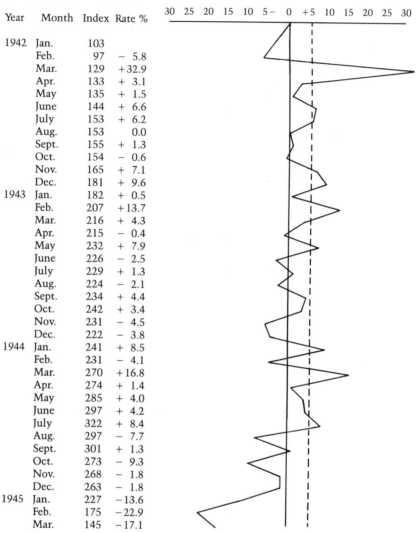

Year	Month	Index	Rate %
1942	Jan.	103	
	Feb.	97	− 5.8
	Mar.	129	+32.9
	Apr.	133	+ 3.1
	May	135	+ 1.5
	June	144	+ 6.6
	July	153	+ 6.2
	Aug.	153	0.0
	Sept.	155	+ 1.3
	Oct.	154	− 0.6
	Nov.	165	+ 7.1
	Dec.	181	+ 9.6
1943	Jan.	182	+ 0.5
	Feb.	207	+13.7
	Mar.	216	+ 4.3
	Apr.	215	− 0.4
	May	232	+ 7.9
	June	226	− 2.5
	July	229	+ 1.3
	Aug.	224	− 2.1
	Sept.	234	+ 4.4
	Oct.	242	+ 3.4
	Nov.	231	− 4.5
	Dec.	222	− 3.8
1944	Jan.	241	+ 8.5
	Feb.	231	− 4.1
	Mar.	270	+16.8
	Apr.	274	+ 1.4
	May	285	+ 4.0
	June	297	+ 4.2
	July	322	+ 8.4
	Aug.	297	− 7.7
	Sept.	301	+ 1.3
	Oct.	273	− 9.3
	Nov.	268	− 1.8
	Dec.	263	− 1.8
1945	Jan.	227	−13.6
	Feb.	175	−22.9
	Mar.	145	−17.1

Source: Wagenführ, *Deutsche Industrie*, pp. 66, 114, 178.

of arms output achieved between 1942 and 1944. Another set of factors acting on the factory floor was decisive.

The secret of Speer's success lay in a myriad of individual efficiencies that together permitted massive savings of all factors of production. A clue appears in the "Newsletter of the Reich Minister for Armaments and War Production" of 9 June 1944.[81] A metal hammering works is discussed at which in the year between 1 April 1943 and 31 March 1944 production had risen by 85 percent while coal consumption had sunk by 41 percent. Energy consumption per ton of finished steel had fallen 40 percent. This development was typical. Between 1941 and 1944 the ratio of unit of raw material input to unit of finished output, measured by weight, had fallen dramatically from 4:1 to 2:1.[82] Labor productivity had also risen. In the metal working industries, value added by each worker per ton of raw material had climbed during Speer's tenure by 18 percent.[83] Labor productivity in final production of all types of goods rose by a third.[84] Most importantly, labor productivity in the crucial armaments sector improved spectacularly (see Table 1.1).

Clearly Speer's efforts using young engineers gathered in the committees and rings had borne fruit. Best methods had been propagated throughout industry, the multiplicity of models and variants reduced, and management initiative encouraged by industrial self-responsibility.[85] The result was a major increase in the production of those weapons most needed by the military.

The examples in Table 1.2 suffice to illustrate the astonishing jump in armaments output. While substantial gains were made in 1940 and 1941 as a result of Todt's reforms, the really significant increases were the product of Speer's centralization measures of 1942 and 1943. They alone permitted the gains in efficiency that enabled him to maintain the German people's standard of living and simultaneously vastly to increase armaments production. These increases were the consequence of Speer's shrewd recognition that the decisions so haphazardly made during the 1930s combined with the prevailing ideological climate prevented him from embarking on a program of major capital expansion and restructuring. Expedients and managerial palliatives were his only alternatives. The creation of the Planning Office was decisive because it ensured that they retained coherence and direction. No central authority, however powerful, can function without mastering the flow

Table 1.1
Index of Labor Productivity in the Armaments Industry, 1941–1944

1941/42	1942/43	1943/44	June–July 1944
100	157	189	234

Source: Wagenführ, *Deutsche Industrie*, p. 125.

Table 1.2
Examples of Increases in Armaments Production, 1940–1944

	1940	1941	1942	1943	1944
Carbines	1,351,700	1,358,500	1,370,180	2,244,100	2,585,600
Munitions (1,000 tons)	865	540	1,270	2,558	3,350
Medium tanks	1,359	2,875	5,595	9,398	12,096
Submarines	40	196	244	270	387
Single engine fighters	1,870	2,852	4,542	9,626	25,860
Explosives (average tons per month)	—	21,775	24,232	34,359	44,009

Sources: For submarines see USSBS, *Overall Report (European War)*, p. 69; for single engine fighters, USSBS, *Aircraft Industry*, figure VI-1, facing p. 93; for explosives see Becker, "German War Economy under Speer," p. 300, table 17, based on "Bericht über den Fortschritt der Arbeiten," BA R25/vorl. 105–8; for rifles, munitions, and medium tanks see RMfRuK, "Ausstoß Übersicht 1940–44. Waffen, Geräte, Munition," 20 February 1945, p. 1, BA R3/1729, f. 2.

of information. That was the Planning Office's contribution. It made possible the gains in efficiency and their mass exploitation.[86]

Measured by this standard, Speer's accomplishment can only be termed brilliant. This does not mean that he and his subordinates did not commit errors. They did.[87] Rather it means that Speer successfully adapted to the prevailing economic, bureaucratic, and ideological environment. He achieved as much as could be expected with the tools at hand. One cannot condemn a man or his generation for not escaping the intellectual and emotional constraints of their era. Nor can one castigate a decision maker for not altering his physical environment. It is the shape of that environment that will occupy us next.

2 The Geographical Division of Labor

The organizational reforms enacted by Speer overlaid the basic industrial structure that had characterized the German economy since the mid-nineteenth century. Trading patterns and regional specialization had developed according to functional and geographical factors resulting in a division of labor that enabled the aggregate to produce more than the mere sum of its parts could have produced independently. The decisive factor was an industry's relationship to the nation's preponderant source of energy—coal. All German industry revolved around one of the two great coal storehouses—the Ruhr or Upper Silesia.

Coal was Germany's only abundant natural resource. From the beginning of the period of its industrialization, German industry had intensively exploited its coal resources to offset its lack of other raw materials and grouped itself around its coal storehouses to cut costs. The first such relationship bloomed in the Ruhr.[1] The pattern repeated itself elsewhere using different technologies and resulting in different trading relationships to create the division of labor as it existed in 1933. By the eve of World War II, the German economy derived over 90 percent of its energy from one form or another of coal.[2] The smelting of every kilogram of iron required the consumption of almost twice its weight in coal. Six tons of coal stood behind every ton of synthetic gasoline. A heavy tank could rumble from the factory only after 115 tons of coal had been burned by a myriad of companies to produce it.[3] Coal was at once the indispensable basis of the German economy and the life blood of its everyday activity.

To the casual observer, coal is a mundane substance easily forgotten when considering gross national product or counting divisions. Its humble origins and ubiquity obscure its crucial importance and the sophisticated technology and distribution system necessary for its exploitation. Coal is an organic sedimentary rock formed by the combined action of pressure and temperature on plant debris. Variations in the intensity of the formative forces and the length of time in which they act result in the creation of a wide variety of coals, each with its own energy content. Two basic families issue from this process—hard coal and brown coal. The most important are the hard coals, known to Americans as bituminous coals.[4] They have the highest energy content and are the easiest to handle.

Ruhr hard coal had energy values ranging from 6,800 to 7,600 calories per kilogram. Upper Silesian hard coals were slightly less potent.[5] Within this broad grouping were ranks, each with its own thermal value and burning characteristics. The industry mechanically shaped these ranks to fit the furnaces of their customers, thus offering optimum thermal qualities and reduced residues.[6] These were marketed by coal traders as types. The critical consideration is that coal was not a uniform product. The many geological varieties and market-oriented permutations handled by German coal traders resulted in a highly complex industry that experienced all of the inventory and utilization problems that one ordinarily assocates with finer commodities. Coals were not easily interchangeable for all of their visual resemblance.

To facilitate its utilization, a number of derivative forms of coal were developed.[7] The most important was coke. A hard, brittle, spongy mass, coke was first used in the Ruhr in the late 1850s. It is devoid of coal's gaseous constituents and is used to line smelters to enable a more uniform and malleable iron to be produced.[8] Coke was the most important hard coal derivative and its introduction triggered the boom in Germany's iron industry that caused iron works to congregate in the Ruhr to obtain coke as cheaply as possible. Other heavy industrial and ancillary industries followed in their wake.

In the coal economy year 1943/44, Germany produced 278.1 million tons of hard coal and 53.3 million tons of coke.[9] Her total assured reserves amounted to 190.6 billion tons.[10] These massive stores were scattered about at six locations. But only three were economically significant and of these two were of overwhelming importance.

Holding a third of Germany's proven reserves, the Ruhr was the leader in German hard coal production.[11] In the 1943/44 coal economy year, it accounted for 45 percent of the Reich's hard coal output. However, the Ruhr's importance rested not just on the enormity of its reserves, but on the abundance of its high-quality coking coal. It was this that had propelled it from a sleepy agricultural area into an industrial giant in just a few decades in the mid-nineteenth century, and it was this factor that assured its predominance during World War II. Over a third of the region's cut went to the ovens comprising fully 63 percent of Germany's coke production.[12]

Approaching the Ruhr in terms of overall output was Upper Silesia. The eastern hard coal region had proven reserves of 114.5 billion tons, almost two thirds of Germany's total.[13] It contributed a third of total production amounting to 101,512,000 tons.[14] But the lower quality of its coal meant that it provided only 13 percent of national coke supplies.[15] It was this factor that put Upper Silesia in the second rank. As will be seen presently, its weakness in coking coal also determined the scale of its contribution in other forms of industrial production and the number of its dependencies.

Together, the Ruhr and Upper Silesia dominated the German hard coal market. Only one other region mattered, the Saar. Located in the southwest near the prewar Franco-German border, it held only 4 percent of Germany's proven hard coal reserves.[16] It accounted for only 8 percent of total hard coal output, its contribution to national coke supplies being of the same order.[17] Although relatively small, the Saar's role was nonetheless significant because it combined in one unit coal and iron ore supplies which were exploited by a long-established, highly developed industry. The first factor meant that unlike the Ruhr it was not reliant on external supplies of ore. The second consideration meant that it was able to exceed Upper Silesia's production of semifinished and finished metal goods. The upshot was that the Ruhr was Germany's most important coal producing region. Upper Silesia was significant only in terms of quantity. The Saar was a self-contained unit incapable of supporting dependencies.

The patterns in which coal was consumed can be understood in two ways: by industry and by region. The two schemas coincide but for the sake of clarity they will be discussed separately.

The single largest consumer of hard coal was the mining industry itself. It used a third of the cut to power its equipment and produce coke. Next was manufacturing which used about 17 percent of supplies. Half of this was drawn from the Ruhr. Third in importance was transportation which used 15 percent of total output and relied on the two major coal regions almost equally. Then came the utilities, which used about a tenth of hard coal supplies. The gas works relied on the Ruhr for almost two-thirds of their needs while the electricity plants drew equally upon the two major hard coal regions.[18] Gas and electricity can be viewed as transformations of coal that allow its energy to be consumed at locations remote from the mines. The use of electrical transmission cables also permitted the second coal family, brown coals, to be exploited on a nationally important scale.

Brown coal, familiar to Americans as lignite, is one of the younger ranks of coal that have been subjected to the geological development process for less time than hard coals. Raw brown coal has a thermal value ranging from 2,000 to 2,500 calories per kilogram.[19] It contains a high percentage of water which renders it fragile. For these reasons, low energy content and fragility, it was generally not economical to ship it long distances or store it in quantity for long periods. Industry adapted to these characteristics in two ways. One was to make brown coal suitable for transport by forming it into briquettes that were more robust and had about twice the heat value per unit of weight as raw brown coal. The other method was to locate plants immediately adjacent to brown coal mines. Unlike hard coal which is won in shafts diving hundreds and sometimes thousands of feet below the earth's surface, brown coal is obtained by strip mining from open pits on the surface. This fact meant that plants generating electricity could be built beside the mines, using conveyor belts to bring the raw coal to the furnaces.[20] Synthetic fuel plants were located near brown coal pits for the same reason.

Germany's brown coal supplies were grouped in two main areas. The most important, with over 80 percent of total reserves, was in the central region near Magdeburg and Leipzig. For administrative convenience, it was divided into the Central German area lying west of the Elbe River and the East Elbian region. The other major producer, accounting for 12 percent of reserves was on the left bank of the Rhine near Cologne.[21] The Central German area was dominant accounting for 45 percent of production in the coal economy year 1943/44. The East Elbian and Rhenish regions both contributed 27 percent of the total. The geographical distribution of briquetting operations was similar.[22]

Brown coal constituted a support for hard coal, but because its heat value was only a third as great and it was difficult to ship, it could never replace hard coal nor substitute for the loss of one of the major hard coal producing areas. However, it did enjoy the advantage of being preponderantly located far from Germany's borders, so that mining and distributing it were less susceptible to external interference. In contrast, both of the major hard coal regions lay perilously near Germany's frontiers.

As we have seen, one of the major consumers of brown coal was the electricity generating sector. It used brown coal along with hard coal and water to build a balanced, redundant, generating system. Hard coal was burned to generate almost half of Germany's electricity, brown coal generated a third, and hydro plants provided a fifth.[23] Large publicly owned facilities were situated near the brown coal fields providing the system's basic capacity. Smaller hard coal plants were located adjacent to large cities and industries when it was deemed more economical to ship hard coal than build and operate transmission lines. Hydroelectric plants were built in southern Germany and Austria to take advantage of fast-flowing rivers. A few others were placed near reservoirs elsewhere. Together they were used as giant storage batteries to meet peak loads.[24] Total generating capacity in early 1944 was 13.3 million kilowatts of which 9.7 million were actually available for use. The difference between capacity and availability was caused by plants shut down for scheduled maintenance and other technical limitations.[25] Total production in 1943 was just over 47 billion kilowatt-hours.[26] It was allocated by the Reich Load Distributor (Reichslastverteiler, RLV), Dr. Richard Fischer, who was also head of Berlin's public utility.[27] Fischer controlled a unified system consisting of the publicly owned plants, which contributed just over half of all electricity generated, and private plants, most of which were associated with heavy industry.[28] Virtually every producer was tied into the national grid that, within certain limitations, allowed the exchange of supplies among regions.[29] By far the heaviest consumer of electricity was industry which used almost nine-tenths of all that was generated.[30] The branches with the biggest appetites were electrochemicals and electrometallurgy, which together consumed almost half of total production. Trailing far behind were mining and heavy industry.[31]

Gas performed a function similar to electricity. But its dependence on hard coal was far greater. It was produced in three basic forms[32] and generally had a heat value of 4,300 calories per cubic meter.[33] It was generated by two industry groups: municipal works and cokeries where it was obtained as a by-product. Total production in 1943 was a bit over twenty-nine billion cubic meters. The cokeries were the most important, providing over four-fifths of the total.[34] All producers were united in a long-distance grid. The biggest consumer from the grid in the Ruhr area, for example, was heavy industry which took two-thirds of available supplies.[35] Iron and chemical industries in the same area consumed three-quarters of the cokery gas produced there.[36] The cokeries were located near their coal supplies. But the municipal works relied on transport, mostly rail, for their coal. Their consumption was enormous. Two typical systems, Duisburg and Berlin, consumed respectively 37,505 tons and 76,736 tons of hard coal per month during early 1944.[37] Stocks varied. In regions near the coal producing areas they were kept low, on the order of enough for a few days, while at more distant places such as Frankfurt/Main or Stuttgart, there might be as much as for two weeks.[38] Allocation of gas supplies to consumers and fuel to the plants was in the hands of the Economic Group Gas and Water Utilities and the RVK under the constant oversight of the Planning Office.

Neither electricity nor gas was plentiful, although neither was so short as to curtail production seriously. Economies were enforced and plans were on the shelf to enable further savings if necessary.[39]

These were the chief coal users when considered in aggregate. Individual branches within industry consumed less, giving a deceptively low indication of their importance. It must be remembered when considering their coal consumption figures that industries were simultaneously using gas and electricity and that the fabrication of subassemblies, while not requiring high direct energy use, was nevertheless an indispensable part of the industrial system. For example, the munitions industry used only about seven-tenths of 1 percent of total coal production. Synthetic fuels used less than a tenth.[40] In contrast the iron sector used well over a fifth.[41] The critical consideration is that coal played a decisive role at every level of the production process, and because that process was highly integrated, the functioning of each component depended upon the smooth operation of every other.

The image of a complex system of mutually dependent parts was very difficult for those involved in it to bear in mind. Consequently Paul Pleiger and the Reich Coal Association constantly worked to ensure that competition for energy did not hinder the functioning of the whole. In 1941 Pleiger established a set of priorities for coal distribution that put transportation at the top along with armaments plants, utilities, cokeries, and the military. A year later, he imposed a limit on coal stocks of two to three months, depending on how it was shipped, in order to prevent hoarding. But the guidelines were vague and not rigorously enforced. Companies relied instead upon established business connections, sometimes involving shipments from distant suppliers, to obtain coal in excess of the stipulations. Pleiger attempted to curb this in April 1941 by dividing Germany into two large areas to be served by the two leading hard coal regions.[42] The country was split along an imaginary line running from Rostock on the Baltic to Stendahl, Magdeburg, Aschersleben, Weimar, Probstzella to the Bavarian border. East of it, industries would turn to Upper Silesia. To the west and in Bavaria, they were in the hands of one of Pleiger's nominal subordinates, the mighty Rhenish-Westphalian Coal Syndicate (Rheinisch-Westfälisches Kohlen-Syndikat, RWKS).

The RWKS was formed in 1893 to protect the Ruhr coal mine owners from competition by pooling resources and limiting production to maintain prices.[43] The syndicate determined virtually every phase of its members' operations and enjoyed unlimited oversight powers.[44] Over the years it drove out or absorbed all competition in the area and established regional representatives throughout western, central, and southern Germany, the Syndicate Trading Companies (Syndikatshandelsgesellschaften, SHGs), to deal with customers. By the mid-1920s, it controlled three-quarters of Germany's hard coal production. Its dominance was reinforced in 1934 and 1935 when the Aachen and Saar mines were put under its sway by the RWM.[45] The acquisition of the Polish sections of Silesia by the eastern region did not fundamentally weaken its position. The RWKS still controlled the nation's primary source of coke and, although the eastern region had its own industry organization, the Upper Silesian Hard Coal Syndicate (Oberschlesisches Steinkohlensyndikat, OSS), the RWKS was incomparably better organized and enjoyed more important political connections in Berlin. Its chairman, Rüdiger Schmidt, was therefore one of the most powerful, if least known, business leaders in Germany.[46] When he saw fit, he could balk government policy. So long as Pleiger allowed the syndicate itself actually to allocate coal there was little friction. But when he intervened, as he began to do more often during the early part of 1944, Schmidt resisted. Like the leaders of the iron and steel industry with whom his relations were also strained, Schmidt was exceedingly suspicious of anything resembling centralized control over the economy that would restrict the prerogatives of private enterprise.[47]

An insight into the power of the RWKS can be gained by examining the process of coal allocation. In general the RWKS, and the other syndicates, distributed coal within the loose guidelines established by the RVK. If a company desired additional coal or coal for a new plant, it forwarded a request to the nearest State Economic Office which made a preliminary evaluation and then passed it on to Berlin. Here the RVK, after consulting the Reich Transportation Ministry (Reichsverkehrsministerium, RVM), determined if the request was justified and if it could be fulfilled. Then the RWKS received it, compared it with information obtained from its own sources, and if it saw fit, allocated coal. Only very large consumers such as the major iron companies and the Reichsbahn could circumvent this process and deal directly with the syndicate. Consequently, because it alone controlled the coal and had its own organization and sources of information, and because its goals did not always coincide with those of the regime, the RWKS actually controlled the distribution of coal and could obstruct government policy. Rüdiger Schmidt could therefore heavily influence the performance of Speer's economic apparatus. He could greatly smooth its operation or severely disrupt it.

Because of its importance to every phase of economic life and because of its strong political position, the coal industry was the decisive factor shaping Germany's economy. It determined, subject to a few modifying influences, the overall scale of industrial activity and its geographical configuration. Two areas, the Ruhr and Upper Silesia, dominated it and developed manufacturing satellites that depended upon them for energy and basic heavy industrial goods and in turn provided them with specialized manufactures and food (see Map 2.1).[48]

Of the two coal hubs the Ruhr was the more important because of the scale and quality of its coal output and its strong business organizations. It was the home not only of mining, but of heavy iron, steel, chemical, and engineering concerns that attracted a horde of supporting industries. Around it revolved dependencies such as Hamburg and the North Sea ports that provided it with light manufactures, imported petroleum products, and iron ore. To the east were Hanover, Kassel, and Brunswick where engineering, vehicle, and other manufacturing industries were grouped. To the

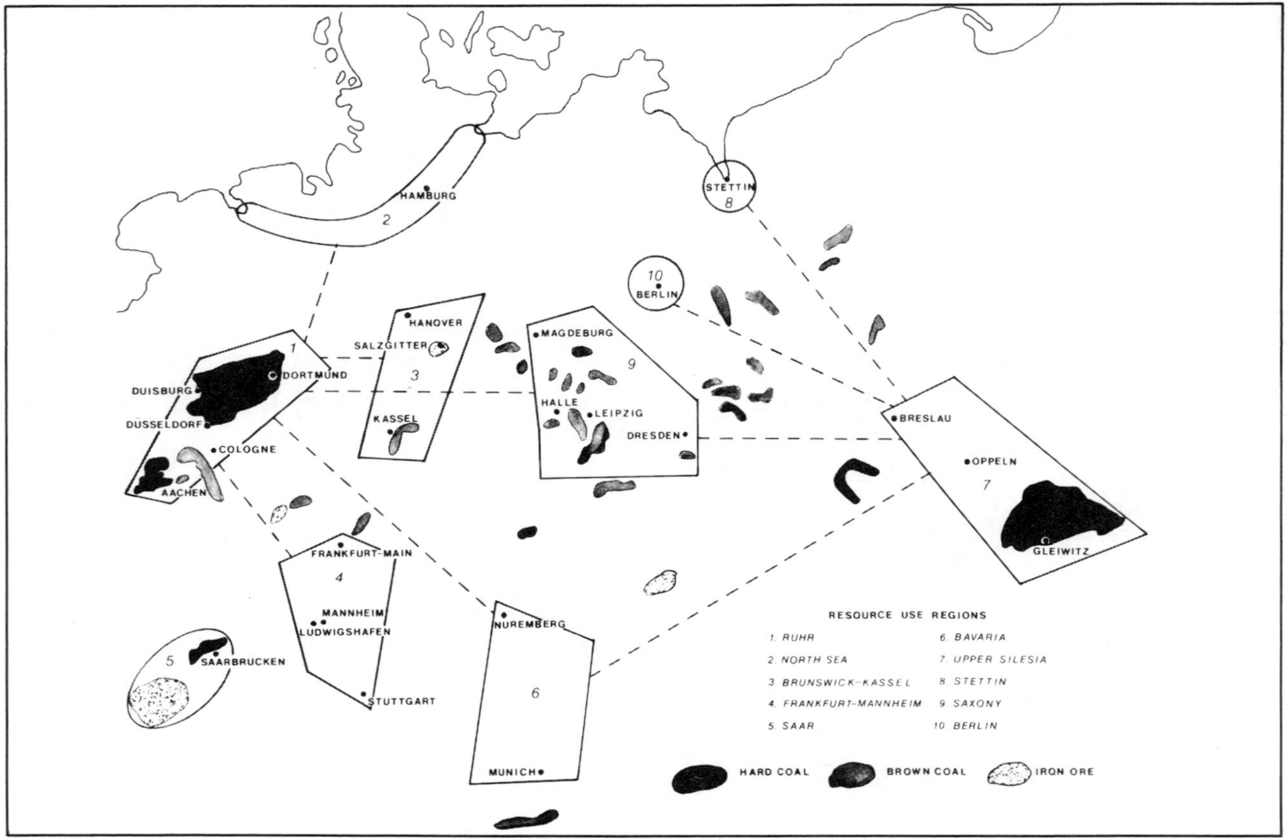

HAMBURG
2
STETTIN
8
10
BERLIN
HANOVER
SALZGITTER
3
KASSEL
1
DORTMUND
DUISBURG
DÜSSELDORF
COLOGNE
AACHEN
MAGDEBURG
9
HALLE
LEIPZIG
DRESDEN
BRESLAU
OPPELN
7
GLEIWITZ
FRANKFURT-MAIN
4
MANNHEIM
LUDWIGSHAFEN
STUTTGART
5
SAARBRUCKEN
NUREMBERG
6
MUNICH
RESOURCE USE REGIONS
1. RUHR
2. NORTH SEA
3. BRUNSWICK–KASSEL
4. FRANKFURT–MANNHEIM
5. SAAR
6. BAVARIA
7. UPPER SILESIA
8. STETTIN
9. SAXONY
10. BERLIN
HARD COAL
BROWN COAL
IRON ORE

Map 2.1 *Germany's Economic Areas*

southwest was the region centered around Frankfurt/Main, the Ludwigshafen-Mannheim complex, and Stuttgart, featuring light and precision manufacturing, electrical engineering, and chemical industries. Finally, in Bavaria industries such as the engineering works at Nuremberg were also within the Ruhr's orbit.

Upper Silesia, because it possessed less coking coal, had a smaller set of satellites. Like the Ruhr it developed heavy manufacturing industries of its own, albeit on a smaller scale. Its chief tributaries were the Baltic port and manufacturing center of Stettin, the aviation, engineering, and chemical works near Leipzig and Dresden, and the electrical engineering, armaments, and vehicle-manufacturing dynamo on the Spree, Berlin.

Examining the economics of energy and raw material supply of functional components of the division of labor can help bring its contours into bold relief. One illustration is the iron and steel industry, which was heavily dependent on the acquistion of iron ore from remote sources. In 1943 Germany obtained over 80 million tons of it with the largest share, 44 percent, composed of minette taken from annexed Lorraine. Imports from Sweden amounted to 12 percent of the total.[49] The latter were greatly valued because of their high iron content and ease of smelting. National ore stocks in 1943 amounted to almost 20 million tons, sufficient for three months of normal operations.[50] Total raw iron production was just over 24,200,000 tons and steel output was 30,600,000 tons.[51]

The dominant force in all of these sectors was the Ruhr. In 1943 it received 26.5 million tons of iron ore of which a third arrived from Scandinavia and almost 18 percent from the minette region. The remainder was drawn from domestic sources.[52] Almost 8 million tons were held in stock, sufficient for about three months of production.[53] The region's output of 9 million tons of raw iron constituted 44 percent of national output.[54] Its steel production was of similar proportions.[55]

Typifying the Ruhr was the giant United Steel Company (Vereinigte Stahlwerke A.G., VSt) headquartered in Düsseldorf. The concern was formed in 1926 to meet the competition offered by large American firms.[56] During the late twenties it modernized and rationalized its facilities which ran the gamut from coal mining to munitions plants. Among its holdings were the Gelsenkirchen Mining Company (Gelsenkirchener Bergwerks AG, GBAG), and famous steel mills such as Thyssen, Ruhrstahl, and the Bochumer

Verein. It was headed initially by Albert Vögler who, though not a
Nazi, was on good terms with Göring and later with Speer. One of
its board members, Walter Rohland, played a major role in Speer's
committee system. GBAG produced 25.7 million tons of coal and
9.8 million tons of coke for its parent in 1943. It retained stocks
equaling about ten days consumption.[57] VSt consumed about 5.3
million tons of iron ore anually. Raw iron production was 5.9 million tons and raw steel output 7.2 million tons, in both cases about
a quarter of the Reich's total.[58] VSt, in its overwhelming scale, integration of production processes and political clout was typical of
the Ruhr's dominance of basic production tied to strong influence
in Berlin. It also illustrates how the steel industry located near its
source of energy, hard coal, relied on distant sources of iron ore.
The cost of transporting iron ore was considered to be lower than
that of shipping enormous amounts of coal.

The central German industrial region, comprising Hanover, Kassel, and Brunswick depended upon the Ruhr for hard coal and semifinished goods and engaged in the manufacture of steel, armaments,
vehicles, and machinery. It controlled its own ore supplies at Salzgitter and could draw upon nearby brown coal resources to supplement energy obtained from the Ruhr. It accounted for 10 percent of
national raw iron output.[59] The dominant factor in the iron and
steel sector was the RWHG. In 1943 it consumed 2.6 million tons
of coal, virtually all of it obtained from the RWKS over the Mittelland Canal and the Reichsbahn. It used 3.24 million tons of iron
ore, most obtained locally, and produced 1.09 million tons of raw
iron, about 5.5 percent of Reich output.[60]

More representative of the region's manufacturing industry was
the Krupp-Gruson plant at Magdeburg. The facility had been purchased by Krupp in the 1880s to help it enter the artillery and armor
plate markets.[61] It produced the Mk IV medium tank, the 75 mm
gun, and artillery shells of various calibers. It received components
for them from Essen and from local subcontractors by rail. It turned
to a diversified range of suppliers for energy. Gas was purchased
from the Reichswerke Hermann Göring and the Magdeburg municipal works, brown coal was procured locally, coke came from the
RWHG and Essen, and all of its hard coal from the Ruhr. The plant
generated most of its own electricity, purchasing the rest from the
municipal works.[62] It kept stocks of coals and coke ranging from
four to seven weeks' worth.[63] In the first quarter of 1944 it pro-

duced monthly an average of 2,592.3 tons of all products including 107 tanks, 137,000 shells, and 47 anti-aircraft pieces.[64] Krupp-Gruson illustrates how even sizable armaments manufacturers in the tributary regions were dependent upon outside suppliers for energy, raw materials, and components to complete their contracts. Not only were these needed in appropriate quantities, but they had to arrive on time to prevent the interruption of production.

A similar situation prevailed in Ludwigshafen on the Rhine at the company of Gebrüder Giulini, which smelted bauxite into aluminum in a converted chemical works. The plant could process 145,000 tons of bauxite per annum, or about a fifth of total German capacity.[65] In 1943 it obtained 303,808 tons of bauxite, all by rail and all from regions outside of Germany, enabling it to accumulate extensive stocks. It purchased 71,655 tons of hard coal from the RWKS local representative, the Kohlenkontor Weyhenmeyer, and 38,107 tons of brown coal from the Cologne area through the Rhenish Brown Coal Syndicate (Rheinisches Braunkohlensyndikat, RBS) which arrived both by rail and by barge.[66] The company operated its own coal-fired electricity generating plant to support its voracious demand for power, a characteristic of the aluminum industry.

The Ruhr's tributaries stretched across western and southern Germany encompassing the bulk of the nation's most important enterprises. All were united in their dependency on the region for energy and to varying degrees by reliance on it for semifinished goods. Together they formed a coherent production unit capable of providing Germany with the preponderance of her war material. The tempo of the unit's activity was set by the coal industry at its heart.

Upper Silesia presided over a similar but smaller system. In 1943 it produced 1.1 million tons of raw iron, just over 5 percent of the national total and 2,350,000 tons or 9 percent of Germany's steel output.[67]

The eastern coal region's major dependency was Berlin. The national capital was the home of major automotive, railroad, aviation, electrical engineering, and armaments plants. A good illustration of the area's energy position was the Berlin Electricity Works (Berliner Elektrizitätswerke, BEWAG, also known as Berliner Kraft- und Licht). BEWAG served all the city's manufacturers and like them was dependent upon the shipment of coal from distant sources. BEWAG operated nine plants in and around the metropolitan area that generated 2.1 billion kilowatt hours of electricity in 1943, or about 179 million KWH per month. It received an average of 129,000 tons of coal each month by rail and water with Upper Silesia contributing 85 percent. The remainder came from the RWKS. Stocks averaged seven weeks' consumption.[68] The utility's head was Dr. Richard Fischer, who was also the Reich Load Distributor.

These firms typified the industries of the satellite regions and their energy relationships to the two hard coal producing centers. It should not be forgotten, however, that many other companies made important contributions to the German war effort. Some were similar in size to those discussed above. Others consumed only a few tons of coal, a few hundred cubic meters of gas, and a few thousand kilowatt-hours of electricity. They produced perhaps only a few thousand kilograms of goods. But they were vital to the system because they provided components and sub-assemblies without which the major firms engaged in final production could not function. Like the great concerns, they relied on the easy exchange of goods to perform their function. Some will be mentioned later, but in the interim their indispensable contribution should be borne in mind.

By late 1943 the German economy had developed a highly complex functional and geographical division of labor steered by the managerial system perfected by Speer. Its strength lay in the close integration and tight coordination of its separate parts. A key to its efficient operation was the grouping of industry around the two great coal centers, the Ruhr and Upper Silesia. The Ruhr predominated because of the high quality of its coal, its more variegated ancillary industries, and its superior political organization. The exchange of goods in a timely fashion among industrial sectors and regions was crucial. The lifeblood of the system was coal, and the fate of the entire organism rested on the conduit that ensured its steady flow, the Deutsche Reichsbahn.

3 Wheels Must Roll for Victory

The Deutsche Reichsbahn

On the warm early summer day of 17 June 1942, Paul Pleiger sat at his desk writing a letter to Albert Speer that would be like the cold blast of winter on the new minister's rosy production plans. Pleiger explained that coal production was rising but shortages threatened to develop among consumers. The Reichsbahn could not ship all the coal that was cut.[1] He calculated that transportation problems caused the loss of over 60 million tons of all types of coal in the preceding year, almost 27 million tons to industry alone.[2] Disaster could be avoided, he argued, only if the Reichsbahn provided him with 22,000 more cars per day.[3] As he had put it in May, "The coal situation can . . . be considered as purely a transportation problem."[4]

The head of the Reich Coal Association was not alone in sounding the alarm. The Reich Iron Association estimated that over 2 million tons of iron would be lost because of a lack of coal in the period from October 1942 to March 1943.[5] Blast furnaces in occupied France and Belgium and many rolling mills in Germany ran well below capacity due to a lack of fuel.[6] On being informed of this Hitler warned Pleiger that "if the output of the steel industry cannot be increased as foreseen because of a shortage of coking coal, the war is lost."[7]

The division of labor that shaped the German economy was based on coal. Distributing coal in sufficient quantity, reliably and in a timely fashion both to users in heavy industry near the mines and to consumers at the end of the production process far removed from them, depended upon the smooth functioning of the transportation system. A coal/transport nexus existed that bound the functionally diverse and geographically separate parts of the economic organism into a coherent whole. It was the foundation of all economic activity in Germany. Equally important was the transportation system's role in the exchange of finished industrial goods among manufacturing centers and in the provision of food to the urban agglomerations where industry was concentrated.[8] With coal German industry could not function, and without adequate transportation it could not have coal. The dependence on transportation was multifaceted and self-reinforcing. It was the very heart of the Reich's military might.

The transportation system consisted of two parts, the national railway (the Deutsche Reichsbahn) and the inland waterway network. Of the two, the Reichsbahn was by far more important. In 1943 it carried over three-quarters of all freight while the waterways bore only one-tenth.[9] Moreover it moved 90 percent of all coal that was shipped.[10] The Reichsbahn was the main constituent of the coal/transport nexus. Because of its flexibility and the wide range of services that it offered it was also the most important prop to the functional division of labor. It could reach more places, more often and faster than the barges. It was the indispensable conduit, the most powerful buttress of the German economy.

The Reichsbahn was fairly new, created only in 1920 through the amalgamation of the numerous German state railways that had survived into the twentieth century. But it was also the legatee of a long and honorable railroading heritage. Its past was personified by Dr.-Ing. Julius Dorpmüller, its head and Reich Transportation Minister. Known for his geniality and engineering expertise, Dorpmüller was seventy-four years old. He enjoyed a wealth of railroading experience including work in China and in Germany's great coal regions. He had been General Director of the DR since 1927 and Transportation Minister since 1937. During the 1920s he resurrected the Reichsbahn from the confusion of hasty unification and the reparations crisis of 1923. He initiated technical and managerial improvements that raised it to the first rank of world railroading. He also imbued it with a philosophy stressing the formation of a solid capital base, the accumulation of excess vehicle capacity, the conduct of operations well within the limits of available equipment, and the provision of a wide variety of services tailored to the broadest consuming public. Dorpmüller was a political conservative who eschewed membership in the Nazi Party. But as a patriotic German, he cooperated with it in its economic and military ventures with the proviso that it not interfere in the internal matters of the railroad.[11]

Dorpmüller's organization was well calculated to handle the rhythms of economic activity and, with sufficient notice, the brief military adventures contemplated by Hitler. It featured advance planning and provision for contingencies in its basic framework. The central organs formulated policy and oversaw daily operations. Regional and local bodies managed the system and actually ran the trains.

At the center, the Transportation Ministry was responsible for all forms of transportation except aviation. It was divided into six sections. The two most significant were for railways and inland waterways. Others dealt with ocean-going commerce, road transport, and general administrative matters.[12] Within the Railway Section were ten sub-sections. For the management of traffic two were of overriding importance: E I, the Traffic and Tariff Section, and E II, the Operations Section. Assisting them was the Main Car Office (Hauptwagenamt, Hwa) established in the Central Office (Zentralamt, RZA) located in Berlin. Regional control was exerted by three General Operating Offices (Generalbetriebsleitungen, GBL). They were responsible for operational affairs within their areas with emphasis on the smooth and punctual flow of traffic. Because of their control of armaments traffic and close cooperation with the military, their existence was a closely guarded secret. They were headquartered in Berlin (GBL-East), Munich (GBL-South) and Essen (GBL-West) and provide a convenient means for observing the broad trends in the Reichsbahn's operations. Associated with them were General Transportation Offices (Generalverkehrsleitungen, GVL) that coordinated waterway, street car, and road traffic with the Reichsbahn's activities.[13]

The basic operational unit of the DR was the Reichsbahn Directorate (Reichsbahndirektion, RBD). In 1943 there were thirty-one of them divided among the three GBLs (see Map 3.1). Each was associated with a Regional Traffic Office (Bezirksverkehrsleitung, BVL). The directorates ran trains, managed their supporting maintenance shops, and had control over locomotives and cars. They were in the most intimate contact with transportation consumers. Within the general guidelines set by Berlin, they exercised enormous power.

The allocation of car space was a cooperative venture accomplished by the Main Car Office, sections E I and E II, the GBLs, and the RBDs. Each day as many as 30,000 freight trains were run. Of them about 17,000 worked to a fixed schedule. The remainder were operated only on demand. Each RBD held a stock of cars and locomotives from which it attempted to meet requirements. Every morning between six and ten it reported its plans and needs to

Map 3.1 *Deutsche Reichsbahn Directorates*

the appropriate GBL and the Hwa. They coordinated movements among the RBDs and allocated cars to those in need. Therefore, each RBD operated independently with the central authorities acting as referees who stepped in to play a direct role only when necessary. The resulting system was flexible, although it suffered from a lack of coordination from the center due to unclear lines of authority between the Hwa, GBLs, and RBDs.[14]

Managing such a complex enterprise, in which the movements of thousands of trains, yard operations, and customers took place simultaneously, demanded the collection of mountains of information quickly, accurately, and reliably. The Reichsbahn had recognized this requirement and fashioned a modern, comprehensive, and redundant communications net consisting of 800,000 kilometers of cable serving over 600,000 telephones and 200,000 teletypes.[15] During the war over 7,700 kilometers of new line were laid.[16] Directorates were connected to Berlin by double cable lines that were buried or carried on poles along the right of way. Stations were tied to the directorates by laying lines about a meter underground, avoiding bridges and viaducts by passing separately under or around obstacles.[17] Equipment was procured by the Central Office in Berlin, repair shops were set up there and in Munich and Vienna, and schools were located in Berlin, Dresden, and Stuttgart.[18] On average, the network carried over 2.5 million conversations averaging 2 minutes each and over .5 million telegrams of 10 words each per day.[19] Rules were enforced limiting the length of messages and conversations. Those deemed inconsequential were cut off.

The telecommunications net was subdivided into three interlocking components. An operational network coterminous with the directorates connected all stations and repair shops and featured telephones every 1,000 meters along the line. Each station had its own exchange that linked all work places in its confines and had special connections to major transportation consumers nearby, such as coal mines and steel plants. Finally, four main nets, consisting of both telephone and telegraph connections, based in Berlin, Essen, Frankfurt/Main, and Nuremberg, provided long-distance services. The technical foundation of the network was the Railway Automatic Connection Apparatus (Bahnselbstanschlussanlage, Basa) that enabled a caller to telephone any other location simply by dialing the appropriate number without contacting an operator. Basas were given to all of the directorate headquarters and other major operating locations such as repair shops and yards.[20]

Special communications repair trains equipped with stores of spares and tools and manned by technicians were kept in constant readiness. Supplies of materials were stored at locations removed from stations and other likely bombing targets. Communications rooms were hardened against blast and splinters. Dispersed sites were equipped with communications apparatus and mobile Basas were set up in freight cars and trucks.[21]

Long before the war it was recognized that whatever precautions were taken, telephone, and telegraph systems remained vulnerable to air attack. Consequently radios were provided to major offices to assure emergency communications links. They were never available in sufficient numbers and the DR fought a losing battle with the Wehrmacht for frequencies.[22] But radio opened another vulnerability that was immediately identified and addressed. The offices in Berlin, each RBD headquarters, and the GBLs were equipped with an Enigma cipher machine.[23] This channel was open only to high officials such as Dorpmüller and his immediate subordinates and the presidents of the RBDs and GBLs.[24] The use of the Enigma by the Reichsbahn was shrouded in secrecy at the time, and virtually all traces of it were intentionally erased by DR personnel just prior to the capitulation in 1945. Yet it is clear that Enigma was used right up until the end and grew in importance as the war neared its conclusion. As fears increased concerning the security of its other channels and as land lines were cut by bombing, the DR relied more heavily upon its supposedly unbreakable cipher.[25]

The care taken to mask its inner workings and to ensure the flow of information despite external interference was matched by the Reichsbahn's preparations to maintain the movement of traffic. Like all public organizations in the Third Reich, the DR created a chapter of the Reich Air Defense League (Reichsluftschutzbund), dubbed the Railway Air Protection Service (Eisenbahn Luftschutzdienst). It monitored the air situation based on information obtained from the Luftwaffe and its own offices and issued air-raid warnings. When attack appeared imminent, trains halted in tunnels and wooded areas and the crews disembarked. No train could enter or leave a yard during an attack. Yards ceased operations during raids but worked until the last possible moment. Then crews took to shrapnel shelters and small concrete bunkers erected near their work places. Occasionally they used the heavier bunkers built to protect the traveling public.[26]

In February 1944 the increased weight of air attack on German industry prompted the DR to establish a central Air Raid Control Office (Luftschutzbefehlstelle) in the Transportation Ministry. It was responsible for allocating manpower and materials to regions struck by air raids.[27] Prior to the war, repair columns had been formed consisting of a total of 16,000 men of whom 5,700 were from the DR itself. They were committed to the restoration of heavily damaged yards.[28] Organic repair personnel handled lesser damage. The DR had always fielded dedicated right-of-way repair trains. They were equipped with special tools and machine shop equipment and were based at major stations throughout the system. During the war they were reinforced and kept at instant readiness.[29] Materials were stored in dumps scattered along the line.

Supporting the DR were outside organizations providing labor and technical services that were beyond its own resources. These included the Organisation Todt, technical troops from the Wehrmacht, and the Repair Service of the Security and Emergency Service (Instandsetzungsdienst des Sicherheits- und Hilfsdienstes, IS) of the Air Raid Protection League.[30] The OT could intervene with thousands of laborers including foreigners and prisoners, while the IS specialized in utility and bridge repairs in urban areas.

Signal repair was a particularly thorny problem and the Reichsbahn took precautions early. Spare parts were scarce due to low industrial priority and the destruction by bombing of the largest supplier, the Vereinigte Eisenbahnsignalwerke located in Berlin-Siemensstadt on 20 January 1944. To repair damaged signal and communications facilities 168 special trains were formed. Mobile signal and switching towers were prepared to enable yards to continue operations until permanent repairs could be completed.[31]

A firm policy was established to guide the actions of repair crews in the wake of a bombing attack. First, through service was restored so as to limit disruption to the particular yard hit. Next, the marshalling section was repaired. Then, freight and passenger loading facilities were tackled and finally, roundhouses.[32]

From the outset it was recognized that these preparations might prove inadequate in the face of concerted attack. Therefore plans were laid to compensate for the temporary loss of major components of the system. They were based on the standard rules for meeting emergencies and included operating line without signals, with only one track open on a two track line, and running opposite to the ordinary direction of travel. In addition, provisions were made for the reallocation of freight loading and traffic handling among yards, including the case of the simultaneous loss of two major yards in the Ruhr.[33]

The Reichsbahn, therefore, possessed a good administrative system and a conservative mode of traffic management beset only by a slight lack of coordination between its center and regional offices. It had executed extensive preparations to meet any conceivable emergency. Not surprisingly, it resented outside suggestions for change and, until the spring of 1942, it successfully resisted them.[34] But then its front crumbled under the pressure of the massive crisis that swept over the entire German war effort and brought Speer to power. The defeat before Moscow and the terrible winter that accompanied it both in the Soviet Union and in Germany unleashed a serious transportation crisis. The long lines of communication leading eastward drained the DR of locomotives and cars. Many were immobilized by the intense cold. By March 1942 available car space could satisfy only about two-thirds of demand, and coal car space was a tenth below target.[35] Plant closings followed and coal piled up at the mines.

Dorpmüller himself recognized the magnitude of the emergency and offered to hand over control of railroad matters to Speer. But the new armaments minister was loathe to shoulder such a heavy burden in addition to his other onerous tasks. He therefore obtained Hitler's approval for personnel and managerial changes that would revitalize the DR and incorporate it into his nascent system of industrial efficiency.[36]

Speer won the dismissal of the heads of the Reichsbahn's Traffic and Operations sections and replaced them with Dr. Fritz Schelp and Gustav Dilli respectively. Schelp was forty-five years old and had been active in the DR for nineteen years. He was trained as a jurist and was a solid administrator. Dilli had an engineering background and was fifty-two years old. He was a specialist in freight train scheduling and had served in the Ruhr, in the occupied territories, and at GBL-West.[37]

The most important of Speer's appointments was the new state secretary and assistant general director of the Reichsbahn, the energetic Dr. Albert Ganzenmüller. At the age of thirty-seven, Ganzenmüller typified the sort of young, committed, and dynamic administrator that Speer prized. He had an electrical-engineering background and had served with distinction in the occupied West. He had volunteered for service in the East and had established his reputation in the Ukraine by mastering the all-embracing winter traffic emergency. Moreover, he was a staunch National Socialist who had participated in the Beer Hall Putsch of November 1923 and had joined the NSDAP in April 1931. He was active in Party affairs and had captured some of its athletic awards.[38] He shunned bureaucratic routine, refusing, for example, to sign memoranda longer than four pages. He was convinced that the Reichsbahn's difficulties stemmed from poor management, not from a lack of vehicles.

Ganzenmüller along with Schelp and Dilli were charged by Speer with infusing the Reichsbahn's fundamentally sound system with new energy. They were to abandon the old conservative, consumer-oriented practices in order to stress speed and efficiency and thus to enable an increase in performance without major additions to capital. Speer did make provision for heightened output of simplified locomotives, but no substantial construction of stations or right-of-way was planned.[39]

Accompanying these personnel changes were organizational reforms through which Speer integrated the DR into his administrative apparatus. Initially he attached transport representatives to his rings and committees.[40] But they proved inadequate. On 21 June 1942 he formed a Transport Office in his ministry, composed of himself; Ganzenmüller; Erhard Milch; Willi Liebel, mayor of Nuremberg, another close friend; Wilhelm Landfried of the Ministry of Economics; Karl Kaufmann, Gauleiter of Hamburg and special plenipotentiary for sea transport; and Wilhelm Meinberg, responsible for coal transport in the Four Year Plan Office.[41] This body was run by Milch with Speer remaining in the background. It instituted measures to speed loading of cars and to shift traffic from the rails to the waterways. Deeming its task accomplished, it dissolved itself in September 1942.[42]

Operating in tandem with the Transport Office was Hans Kehrl, who was named Special Representative for the Reichsbahn. Kehrl also concentrated on reducing loading time and eliminating unjustified shipments. Among the latter were goods sent over long distances that the purchaser could have obtained locally. Ending such shipments saved transport both by shortening the average flow of goods and by eliminating the phenomenon of similar products passing each other on the rails, headed to adjacent consumers and shippers. Kehrl also sought to limit overall demand by concentrating transport on the most important goods, such as coal and steel, and reducing or eliminating transport of other types of freight.[43] To make shippers more aware of the program, the Reichsbahn initiated an advertising campaign with the theme "Wheels must roll for victory."[44] Like the Transport Office, Kehrl ended his intervention in transportation affairs in the autumn of 1942.

Of somewhat longer-lasting significance was the Bureau for Transportation Organization. It functioned from November 1942 until 1 September 1943 under contract with the RWM to continue

Kehrl's program based on studies it had previously conducted independently. As of September 1943 it was incorporated in the ministry and thereafter lost influence. It examined the economic relationships of the Reich's industrial regions and instituted measures that rationalized freight flows.[45]

All of these organizational measures initiated by Speer were transitory in nature although they did greatly assist the Reichsbahn in overcoming the 1942 crisis. More permanent was the Central Transportation Directorate (Zentralverkehrsleitstelle, ZVL). It was the direct analogue to his industrial committees and rings, and its formation fundamentally altered the means of controlling transport in the Reich. The ZVL was headed by the fifty-six-year-old Ernst Emrich, who had begun his railroad career in 1912 and was simultaneously head of GBL-East.[46] Formed in June 1942, the ZVL was composed of representatives of all ministries involved in economic affairs. Heads of important offices in the Reichsbahn and the Inland Waterway Section of the RVM regularly reported before it on traffic conditions. While the ZVL possessed no statutory powers, because of the importance of its membership, its uniqueness as a forum where providers and consumers of transportation services could meet directly, and because it enjoyed Speer's imprimatur, it was the most powerful administrative organ influencing transport policy in the Reich. It alone allocated space among groups of users and relied on Dilli and the Main Car Office to set specific quotas. One exception was coal transport where the ZVL constantly maintained the closest supervision.[47]

The net result of these personnel and administrative reforms was that the Reichsbahn weathered the 1942 winter crisis and markedly improved its performance afterward. It provided the necessary support for Speer's armaments expansion by increasing the tonnage it carried through enhanced efficiency, not through the provision of greater car space. This enabled Pleiger to conclude after the Central Planning meeting on coal matters on 30 April 1943 that the situation was satisfactory.[48]

While managerial changes could wring increased performance from it, ultimately the Reichsbahn's limits were set by its fund of physical assets. In 1943 it was manned by about 1.5 million people, about 12 percent of whom were foreigners and prisoners of war.[49] They operated 78,879 kilometers of line, of which 55 percent was considered main line suitable for the heaviest traffic. Two-thirds of the main line was double tracked, and a further 3 percent had three or more tracks. About 3 percent, primarily in southern Germany, was electrified.[50] (For the main freight arteries see Map 3.2.)

The vehicle park that moved on the Reichsbahn's extensive and well-maintained rail net was massive by any standard. As of July 1944 it included 34,545 locomotives of which 32,295 were steam powered.[51] They were housed at 740 Operating Works (Bahnbetriebswcrke, Bw) backed by 95 Repair Works (Reichsbahn Ausbesserungswerke, RAW). The RAW were veritable factories capable of performing the most extensive repair projects.[52] Some had staffs of over a thousand people.[53]

Like the rest of the economy, the Reichsbahn was heavily dependent on coal. Its locomotives consumed over 32 million tons of hard coal in 1943.[54] Stocks were maintained at twenty days.[55] Coal was purchased by the Central Office directly from the syndicates. Only certain types were acceptable and engineers went to the mines to select them.[56] The chief supplier was the RWKS, which provided about 43 percent of the Reichsbahn's needs with Upper Silesia satisfying about 40 percent.[57]

The voracious locomotives pulled an aggregation of 1,208,438 freight cars of which the DR owned 973,045.[58] There were two basic types. Box cars, about a third of the total, were employed to move perishable or high unit value freight, while open cars, comprising two-thirds of the park, were used to ship bulk commodities such as coal. Both types had an average capacity of twenty tons. However, as of 1942 they were regularly overloaded with an additional one to two tons.[59]

A broad range of services was offered, adapted to the dictates of running trains and to the needs of the market. Through trains passed only between major distribution centers, not stopping at lesser stations. Others collected freight and distributed it among the myriad of small yards, freight acceptance sheds at passenger stations, and company loading facilities.[60] Almost a third of all trains ran empty since return cargoes could not always be arranged despite energetic efforts to do so. Trains carrying mixed freight averaged 39 cars in length.[61] Average load was about 300 tons.[62] Coal trains were about 40 cars long and carried about 800 tons, though many, consisting of special large capacity cars, weighed over 1,000 tons.[63] Most freights traveled at about 50 KPH but a third moved at 60 KPH.[64]

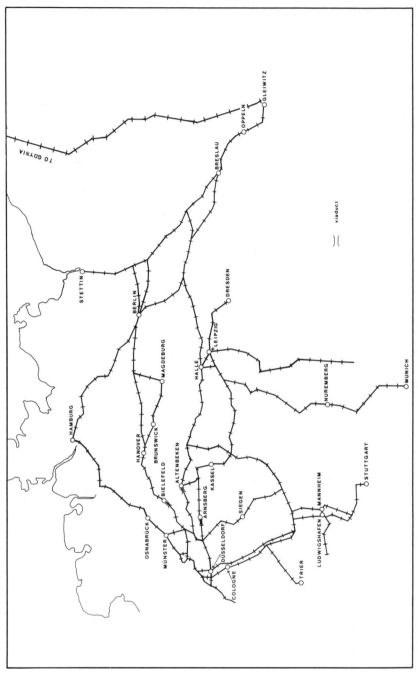

Map 3.2 *Main Freight Arteries of the Deutsche Reichsbahn*

All of this bustling traffic was orchestrated from what was universally recognized as the Reichsbahn's heart, its most sensitive point—its marshalling yards.[65] The marshalling yard was the physical embodiment of the economic division of labor. Freight from a host of origins was directed to equally numerous destinations through a complicated method of sorting that functioned to a strict schedule both within single marshalling yards and among them. Cars were not loaded at marshalling yards. Instead small consignments were brought to loading sheds adjacent to them or near main passenger stations. Larger shipments were put aboard cars at loading docks operated by manufacturers connected to the main line by spurs. All major heavy industries and coal mines possessed their own loading facilities. At this point each car was given a card which was inserted into a pocket on its outside. It would accompany the car to its destination and be used in the sorting process. The card bore a stamp indicating the load's priority with a code word such as "Panzer." Cars were gathered by local trains and brought to a nearby marshalling yard where they were left in a set of tracks shaped like a gridiron called a reception group. The locomotive moved away for servicing. A small yard locomotive then pushed the line of cars, which had been uncoupled by workers, over a hump, a dirt mound over which track had been laid. Their own weight and gravity pulled them toward a second gridiron in which each track represented a route. Cars were lined up on the tracks of this sorting group in the order in which they would be dropped off. Remotely controlled switches and brakes called retarders, directed them to the proper tracks and prevented them from crashing into each other. Once they had all been sorted, yard locomotives pulled the cars to a departure group where a line locomotive would take them on their way. All of this highly complex and dangerous work occurred at night to enable completed trains to depart during the early morning to deliver the freight during business hours. The entire marshalling process could be vastly more complicated if a yard served traffic flows coming from intersecting directions or if it was near a port. In any case, it was an exceedingly complex and delicate affair subject to disruption by weather and human error.[66] Problems at one yard reverberated to others. For this reason unit trains (Ganzzüge) carrying just one type of freight, usually coal or ore, were used. They took longer than ordinary trains to form and for that reason were initially disliked by the Reichsbahn. But their advantages in terms of reduced marshalling grew in importance and they were used more frequently with every passing month.[67]

The importance and sensitivity of the marshalling process meant that the ZVL and the other offices responsible for the allocation of car space scrutinized their operations very closely. Inevitably most of their attention fell on three critical directorates that together set the pace for the entire Reichsbahn. They mirrored exactly the geographical division of labor since they were the hubs of coal traffic.

The most important was RBD Essen (see Map 3.3). Alone it accounted for a tenth of all marshalling activities and more importantly, originated 38 percent of the Reichsbahn's hard coal movements. It held five of the DR's ten largest marshalling yards. But sheer size was not the sole determinant of a marshalling yard's importance. Also crucial was its location in relation both to industry originating traffic and to recipients. Consequently a few yards in RBD Essen and in the surrounding directorates were of overriding importance. They were identified by Rüdiger Schmidt of the RWKS and, along with the Reichsbahn, he agonized daily over their well-being because they regulated the flow of coal from the Ruhr to its dependencies.[68]

The largest such Ruhr gateway, situated in RBD Essen on the eastern edge of the region, northeast of Dortmund, was Hamm. It could assemble up to two hundred fifty-car trains per day (10,000 cars in all) making it the largest marshalling yard in Germany. It controlled the high density four-track line passing over the Bielefeld Viaduct to Hanover and Berlin. This was the most heavily traveled route in Germany. At Hamm local trains from within the Ruhr were combined for dispatch east and incoming long distance trains were broken up for distribution of their contents within the region.[69]

To the south in RBD Kassel was Soest, which could handle 4,000 cars per day. It paced the flow to the Ruhr's satellites in Saxony, which ran on the line using the Altenbecken Viaduct. Farther south was Geisecke which, with a capacity of 3,000 cars per day, controlled movement eastward over the Arnsberg Viaduct to Kassel. Yet farther south and to the west was the railroad complex at Hagen of which the most important yard was Vorhalle with a capacity of 3,800 cars per day. This was the gateway to the famous Siegen Stretch that ran south through the Ruhr's historic source of iron ore

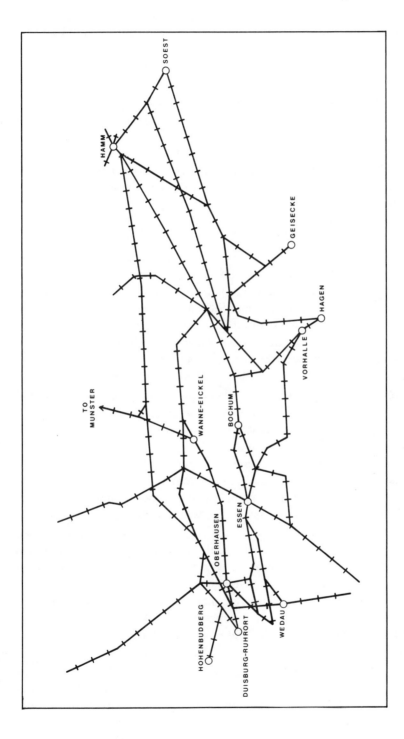

Map 3.3 *RBD Essen and the Coal Gateways*

to Frankfurt/Main. It and Geisecke were administered by RBD Wuppertal.

At the opposite corner of the Ruhr was Wedau in RBD Essen, which could process 7,200 cars each day. It regulated the flow from Duisburg, Oberhausen, and Essen southward along the right bank of the Rhine to Düsseldorf and its Derendorf yard and ultimately to Mannheim.

North of Wedau on the left bank of the Rhine in RBD Cologne was Hohenbudberg. It could manage about 6,000 cars per day and manipulated the traffic moving down the left bank of the Rhine to Cologne.

Finally, in the directorate of the same name, was Münster which, though capable of processing only 2,000 cars per day, regulated the northward flow to the North Sea ports from the massive freight and coal yard at Wanne-Eickel.[70] There was also a significant reverse traffic in manufactured goods, food, and iron ore.

The second coal pivot, Upper Silesia, was served by RBD Oppeln. Traffic here was much simpler, generally flowing out of the region westward over the so-called Coal Railway to Berlin and Saxony. Almost as important was the traffic passing northward on the Magistrale line to Gdynia on the Baltic. Coal was dispatched from there to the North Sea ports and Scandinavia. The Magistrale carried 60,000 of Upper Silesia's daily export of 160,000 tons of hard coal.[71] RBD Oppeln's most important yard was at Gleiwitz in the midst of the coal field. It could marshal 6,800 cars per day. Overall RBD Oppeln accounted for 12 percent of general freight car traffic and originated a third of hard coal movements.[72]

Acting as an intermediary between the two major coal regions and the industrial groupings to the west, north, and east was RBD Halle. It accounted for 7.5 percent of freight car traffic and originated 45 percent of all brown coal shipments.[73] Its importance is belied by its overall freight car placing share since its operations were highly complex and were executed under extreme time pressure so as not to disrupt movement elsewhere. Its most important yards were at Halle, with a capacity of 4,800 cars per day, and Falkenberg, which could handle 7,000 cars daily.[74]

These three pivotal directorates, Essen, Halle, and Oppeln, determined the overall scale and pace of the Reichsbahn's operations. They performed this role because of their association with the coal trade and because their geographical location made them originators or intermediaries for traffic in manufactured goods. Two directorates at the geographical extremities and one in the center were crucial factors determining not only the DR's fate but that of Germany as well since they made possible the smooth functioning of the division of labor.

Special importance was accorded by Berlin to their mastering of coal traffic. RBDs Essen and Oppeln were given wide operational latitude in the matter. But the Main Car Office and the ZVL watched developments closely and maintained a reserve of coal cars in RBDs Halle, Berlin, and neighboring areas to overcome any irregularities in the traffic. A special effort was made to ship coal in unit trains, with regular runs rigidly established in the schedule and given priority over other trains.[75]

A complicating factor was the seasonal variation in traffic patterns. The summer was the quietest period as demand for coal was lowest. Then the pace quickened in September as firms rushed to accumulate stocks for the winter. A few weeks later a heavy, urgent demand for cars developed in the East to move the harvest westward to the urban areas before it spoiled. This was the most difficult time of the year for the Reichsbahn. After the harvest, traffic remained heavy until warm weather in the spring reduced the demand for coal and therefore for transport. The Reichsbahn continuously warned consumers to accumulate stocks during the summer months when car space was plentiful. But inevitably they failed to seize the opportunity.[76]

To trace the Reichsbahn's activities in the three GBLs and the three pivotal directorates, four indices have been selected, all of which were used for the same purpose by the DR itself. The most revealing is car placings. It measures the operation of the heart of the system, the marshalling yards. A car placing was the insertion of one car into a train. It was not synonymous with loading.[77] In 1943 the Reichsbahn achieved its highest car placing total since 1916 by putting 48,614,078 cars into trains.[78] The largest share went to coal, which amounted to almost a third of the cars.[79] In 1943 about 14.5 million coal cars were placed. To facilitate comparison among the various sizes of coal cars they were discussed in terms of ten-ton units. By that measure, the one that will also be used througout this account, 26,266,876 were placed.[80] Measured by weight, just to put these figures into perspective, coal accounted for 43 percent of the DR's total freight burden.[81] The Reichsbahn placed an average of 81,696 coal units per day in November 1943 of which 57,197 were for hard coal and 21,499 were for brown coal.[82] The overall target fluctuated between 81,000 and 83,000, depending upon the season and other circumstances.[83]

A second major measurement was backlog, that is, trains delayed more than two hours after scheduled departure time. In 1943 the average daily backlog system wide was 282 trains.[84]

Another revealing yardstick was the amount of time necessary to unload and reload a car. This turnaround time stood at six and a half days in November 1943.[85] The faster cars were turned around the fewer would be needed to run a given volume of traffic.

Finally, the stock of coal available for use by the DR's locomotives measured in number of days consumption will be observed. It provides a very reliable indication of the state of coal traffic in general, since Reichsbahn coal shipments enjoyed first priority. It is also an accurate measure of the health of locomotive service. The emergency stock level was ten days.[86] In the summer of 1943, service coal stocks hovered around the nineteen-day level.[87]

The Reichsbahn achieved its best performance of the war in 1943. Speer's managerial reforms had enabled it to realize its full potential in concert with the increase in armaments production. The system was now personified by Ganzenmüller. He infused new energy into the DR and banished the old conservative managerial and operational practices embodied by Dorpmüller. The historical division of labor which bestowed special importance on RBDs Essen, Halle, and Oppeln was thereby adapted to the new situation.

Nevertheless, performance remained inadequate in light of the additional increases in production sought by Speer. Car placings were consistently about a quarter below demand.[88] Of the 200,000 cars per day requested by industry, probably about 165,000 were genuinely needed.[89] But actual car placings averaged 158,352 per day in 1943—close but far enough below demand to put a cap on production.[90] Coal car placings were also near target, but the overall tonnage sought by the RVK, 275 million for the coal economy year 1943/44, was not met by almost 5 percent.[91] Again this was close, but given the need for ever-increasing amounts, every kilogram of coal not delivered meant a real production loss.

Two reasons can be adduced to explain the DR's inadequacy. First was the increase in the average length of a trip from 183 kilometers in 1938 to 375 by the end of 1943. This was caused by the expansion of the geographical area served by the Reichsbahn as a consequence of Hitler's territorial acquisitions and by the dispersal of industry to escape air attack. Much of the dispersal program was carried out in a haphazard fashion with little attention given by the companies involved to transportation requirements. A frantic rush developed in March 1944 when the aviation industry was scattered broadcast to escape the American air raids conducted against it in February. The result was a temporary respite for the factories and an increased burden on the marshalling yards which were given more destinations to serve. Longer runs to remote locations kept cars en route longer, requiring more cars to move a constant volume of freight.[92]

The decisive reason, however, was that the war had mushroomed far beyond the proportions originally contemplated by Hitler. Reichsbahn officials at the time and after the war, and many historians as well, have concluded that the DR was not adequately prepared for war.[93] They cite the greatly increased demand for transport that allegedly exceeded the Reichsbahn's capacity as early as 1938. In fact, the DR was well prepared for the short wars of conquest envisioned by Hitler. It had untapped potential idled by the Depression and left unexploited by its own inefficiency. Its capacity had been increased through capital improvements carried out before the war. Governmental investment in transportation and especially in the Reichsbahn rose by 40 percent from 1937 to 1938.[94] Extensive improvements were made to lines.[95] Throughout the 1930s the Reichsbahn had fought to increase the speed of its passenger service between major urban areas such as Berlin, Hamburg, Cologne, Frankfurt, and Stuttgart, the very centers of economic activity. To accommodate the crack expresses, roadbeds and signals were improved. This also benefited freight traffic as its average speed increased by a third.[96] An extensive series of improvements was made to marshalling yards beginning in the 1920s and culminating in the extension and modernization of yards in eastern Germany between 1940 and 1942.[97] Operations were mechanized to the latest standard with retarders, remote control switches, and radios.[98] The number of marshalling locomotives was increased fifteenfold between 1932 and 1938.[99] In comparison with 1913 (see Table 3.1), in 1938 the DR possessed more freight cars and fewer but more powerful locomotives, placed more cars in trains, and carried a third more freight. This was in spite of an increase in average haul by more than half and a rise in turnaround time by a third. Whereas in 1913 German railways were operated by the various states, the Reichsbahn was able to provide greater service with a similar capital base because it was unified, because it had more modern, more productive equipment, and because it was administered more effectively. For the same reasons it was able to improve its performance still further during the war. When the war began, contrary to the generally accepted view, the Reichsbahn had a large fleet of modern vehicles run on solid, beautifully maintained right-of-way with an extensive maintenance organization supporting both. It enjoyed the reputation of being one of the best railroads in the world. Ultimately it was overwhelmed by the enormous demands placed upon it by Hitler's megalomania. Nevertheless the Reichsbahn performed admirably and fought doggedly against long odds until the end.

Even under optimum circumstances the Reichsbahn could not have satisfied all the demand for transport space unaided, especially for bulk commodities. Since the turn of the century, transport planners had intended that the inland waterways help the railroads. During the 1930s both the Weimar Republic and the Nazi regime engaged in an extensive program aimed at expanding the net's capacity by improving rivers and adding to the canal system. Yet by 1943 the inland waterway network had fallen badly behind expectations. Its share of overall transport tonnage and its share of coal traffic had steadily declined since the start of the war. Moreover its performance in real terms had also fallen.[100] There were three major causes for the deterioration. One was the loss of ship personnel to the Wehrmacht. Another was the decline in maintenance standards. The most important was poor organization.

Traffic on Germany's rivers and canals was nominally under the overall control of Werner Hassenpflug, head of the Inland Waterway Section of the Ministry of Transportation.[101] He had assumed this responsibility in 1942 during Speer's reform effort. His brief was to energize the sluggish waterways administration, but the inherent qualities of the shipping business and the vagaries of the weather defeated him. Unlike the Reichsbahn, which was operated directly by the state, waterway traffic was in the hands of boat owners and forwarding agents, who ran for profit.[102] They had been incorporated into the Economics Ministry's framework of trade groups in

Table 3.1

*Comparison of German Railroad Performance in
World Wars I and II*

Year	Freight cars	Locomotives	Tonnage[a]	Car placings[a]	Average daily car placings	Net ton kilometers[b]	Average haul[c]	Turnaround[d]
1913	617,748	27,214	501	40.7	133,433	67.7	119	3.05
1938	650,229	25,183	547	47.2	154,521	92.8	182	4.2
1916	711,507	31,038	416	51.4	167,213	—	164	4.6
1943	973,045	36,329	675	48.6	158,352	178.0	269	7.6

Sources: Kreidler, *Eisenbahnen*, pp. 284, 335, table 3.1, 336, table 3.2, 337, table 3.3, 338, tables 3.5 and 3.6; Sarter, *Deutschen Eisenbahnen im Kriege*, p. 276, table A, 278, tables E, F, and G; Wehde-Textor, "Dokumentarische Darstellung," p. 43, BA R5 Anh I/11; USSBS, *German Transportation*, pp. 74–75, exhibit 72.
  a. In millions.
  b. In billions.
  c. In kilometers.
  d. In days.

1935 and retained ties to their historic private organizations.[103] But they had evaded strict government control. There were simply too many individual boat owners to be harnessed by any regulatory body. All of them were jealous of their freedom and could sail as they pleased, given the long stretches of unsupervised waterway and the bustle of the ports. They could embark when they chose, negotiate for lucrative cargoes, tie up their vessels, and rent them out as storage space if that promised greater returns, or if they thought an area too dangerous they could avoid it altogether. The medium in which they traveled was so different from that of the railroad with its fixed rails, and the tradition of private trading so deeply rooted, compared to the centralized control and scheduling common to all railroad operations and the German railways' long and intimate ties to government, that the Transportation Ministry's local offices did little more than collect statistics.

The nation was divided into twelve shipping regions administered by Waterway Directorates (Wasserstrassendirektionen). Shipping Offices were established subordinate to them to oversee traffic and nominally to establish priorities. At important ports and places where waterways met, Shipping Control Stations were set up to regulate movement, issue permits, and maintain records. All of these offices were in contact with the Reichsbahn through the GVLs and the BVLs.[104]

This weak and loosely organized apparatus administered a fleet of 19,248 vessels of 8,262,170 tons burthen. They were manned by 45,858 people of whom about 6 percent were female and almost a third foreigners.[105] Altogether they moved 82 million tons of freight in 1943.[106] Their most important cargo was coal, accounting for 37 percent of their load.[107] On the western canals about 40 percent of barge capacity was occupied by coal and on the Rhine, 60 percent.[108]

The configuration of the system (see Map 3.4) reflected its role in the division of labor. The Rhine supported north-south traffic between the Ruhr and its southwestern tributaries. On the more than 1,300 kilometers of its navigable length plied 4,177 vessels. Barges averaged 1,000 tons capacity. Total available space on all types of vessels amounted to 3,238,074 tons.[109] A large number of ports operated along the great river; however, a few of these illustrate the nature of its traffic and will be watched throughout this account.

The most important was the sprawling Duisburg-Ruhrort complex. In 1943 it handled about 10 million tons of freight of which almost half was coal.[110] It contributed about three-quarters of all coal shipments from Ruhr ports on the Rhine.[111] At the receiving end of this flow was Mannheim which accepted about 70 percent of all coal shipped southward from the Ruhr. Its port had its own briquette factory to process brown coal and was easily accessible by rail from all of the nearby industries. In 1943 it processed over 4 million tons of freight of which about three-quarters consisted of coal arriving from the Rhine-Ruhr region.[112]

Serving the Ruhr's dependencies to the north and east and acting as its conduit for iron ore from Scandinavia was the Dortmund-Ems Canal (DEK). It was completed in 1899 to accommodate barges of 750-ton capacity and was rebuilt after World War I to accept vessels up to 1,500 tons burthen.[113] About 1,400 craft operated on it with a combined capacity of over a million tons.[114] It served a large number of ports including Dortmund and the colliery harbors along its southern stretch and on the Rhine-Herne Canal (RHK) that tied it to the Rhine.[115] A convenient location to measure its activity is the

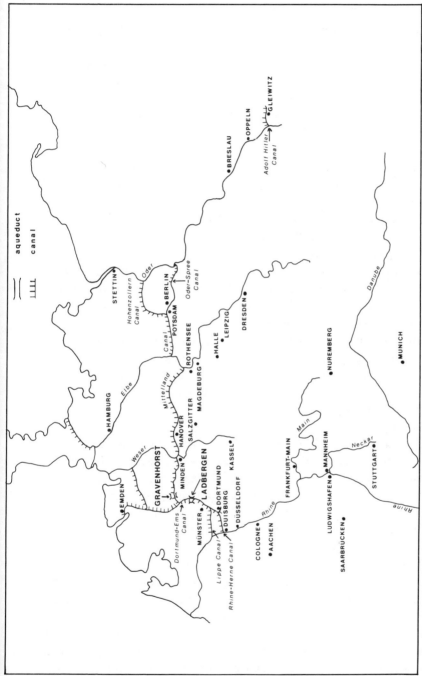

Map 3.4 *Germany's Inland Waterways*

Münster lock just south of where it connected with the Mittelland Canal. At that point a total of 13,749,308 tons of freight passed in 1943. Sixty percent was hard coal moving north and east and 39 percent was iron ore headed south to the Ruhr's smelters.[116]

Completing the western waterway system was the Mittelland Canal (MLK) finished in 1938, which could accommodate vessels of up to 1,700 tons displacement.[117] The MLK was traveled by the same group of barges that operated on the Dortmund-Ems Canal. It connected with the Elbe at Minden via locks and passed over the river by an aqueduct. Its principal ports were at Hanover and Salzgitter, the latter serving the Reichswerke Hermann Göring.[118] Using the spectacular shiplift at Rothensee near Magdeburg and then navigating the rivers Elbe and Havel and associated canals, barges could reach Berlin. The MLK carried about 18 million tons of freight, half of which was coal, as measured at Minden.[119]

Berlin was primarily dependent for its waterborne trade on the Oder via the Oder-Spree Canal. The predominant traffic was hard coal from Upper Silesia with brown coal from central Germany playing a lesser role. The Oder was home to 2,343 vessels with a combined payload of 854,135 tons. They were smaller than the Rhine and west German canal barges averaging 430 tons capacity. Nearby canals were plied by 2,413 craft capable of toting 577,882 tons of freight. They too were relatively small barges having a median capacity of 307 tons.[120]

About 13.5 million tons of freight were handled by Berlin's ports each year with coal constituting almost 29 percent of the total. Two-thirds of the coal originated in Upper Silesia. The source of most of the flow was the port of Gleiwitz. It was connected to the Oder by the Adolf Hitler Canal completed in 1940 and capable of accommodating 750-ton barges.[121] Virtually all of its traffic was in coal shipments which amounted to about 4.5 million tons per year.[122]

The full potential of the web of waterways was never exploited because of the administrative obstacles mentioned earlier. Their value was further limited by their susceptibility to interference by the weather. Traffic was halted for a few weeks each winter due to ice and was restricted during summer by low water. Aside from the objections of the boatmen, it was difficult to utilize ships built for one waterway on another because of their different characteristics.

Finally, because of topographical limits on where they could be constructed and the given locations of navigable rivers, barges could serve only a limited portion of the market. They were not suitable for express freight, component parts of machinery, and other relatively small shipments. Their major contribution was in moving coal and ore but even here they were an adjunct to and never a potential replacement for the Reichsbahn. Their physical and organizational limitations combined to cause the failure of the waterways to meet the needs of Speer's arms production scheme. In the coal economy year 1943/44 the barges and tugs moved almost a quarter less coal than in the preceding year and almost a tenth less than in 1940/41.[123]

It was against this somber background that Speer's carefully balanced mechanism was beset by a new crisis beginning in the spring of 1944. Coal production was a tenth below expectation and coke output fell 5 percent behind its target.[124] The Reichsbahn narrowly failed to meet its goal and the waterways were far away from theirs.[125] The result was a marked tightening of industrial coal supplies. The usual restoration of stocks during the spring did not occur.[126] To discuss the matter Speer called a meeting of Central Planning on 25 May 1944.

The gathering erupted into one of the stormiest of the war. Pleiger painted a bleak picture of coal production hamstrung by lack of transport, stocks at factories shrinking to half of what they had been a year before, and piles at the mines mushrooming. The downward slide was accelerating, he warned, and drastic action was needed to arrest it. He demanded 86,000 coal cars per day; 25,000 for the Ruhr and 28,000 for Upper Silesia.[127]

There followed a chorus of appeals for coal and impassioned accounts of failing transport. The common theme was that Allied bombers were battering marshalling yards in France and Belgium and had disrupted the flow of coal there. The Reichsbahn was even sending in coal from the Ruhr. This created a drain on its strength because many of its cars were being swept up in the turmoil and never returned to Germany.[128] Kehrl cautioned that the Reich was on the verge of plunging into a major coal emergency.[129]

Speer agreed that Germany was on the brink of a crisis which could determine the outcome of the war. He predicted that violent attacks on marshalling yards in Germany would begin soon. Although he hoped for a vigorous defense by the Luftwaffe he emphasized that the key would be how well the Reichsbahn and especially its repair crews in the critical Ruhr marshalling yards would weather the storm.[130] The fate of coal supplies and with them Speer's entire finely balanced industrial organism lay with the Allied bomber commanders. It is to them that we turn next.

4 Controversy and Compromise

The air attack on the Reichsbahn that seemed inevitable to Speer was actually the product of an unstable compromise among Allied air leaders and could very well not have occurred. Powerful organizations and personalities ranged themselves against the notion of a transportation offensive. In part they did so because the problems confronting the German war economy and the vulnerability of its transportation system were not clear to them. Reliable, detailed information on current economic activity in the Reich was scarce. Yet the basic configuration of Germany's economy, the role coal played in it, and the function of the transportation system had not changed since the beginning of the war and could have been understood from the study of open sources. Moreover, by 1944 entirely serviceable appreciations of the Reichsbahn and the inland waterway system stood ready on the shelves of Allied air intelligence officers. The major obstacles to a coherent attack on the German transportation system were bureaucratic in nature. Competition within the air intelligence apparatus and among the armed forces skewed appreciations. Almost as important was the understandable fear on the part of the air commanders of diverting their forces from what they considered to be more remunerative target systems and the lack of clarity concerning what bombers could actually accomplish. The Americans in particular had considerable difficulty understanding an economy that was very different from their own. It must also be kept in mind that the Allied air commanders had no historical precedents to turn to for guidance and such theories as had been developed before the war were not blueprints for success. Nevertheless, after bitter debate a workable compromise was achieved. It had to be constantly renewed. It was not elegant. It was less effective than it might have been. But optimum results in war can never be achieved.

When Allied air commanders confronted the problem of formulating a strategy for defeating Germany, they were very conscious of the fact that what they were doing was wholly without precedent.

Unlike army and navy commanders, they could not turn to historical examples for guidance. There were no theoretical guides based on experience to show them the way. What they had instead were the lessons that they themselves had learned during the current war and the speculations of a few writers who had addressed the problem during the interwar years. The most prominent of these was the Italian Giulio Douhet whose work, *The Command of the Air,* was published in 1921. Unfortunately, Douhet provided no set of rules for building an air force and employing it in battle. Rather, using his limited observations of the effects of German bombing of Italian cities during World War I and his own speculations, he offered an idealized scenario to a future air commander. Douhet argued that the vital prerequisite for a successful air offensive was winning air superiority. This could be achieved only by offensive action: by operating over enemy territory and defeating the opposing air force. Only then could the assault on the kernel of the enemy nation's strength begin. But the problem of how to exploit this opportunity would be immense. Douhet emphasized that the choice of targets would be the most important task facing air commanders because the result of the entire campaign would turn on these decisions made at the outset. Douhet was convinced that if correct selections were made, taking into consideration the entire social, economic, and organizational framework of the enemy state, air forces could win the war alone. For this to occur, to prevent the air force's resources from being diverted to secondary targets, it was vital that it achieve organizational independence. Although he admonished air commanders to cooperate with the army and navy, he stressed that the air force should act independently of them. Only in this way could it achieve the mass and concentration that would be decisive. Douhet, in his discussion of an imaginary air offensive, visualized a mighty, remorseless attack on the production centers of the opposition and its population. He speculated that the psychological impact of this offensive would exceed its physical effects and ultimately lead to the collapse of the opposing state.[1]

The shining vision of a quick and decisive air offensive that would prevent the agony of the trenches from recurring proved extremely seductive. Two states embraced it. In 1918 Britain created an independent air force, the Royal Air Force, largely to prosecute a "strategic," or independent air offensive against Germany. When rearmament began in 1936, the RAF, and especially its strategic offensive arm, Bomber Command, received the highest priority in resource and financial allocations. British strategists reasoned that the small island country could not liberate the continent until after Germany's fighting power had been reduced by blockade and bombing. This did not coincide with Douhet's precepts. Nor did it agree with the prescriptions laid down by the organizational and intellectual father of the RAF, Hugh Lord Trenchard. But it did open the door for a powerful air offensive against German urban areas, which the commander of Bomber Command from February 1942, Sir Arthur Harris, believed would result in Germany's defeat without a major land campaign.[2]

One other prerequisite for victory set by Britain's strategists was the formation of a great coalition against Germany. The key member would be the United States. In America the concept of victory through strategic bombing had also been adopted by the U.S. Army Air Corps (U.S. Army Air Forces after 20 June 1941). Here the attractions were its technological nature, its appropriateness for attacking a modern, complex economy, and the dynamic that it would initiate for the creation of an independent air force. It was of crucial importance that the U.S. Army Air Corps was not an independent entity. Its formal subordination to what it perceived to be the staid land army would color its position on strategic issues throughout the war. Initially, Douhet's ideas, along with the similar theories developed by William Mitchell, were incorporated unchanged into American air doctrine. But from 1935 the Air Corps Tactical School at Maxwell Field, Alabama, modified their concepts into a doctrine stressing "daylight precision" bombing of industrial objectives to defeat the enemy unaided. From the outset it was anticipated that the enemy would be Germany.[3]

All of this was extremely vague. No evidence of the effectiveness of bombs, no historical precedents could be marshalled to prove these theories. Air strategists in Britain and America reasoned from first principles and relied on expectations of what airplanes could do in situations that could be only hazily imagined. They assumed that economies would react to bombing in certain, favorable ways. In short, much of strategic bombing theory was based on faith. Adherence to that faith was deepened during the brutal struggle for existence that both the RAF and the USAAC fought during the 1920s and 1930s. Challenges to the theory of strategic bombing were rejected as being attacks on their very organizational existence, present or future. The leaders of the two air forces, especially the Americans, belonged to the first generation of aviators who were much more attuned to flying than theoretical speculation. They were not intellectuals. They were dynamic leaders, men of action, who were impatient with the subtleties of intelligence analyses or economics. The combination of novelty, fear, and dynamism meant that the selection of targets during the war was done haphazardly. Allied air strategists learned as they went along while operating in a highly competitive bureaucratic environment. Throughout, faith was more important than contemplation.

Confronted with the reality of the Nazi economy and the competing calls for resources from the other services, the problem arose of defining the mission of the strategic bomber forces. It became necessary to determine just what would be considered success. This in turn raised critical questions of how the bomber offensive would fit into overall strategy and especially of how to judge the time element. Considerations of how long the war would last and how Germany would be defeated played a decisive role in determining the selection of target systems. An initial attempt to clarify these issues was made at the Casblanca Conference of January 1943. President Roosevelt and Prime Minister Churchill affirmed that an invasion of the continent of Europe would be necessary to defeat Germany. They also agreed that a preliminary air bombardment would be necessary to weaken the Luftwaffe and the Reich's industrial capacity. The mission that they assigned to the strategic air forces was intentionally vague. The RAF and the USAAF had lobbied vigorously to retain their freedom of action. In large measure they succeeded. The task that they were given was "the progressive destruction and dislocation of the German military, industrial and economic system, and the undermining of the morale of the German people to a point where their capacity for armed resistance is fatally weakened."[4]

This brief effectively allowed both air forces to pursue their own strategies for defeating Germany independently. No time limit was set. Undermining the German people's ability to wage war could be interpreted as weakening the Wehrmacht directly or ruining the war economy. Nowhere was it stated what level of decline in fighting power or production constituted "fatally" weakening. Churchill and Roosevelt set broad guidelines which allowed them to adjust plans to subsequent developments. The air forces refined their target priorities during 1943 but never came to a clear, universally accepted definition of victory. This prevented them from adequately evaluating their actions. It also makes it very difficult in retrospect to gauge the success of the strategic bombing offensive. It might be useful, then, to establish a rough standard by reviewing the overall strategic situation and the comparative economic power of the two sides fighting in Europe at the end of 1943 (see Table 4.1).

Germany suffered from an inferiority in manpower that prevented it from fielding armies on the scale of its opponents. While occupied Europe offset Allied preponderance in population, the conquered territories, except France and Bohemia, could not produce sophisticated armaments. Nor could they provide raw materials and agricultural goods in sufficient quantities to free enough assets in Germany that might have balanced the Allied advantage. Most of the workers of Europe labored for the Third Reich unwillingly and therefore comparatively unproductively. During the war French output never attained its prewar level.[5] What contributions were derived from these quarters, except Bohemia, were lost to Germany from August 1944.

A moderating factor was that about a fifth of the American war effort was directed against Japan. Furthermore, Germany was fighting on interior lines. With every step forward the enemy moved farther from its sources of supply while the German armed forces moved closer to their own. The more the enemy lost in maintaining long lines of communications, the more Germany gained, along with the ability to switch its military forces among the various fronts more easily. Moreover, the German army remained tactically superior to its opponents almost until the end.[6] Nevertheless, even considering these moderating factors, Germany required every ton of steel, every airplane, and every tank that it could produce. Speer and Ganzenmüller recognized this. Given the unquantifiability of the modifying factors, to say nothing of the quality of political and military leadership on the two sides, it is impossible to calculate with precision what reduction in production short of total collapse would have been decisive. A conservative estimate shows that in 1943 Germany was outnumbered 3:1 in tank production. Would a 4:1 ratio have made a difference? Would an advantage of 6:1 or 7:1 in aircraft instead of 5:1 have accelerated Allied victory?[7] No one can say. But if strategic bombing could reduce arms output by a quarter or a third, not below targets but in real terms, then it could

Table 4.1

*Comparative Economic Power of the Warring States
in Europe, 1943*

	Population (millions)	Steel production[a]	Hard coal production[a]	Aircraft production (units)	Tank production (units)
Britain	42	13.2	202.1	26,263	7,476
United States	137.3	82.1	535.3	85,898	29,497
Soviet Union	170.5	8.4	92	34,900	24,012
Germany	81.1	30.6	268.3	25,200	19,824

Sources: Population—for Britain, Mitchell, *European Historical Statistics*, p. 8, table A1, estimate; for the United States, Department of Commerce, *Statistical Abstract of the United States*, p. 6, table 2; for the Soviet Union, Mitchell, *European Historical Statistics*, p. 7, for 1939; for Germany, USSBS, *German War Economy*, p. 202, appendix table 1. Steel—for Britain, Mitchell, *European Historical Statistics*, p. 225; for the United States, Bureau of the Census, *Historical Statistics of the United States*, 2:693; for the Soviet Union, Milward, *War, Economy, and Society*, p. 95, table 19; for Germany, USSBS, *German War Economy*, p. 251, appendix 71. Hard coal—for Britain, Mitchell, *European Historical Statistics*, p. 192; for the United States, Bureau of the Census, *Historical Statistics of the United States*, 2:588; for the Soviet Union, Milward, *War, Economy, and Society*, p. 95, table 19; for Germany, RVK, Statistischer Bericht Nr. 13, p. 3, BBA 15/1103. Aircraft—for Britain, Postan, *British War Production*, 2:485, appendix 4; for the United States, Holley, *Buying Aircraft*, p. 555, table 14; for the Soviet Union, Moscow Institute Marksizma-Leninizma, *Geschichte des Grossen Vaterländischen Krieges der Sowjetunion*, 6:60, obtained by multiplying the monthly average by twelve; for Germany, RMfRuK, "Ausstoß-Übersicht 1940–44. Waffen, Geräte, Munition," 370-293/45 g. Rs., Geheime Reichssache, February 1945, p. 1, BA R3/1729, f. 2. Tanks—for Britain, Milward, *War, Economy, and Society*, p. 91, table 16; for the United States, Thompson and Mayo, *The Ordnance Department*, p. 263, table 21; for the Soviet Union, Moscow Institute Marksizma-Leninizma, *Geschichte des Grossen Vaterländischen Krieges der Sowjetunion*, 6:60, by multiplying the monthly average by twelve; for Germany, RMfRuK, "Ausstoß-Übersicht 1940–44. Waffen, Geräte, Munition," p. 1.

a. Expressed in millions of metric tons.

conceivably cause the finely balanced, highly strained German industrial-military system to topple. Therefore, as a rough guide, this measure, one-quarter to one-third reduction, will serve as a standard against which to measure the results of the transportation offensive. Because the availability of weapons to the military is a function of stocks as well as production, they too must be taken into account. As a crude guide, the pipeline, a further complicating factor, will be taken as having a three- to eight-month duration depending upon the weapon or commodity.[8] Production declines caused by territorial losses can also be calculated. Losses due to direct damage to factories cannot be disaggregated from overall production statistics. However they can be for specific factories on some occasions. Impressionistic evidence from plant officials can supplement statistical data. But it must be borne in mind that during the fall of 1944 and after, the synergistic effects of direct damage and the loss of transport can not be quantified. They can only be hinted at. The one-quarter to one-third standard is useful equally for measuring the bombing offensive's accomplishments against either the standard of complete collapse or of paving the way for a ground offensive. Speer's finely balanced system was rocked by smaller setbacks and it is hard to imagine how a 25 to 33 percent reduction in the number of divisions facing the Red Army and the Western Allies could not have greatly accelerated their advance. Moreover, in light of the information available from sources open to Allied air intelligence staffs, leaving out that obtained from covert sources, it is also reasonable to argue that they could have used a similar standard at the time.

There can be no doubt that the task outlined above was a formidable one. Yet the strategic air forces confronting Germany during the spring of 1944 were enormous. Bomber Command had at its disposal 1,023 bombers in April 1944. Among them were 614 superb Avro Lancasters capable of carrying up to 22,000 pounds of bombs, though half that was normal.[9] Operating in conjunction with Bomber Command were the 4,085 bombers of the United States Strategic Air Forces (USSTAF). They were divided between the Eighth Air Force with 2,788 bombers flying from England and the Fifteenth Air Force with 1,297 bombers operating out of Foggia in Italy.[10] The Americans used the B-17 Flying Fortress and B-24 Liberator four-engined aircraft, both of which carried an average bomb load of 4,000 to 5,000 pounds.[11] The reason that the American aircraft carried smaller bomb loads was that they were more heavily armed and armored than their British counterparts. They were intended to fight their way to their targets in daylight without fighter escort whereas Bomber Command aircraft attempted to avoid interception by flying at night and therefore carried much lighter defensive armor and armament. By April 1944 the Americans had recognized the need for fighter escort and had built a force of 1,942 P-51 Mustangs, P-47 Thunderbolts, and P-38 Lightnings to protect their bombers. The Eighth Air Force controlled 1,242 and the Fifteenth 700 of them.[12] The fighters could contribute little to the weight of bombs dropped on Germany, although they could strafe targets such as locomotives. Their importance lay in the shield that they gave to the bombers and the casualties that they inflicted on the Luftwaffe. The crucial feature of these forces was their overwhelming size. By a conservative estimate, the Allied strategic bomber forces could deliver an average of over 100,000 tons of bombs per month.[13] This meant that a single target system could be inundated with explosives or that simultaneously a number could be struck heavily. The power of the forces at their disposal by the spring of 1944 was not understood by the Allied bomber commanders. Their attitude was shaped by memories of 1942 and 1943 when their forces had been raided for aircraft to reinforce the North African theater and the Pacific and to counter the U-boat threat. But by 1944 scarcity had given way to abundance. The Allied bomber commanders fought to concentrate their forces against a limited number of target systems and objectives. In doing so they underestimated what their forces could do. This fear of dispersal of effort, combined with their desire to win the war alone, heavily influenced the reaction of the Allied air commanders to suggestions that they devote their resources to hitting new target systems.

The command structure created by the American and British Chiefs of Staff gave ample scope for the strategic air commanders to follow their own ideas. Nominally, both Bomber Command, under Air Chief Marshal Sir Arthur Harris, and USSTAF, under Gen. Carl Spaatz, were subordinated to Marshal of the Royal Air Force Sir Charles Portal, Chief of Air Staff, RAF, acting as agent for the Combined Chiefs of Staff.[14] The Eighth Air Force was commanded by Maj. Gen. James H. Doolittle and the Fifteenth by Lt. Gen. Nathan F. Twining. This situation was due to change with the approach of the invasion of the continent, Operation Overlord. The Supreme Allied Commander, Gen. Dwight D. Eisenhower, would be given command of all forces, including air units, participating in the assault. An Allied Expeditionary Air Force had been created under Air Chief Marshal Sir Trafford Leigh-Mallory to support the invasion. Neither Spaatz nor Harris thought that the invasion would succeed and each hoped to win the war through air power alone. Therefore both felt the onset of the invasion as a goad to finish off the Germans. Both also struggled to avoid submitting to the authority of Leigh-Mallory, whom they mistrusted as a man experienced only in the use of fighters and who they feared would therefore misuse their bombers.

A compromise was hammered out to satisfy Harris and Spaatz. On 29 February, Churchill ordered that Eisenhower's deputy, Air Chief Marshal Sir Arthur Tedder would have authority over all three air commanders and would prepare a plan for using both the strategic and tactical air forces to support the invasion. The strategic air forces would come under Tedder's authority only when the air plan for their use was agreed.[15] Consequently, Spaatz and Harris were given the power to block or at least delay any employment of their forces with which they disagreed.

The pressures bearing upon the two stratetic air force commanders in March 1944 were immense. Both saw Overlord as a threat to their organizational freedom and to their dream of victory through air power. With every day that passed, as Overlord loomed closer, their fears increased. Harris had been pummeling Germany's cities since 1942. He pleaded that just a few more blows would bring the Reich's economy crashing to the ground. But his bombers were suffering increasing losses which culminated in the disaster over Nuremberg of 31 March.[16] In contrast, in the last week of February and the first week of March, the Eighth Air Force's escort fighters had dealt the Luftwaffe a shattering defeat over Germany. The American bombers could now range over Germany and strike targets of their commanders' choosing without fear of crippling losses. Winning air superiority over Germany created the preconditions both for a concerted strategic air offensive against economic targets and for the invasion. Spaatz, therefore, thought that he had a golden opportunity to realize his dreams. But the door had also been opened for what he feared could be the greatest diversion of all. A crucial turning point had been reached. Fundamental decisions had to be made concerning how the strategic bombers would be used. In making these decisions, intelligence concerning the German economy would play a significant though far from decisive role.

The information available to the Allies concerning Germany's economic war effort was abundant but of varying quality. The crucial factor in determining the exploitation of this intelligence was not its content but the preconceived notions brought to it by the analysts and the ability of intelligence organizations to function effectively in the highly competitive bureaucratic-political environment surrounding the air decision makers.

Two basic types of information were available: overt and covert. Overt data were gleaned from publicly available sources such as professional and business journals, newspapers, product brochures, telephone books, and railway schedules. Covert information was obtained by methods about which the enemy was unaware. The primary means of covert intelligence gathering were photo reconnaissance, interrogation of prisoners of war, and the interception of encoded and encrypted radio transmissions. Photo reconnaissance was the source of the most voluminous and in many ways the most reliable information.[17] Black and white and infrared photography could depict the location of factories, give clues about their activities by showing stockpiles of raw materials or finished goods waiting on loading docks, and provide information on bomb damage. The exploitation of imagery was handled at the Allied Central Interpretation Unit at Medmenham. Here photos were developed and interpreted for both the British and the Americans.[18] Prisoners and travelers could be interrogated to provide clues about the thoughts and plans of decision makers and about activities in laboratories or sections of plants that could not be seen by the cameras. But such informants had a limited field of knowledge and frequently gave very impressionistic accounts.

The third form of covert intelligence, signal intelligence, played little role in shaping air strategy before the spring of 1944. Its most important form was Ultra, the system for decrypting high-grade German cipher traffic generated by the Enigma machine. Ultra provided a wealth of data on military movements. But it told little about economic events because such information flowed over land lines or by mail.[19] However, the Reichsbahn did use Enigma and in February 1941 its cypher, code-named "Rocket" and later "Reichsbahn" by the British, was solved.[20] Therefore, Ultra was potentially a source of economic information of great value. But again, so long as the Reichsbahn could use its land lines, little could be gained from Rocket. A complementary source of signal intelligence was the MAGIC decrypts of the reports transmitted to Tokyo by the Japanese ambassador in Berlin. Occasionally these provided a glimpse of events in Germany. Their value was reduced by the diplomats' lack of expertise in economic matters and because the

Germans intentionally misled the military attachés. MAGIC was available to the American planning staffs in Washington and through them to the Ministry of Economic Warfare (MEW) in London.[21] Ultra was made available to combined headquarters, to the Army Air Forces commander Gen. Henry H. Arnold and his intelligence officers, to air force commanders and their intelligence officers, and to air division and even group commanders.[22]

A major problem confronting the Allied air command was the sheer volume of information available and the even greater demands for additional data. Hundreds of photo reconnaissance missions were flown monthly and a veritable horde of prisoners waited to be screened. But the number of aircraft available to photograph targets was limited, and prisoners and business travelers did not always come from the right area or have access to the types of information desired. So too with Ultra. During 1943 an average of 84,000 Enigma messages was decrypted monthly by the Government Code and Cypher School at Bletchley Park, which was responsible for decrypting all Enigma in the European theater.[23] But many more were either not decrypted or decrypted only after a delay. The decisions about what places would be photographed, which prisoners would be questioned first, and what Enigma messages would have priority were made by the organizations that would use the information to be obtained.[24] In this way, those in the best positions to know what was important were able to focus the Allies' limited assets on obtaining the categories of data that they needed most. But there was a negative aspect to this arrangement. Organizations charged with evaluating information also frequently develop an interest in the way it will be used. They become loyal to a particular strategy, seek information that confirms their choice, and attempt to exclude or deprecate information that challenges their position. This bureaucratic egotism played a significant role in Allied air intelligence and decision making.

There was a superabundance of organizations charged with evaluating intelligence in the spring of 1944. A highly complex collection of ministries, offices, boards, and committees had developed. Competition among them was fierce, and mutually agreed appreciations of the German economy were frequently more the result of a form of bureaucratic scholasticism than reasoned analysis.

On the British side, the apex of the intelligence pyramid was the Joint Intelligence Sub-Committee (JIC) attached to the Chiefs of

Staff. JIC was composed of the directors of the three military services' intelligence sections and representatives of the Foreign Office and the Ministry of Economic Warfare. It had liaison with the American JIC. Formed on 15 May 1941, JIC guided British intelligence policy, supervised the administration of interservice committees, coordinated, assessed, and disseminated strategic interpretations. It produced its reports using papers written by subordinate bodies and what it could learn from its direct access to Ultra.[25]

An office in the Air Ministry also assessed potential target systems and the results of bombing attacks. AI3(c) supplied basic information on targets to all air forces down to group level including the Americans. It had access to Ultra, photo reconnaissance, prisoner interrogation reports, and overt intelligence. Results of raids were evaluated by the Assistant Chief of Air Staff (I), Air Vice Marshal F. F. Inglis. In addition, the Deputy Director for Bomber Operations, Air Commodore Sidney O. Bufton, monitored the progress of the bombers and proposed new target systems. Sir Arthur Harris chafed at Bufton's interventions and mistrusted the Air Ministry. In response he set up his own intelligence organization at his headquarters at High Wycombe.[26]

A major player in the intelligence struggle was the Objectives Department of Enemy Branch in the Ministry of Economic Warfare. Formed in 1942 and headed by Oliver L. Lawrence, Objectives Department evaluated data on the German economy and recommended target systems for attack by bombing. It favored selective strikes on key sectors, realizing that results could be obtained only over time. MEW also produced general appreciations of Germany's economic performance every six months, supplemented by summaries of current economic intelligence data twice a week. In April 1944 Enemy Branch was transferred to the Foreign Office and seemed to gain in prestige as a result.[27] MEW had access to all overt and covert sources of information.

A constituent of MEW was the Railroad Research Service headed by C. E. R. Sherrington. RRS was created by the British railway industry at the outbreak of the war to provide advice to the Air Ministry.[28] It too received all types of information and was instrumental in solving the Reichsbahn's cipher.

The intelligence structure serving the American air forces was newer and in many ways less developed. At the outbreak of the war, the Army Air Corps did not have an intelligence organization. It

relied upon the army for data and profited from private study undertaken by the officers at the Air Corps Tactical School at Maxwell
Field, Alabama. When war began, the Americans hurriedly built an
intelligence apparatus. But they relied on the British throughout
the war both for facilities and for information. The haste with
which the Americans formed their intelligence system dogged
them until the end of the war. Arnold drew upon both his officer
corps and civilians to form a number of ad hoc agencies to provide
him with intelligence quickly while his regular organization was
taking shape. Two of these, the Air War Plans Division (AWPD) and
the Committee of Operations Analysts (COA), exerted an important if fleeting influence on U.S. intelligence appreciations. Of
more lasting importance were three other bodies, one civilian, one
military, and one composed of civilians in uniform.

The civilian body was the Research and Analysis Branch of the
Office of Strategic Services in Washington (OSS, R&A). R&A came
into existence during August 1941 under the auspices of the Library
of Congress and Archibald MacLeish. It was composed of academicians drawn from a broad range of universities solely for their com-
petence and specialized knowledge. R&A had access to a wide variety of overt sources, including America's libraries and the holdings
of business and trade organizations. It also received at second-hand
prisoner interrogation reports and captured documents. It did not
obtain Ultra.[29]

During the spring of 1942, OSS established a branch office in
London dubbed Economic Warfare Division. EWD in turn formed
the Enemy Objectives Unit in April to provide targeting information to the Eighth Air Force.[30] EOU produced aiming point reports
based on overt sources and some classified data but no Ultra.[31]
Manning the unit were academics who were given military rank for
the duration. EOU therefore existed somewhere between the civilian world and the military. Its civilians in uniform were anxious to
win the confidence of their military counterparts. They carried over
from civilian life the academic's skill in and love of bureaucratic
politics. EOU had a stormy birth and would struggle with every
intelligence organization that it encountered. Its unique degree of
egotism made it a bitter opponent of all who disagreed with it and
prompted it to subvert even those whose views coincided with its
own.

The purely military intelligence organization supporting the

American segment of the strategic air offensive was the office of the Assistant Chief of Air Staff-Intelligence (AC/AS A-2). It was created during 1942 and had an analysis division with a European branch headed by Maj. Gen. James P. Hodges, a former bombardment group commander in the Eighth Air Force.[32] Similar A-2 organizations were formed at every subordinate command level including USSTAF where it was headed by Brig. Gen. George MacDonald. A-2 in Washington and its subordinates relied primarily on data and appreciations generated by other agencies. AC/AS A-2 in particular was so far removed from the theater of war that it exerted little influence on events. On those occasions when it might have, it was by-passed by the impulsive General Arnold. A-2 at USSTAF did play a significant role, though its mood was dominated by EOU.

AWPD was created in June 1941 with officers drawn from the Air Corps Tactical School. On 3 July it was given the urgent task of preparing an aircraft production plan for President Roosevelt.[33] Because the number of aircraft to be built depended on the purposes to which they were to be put, AWPD proposed a full-fledged strategy for using air power to defeat Germany. It produced an intelligence appreciation to support this based on overt sources of data and what the officers in it had turned up on their own before the war. AWPD was then dispersed, recalled in 1942 and broken up again.

COA was created at the order of General Arnold on 9 December 1942. It was composed of prominent lawyers, academicians, and businessmen in and out of uniform along with a few regular officers.[34] Arnold had been disappointed with the level of AWPD's economic analysis and with the appreciations developed by his uniformed subordinates. COA was to provide a comprehensive analysis of the German war economy in time to guide the proposed combined bomber offensive. It relied on open sources and interviews with experts in and out of the military. It rendered a report on 8 March 1943 and then, although it remained in existence, directed its attention toward the Japanese economy for the rest of the war.

The conceptual problems facing these organizations were enormous. At the most basic level, they had to formulate a general picture of the structure of the German economy and its overall level of output. They also had to determine the relative importance of the various sectors of that economy and gauge their vulnerability to disruption by bombing. While doing this they had to keep in mind the broad outlines of Allied strategy. There were two crucial aspects to the latter consideration. The decision had been made to land on the continent, confront the Wehrmacht, and deal it a death blow in open combat. But through all of 1943 no date had been set for the final reckoning. This, along with the lack of a clear definition of what would constitute success, greatly complicated the air intelligence analysts' problem. If the goal of the air offensive were simply to weaken the Wehrmacht in conjunction with land campaigns, then target systems fairly late in the production cycle would be selected. That is to say, they would choose the sites of final production of armaments or the manufacture of components closely related to completed products because their loss would have direct military effects in fairly short order. But if the invasion would be long postponed, the goal could become the general weakening of the Reich economy because more time would be available. Then they could select target systems deeper in the economy, which were farther removed from final production and where greater stockpiles were kept. A successful attack on these systems would take longer but would result in a more complete disruption of the German economy. These considerations demanded a very clear definition of options concerning not only target systems but also types of attack. Tactical considerations related to the way a target was attacked, that is, by night or day, from high altitude or low, or in a dive. Tactical considerations also dictated whether an area would be drenched with bombs or a precise target, for example, a factory, would be hit. Among the strategic airmen, the term "tactical" was used to mean a type of target directly related to the outcome of a specific ground engagement. Strategic attack focused on the sources of enemy strength. Strategic issues included the crucial question of whether to pursue general or selective attack. In a general attack, an entire economy or society would be the object for destruction. Selective attack, in contrast, would seek to disable only vital sectors of the economy and thereby paralyze the entire system.[35] In the spring of 1944, USSTAF favored a selective attack using daylight precision tactics. Bomber Command employed general attack with night area tactics. Both sought to bring down the entire German economy. MEW and the Air Ministry favored a selective attack to achieve the same purpose. OSS R&A generally advocated selective attack without expressing any preference as to the ultimate goal. EOU vehemently advocated selective attack that would have direct, short-term consequences on the military situation.[36] COA shared this view.[37]

This diversity of opinion greatly complicated target selection especially since EOU's difference with General Spaatz was not made explicit. Moreover, EOU came into conflict with the two new actors who appeared on the scene in connection with Overlord, Sir Arthur Tedder and his scientific advisor on planning, Dr. Solly Zuckerman. The dispute that flared between them was in part a product of differing bombing philosophies, in part due to EOU's misunderstanding of Tedder's goals, and EOU's bureaucratic egotism. The decisive factors, then, in determining what targets were attacked by the Allied strategic air forces were the views of the decision makers, especially Harris, Spaatz, and Tedder, their advisors' access to them, the credibility that the intelligence agencies enjoyed with them, and what was known about the German economy, especially its energy and transportation sectors.

The overall image of the German economy held by the Allies—its output, organization and division of labor, and the implications of these factors for the strategic air offensive—was highly imperfect. The general conception held by MEW and JIC up to the middle of 1943 was wholly unreliable. They emphasized that the German economy was stressed to the limit, and that no reallocation of resources in it or expansion of armaments output was possible. They repeatedly predicted its collapse and consistently exaggerated the effects of strategic bombing. MEW even argued that industrial capacity was being shifted from armaments production to the output of civilian goods. AWPD shared MEW's basic assumption that the German economy was stressed to the breaking point. COA, in its haste, elected not to question this assumption.[38]

In mid- and late 1943 this unrealistic picture was changed. JIC and MEW argued that now there was no evidence of a general collapse on the horizon, and that reserves of manufacturing capacity apparently existed.[39] JIC stressed that no reliable standard of measurement was available. But by February 1944 MEW was again arguing that armaments production had actually declined, and that there were no reserves to shift to weapons output.[40]

An important reason for the failure to gauge German output accurately, aside from the errant initial assumption that the German economy had been fully and carefully mobilized at the outset of the war, was the inability of MEW and OSS R&A to assess Speer's programs accurately. MEW never detected the existence of Central Planning, one of the keys to Speer's success. The other bodies were identified but their purpose escaped MEW. It thought that they only added complexity to his managerial apparatus and doubted that they could be effective.[41] Since it did not understand the overall context, it could not appreciate Speer's initiatives. R&A did only a bit better. Very soon after the formation of the RMfRuK, it noted the changes accurately. It considered Speer a genuine Nazi, a technocratic "monomaniac," and the key figure in the German economy.[42] R&A also noted the vicious competition raging within the Nazi bureaucracy. It identified Kehrl as a crucial figure and realized that Speer's organization had superseded those of the Ministry of Economics and the OKW.[43] R&A concluded, though, that it would be "impossible for the new organization to increase arms output."[44] It argued that the rings and committees would exacerbate the friction between the Nazi Party and business and reduce managerial efficiency. Elements of these analyses were very insightful but the basic conclusion of increasing confusion and stagnating production was wrong.

In judging Germany's raw materials position MEW groped badly. Up to the end of 1942 it overestimated the decline of stocks. Yet it considered supplies of iron, steel, and coal to be satisfactory for the moment. After the change in its position in 1943 it presented a very confusing picture, underestimating available stocks but suggesting that no shortages would arise that would inhibit arms output.[45] In short, in relation to the crucial issues of stocks and the pipeline, both extremely important considerations in selecting bombing targets, MEW simply did not know what was happening.

MEW estimates of specific types of output were only slightly better. It badly misjudged the number of machine tools available to the German economy and the number of workers using them.[46] Consequently it was in no position to estimate the efficiency of industry in the Reich and therefore could not appreciate Speer's measures. Admittedly a correct judgment would have been very difficult to formulate. But simply projecting British practices onto German industry caused MEW to misinterpret the clues that were available from captured documents. MEW also vastly overestimated German aircraft output until the last half of 1942 and then after the last half of 1943 underestimated fighter production by 58 percent and total output by a third.[47] It had greater success judging tank output. During 1940, it overestimated it by 39 percent. But by June 1944 it was underestimating it by only about 7 percent.[48]

MEW estimates of overall German economic performance and war production were used by both the British and Americans. The two Allies developed a wide variety of interpretations of the geographical division of labor prevailing in Germany and transportation's role in it. Among the Americans, AWPD considered the Reichsbahn to be operating at near capacity and to be an inviting target. In its view, not unreasonably, it saw the Ruhr as the hub of the system and the marshalling yards as its most crucial components. It fully appreciated the importance of the inland waterway system and strongly recommended attacking it. COA developed a completely false picture of the DR. It considered locomotives to be the decisive factor determining a railroad's capacity. It underestimated the share of freight carried by the railway, pegging it at half of all freight movements, and suggested that Germany could dispense with a third of current freight traffic. COA concluded that 17,500 locomotives would have to be destroyed to harm the German economy, a task beyond the capacity of the air forces.[49]

With the approach of Overlord, USSTAF anticipated calls for bombing railways in Europe. General MacDonald asked Maj. W. F. R. Ballard of the intelligence section of the Mediterranean Allied Air Force (MAAF) to provide him with an appreciation based on experience gained during attacks on railways in Sicily and Italy. Ballard replied that transportation bombing could only help the ground advance, that it could not disrupt an economy because insufficient aircraft were available to conduct a comprehensive attack and because considerable industrial capacity in Germany was idle. He also thought that railways carried an insufficient share of freight in Germany to matter.[50]

EOU itself never studied transportation, let alone the Reichsbahn.[51] Instead it relied on papers prepared by others such as MAAF. On 8 February 1944 it counseled USSTAF that the delay incurred by attacks on marshalling yards was "immaterial." It underscored the "vast cushion of excess capacity" available to the railway and the economy in general.[52] It could make this argument because it valued only purely military traffic. Its rejection of general attack led it to conclude that disrupting economic traffic would be irrelevant because of the delayed effect it would have on the

Wehrmacht. In light of the frantic hunt for every ton of coal and steel in Germany, this view can only be called astonishing.

A special Army Air Forces Evaluation Board consisting of intelligence officers drawn from Washington, Britain, and the Mediterranean also gave its interpretation. It too concluded that marshalling yards were not suitable targets for cutting the flow of traffic and stressed the surplus of vehicles enjoyed by the Reichsbahn. In its view, bridges in general offered far better potential for interrupting the flow of traffic.[53] Given these wildly inaccurate assessments, one might conclude that there was a dearth of information available about the Reichsbahn. But AWPD and others did come to accurate appreciations. They were based on overt sources, many of which were available before the war. MEW was hard at work during the spring of 1944 on a set of very comprehenisve handbooks on the German economy that presented an accurate picture of the coal industry and the role of the Reichsbahn and the inland waterways.[54] Even earlier, in December 1942, MEW had pointed out that the coal-mining sector was especially vulnerable to disruption from indirect causes such as transportation snarls.[55] The RRS produced a number of accurate portrayals of the Reichsbahn and its economic importance. In November 1940 Sherrington sent Bomber Command a report, later forwarded to the Eighth Air Force, which emphasized that marshalling yards were the heart and most vulnerable part of a railway. He especially underscored the importance of those in the Ruhr.[56] In another report prepared at the same time, he deprecated attacking locomotives, even bombing their servicing sheds and facilities, unless the assault were part of an offensive against marshalling yards.[57] In March 1941 Sherrington completed another paper that was distributed both to Bomber Command and later to the Eighth Air Force, in which he advocated attacking railroad centers, those key locations where marshalling and vehicle servicing took place. He emphasized that since the Reichsbahn was the primary carrier of Ruhr coal, it was the most important single element in the German economy.[58] Sherrington's reports were concise and generally accurate. They can be faulted only for not noting the importance of RBDs Halle and Oppeln. But they were very useful contributions. In November 1943 the technical intelligence section, TN 1(c) of Military Intelligence, MI 8, in the War Ministry, produced a basically accurate appraisal of the Ruhr and its railways.

Although it missed the role of marshalling yards, it did highlight the importance of the region's coal traffic and the role played by RBD Halle. Overall, it considered the Reichsbahn to be "the greatest single factor in maintaining the economic life of the nation."[59]

At the same time, OSS R&A completed a series of very valuable reports on the Reichsbahn. It correctly asserted that the DR was under great pressure but had nonetheless barely succeeded in fulfilling Germany's transportation needs up to late 1943. The Reichsbahn's main role in the eyes of R&A, was to move coal and other raw materials between the Ruhr and its hinterland. The keys to these movements were the marshalling yards. The report provided accurate, detailed information on the location and capacity of the DR's major marshalling yards. It even identified and correctly interpreted the role of the ZVL. In its view trucks were unimportant and the canals were being used to try to relieve the railway. It suggested a series of attacks to isolate the Ruhr and Upper Silesia but paradoxically emphasized bridge targets and line cuts.[60] In an appreciation of the Reichsbahn's political position, it argued the the DR was not heavily nazified, but that it was fundamentally politically conservative and would be a reliable, patriotic supporter of the regime.[61]

In sum, no single report by any of these agencies presented a completely accurate image of the Reichsbahn or the division of labor. But many made good approximations. As a group they offered almost all the components for a useable assessment. During the war the basic division of labor in Germany had not changed. Only the nuances were new. Therefore these reports based on pre-war information, lacking accurate, detailed, current statistics, could nevertheless have formed the intellectual basis for an effective air offensive against the German transportation system. The main difficulty lay in the faulty assessments of the overall performance of the German economy. The reasoning was that if the German economy still had control over vast reserves of unused capacity, then transportation bombing would take too long to pay dividends. Coupled with this was the mistaken conclusion that the Reichsbahn also had surplus potential. Equally important was the superheated atmosphere of bureaucratic competition that prevailed in Allied air headquarters.

The temperature rose to fever pitch when the two newcomers, Tedder and Zuckerman, appeared around the end of 1943 and proceeded to advocate a target system that was anathema to both Harris and Spaatz. Tedder and Zuckerman were the main protagonists of transportation bombing during the months to come. Tedder engaged in a duel with Speer over the fate of the German war economy. While waging the contest, both the Deputy Supreme Commander and the Armaments Minister had to fend off difficult bureaucratic opposition in their own camps.

Tedder and Zuckerman did not conform to the image of air strategists. Tedder, although a career RAF officer, was a taciturn intellectual, not given to the bluster of the cockpit types. He disdained formalities and loathed the process of decision by committee and the creation of intelligence appreciation by scholastic compromise that dominated the Allied command. Zuckerman was a civilian whom Tedder retained personally to assist him in planning. He had been born in South Africa and educated in zoology at Oxford where he later taught the subject. Zuckerman looked at problems as wholes and considered their individual components as parts of a complete organism. He was a difficult man, convinced of his intellectual prowess and accustomed to the cut and thrust of debate. This team of the unconventional flyer and the feisty academic confronted the entrenched air intelligence agencies in Britain with a scheme that the latter found difficult to grasp and almost impossible to accept.

When Zuckerman arrived in England, he was confronted by a plan prepared by the SHAEF Joint Planning Staff that called for the bombing of twenty railway targets fifty to sixty miles behind the landing beaches. He immediately recognized that it was inadequate. After studying the information available concerning the German defences in western Europe, Zuckerman evolved a plan calling for a concerted attack on seventy-six "railway centers" in France, Belgium, and Western Germany. The immediate goal was to cut the overall potential to generate traffic of the railways serving the invasion area. By reducing the efficiency of railway centers, he hoped to decrease the volume of traffic and canalize it. Then it could be lowered further by bombing bridges, cutting lines, and strafing locomotives at the appropriate moment shortly before the landing. Although some rail movement would continue, the Wehrmacht would be prevented from rapidly moving reinforcements on a large scale into the region behind the beachhead. But that was not all. Tedder and Zuckerman understood that rail transport was vital not only to the Wehrmacht but also to the German economy. Attacks on rail centers in western Germany would contribute both to reducing the volume of military traffic flowing westward and to restricting and ultimately halting industrial activity in the Reich. Here was a breathtaking conception. Tedder sought to help the armies in the short run and paralyze the German war economy over the long run. He would fulfill his responsibilities for the invasion and simultaneously realize the old dream of strategic bombing theorists of bringing down the enemy economy.[62]

Tedder typified his idea as the "common denominator." He and Zuckerman selected a target system that all types of aircraft could attack and that could achieve both short-term military and long-term economic results. His strategy called for a conceptually and geographically concentrated selective campaign using bombing tactics that required a moderate level of accuracy. He saw attacks on other systems, especially synthetic oil, as complementary. The key issue here would again be timing and allocation of bombing effort.

This conception was based in large measure on Zuckerman's findings from a study of the bombing of the Sicilian and Italian railways that he had completed in December 1943.[63] Using captured Italian railway records and impressions gained from his own inspection of yards, Zuckerman concluded that the most vulnerable components of a railway system were its centers of operation comprising repair shops, locomotive sheds, and control facilities. Destruction or incapacitation of such centers would gravely reduce a railway's basic ability to generate traffic. He contended that since a railway was a complex organism composed of mutually interdependent parts, throwing these components out of equilibrium would generate shock waves that would reverberate throughout the system and lead to its paralysis. Zuckerman realized that pinpoint accuracy could not be achieved by bombers. Particular sections of yards could not be singled out for attack. So he suggested that "railway centers" should be bombed as units. All of the key features of the railway system would be assailed simultaneously where they were grouped together. Zuckerman also noticed that a coal shortage had developed in Sicily and southern Italy at the same time the transportation attacks had taken place. He could not pinpoint its cause. But he discerned that it had dire consequences for the economy. This was suggestive. He and Tedder were well aware of the importance of the Ruhr. They hoped that if attacks could be extended eastward into Germany they would also prevent the Ruhr from supplying coal to its dependencies. Under the pressure of events Zuckerman had not formulated a completely accurate picture of the system that he hoped to attack, underrating the importance of the marshalling process. But he understood enough to nominate it for destruction as part of the railway center and to convince Tedder of the correctness of his choice. Moreover, he continued to develop his ideas in light of newly available evidence. Speer's worst fears were being embodied by the Deputy Supreme Commander and his advisor.

While Tedder and Zuckerman were perfecting their scheme and shepherding it through the various intelligence and command echelons, EOU prepared a plan of its own. EOU had reacted violently against the transportation plan as soon as it learned of it.[64] In its view, the scheme was of a purely tactical nature since no attack on a railway could possibly achieve strategically meaningful results. A few weeks later, EOU prepared a comprehensive plan for the use of the Allied strategic air forces. It correctly perceived that the Eighth Air Force was seizing air superiority over Germany during the last week of February 1944. It proposed to exploit this unprecedented opportunity by launching a massive attack on Germany's synthetic fuel refineries and supporting crude oil processing facilities. It predicted that Germany would be denied over half of its petroleum reserves within six months of the start of the assault if fifty-four targets were disabled and revisited periodically to prevent the completion of repairs.[65] EOU argued that oil was the decisive factor in German economic life as well as the foundation of its military operations. According to EOU, the civilian sector consumed a third of the Reich's liquid fuel output.[66] It promised a rapid end to Wehrmacht operations, the collapse of the civilian economy, and the erosion of the morale of the German high command if its plan were implemented. It concluded that "oil alone, among the remaining target systems, offers the opportunity, if completed, of bringing the German war effort to a close."[67] In a comprehensive review of other prospective target systems, EOU rejected all of them. It condemned railways because there was too great a "cushion of civilian and long-term industrial use" between them and the fighting units.[68]

But EOU's analysis erred. Undoubtedly the denial of fuel to the Wehrmacht would have major military consequences. However, EOU promised this only six months into the future and Overlord was only two months away. Tedder's plan promised faster results at the tactical level. The notion that liquid fuel was crucial to German industrial activity was wholly erroneous. As we have seen, the German economy derived 90 percent of its energy from coal. The hope for a break in the morale of OKW utterly ignored the role of Hitler and the loyalty that he still commanded both in the Wehrmacht and among the German people. Undoubtedly, gauging the latter factor correctly would have been difficult or impossible under the circumstances. But to argue that an oil campaign would ruin the German economy was more the result of projecting the image of their own economy onto that of Germany than careful intelligence analysis. Information concerning Germany's dependence on coal, as noted above, was easily available in classified publications and in open, unclassified sources dating from before the war.

Oblivious to these flaws in its scheme, EOU launched a bureaucratic guerrilla campaign against the transportation plan.[69] Tedder relied on his good relations with Eisenhower and Portal to counter it. The result was a compromise that provided for attacks on both transportation and oil. This was possible because Tedder anticipated using only about half of the bombing capacity available from the strategic air forces. The oil compaign, with its roughly fifty targets, could be accommodated by remaining capacity. Many of the railway center targets in western Germany were casualties of the compromise, however. This had no effect on the tactical aspects of Tedder's plan. But it did imperil the attainment its long-term strategic goals.

The compromise was fashioned between March and May. Harris's objection that his aircraft could not hit targets as small as marshalling yards was eliminated first. On 4 March, Eisenhower ordered a series of test attacks against yards in France. They proved highly successful.[70]

On 25 March a major meeting was attended by all of the key players. During the discussion, Eisenhower and Portal exposed one of the crucial weaknesses in the oil plan: it would not become effective in time to help the invasion. They ordered the acceptance of Tedder's transportation plan.[71] Spaatz, however, saw the oil plan as his last opportunity to show what air power could do and to upstage Harris and win the war alone.[72] Morever, he believed that Overlord would fail.[73] So on 31 March he offered to attack transportation targets in France if he could use the remaining bombers to strike oil and ball-bearing targets in Germany.[74] Meanwhile, Churchill objected to Tedder's plan because he feared that it would inflict too many casualties on the French population living near the railyards. But the assurances of the spokesman of the Free French in Britain, Maj. Gen. Pierre J. Koenig, and finally of President Roosevelt stilled the prime minister's opposition in mid-April.[75] On 19 April, Eisenhower gave verbal permission to Spaatz to use the Eighth Air Force against Germany's synthetic fuel industry so long as he fulfilled his obligations under the transportation plan.[76] Two days before, Eisenhower had assumed command of all Allied air forces in Europe and delegated authority over them to Tedder. The deputy supreme commander issued a directive in which German industry and the Luftwaffe were given the highest priority with the Overlord transportation plan second in line.[77] He ensured that a balance was maintained between transportation and oil attacks.[78] In late May the Eighth Air Force vented its full fury on the rail lines leading to the front and on the Reichsbahn along the western edge of Germany. Tedder ordered bridge and strafing attacks to complement the destruction already meted out to marshalling yards.[79] Both in the final days before the invasion and immediately after the landings, Tedder protected the unstable compromise against continued sharp criticism. Meanwhile, on the other side of the line, Speer's resources were disappearing rapidly. To him, the meaning of the dual offensive was painfully clear.

5 Living for the Present

The compromise worked out by the commanders of the Allied air forces loosed a deluge of explosives on the marshalling yards of the French and Belgian railways. The disaster lapped up against the western edge of the Reichsbahn. The Münster, Geisecke, and Wedau coal gateways were hit either at their source or along their tributaries. By the time the troops hit the beaches on 6 June, the strategic air forces had dropped 56,930 tons of bombs on transportation targets in support of Overlord in France, Belgium, and western Germany.[1] Then through the summer, the focus of the assault shifted eastward in conjunction with the advance of the armies. In July and August an average of 2,400 tons of bombs per month was dropped on transportation targets in Germany.[2] During the first two weeks of September the pace accelerated. Against the onslaught, the Luftwaffe's fighters could mount only feeble resistance. Priority was given by the Luftwaffe High Command to protecting the synthetic fuel plants in central Germany. But even here, the defense was anemic owing to the crushing losses suffered during the spring defending these targets and trying to stem the invasion.[3] Flak was also concentrated near the hydrogenation plants in the Leuna and Leipzig regions near RBD Halle.[4] But with the growing shortage of powder, itself due to the attacks on oil, restrictions were placed on the expenditure of ammunition.[5] This weakness meant that the issue in the transportation sector resolved itself into a race between the bombers' ability to inflict damage and the Reichsbahn repair crews' ability to make it good. A competition had opened between the military force led by Tedder and the economic apparatus led by Speer and Ganzenmüller.

Least affected by the first wave of air attacks was the inland waterway system. It was not struck directly although it was influenced by car shortages at ports and by the RVM's and RWKS's attempts to shift traffic from the Reichsbahn to the barges. Overall tonnage moved by the waterways during the third quarter of 1944 was about 15 percent lower than during the same period of the preceding year.[6] Coal shipments along the Rhine were actually slightly above normal.[7] The decline in overall movements was caused by low water during the spring and summer and the chronic disorganization of the boatmen. Indeed, although bargespace was short, in some places boats had been laid up and were being used as warehouses by shipowners looking for higher profits.[8]

Lacking the ability or the time to build more vessels, both the Armaments Ministry and the Transportation Ministry resorted to organizational measures to increase the tonnage carried on the waterways. When faced with a crisis, complex organizations resort to responses that have served them well in the past. That is what happened in this instance. On 30 June, Speer ordered that bargespace be used more efficiently.[9] On 13 September the ZVL relieved the waterway plenipotentiaries who had been appointed in 1942 and vested their responsibilities in the shipping offices. These offices were ordered in turn to report directly to the ZVL. In addition, many of their heads were replaced in hopes of increasing control from the center.[10] Meanwhile, in June, Adolf Sarter, head of GBL-West, appealed to the RWKS to transfer some of its coal traffic to the waterways. Initially, though, the syndicate balked.[11]

From the ZVL's position in Berlin, the situation by mid-August appeared ominous. Emrich considered air attacks on marshalling yards to be the greatest threat followed by the retreat in the east. Together these pressures prevented the Reichsbahn from meeting the coal car target.[12] In response, on 23 August the ZVL held a crisis meeting at which Ganzenmüller and Speer's assistant Willi Liebel set the direction for the entire transportation system for the foreseeable future. Ganzenmüller stressed that Speer was planning a major increase in armaments production to make good the Wehrmacht's losses of the preceding summer and to prepare for the defense of Germany. The minister's plans could be fulfilled only with a maximum effort by the Reichsbahn and the bargemen. Especially important was the shipment of coal. Industrial stocks had shrunk in some places to as little as three weeks. Lost opportunities to move coal during the summer could never be made good. Therefore every chance, every potential avenue had to be seized. Ganzenmüller ordered that military shipments to front line units should enjoy first priority. Next, coal would be moved. Then would come the harvest. Liebel informed the ZVL that beginning immediately, arms shipments would be directed to units in the general areas of the factories. Shipments to depots would cease. Stocks at plants would be used to continue or increase output and shipments of raw materials would be cut to free up space for finished weapons. Every car would be used, open or covered, for whatever freight was at hand. Liebel underscored Ganzenmüller's warning that the Reich faced a dire emergency and warned that it could be overcome only with the assistance of the Reichsbahn.[13]

Help was made available to the DR to accomplish this task. In June, Hitler ordered the OT to leave France and move to the Ruhr to repair damaged railway facilities. In July the Reichsbahn agreed to plans that provided for manpower from the Wehrmacht, the Reich Labor Service, and even from factories to be committed to restoring marshalling yards.[14]

But problems continued to crowd in on the DR. The Reich Iron Association clamored for additional car space to deliver iron ore to the smelters. In the east, the grain, beet, and potato harvests were in, waiting for cars to bring them west. The Food and Agriculture Ministry warned that delays could cause most of the crop to spoil. On 6 September, Speer and Ganzenmüller decided to give food shipments from the east first priority for the next two weeks.[15]

Similar problems faced coal shippers. Despite Ganzenmüller's call, the volume of car space available for coal continued to decline, preventing factories from accumulating stocks for the winter. What the head of the DR had warned against had happened. Attempts were made to restructure traffic to increase the movement of coal. The RWKS reluctantly agreed to make greater use of unit trains and to form them at the mines as was being done in Upper Silesia.[16]

The issue of iron ore shipments exploded during the summer. The RVE claimed that it was being shortchanged in the allocation of car space and that any reduction in ore supplies would mean a decline in iron and steel output. During July, ore receipts from Sweden dropped as a result of Stockholm's decision, taken under intense pressure from the Allies, to cut off supplies to the Reich. The RVM and Röchling agreed to compensate by increasing shipments of minette.[17] But during August, overall ore movements fell by a quarter. Shipments by water, especially on the Rhine, held steady but railway movement declined by 28 percent.[18]

The cause and the most important problem confronting German industry by the end of August was the decline in the powers of the Reichsbahn. Overall freight car placings during the third quarter of

1944 were only 4 percent below the level of the same period during 1943. But coal car placings were 16 percent lower. Placings for brown coal fell by 9 percent.[19] There was no shortage of cars or locomotives. The difficulty was in marshalling. The attacks in France and Belgium had created chaos that reverberated eastward into Germany. The Reichsbahn was compelled to feed cars into the inferno in the west to support the military. The result was that the most important coal pivot, the Ruhr, and along with it the Saar, was swept up first in the spreading chaos. During the third quarter of 1944, car placings for hard coal in the Ruhr were off by 7 percent. Given the dire need for every ton of coal, this was ominous enough. But brown coal car placings in the region west of Cologne also dropped by 18 percent, although production continued at normal levels.[20] This had major implications for the industrial region around Mannheim and put a greater burden on hard coal suppliers in the Ruhr. In the region itself, coal production proceeded normally. However, stocks of both coal and coke at the mines and ovens began to rise when they ordinarily sank to their lowest.[21]

RBD Saarbrücken suffered the greatest setbacks. The backlog of trains mounted and delays increased. Coal trains destined for France clogged the sidings. Trains that were sent into France frequently did not return, thus creating a shortage of empty cars.[22] During the third quarter, freight and coal car placings were a third below normal.[23] The most immediate effect of this was a fuel shortage in the Saar and a decline in minette arrivals of 98 percent.[24] The iron and steel industry was forced to consume stocks to maintain production. But iron output dropped by 43 percent and steel production by 40 percent.[25] Since the Saar contributed almost a third of national iron production and a quarter of steel output, these losses represented a major blow to Speer's production plans. The Saar ceased to be a significant factor in German industrial life. But the Ruhr continued to work at a high pitch. Steel output continued normally into September. This was accomplished at the expense of stockpiles. Arrivals of Swedish ore began to decline only in September. Minette supplies virtually ceased at the end of August.[26] Since the Ruhr was not heavily dependent on minette, this was not important by itself. However, with the impending cessation of Swedish deliveries, it was a harbinger of problems lying just over the horizon. Stocks were reduced in August to 22 percent below normal.[27] Raw iron output in August declined by only 4 percent.[28] The case of Vereinigte Stahlwerke illustrates the situation nicely. Iron and steel production both proceeded satisfactorily compared to the monthly average of the previous year. Coal and coke output by GBAG were also normal. But coal stocked at the mines had quadrupled and coke holdings at the ovens had quintupled. Coal and coke stock at the mills had not changed dramatically. But ore stocks were down by a quarter and supplies of Swedish ore were half of the level held ordinarily.[29] The result was that the leaders of the Ruhr steel industry clamored for increased car space for iron ore. They did so primarily not because they faced an impending decline in output but because they refused to exhaust their stockpiles to support the Nazis.[30] Vögler, Rohland, and the rest had long been disenchanted with the Hitler regime, and now that defeat was closing in, they were positioning themselves for the postwar economic and political environment. They sought to keep their plants intact as much as possible, maintain old business connections, and keep on hand a supply of raw materials that would permit them to resume production as soon as possible after the surrender. Elsewhere in the Ruhr, while the storm neared from the west, production continued as usual. In Düsseldorf no major production difficulties appeared among either utilities or armaments works.[31]

In the Ruhr hinterland to the south, the problems confronting RBD Saarbrücken were repeated at Mannheim, Karlsruhe, and Stuttgart. GBL-South reported in early September that, although it had sufficient locomotives, marshalling difficulties were badly snarling traffic. Telecommunications were seriously disrupted and train movement was restricted to the nighttime.[32] The inevitable result was a coal shortage. At Ludwigshafen, for example, of eleven major plants monitored by the local Armaments Inspectorate, four suffered from declining coal stocks. These were directly dependent on supplies brought by rail from harbors on the Rhine.[33] Mannheim harbor functioned with few interruptions throughout the summer, but moving the coal from the storage bins near the wharves was becoming increasingly difficult.[34] A few slight problems arose obtaining components. The statistics concealed the strains under which plant managers struggled in order to find car space to get parts and ship their output.[35] A feeling of impending catastrophe pervaded the area.

Overall then, basic goods and armaments production in the west continued satisfactorily. But already reserves of raw materials, components, and expedients were being called upon just to keep pace. Only in the Saar had a disaster occurred. It was significant because of the speed with which it developed. It also bode ill for the Reich economy because it placed a heavier burden on the Ruhr steel and coke industries, which were already highly strained. In effect, the Saar had been eliminated and there was nothing that the Ruhr could do to compensate. In the Ruhr itself the leadership of the steel industry and Schmidt of the RWKS were chafing at the measures being undertaken by the regime to counter the growing transporation problem. The RWKS in particular resented them as restricting its prerogative to service its customers as it saw fit even in time of national emergency.

With the weakening of the west both physically and psychologically, the central and eastern industrial regions assumed greater importance. Those areas of central Germany that were tributaries of the Ruhr were well provided with coal by the canal system and, to a lesser extent, by the increased shipments from Upper Silesia. Both the Dortmund-Ems and Mittelland canals carried coal eastward at about normal levels. In addition, brown coal mining in the Elbe region continued without interruption. RBD Halle had increasing difficulties supporting the latter flow. Its overall car placings dropped by almost 9 percent during the third quarter and its car placings for brown coal fell by 6 percent. These declines came about as a result of delays in traffic moving through the region to the west and disruption caused by air attacks on the nearby hydrogenation plants. Slight as they were, they resulted in a small reduction in raw iron production. In the Ruhr's Hanover dependency, no energy problems developed and arms production targets were met, though with increasing difficulties due to dwindling supplies of components. Stocks of coal for the winter could not be accumulated. Armaments output at both the RWHG and Krupp-Gruson was not affected.[36]

One reason why production continued almost undisturbed in the Ruhr's hinterland in central Germany was the help given to the RWKS by the other syndicates. The Upper Silesian and Lower Silesian hard coal syndicates stepped in to supply many of the RWKS clients in the area. Consequently, coal stocks at the RWKS local trading companies were satisfactory although below the desired winter level. Generally, they ranged from three to five weeks. Another major reason that the RWKS was able to supply so many of its customers was the smooth functioning of the waterway system. Bending to the pressure exerted by Sarter and the RVM, the RWKS increased the share of its coal sales shipped by water from a fifth in January 1944 to more than a quarter by September. Rüdiger Schmidt hoped to raise this to a third.[37]

To the east, GBL-East encountered problems with traffic moving to directorates to the west.[38] By early September, operations were strained because of difficulty exchanging traffic with GBLs West and South. In RBD Oppeln problems arose due to the need to handle traffic moving west to escape the onrushing Red Army.[39] This was a new factor. Its importance would grow during the coming months. For the moment, the eastern coal pivot suffered a loss of 16 percent in overall car placings and 18 percent in hard coal car placings in the third quarter of 1944.[40] Traffic on the Oder at the coal ports of Oppeln and Gleiwitz ran normally, preventing a major emergency.[41] Hard coal cut in the region fell 4 percent below the previous year's standard during August.[42] Iron production declined by 5 percent.[43] Coal stocks at armaments plants remained satisfactory though some types were unavailable. Supplies of components were adequate and the region's armaments plants met their targets.[44] At Upper Silesia's major dependency, Berlin, the satisfactory functioning of the waterways enabled production to continue uninterrupted.[45] BEWAG had no difficulty meeting electrical demand.[46] Coal stocks approached two months. Arrivals from the Ruhr were sharply reduced but supplies from Upper Silesia had compensated. So too in the city's armaments plants. Speer's armaments inspectors detected no major difficulties into September.[47]

The Reich economy had withstood the intitial shocks of transportation bombing remarkably well. It had done so by using stocks and by shifting priorities in the employment of labor, components, and materials. Only the Saar had suffered a major collapse. The effects of this were not immediately felt in final production. But the region's loss reduced the nation's overall armaments potential because of the role it played, second only to the Ruhr, in steel production. No significant difficulties arose in hard coal output which declined by only 2 percent. Brown coal output fell by 5 percent due to the disruption of transport west of the Rhine. Coke production was off by only 1.5 percent.[48] Electricity and gas supplies were also adequate.[49] The key indicator was the rise in stocks at the mines. Hard coal stocks jumped 462 percent, coke holdings at the ovens

580 percent, and brown coal at the pits 400 percent compared to summer 1943.[50] Although production was not interrupted, the fruits of the miners' labors could not be sent to the mills and factories. They were forced to dip into their stockpiles to compensate. As yet the decline in stocks among consumers was not serious. But when it is recalled that this was the time of year when they should have been accumulating, then the peril for the future becomes glaringly obvious. The same held for iron ore. Stocks at the steel works were only half as great as during the preceeding year.[51] The cause was the drop in minette shipments from Lorraine, and the major loser was the Saar. Reich raw iron production fell in August by a quarter compared to the preceding year.[52] This was due almost entirely to the disaster in the Saar. Steel production did not fall in tandem since both in the Saar and elsewhere scrap could be substituted for high-content ore.[53] Consequently steel production fell by 16 percent.[54] While basic industries sustained their first setbacks, armaments final production, using materials and components that had entered the industrial process months before, continued its second great wartime boom. In July 1944 the armaments final production index peaked at 322. Only the initial spurt between February 1942 and May 1943 exceeded the March–July 1944 period in rate of monthly growth.[55] These months saw production of many important weapons—the Panther tank, 88 millimeter anti-tank ammunition, 105 millimeter Flak, and the K98 carbine—reach the highest levels of the war.[56] This astonishing success was possible because Speer and Kehrl had fashioned an organization that could exploit Germany's limited resources relatively efficiently. But they understood the implications for the future of the transportation attacks that gradually spread eastward during June. Consequently, they took precautions immediately after the invasion to counteract their anticipated effects.[57]

The first intiative taken by Speer was to have Hitler sign an order for the "Concentration of Armaments and War Production."[58] It provided for a drastic reduction in development work on new weapons. This would allow engineers to be transferred to other industries where they could develop means to save raw materials by introducing new production processes and simplifying weapons designs. Commissioners would be named to supervise the implementation of the order. A week later Speer ordered that iron and steel allocations to manufacturers of machines, vehicles, and armaments be slashed and that they consume their plentiful holdings of these materials.[59] The RMfRuK estimated that stocks of iron and steel at the factories had almost doubled during 1943 and reached a level that would suffice to maintain output at the current rate for six to eight months.[60] On 13 July, Speer named inspectors whom he empowered to enter factory premises unannounced to check inventories.[61] The purpose of these measures was to maintain or increase final production of weapons and simultaneously to reduce the burden on the Reichsbahn. The dwindling car space that was available would be used to ship finished armaments. The entire scheme was predicated on achieving short-term results. At his regular conference with Hitler on 20 August, Speer counseled, and Hitler agreed, that industrial planning should focus only on the next nine months. Long-term planning was irrelevant.[62] Implicitly, Speer and Hitler admitted that Germany was in a fight for survivial in which the next few weeks would be decisive. Major setbacks had so far occurred only in the Saar. But Speer gave the Allies credit for a consistency of command that they did not possess. He anticipated a major new series of air attacks on the synthetic fuel industry and especially on the Reichsbahn. The latter was his greatest fear. While fending off these blows, he faced the urgent task of reequipping the Wehrmacht streaming back to Germany from France and Poland. To do so, like Ganzenmüller and the Reichsbahn, he used methods that had proven themselves over the preceding two and a half years. On 1 August Speer abolished the highly successful Fighter Staff and reconstituted it as the Armaments Staff.[63] He hoped to tap the energy of its dynamic chief, Karl Saur, for the benefit of the entire armaments industry. Unfortunately, Speer's method of creating special commissioners and staffs had outlived its value. Saur's crude methods soon increased confusion and alienated factory owners. Moreover, Saur harbored growing ambitions to supersede Speer. The armaments minister's bureaucratic and political position also came increasingly under attack from other quarters. The SS resented his disdain for Nazi ideology. The Party, especially the Gauleiters and Bormann, was jealous of the power that he wielded over factory labor and criticized his close ties to the old business elites. Nevertheless, on 1 August, Speer created Armaments Sub-Commissions to coordinate the actions of the Gauleiters, who had an interest in economic matters as Reich Defense Commissioners, and his Defense Economics Officers. At a speech in Posen announcing these measures, Speer stressed the need for improvisation and cited production statistics to demonstrate that only his system of industrial self-responsibility could win Germany the production increases that it so desperately needed. But Bormann and the Gauleiters were unimpressed. In a note to the Gauleiters, attached to Speer's decree creating the Sub-Commissions, Bormann stressed that in the event of disputes with Speer's armaments officers, they should turn to him alone for a final decision. The Party saw Speer's initiative as an opportunity to infiltrate his apparatus. In the wake of the 20 July assassination attempt on Hitler and Goebbels's appointment as Commissar for Total War Measures, the Party attacks had gained new impetus. Bormann and Goebbels had formed a temporary alliance. This was the power constellation that stood behind Bormann's readiness to "cooperate" with Speer. The armaments minister soon realized that his gambit had failed. On 6 September, in a meeting of section chiefs of his ministry, Speer complained that the Gauleiters were ruining his production schemes. Key workers were being taken from factories, even engineers from the Reichsbahn's locomotives, to dig trenches. In a fit of pique, he threatened to dump all responsibility for managing the war economy into the laps of the Party chieftains.[64]

But he soon recovered his poise. Speer would not so easily loosen his grip on the apparatus that he had fashioned with such great care and effort. On the same day, 6 September, he began to move against the Party and the renegades in his own ministry. He ordered that in the the future all plenipotentiaries would be confirmed in their posts by the Central Office of his ministry. Too many Party officials simply proclaimed themselves plenipotentiaries for war production and without permission had taken upon themselves the mantle of authority of his ministry. Many of his own subordinates had also arrogated to themselves power not authorized by Berlin.[65] Clearly, Speer had realized that the practice of naming special commissioners with extraordinary powers was counterproductive. Probably the most notorious case was that of Heinz Kammler, who was given full powers under Himmler's auspices to expedite production of jet aircraft and transfer the armaments industry underground.[66] Kammler seized men and resources without consulting Speer, spreading confusion and consternation.

Speer also moved against Hitler's orders to destroy factories and evacuate industrial areas before the advancing Allied armies overran them. While touring the west in the second week of September, he ordered that plants should work to the maximum of their capacity until the last possible moment before they were lost.[67]

Contrary to Party suspicions, Speer's relationship with industry was deteriorating. The RWKS resented his attempts to intervene in its market relationships. Rüdiger Schmidt considered the attitude of the Berlin authorities unfriendly and warned his board of directors that the RWKS was faced with a fight for its existence. By this he meant that it would be forced to defend "free enterprise" against the government, not dissolution by invading armies. During September, Schmidt openly defied the coal allocation priorities established by Speer and Ganzenmüller. For example, he ordered that sufficient coal be given to private homes in the Ruhr to satisfy all their needs. This was justified in his view because the coal could not be shipped to industries outside of the Ruhr in any case.[68]

Because their initiatives were fast being overtaken by events, assailed from within, and bombarded from outside, Speer and Kehrl again moved decisively to meet the deteriorating situation. On 9 September, Speer issued an "Armaments Order" that was of crucial importance for the future of the Third Reich's economy. He laid down that all completed weapons should be shipped to the Wehrmacht immediately. Raw materials stocks except coal should be reduced to two weeks supply. Stocks of components were to be reduced to a mere eight days. Those factories that possessed supplies in excess of these limits were not to share them with factories that were below the standard. Instead, to save transport space, they would draw them down by producing arms and would receive no additional supplies until they complied with the limits that he had stipulated. The goal, Speer emphasized, was to produce the maximum number of completed armaments in the shortest time and to ship them to front-line units as quickly as possible.[69]

Accompanying the Armaments Order was the "Coal Saving Action" that Speer promulgated on 20 September.[70] The minister demanded that coal be used as efficiently as possible to heighten production, reduce the burden on the Reichsbahn, and bridge the current period of unreliable supplies. Additional rationalization measures would be used to save energy. Heating would be ruthlessly curtailed and alternative sources would be pressed into the breach. Each plant would name an energy expert who would participate in regional and national organizations that would share experience and propagate best methods.

The Armaments Order and the Coal Saving Action of September 1944 mark the point at which the German economy stepped over the precipice into chaos. Speer had explicitly called upon elasticity of supply to carry the economy through the impending coal emergency. That done, new plans would be formulated in the future. To an extent his scheme was a rational response to a very dangerous situation. The Wehrmacht was badly in need of large quantities of new equipment to replace the staggering losses that it had sustained during the summer. At the same time, because of the bombing of marshalling yards and the implications of these attacks for the future, the economy's ability to satisfy these needs was diminishing. So Speer gambled. He gambled that the new and refurbished divisions equipped with the weapons his system produced would stop the onrushing British, American, and Soviet armies. He gambled that General of Fighters Adolf Galland's plan to stop the American daylight bombing would succeed or that the Allied air commanders would fail to press home their advantage as they always had in the past. But these risks were wildly unrealistic. The size of the enemy armies and air forces and the industries standing behind them was overwhelming. The German people had already suffered terrible losses and the economy was strained to the breaking point. Now, due to the bombing of transportation, the fragile edifice that Speer had created to guide armaments production was cracking. Not only had output in a few areas, and the performance of the Reichsbahn, begun to slip. But the political tensions fostered by the Nazi regime were beginning to rip the system apart from within. Cooperation was becoming increasingly difficult, centralized control less feasible. An unexpected side effect of the transportation bombing, the rapid deterioration of the electronic communications network, abetted this process. Because the public telephone exchanges were located adjacent to major railway stations, when the yards were bombed the exchanges were often hit as well, putting the telephones out of service. Speer and Kehrl agreed that Berlin was rapidly losing its importance as a central economic command post because of transportation bombing. In recognition of this, in May the Reich Coal Association had transferred its offices from Berlin to Ludwigslust, 150 kilometers to the northwest. The

RWKS along with GBAG, Ruhrgas, and the Rhenish-Westphalian Electricity Works established dispersed reporting locations in the Ruhr on 12 September.[71] Speer had decided to have the German economy live solely for the present in the realization that failure to survive the present would mean the end to all hopes for the future.

The astonishing aspect of Speer's plan was that it could very well have succeeded in view of dissension in the Allied air command. The intelligence sources bearing on the German economy did not speak in unison. But they did provide sufficient indication of what had happened in France as a result of transportation bombing and what was beginning to envelop German industry. The decisive question was which group would prevail in the brutal bureaucratic infighting that raged throughout the summer.

Information gleaned from photo reconnaissance clearly showed the results of the raids on marshalling yards in France, Belgium, and western Germany. However, the photos could give only an approximation of how the overall level of traffic had been affected and, in particular, what types of movement had been reduced to allow military traffic to continue flowing. Moreover, the pictures could not resolve questions about whether marshalling yard or bridge attacks had been the most effective.

Ultra partially filled the breach. In April and May it laid bare army and Luftwaffe communications that clearly showed that the volume of rail traffic had fallen dramatically and that military movements had not been spared. At the same time, GC and CS solved the cipher used by the German police.[72] With the deterioration in telephone service, coal, steel, and chemical companies increasingly used the police radio net to transmit information to Berlin. But neither of these sources was fully exploited because the bodies interpreting them were locked in bureaucratic political strife.

On 27 May, EOU attempted to preempt its opposition by presenting to Spaatz a proposal for the use of the strategic air forces after the solidification of the lodgement in Normandy. It suggested that limited efforts be made to strike aircraft factories and airfields to weaken further the Luftwaffe. In addition, two arcs of interdiction should be created, one along the Seine-Loire line and the other along the Albert Canal and the Meuse to choke off rail traffic. The specific targets would be bridges. Finally, a concerted assault on Germany's petroleum industry would be launched, supported by raids on ball-bearing, ordnance, and tank engine plants. "The heavy bomber force could make no greater contribution to the victory on the field," concluded EOU, "than to press home the attack against German oil production."[73] Two days after the landings in France, Spaatz implemented this scheme, giving oil first priority.[74] But he had moved too soon. Eisenhower and Tedder made heavy demands on the bombers to support Montgomery's precarious toehold on the continent, so Spaatz's initiative was stymied.

A critical factor bearing on how the strategic bombers would be used was the picture of the overall performance of the German economy developed by MEW. In its six-month summary issued in June, MEW gave a reasonably accurate estimate of German coal production and the implications of the anticipated loss of Swedish ore supplies. It saw no change in armaments production, though it discounted the possibility of any substantial increases. MEW did detect growing transportation problems and saw the Reichsbahn in particular as being in difficulty. But it did not know what this meant for the future. It was certain, however, that dispersal had increased the vulnerability of the economy to disruption of transportation.[75] MEW's appraisal was basically accurate but because of its many qualifications, it was hardly useful in the bureaucratic struggle where shrewdness, bolder assertions, and more specific information would prove decisive.

EOU attempted again to land the first blow by sending Kindleberger to France to gather data on the effects of the Overlord transportation campaign. On 19 June he reported to Twenty-first Army Group and EOU that none of the evidence that he had obtained showed that the Germans had been handicapped by raids on railway centers. Instead, cutting bridges had exerted a noticeable influence on traffic.[76]

A bit over a month later, on 25 August, Solly Zuckerman received an urgent telephone call from Maj. Derek Ezra. Zuckerman had followed Tedder to the continent and was then in Paris directing the search for information on the impact of the transportation plan on the French and Belgian railways. Ezra had been seconded to Zuckerman's Bombing Analysis Unit (BAU) from SHAEF G-2. He was a vociferous opponent of Zuckerman's plan. He asked the scientist to come to his office immediately. There Ezra showed him two long rolls of what appeared at first glance to be wallpaper. They were actually the traffic flow charts of the French National Railway

(Société Nationale des Chemins de Fer Français, SNCF) from 1940 to the end of May 1944. Zuckerman snatched them and raced to Tedder's office. He and the Deputy Supreme Commander sprawled on the floor in the antechamber and pored over them. They showed clearly that French railway traffic had declined precipitately soon after the bombing began. The most striking feature of the charts was the unmistakable, catastrophic drop in coal shipments.[77] Subsequent investigation showed that a brutal coal famine had swept the country. Coke traffic disappeared and minette shipments to the Saar and the Ruhr were reduced to a trickle. Inspection of yards hit by the bombers made clear that the decisive factor was the disruption of marshalling. Analysis of other SNCF records demonstrated that by 26 May, that is, before the attacks on the Seine bridges, the volume of rail traffic in France had fallen to just over half of the January 1944 level. By D-Day it was 70 percent lower and by the end of July a staggering 90 percent lower.[78] There had never been a car shortage. Nor had there been a lack of locomotives. The vehicles available, and the Reichsbahn had constantly fed more into the system from Germany, could not be used because marshalling was in disarray.[79] Captured documents proved that even military movement had been badly delayed. The First SS Panzer Division had required seven days to travel from Louvain to Paris, a distance of only 300 kilometers.[80] Of the 100 supply trains from Germany needed by the armies in France each day, by May an average of only thirty-two actually arrived.[81] Tedder's plan had accomplished its purpose of slowing and reducing the scale of logistical support and reinforcement to the units thrown against the Allied landing. But it had also spread far greater chaos in the French economy than Tedder or Zuckerman had imagined possible beforehand. They now fully realized the importance of marshalling yards both to railway activities and to coal supplies. They perceived that similar attacks would have dire, possibly decisive effects on the German economy. They were more firmly convinced than ever that the transportation offensive should continue unabated and that it should be extended eastward into Germany as far and as soon as possible. In the meantime, Tedder had become very dissatisfied with the quality of the intelligence analyses that he was receiving from the Air Ministry and other agencies. Therefore, he ordered SHAEF G-2 to begin preparing weekly summaries of intelligence bearing on the transportation offensive in mid-July.[82]

EOU was not susceptible to the evidence uncovered by Zuckerman. It had adopted the oil alternative and now defended it as an
article of faith. No one can doubt that the oil offensive was extremely effective in reducing the combat power of the Wehrmacht
and especially the Luftwaffe. Nor can it be doubted that it exerted
no influence on the operations of German industry. The issue then,
as it had been before Overlord, turned on how much of the Allies'
massive bombing capacity would be devoted to each. One can sym-
pathize with Spaatz's staff, beleaguered as it was with requests for
support from the army, attacks on V-Weapon sites, and submarine
pens. But it was their business to form an accurate appraisal. In this
instance that meant seeing that attacks on oil and transportation,
as Tedder had made clear, were complementary, not contradictory
or competing strategies.

EOU resorted to its usual gambit of attempting to preempt the
opposition by submitting a new bombing proposal in July. Its primary purpose was to assist the ground forces in what it considered
to be the last offensive of the war. Again it tapped oil as the most
important target system.[83] Its plan reflected the optimism, almost
euphoria that swept through the Allied command during July and
August as the British and American armies raced across France.
Portal repeatedly suggested that a massive blow be launched at the
urban areas of Berlin to convince the population and the government to capitulate.[84] Spaatz opposed these plans, but only because
he thought that Germany was about to succumb to his oil offensive. On 1 September he issued a new priority list that called for an
intensified attack on oil plants. In his introduction to the plan,
clearly reflecting the influence of EOU, Spaatz claimed that the
German economy was about to "collapse for lack of fuel."[85] Nothing could have been further from reality. Germany's economy was
not dependent on petroleum and there was no coal famine yet.

It was of the utmost importance under these circumstances that
Eisenhower relinquished control of the heavy bombers on 6 September. Arnold and Portal were again to act as the agents of the
CCS with Air Marshal Sir Norman Bottomley, Deputy Chief of
Staff, RAF, and Spaatz serving as their intermediaries. The future of
the transportation offensive was imperiled. Portal canvassed a plan
under which oil and popular morale would be the primary targets
and transportation would be excluded.[86] But Tedder had created a
web of relationships that enabled him to dominate the air com-

manders' conferences that met at SHAEF two to three times weekly to select targets. At the meeting of 12 September, Tedder won Harris's and Doolittle's approval for raids on marshalling yards in the Rhineland and Ruhr.[87] This was the genesis of the special priority that was accorded transportation in the directive issued by the Octagon Conference at Quebec on 14 September.[88] Oil continued to enjoy first priority. But transportation was raised to a special position, depending on weather conditions that effectively gave it second priority. The agreement, informally reached at SHAEF on 13 September between Spaatz, Bottomley, Harris, and Tedder, was presented to the CCS by Portal.[89] When cloud obscured the synthetic fuel plants, which Spaatz insisted must be attacked visually, the bombers would use radar to hit marshalling yards. At the air commanders' conference of 19 September, Tedder agreed with Harris and Doolittle that marshalling yards near Koblenz, Cologne, and Soest should be bombed.[90] Harris intimated that he was also contemplating strikes against the canal system. The deputy supreme commander warmly encouraged Bomber Command's chief.

Tedder had shepherded transportation to a high place in the priority list by assiduous political preparation, relentless struggle, and maintaining good personal ties with Eisenhower and Portal. He also knew that Spaatz and Harris did not agree with his ideas. But they could not cooperate with each other and were checkmated by superiors who supported Tedder. The deputy supreme commander improved his position by his pragmatism. Unlike EOU, he did not exclude alternatives to his own preferences. He advocated transportation bombing, but also saw the merits of attacking Germany's oil supply simultaneously. A new compromise had been reached. As additional strains impinged on the Allies during the coming weeks, the fragile understanding would threaten to collapse. Tedder would be hard pressed to preserve it. Throughout, in contrast to his opposition, he emphasized cooperation and the mutually reinforcing nature of transportation and oil raids in both the strategic and tactical spheres. Speer had cobbled together a scheme to meet Tedder's threat. His worst fears were about to be realized, but by a margin so thin that he would have been astonished had he known.

6 Debilitation

The special priority given to transportation targets, combined with the bad weather that prevailed over Germany during most of September and October 1944, resulted in a deluge of explosives falling on the Reichsbahn. A new dimension was the assault on the waterway system. In October, 35,000 tons of bombs were dropped on transportation targets by the strategic air forces.[1] Significantly, 95 percent was dropped blindly, using radar.[2] The Eighth Air Force alone contributed 18,844 tons.[3] The cloudy weather caused the Eighth to put the emphasis on transportation targets in October, dropping the preponderance of its bombs on such targets. Oil targets received only one-third the tonnage. The Fifteenth Air Force dropped 4,657 tons of bombs on railway targets in southern Germany during October.[4] Bomber Command resumed its offensive against urban areas in September but with a critical difference: it shifted its aiming points in urban raids from city centers to marshalling yards. Simultaneously, using the superior carrying capacity of its Lancasters, it attacked the canal system. Impetus was added to this by an operational order issued by Bottomley on 13 October 1944.[5] It set in motion Operation Hurricane I. As with every bombing directive, this one also was a compromise. But it was a compromise with an important new feature: it confirmed the existing target priorities but ordered greater concentration of effort both geographically and in time. All air forces were to focus the heaviest possible attack on the Ruhr in order to demonstrate Allied military and air superiority to the German people and to create the maximum disorganization of the communications and administrative apparatus of the region. To this end, the bombers were ordered to hit marshalling yards, viaducts, and the area's canals. The high operational proficiency of the Allied air forces allowed them to respond to this order immediately. The pounding from the air virtually stopped waterway traffic serving the region and gravely weakened rail service. The result was a severe drop in the production of basic goods in the Ruhr itself and the spread of a deadly coal famine to its dependencies in south and central Germany. The distribution of components and the delivery of finished goods were disrupted. Final production in sectors selected by Speer continued at a very high level but only at the cost of depleting stocks of fuel and components. The Reichsbahn was forced to struggle on without the help of the waterways or the Luftwaffe.

Allied air superiority left both the DR and the inland waterways naked to attack. As Ganzenmüller put it to a gathering of operations officers on 20 October, "We cannot rely on our Luftwaffe, but on our own powers of resistance."[6] Three sharp blows, one of which was a lucky break, sufficed to sever all of the Ruhr waterway outlets. On the night of 22–23 September, Bomber Command attacked the Dortmund-Ems Canal at Ladbergen, using 12,000-pound bombs. The embankments were broken and the waterway drained, sweeping barges into the surrounding countryside. All traffic was halted, and 130 vessels backed up on the DEK south of Münster. Making matters worse, the raid also cut telecommunications to the area, slowing the repair effort.[7] The synergistic effects of transportation bombing now made themselves felt. The 2 October attack on the marshalling yard at Hamm destroyed fifteen carloads of repair tools destined for the DEK.[8] Other raids on Münster and Osnabrück delayed the arrival of materials and workers.[9] Disputes arose among the various contractors engaged to do the actual repairs.[10] When work did begin it was hampered by pesky Allied fighters that strafed the repair crews. While the DEK was closed, the ZVL gathered barges from the Ruhr in hopes of surging them through when the waterway reopened.[11] Despite the obstacles, one of the two DEK passages was reopened on 21 October. The loss of a month's traffic and the restricted capacity of the waterway when it did reopen meant that hard coal traffic north and east, as measured at the Münster lock, was 89 percent lower in October than during the preceeding year.[12]

Just when it seemed that the Ruhr link to central Germany would be restored, the Eighth Air Force cut the MLK at Minden on 26 October.[13] The B-24s struck the waterway as it passed over the Weser River, causing not only a long section of the canal to drain, but also unleashing a torrent that created a sandbar that restricted passage on the river as well. Speer intervened immediately by sending his own representative, Dr. Friedrich Lüschen of the armaments staff, to impart his energy to the effort, and by offering bonuses to the repair crews for an early reopening.[14] The Reichsbahn attempted to redistribute the freight from the barges backed up on either side of the cut but was hindered by the lack of car space.[15] Coal-carrying barges to the west of the break were redirected to the Dortmund-Ems Canal on which they then sailed north to Emden, then east along the Coastal Canal to Leer and Oldenburg, and finally back south on the Weser where they could redistribute their loads.[16] Some made the journey to Bremen where they were sent east to Hamburg or Berlin.[17] These roundabout expedients prevented only the worst disasters. They entailed a great loss of time and effort. The result was that coal and iron ore traffic eastward on the MLK virtually ceased after late September.

The third blow was landed on 14 October. The Eighth Air Force was unable to attack synthetic fuel targets in central Germany due to cloud cover so it chose to implement Hurricane I with a series of massive raids against railway facilities in the Cologne area. Two of the raids were made against the Cologne-Gereon marshalling yard on the left bank of the Rhine within walking distance to the north of the great cathedral. During one of the attacks, onlookers were shocked to see the massive Cologne-Mülheimer Bridge erupt in smoke and flame and then tumble into the Rhine, its roadway in one piece. The 14,808-ton, 695-meter-long bridge had been prepared for demolition in anticipation of the onrushing Allied armies. The triggers for the charges were in the Gereon marshalling yard. One of the raids had tripped them. Through a stroke of sheer luck, the bridge had been neatly dropped into the river, severing the vital coal artery to southern Germany. High priority was given to the repair effort. The crews encountered difficulty in obtaining heavy equipment, which was in short supply in Germany, and in approaching the structure through the bomb-battered urban area surrounding it. On 19 October, the Organisation Todt began trying to blast a passage through the tangled mass of girders and the eighteen-foot steel beams that supported the roadway. Charges weighing up to seventeen tons were tried, all to no effect.[18] Work continued unsuccessfully and south Germany's coal supplies were severely reduced. They were subject to the vagaries of the level of the Rhine, which if high enough would allow barges with small loads to float over the wreckage, and to the uncertain service of the Reichsbahn.

But the black day of the Ruhr, 14 October 1944, held more in store. Bomber Command pummeled Duisburg with a total of 9,329 tons of explosives and incendiaries in two raids. The harbor was devastated and the coal gateway at Wedau closed. Telecommunications were cut. Repair crews and damage clearance parties were hurried to the scene, but the damage was too great. Operations at Duisburg harbor and Ruhrort fell by half in October, almost all of the loss coming after the black day. Traffic from the DEK was down by 82 percent.[19]

There was little that the Transportation Ministry could do to counter these shattering disasters other than exhort the repair crews. In September it had increased movement on weekends. In late October it finally established freight priorities for the waterway system. And with winter fast approaching the ministry was compelled to bestow highest priority on the harvest. Second place was reserved for coal.[20] But these measures were overwhelmed by the destruction wrought by the bombers. The Ruhr's waterway connections to the rest of the Reich had been severed. Practically the entire burden of keeping Germany's industrial body intact now rested on the Reichsbahn.

But the Reichsbahn itself was reeling under the relentless pounding from the air. Nowhere was the situation worse than in the Rhineland and the Ruhr itself. The Eighth Air Force followed up its 14 October success at Cologne by blasting the city's marshalling yards on eight further occasions during the next four days. Other attacks focused on GBL-West and the western reaches of GBL-South. All the vital coal gateways were struck either at their sources or along their tributaries. The Hohenbudberg route was bombed on twenty-four occasions, largely because it was on the left bank of the Rhine and closest to the area of ground combat. Therefore it enjoyed the combined attentions of both the strategic and tactical air forces. It was out of service throughout the period of special priority. Wedau was bombed twice, and yards along its route eight times. The RWKS maintained a temperature chart of the gateways between 16 September and 18 October, that is, for thirty-three days. The Wedau gateway was closed for two-fifths of this period. Soest, which was bombed once, was closed for half of the period as well. The Geisecke gateway, struck at Frankfurt/Main, was closed for two-fifths of the period. The Hamm route received an extraordinary amount of attention: Hamm itself was battered, and Hanover and Bielefeld were also hit hard. The result was that this crucial gateway was unavailable for two-thirds of the period. The Münster gateway to the north was bombed twelve times, on six occasions at its source. This sufficed to close it for a third of the period. Finally, the Vorhalle line was not attacked but because of congestion caused by raids elsewhere in the system, it operated at only half capacity. Using this crude accounting, it can be surmised that the Ruhr's crucial coal gateways were available on average for only about half of the period of special priority.[21]

The consequences were severe. All coal traffic going south by rail from the Ruhr stopped from 14 to 18 October. Afterwards, instead of the one hundred coal trains for industrial consumers that ordinarily left the region daily, only about twenty could find their way out.[22] Central Planning considered this to be the greatest coal crisis since the beginning of the war.[23] Meeting on 27 October to discuss armaments issues, Speer and Kehrl agreed that the bombing of the Reichsbahn was the most difficult problem confronting them.[24] To meet the crisis they decided that it was essential to maintain control of policy formation from the center and to allow local and regional authorities greater latitude in implementing it. Therefore they would extend their influence over the Reichsbahn. They recognized that there was a real possibility that Germany would disintegrate into a number of uncoordinated economic areas. But they were faced with the stark reality that there was little that they could do to prevent this. Only the defeat of the bombers could fundamentally change the situation and they knew that no such event was in the offing. All they could do was adapt to circumstances. Hitler had already ordered that the Ruhr attempt to maintain production by relying on resources available internally.[25] Speer also took the dangerous step of reorganizing the lower reaches of his administration. He combined his regional armaments inspectorates with the Economics Ministry's local offices through an agreement with Franz Hayler.[26]

In contrast, the Reichsbahn adhered to its proven system and simply pressed forward grimly with the daunting task of repairing damage and moving trains. Hordes of people were thrown into the repair effort. On 18 October, at Speer's request, Hitler ordered that the repair of marshalling yards be given first call on labor even before fortification work. The Ruhr Staff ordered factory owners to form railway repair columns, fully equipped from their own resources. One team of 125 men would be created for each 5,000 employees. During the last week of October, 76,800 people were engaged in clearing rubble and repairing facilities in Reichsbahn labor teams alone.[27]

By announcing embargoes, the DR also attempted to reduce the volume of freight to correspond to the amount of car space available. Certain types of cargo in designated areas would be excluded until the freight backlog caused by the disruption of traffic was cleared. The first such embargo was proclaimed on 22 September and affected the left bank of the Rhine. Only armaments, coal, food, and ore were allowed. But the continuing deluge from the air caused this relatively limited restriction to be progressively sharpened. On 14 October, the black day, Embargo 41 banned shipments to the west, though there were exceptions for important goods. By the end of the month the number of restrictions was reduced and their content altered. Repair materials for the Reichsbahn itself were added. Coal and ore were also permitted, although parts with priority under the Panzer program were excluded.[28]

The crippling of the coal gateways was just one feature of the problem facing the Reichsbahn. Heavy air attacks on marshalling yards in the Frankfurt/Main and Mannheim areas had also thrown operations there into chaos. The DR countered these setbacks with the Special Measures West program of 19 September. It provided for the increased use of unit trains especially to carry coal and for additional night running. Hohenbudberg and Mannheim were relieved of responsibility for handling long-distance trains. Passenger trains were slowed to the same speed as freights to ease scheduling problems. A danger zone, during which daylight running was prohibited, was proclaimed west of a line running from the Dutch border to Rheine, Osterfeld-Süd, Wedau, Wuppertal-Vohwinckel, Limburg, Frankfurt/Main, Heidelberg, Darmstadt, and Pforzheim to the Swiss border. Three days later all shipments to RBD Frankfurt/Main were embargoed. A special effort was made to reduce the backlog by breaking up trains and reallocating marshalling responsibilities to other directorates.[29]

The Reichsbahn took additional stringent measures to restore the flow of coal and other freight. It redistributed and rationalized responsibilities for serving particular mines and factories among the Münster, Hamm, Soest, and Geisecke gateways.[30] On 11 October, in a major departure, it abandoned its usual practice of returning backed up freight to the shipper. Now the Reichsbahn alone would decide where to send delayed goods, especially coal and perishables.[31] Late in the month it designated six marshalling yards in RBDs Regensburg and Schwerin for the formation of unit trains to ship freight westward.[32] This move typified the way in which the Reichsbahn used GBL-East as a sanctuary to sustain operations in the west. It also began a program of equipping cars with light anti-aircraft guns as protection against strafers.[33]

The ZVL engaged in the intricate process of altering priorities and allocating car space in light of rapidly changing conditions. At the outset of the period of bombing under special priority, as of 21 September, armaments shipments had first call on car space, followed by the harvest.[34] By the middle of October, after the setback of the fourteenth, coal had moved into the spotlight with the ZVL refusing to shift car space from the mining regions to the east to carry the harvest.[35] On 20 October the ZVL bowed to circumstances and reduced the coal target to free up space for grain and sugar beets.[36] This meant that the goal for daily coal car placings was cut from 69,200 to 49,000 units. The Ruhr quota was slashed from 16,000 to 11,000.[37] The sacrifice was more apparent than real because the marshalling yards could not meet even these low targets. Nevertheless, the transfer was reflected in the share of space devoted to food transport. Food occupied 27 percent of available space in boxcars by the middle of October, compared to 20 percent at the end of September. Moreover, after having given no space at all in open cars for food transport, by mid-October nearly 5 percent of such cars was used to carry food.[38] The changes were incremental, but they did contribute to postponing urban starvation. The Reichsbahn was capable of little more. Its options were rapidly dwindling.

The Reich Coal Association and the Speer ministry attempted to help by reducing demand for coal and establishing priorities for the allocation and consumption of what was available. Those firms adjacent to the mines and not reliant on the Reichsbahn were allowed a full supply. Among all other plants served by the RWKS, those that had exhausted their stocks would be served first. Then the Reichsbahn's needs would be satisfied. Next the gas works supplying industrial regions, the Wehrmacht, electrical works, and armaments plants would be catered to, in that order.[39] Emphasis was placed on final production and means of distribution rather than on industries early in the production process. These coal priorities best fitted Speer's scheme of seeking immediate results by drawing down stocks in hopes of stabilizing the battlefield and air situations.

All of the ZVL's measures were intended to overcome the grave weakening of the marshalling yards in the west. Two mutually reinforcing problems developed. One was the reduction of the marshalling capacity of the key yards governing the gateways. The other was the disruption of marshalling in the dependencies to the south. The result was that the Ruhr's capacity to ship coal and other goods was reduced. Simultaneously empty cars were immobilized in the areas around Frankfurt/Main and Mannheim. Without these empty cars, RBD Essen could not fully exploit even its reduced marshalling capacity.

Typical of the situation in the Ruhr was the great marshalling yard at Hamm. It was struck seven times. On each occasion the repair crews, averaging about 200 Germans and additional contingents of foreigners, fought to restore the sorting grid. But the bombers always returned to spoil their work. By the end of October, this crucial nodal point was operating at only a quarter of capacity.[40]

Maximilian Lammertz, head of RBD Essen, badgered Berlin to send him more empty cars,[41] but they never came. It was not that the DR lacked cars. The reverse was the case: the Reichsbahn suffered from a glut of freight cars. For example, 6,400 oil tank cars were switched to carrying grain because they were surplus to the needs of the refineries, given the latter's declining output.[42] GBL-East was putting freight cars aside en masse—38,093 by the end of October.[43] Yet the Ruhr could not ship coal in the quantity necessary. By the third week of October the Reichsbahn could carry only a quarter of its former daily average of 100,000 tons out of the region. The Reichsbahn itself claimed all but 2,000 tons of this.[44] The problem was that sufficient cars could not be brought to where they were needed because of marshalling difficulties. The cars existed, but they simply could not be distributed properly because of the bombers.

The RWKS felt the disruption immediately. But because of the paralysis of the waterway system it was actually forced to increase the share of its shipments moving by rail from two-thirds to three-quarters in October. Overall shipments were down substantially. In the Ruhr itself, stocks at the syndicate's trading companies held steady. But in regions dependent upon it, stocks dwindled to eight to ten days.[45]

Again the RVK arranged for the other syndicates to help the RWKS. It called for the Upper Silesian Hard Coal Syndicate to provide 700,000 tons of coal to RWKS dependents and the Central German Brown Coal Syndicate to supply 200,000 tons of brown coal. Some consumers were compelled to switch from hard coal to brown coal, with all of the difficulties and inefficiencies that entailed. But the ubiquitous problem, the weakness of the Reichsbahn, interposed itself. RWKS customers in Hamburg, Hanover, Kassel, and the RWHG at Salzgitter, all well within the syndicate's hinterland, received only about half of the relief consignments intended for them.[46]

The coal emergency was exacerbated by the confrontation that developed between the RWKS and various government agencies. At an advisory board meeting held in Essen on 19 September, Schmidt attacked Sarter and expressed his desire to work with Lammertz of RBD Essen instead. More importantly, he refused to allow the Reich Coal Association, Speer's Armaments Commands, or the Gau Economics Chambers to interfere in the distribution of coal. He had browbeaten Pleiger into agreeing to stay out of coal distribution, leaving it to the RWKS's local traders. They in turn would deal directly with the nearest Reichsbahn directorate.[47] The Reichsbahn moved decisively both to increase the movement of coal and to placate Schmidt. On 7 October it finalized an arrangement with the RWKS to form coal unit trains for use within the Ruhr and for shipments outside of it. On 28 October the region's coal car target was reduced to 8,000 per day, all moving in unit trains formed at the mines themselves. Finally, on 19 October, in a meeting at RVK headquarters, Schelp laid down that distance from a mine should be the determining factor in what plants would be supplied. The area served by Upper Silesia should extend no further than 300 kilometers. Industries in that area should be run at the maximum, others shut down. Shipping coal from Upper Silesia to Hamburg and other places as far west was a mistake, Schelp explained, because the cars were never returned, thus weakening the entire transportation system and ultimately hurting the RWKS.[48] Schmidt could not contradict Schelp on this issue. The Reichsbahn prevailed. But the syndicate and its leader stubbornly continued to defend its market rights in spite of the threatening military situation.

Despite these palliatives, the battering of the marshalling yards had its effect. In October car placings for hard coal in RBD Essen declined 54 percent below the level of the previous year.[49] Inevitably, coal stocks at the mines skyrocketed to six and a half times the October 1943 amount. Coke stocks at the ovens rose in the same fashion. Because production could not be transported, the coal cut fell by a third. Coke output declined by a quarter.[50] This had a direct effect on gas supplies, which fell by half. Complicating the problem was destruction of the administrative offices of Ruhrgas by bombing and the many cuts in the mains from the same cause. At Speer's orders, Pleiger transfered men from the coal mines, where they were redundant due to shipping difficulties, to teams repairing gas lines.[51] Electrical service in the area also deteriorated sharply. But in this case there was no coal shortage. Numerous line cuts and the destruction by bombing of the major brown coal generating station at Goldenberg on 21 October were the culprits. A total of 80,000 kw were lost. Attempts to transfer power from Berlin and central Germany were impeded by the limited capacity of the grid and because BEWAG had no surplus coal. The results were major cuts to industries, including United Steel, and the breakdown of the area into a number of power islands.[52] Car placings for brown coal in the region on the left bank of the Rhine fell by 70 percent due to its proximity to the front and the attacks on marshalling yards in Cologne.[53] Brown coal production fell by half.[54] The difference can be explained by the use of conveyor belts to carry brown coal from mines to many generating plants.

The shattering decline in coal supplies due to transportation bombing in the Ruhr bore dire implications for the region itself and its dependencies in central and southern Germany. Indirectly, it also placed an added burden on Upper Silesia and therefore influenced the economy of the entire Reich. Less directly affected by the coal famine was industry in the Ruhr itself. The iron and steel sector did suffer from a decline in fuel supplies but its main worry was the failure of its ore resources. Rohland of the RVE and United Steel and Hans-Günther Sohl, also of VSt, subjected Ganzenmüller, Dilli, and Schelp to a veritable blizzard of minatory letters on the subject. Sohl developed his own transportation plan calling for 4,300 car placings per day for domestic ore and 2,700 for scrap. Rohland warned Ganzenmüller that "each ton of ore or scrap not shipped means an effective drop in production."[55]

The ZVL attempted to meet the industry's demands by organizing special runs to bring domestic ore to the region and raising the priority for ore space.[56] But the bombers vetoed this plan. Between 6 and 10 October only one of fifty scheduled ore trains arrived in the Ruhr.[57] The ZVL responded by excepting ore from its embargoes and even raised its priority above that of coal on 14 October. In addition, arrangements were made to ship 35,500 tons of steel shavings and splinters to the Ruhr monthly.[58] Ten days later, Schelp ordered that the full demand for car space for scrap be met.[59] The Speer ministry weighed in by cancelling 204,700 tons of old iron plate orders.[60] The effort to relieve the burden on the steel industry and satisfy its needs, however, slowed and eventually came to a halt. Speer's inspectors discovered that manufacturers still held stocks of 5 million tons of iron and steel. He prohibited new orders as a result and, following up the iron action of the summer, ordered an additional drastic reduction in holdings before new orders could be let.[61] He also decreed that iron stocks be reduced to the five-month level by the end of November 1944 by consumption and transfer to needy companies.[62] In light of these ample supplies of semifinished iron and steel, the need for new production was limited and on 21 October Dilli restored coal to first priority.[63] Schelp and Dilli visited the Ruhr on 28 October and prevailed upon Sohl to accept restrictions on movement within the region when the gateways were open. This would allow vital coal supplies to be rushed to the Ruhr's dependencies. When the gateways were blocked, car space could be given to the steel industry.[64]

In retrospect, it is clear that the steel industry's demands were not entirely justified. In addition to the rich supplies of unused steel in the yards of manufacturing companies, the iron and steel companies themselves were not on the brink of disaster due to a lack of iron ore. A very complex situation had developed in the Ruhr, composed of problems in distributing coal, direct damage to the mills by air raids, a decline in ore supplies, and the reluctance of the iron and steel company owners to exert themselves for the Nazi regime.[65] In the latter regard, Rohland cynically exploited his close relationship with Speer and the businessmen and technocrats who manned his ministry to attempt to gain favors for his company and its allies. A brief look at the resource situation in the industry demonstrates this. Ruhr iron and steel production in October 1944 were 36 percent and 28 percent lower respectively than during 1943.[66] Ore stocks in the industry were 35 percent lower.[67] So real losses had been sustained. But to exclude fluctuations in these indices that occurred during 1943, figures for September and October 1944 can be compared. In October, iron ore arrivals were 46 percent lower than in September. But stocks were not drawn down correspondingly to compensate. By the end of October they had declined by only 15 percent. The key was that consumption was reduced by 34 percent. This husbanding of reserves caused a 39 percent drop in both iron and steel production.[68] The production loss did not correspond to the fall in ore supplies. Indeed, based on the rates of consumption for each month, stocks actually rose. In September they sufficed for 3.7 months, in October for 4.8 months. In part the discrepancy can be attributed to damage to production facilities inflicted by bombing. But much of it must be ascribed to the iron and steel masters' withdrawal of support from the Hitler regime.

The complexity of the situation prevailing in the Ruhr steel industry can be clarified by one additional example. United Steel began to experience a coal shortage. Coal stocks at the mines of its GBAG subsidiary jumped by 1,000 percent and coke stocks were a fifth higher. Meanwhile, coal stocks at the mills were slightly lower and coke stocks one quarter lower than at the same time in 1943.[69]

The strain of constant air attacks, disputes, and searches for expedients led to the beginning of the disintegration of Speer's apparatus in the region. Coordinating components deliveries with final production became extremely difficult. The Ruhr Staff found cooperation among companies and with itself ever rarer. Even members of the Ruhr Staff and Speer's transport plenipotentiaries were collapsing under the pressure. It cannot be surprising then that the Ruhr's contribution to the Reich war effort in terms of finished goods fell sharply. The final production of armaments was badly disrupted. Those goods that were completed often could not be shipped. Klöckner shipped a fifth less in October than during the same month of the preceding year. The small Fritz Hulvershorn plant engaged in making heads for 80mm mortar shells was unable to ship any of the 30,000 that clogged its warehouse and grounds.[70] In short, transportation bombing—attacks on marshalling yards and canals—had substantially reduced the Ruhr's iron, steel, and armaments production, gravely disrupted shipments of completed weapons, and upset the exchange of components with other regions. In addition, the Ruhr's administrative apparatus was crumbling. Most importantly, the region's key contribution to the operation of the geographical division of labor as energy supplier to central and southern Germany was rapidly waning. The incessant bombing was prying out of place the lynchpin of the Reich economy.

In the areas dependent on the Ruhr, the coal situation was deteriorating rapidly. Many of the few trains that managed to leave the area were eventually lost in the morass in the marshalling yards. For example, of thirty trains dispatched by the RWKS between 13 and 28 September, ten were never heard from again. The result was that coal stocks dwindled to about four weeks in the Ruhr's dependencies. In some cases production was already being cut back. Speer's assistant, Liebel, toured the southwest to check the pulse of industry there in late October. He found conditions bordering on panic. Frantic plant managers implored him to intercede on their behalf to obtain coal, otherwise mass closings would ensue immediately.[71]

The causes of the emergency were the problems in the Ruhr and the dislocation of rail operations in GBL-South. Telecommunications at the regional headquarters had collapsed on 4 October, forcing it to be transfered temporarily to Augsburg. The area's key marshalling yards at Karlsruhe, Mannheim, and Stuttgart-Kornwestheim were either shut or operating at reduced capacity. Space for putting aside cars and trains in the yards was exhausted so one track on double tracked lines was used to hold trains that could not be marshalled. Locomotive coal supplies were dangerously low— twelve days by the end of October.[72] The waterways were unable to step into the breach. Coal arrivals at Mannheim collapsed after the Cologne-Mülheimer Bridge disaster halted navigation, thus causing an 11 percent fall in total receipts in October.[73] The Reichsbahn attempted to compensate by accelerating the movement of coal stored at the port but the lack of car space stymied this gambit.[74] The ZVL, as we have seen, directed coal trains to the southern Rhineland from Upper Silesia and central Germany. Whenever RBD Oppeln could place more than 17,000 cars for coal, space above this level would be used to supply the Mannheim area.[75] But by 14 October, a week later, the Reichsbahn had to reduce its help to seven trains daily with the proviso that it determine their destinations.[76] This directly challenged the RWKS's prerogatives. But there was little that the syndicate could do. In its southern hinterland, the Messerschmitt aircraft plant at Augsburg and the Dornier airplane factory at Friedrichshafen had already exhausted their coal supplies by 1 November.[77] Although armaments output in the Mannheim area was delayed by the transport crisis, fuel and components remained sufficiently available to avoid major production losses.[78]

The situation near Hanover was more serious. Here the first major production drops occurred. The key was the cessation of shipments on the Mittelland Canal. Coal arrivals by water at Hanover were down by half. Including assistance from Upper Silesia and the Central German Brown Coal Syndicate, which depended on the Reichsbahn, overall coal receipts were off by 80 percent. Coal stocks were confiscated and production losses were appearing even among armaments plants.[79] At the Reichswerke Hermann Göring coal supplies were at the eight to ten day level by the end of October. Consequently, operation of the cokeries was reduced by up to two-thirds.[80] Yet, reflecting the government's direct control of this facility, production of iron increased 24.2 percent and that of finished goods by 134.8 percent compared to the average for the fourth quarter of 1943. This was done by rifling stocks. Coal consumption rose and scrap usage was up by almost half. Not surprisingly in light of its own increased energy demands, the complex cut sales of electricity to outside consumers by a third.[81] The end result was that the attempt to use central Germany to compensate for the losses sustained in the Ruhr only partially succeeded. Pig iron output actually rose slightly.[82] But it was far from enough to offset the setback suffered by the giant in the west.

Eastern Germany was also used to sustain the Reich economy during the Ruhr's decline. The Reichsbahn and the Speer ministry alike used this ploy. The situation of GBL-East was far better than that of the two other GBLs. But it deteriorated during the period of special priority nonetheless. There were two causes. One was the spread eastward of the chaos reigning along the Rhine. Directorates in the west refused trains steaming from the east, causing backups to reverberate through RBDs Hanover and Regensburg into the region. The intimate interdependence of the components of a railway system cannot be better demonstrated than by these events. The second reason was the disruption caused by air attacks falling in the area itself. They were not directed against marshalling yards in GBL-East as such but against synthetic fuel plants near Leipzig and Gleiwitz. They had the unanticipated result of disrupting marshalling at the nearby yards at Halle and Gleiwitz. Moreover, the region was also affected by the universal telephone problem. GBL-East countered by sending locomotives to RBD Halle, transferring marshalling to quiet areas such as Posen from Halle, and expediting coal shipments to the west.[83] The region was used as a holding area for trains that could not move westward and as a reservoir for cars and locomotives to be fed to the ailing directorates along the Rhine.[84] The penalty was a decline in performance in the region. The backlog of trains more than doubled to 256 during the last week of October.[85] In RBD Halle, freight car placings held steady but brown coal car placings, crucial if losses suffered by the RWKS were to be countered, actually fell by 7.5 percent during October compared to the monthly average for the fourth quarter of 1943.[86] This was due entirely to the disruption of marshalling because the supply of locomotives simultaneously increased.[87]

The coal situation in the region was unstable. Brown coal production was steady in the East Elbian area farthest from the bombing, but in the Central German area it fell by 10 percent due to lack of car space from RBD Halle.[88] The damage to the area's synthetic fuel plants permitted the redisposition of their coal supplies. But hampered by scarce car space, this remedy was only partially effective.[89]

In the other major hard coal pivot, Upper Silesia, RBD Oppeln struggled against the paralysis infecting the region from the west, disruption from air attacks in its own region and the waves of dissolution sweeping westward before the advance of the Red Army. Overall freight car placings declined here by 17 percent. More ominously, the all-important coal car placing figure dropped by 39 percent in October, compared to the average for the fourth quarter of 1943. Again the cause was confusion in marshalling for the number of locomotives in service increased.[90] Hard coal production, measured on the same basis as car placings, fell by 18 percent in October. Coke production, especially valuable in light of the losses suffered in the Ruhr, was sustained with only a 4 percent loss. But again, the weakening of the DR was highlighted by the alarming increase in coal stocks at the mines by 176.5 percent and coke stocks by 720.5 percent.[91] Coal production was reduced due to lack of storage space at the mines.[92] Raw iron production was pushed despite all hindrances and suffered a loss of less than 2 percent.[93] But as in the west, the mere production of an article did not ensure that it could be used. The Oberhütten Gleiwitz complained as early as 27 September that it lacked car space to ship components graced with Hitler's special "Panzerblitz" priority.[94]

Upper Silesia's dependencies were better supplied than those of the Ruhr and so were able to continue operations at near normal levels. But even here, distressing signs of weakness began to appear. Coal traffic on the Oder was reduced in September and October due to low water.[95] Movement on the Adolf Hitler Canal was blocked by Fifteenth Air Force raids on the nearby Blechhammer synthetic fuel plant.[96] At Berlin, coal arrivals from the west through Stettin were down by 40 percent during September while shipments from Upper Silesia were off by a quarter.[97] In October, brown coal traffic also fell a quarter below normal.[98] Nevertheless, through conservation coal supplies in Berlin were maintained or even increased as was the case at the city's gas works.[99] BEWAG suffered a 15 percent drop in supplies. Stocks fell by 9 percent. Consumption rose so that by the end of October stocks sufficed for one and a half months' production.[100] But a new factor limited the nominal value of these stocks. Supplies from Upper Silesia continuously deteriorated in quality causing the jump in consumption.[101] Actual electricity generation by BEWAG was 4 percent lower than the monthly average during the fourth quarter of 1943.[102]

When viewed from the national perspective, it can be seen that the Reich inland waterway system was decisively weakened by the three raids in the west. The Reichsbahn, in spite of the efforts of the repair crews and GBL-East, had sustained crippling losses, and the armaments industry had continued to produce very large quantities of weapons by ruthlessly depleting its stocks. A few key indicators lend substance to this picture.

The Reichsbahn placed 20 percent fewer cars in freight trains during the period of special priority, 16 September to 31 October, than during the same time frame in 1943. More significantly, coal car placings were a staggering 39 percent lower in October. Brown coal car placings were 40 percent lower.[103] The Main Car Office calculated in September, before the worst losses were sustained, that the DR satisfied only 56 percent of nominal demand for car space of all types. This was a third less than in September 1943.[104] The backlog had mushroomed to an average of 1,155 trains per day during the last ten days of October.[105] Put differently, this meant that 307,000 cars were caught in backlogged trains and were therefore unavailable. A further 62,000 were delayed in loading and unloading because freight car turnaround time was up to 12.7 days in October, a quarter more than during the previous year.[106] The effort to repair freight cars was actually reduced because there was no freight car shortage.[107] In effect, the Reichsbahn had lost access to over a third of its entire freight car park simply through disorganization in marshalling. Nor was there a locomotive shortage. By the end of October the size of the DR locomotive park was 2 percent higher than at the beginning and the reserve was 39 percent greater.[108]

There was no vehicle shortage and the strafers were irrelevant. The problem was marshalling. Cars could not be brought to where they were needed because marshalling in the Ruhr and along the Rhine was in chaos and in Halle and Oppeln it was tottering. The result was a major coal famine that did not spare the Reichsbahn itself. By the first of November its stocks of locomotive coal were down to just twelve days, 40 percent below the minimum.[109] Despite these problems, it was the Reichsbahn's task alone to supply the country with coal. By late October the waterways were carrying a mere 7 percent of all coal shipments. Local sales accounted for 14 percent. Even in its weakened state the Reichsbahn still moved three-quarters of the nation's coal traffic.[110] The geographical division of labor was disintegrating. Transportation troubles, cuts in the waterways serving the Ruhr, and the bombing of marshalling yards in the west were prying apart the interdependent regions of the Reich economy. The Ruhr could no longer sustain its dependencies and Upper Silesia was prevented from stepping into the gap. Through the conscious exploitation of elasticity of supply, however, Speer and Kehrl managed to maintain output of selected weapons at a very high rate. The overall armaments production index declined by only 9 percent during the period of special priority.[111] By comparison, national hard coal production tumbled by 31 percent.[112] The difference is explained by the consumption of stocks of coal and components. In this way assault gun output, easier to sustain than that of tanks due to its lower demand for steel, actually rose by a third from August.[113] Output of the 88mm PAK 43 antitank gun was a fifth higher than in August and twice as high as during the previous October.[114] But again the transport problem interposed itself. Many armaments firms were unable to ship their output and some were forced to curtail operations because their production areas were clogged with shipping crates.[115] As we have seen, output of the 88mm PAK 43 rose substantially. But acceptances by the army actually declined in October compared to August by 55 percent. The Army Armaments Office attributed the shortfall exclusively to "transportation difficulties."[116] Considering that the

Army was in dire need of every weapon that it could lay its hands on after the defeats of the summer of 1944, it is clear that transportation bombing was already exerting a direct if far from decisive influence on the actual combat power of the Wehrmacht. By late October 1944 the bombing of marshalling yards and the cutting of the Ruhr waterways had caused a severe reduction in Germany's coal supplies, substantially reduced iron and steel output, forced a slight contraction of armaments production but not of key weapons, and gravely hindered the exchange of goods within the economy and the delivery of weapons to the Wehrmacht. It had also imposed extraordinary strain on Speer's administrative apparatus, causing it and the Reichsbahn to begin to disintegrate.

In Germany there were few people who fully understood what was actually happening to the Reich economy. The decline in the operations of the Reichsbahn and the barges was apparent to all, but the consequences were not. Only Ganzenmüller, Speer, Kehrl, and a few others at the highest levels of the RMfRuK, the Transportation Ministry, and in industry clearly understood how the fragile division of labor was being ripped apart. It is not surprising then, that Allied intelligence, lacking the information available to Speer and the others, encountered extraordinary difficulty in deciphering what was happening in Germany. They also engaged in bureaucratic infighting that reduced their ability to interpret accurately such information as they did uncover. The strengths and weaknesses of intelligence organization among the democratic western Allies were highlighted during this period. The multiplicity of bodies ensured a lively debate that might have resulted in a balanced interpretation. Information was shared among the various entities freely. But this resulted only in acceptance, not questioning of dubious assertions. Mere frequency of repetition added to their credibility. Indeed, the debate actually led to the suppression of evidence. All of the Allied air intelligence agencies agreed that photoreconnaissance provided insufficient information to evaluate the transportation offensive.[117] The very clouds that intensified the attack concealed its results. They were also unanimous in pinpointing the lack of reliable ground sources.[118] The Special Measures West instituted by the Reichsbahn in September were finally mentioned in RRS and SHAEF appreciations in early November. They concurred that this meant a reduction in the DR's overall capability.[119] But RRS and MEW considered the DR to be moving the same volume of traffic as during the same period in 1943.[120] SHAEF and OSS, based on prisoner interrogations, both argued that morale among the Reichsbahn train crews was sinking.[121] No one on the German side was aware of this. MAGIC provided no useful evidence.[122] OSS agents and PW interrogators did learn that the Hamm and Soest gateways were closed at the end of September.[123] Ultra had no impact on the formation of policy for reasons that will become clear shortly.

No less than EOU, SHAEF engaged in policy-directed intelligence appreciation. While it recognized the importance of marshalling, it interpreted the available evidence to conclude that a major locomotive shortage afflicted the DR due to the destruction of repair facilities.[124] The difficult problem of piecing together the complicated puzzle to form a reasonably accurate image of the German economy remained beyond most Allied intelligence agencies. Consequently, they relied upon the ideas that they had developed during the preceding months. The influence of hard, current data upon this phase of the strategic bombing debate was surprisingly slight.

The overwhelming factor shaping Allied strategic air planning during September and October 1944 was the notion that the war in Europe would be won in a few weeks. In September, EOU thought the war would end in October, USSTAF within three months, and MAAF sometime very soon.[125] When the attempt to leap across the Rhine at Arnhem failed, the desire to end the war rapidly did not fade. On 19 October, General Arnold set 1 January 1945 as the target date to finish the conflict with Hitler and questioned current bombing priorities.[126] Two days later, Gen. George C. Marshall, chairman of the American Joint Chiefs of Staff, asked the air forces to present a coordinated plan to end the war during 1944.[127] At the Air Ministry, Air Commodore Bufton also pressed for an air strategy to end the war during 1944.[128] A complicating factor was that not only Harris but Spaatz as well hoped to win the war alone in the immediate future through bombing.[129]

The search for the key that would rapidly end the war began with extraordinary intensity. Maj. Gen. Lawrence Kuter, Arnold's assistant for planning, disappointed his chief in response to his query by arguing that it was too late for strategic bombing alone to end the war during 1944. He suggested that tactical and transportation targets just behind the front would be the most profitable objectives for the heavy bombers.[130] This note of disappointment and the absence of new alternatives influenced the struggle over bombing strategy for the remainder of the war. The two most prominent alternatives were oil and transportation, and each had its advocates —EOU and Spaatz on the one hand and SHAEF and Tedder on the other. The ensuing debate over Tedder's transportation proposal revolved around three issues. Its opponents contended that there was insufficient time for it to exert an appreciable effect. They emphasized the Reichsbahn's ability to withstand an attack, and, finally, they purported that an economic collapse was about to occur due to the oil offensive. The first two objections were made in ignorance of the substantial weakening already suffered by the DR, and the latter was the product of the fundamental lack of comprehension of how energy was used in Germany that reigned at EOU.

On 5 October 1944 the Combined Strategic Targets Committee was formed to improve coordination and finalize an air strategy to help end the war. The body was composed of representatives of MEW, RRS, EOU, the Air Ministry, USSTAF, and SHAEF.[131] Tedder immediately realized that the board was loaded in favor of oil.[132] Consequently, much to the chagrin of the CSTC which bitterly resisted his move, Tedder compelled it to form a transportation working committee on 25 October.[133] This gambit can be interpreted as an attempt by Tedder not only to balance the committee but also to ensure that the air commanders' conferences retained the final policy-making and executive authority in the strategic bombing arena.

Having dealt with the CSTC, Tedder took the initiative behind the scenes and turned to Portal to argue his case. The support that Tedder enjoyed from Portal and Eisenhower was the decisive factor in his ability to prevail in the bureaucratic struggle that swirled in the Allied command. In a masterly summary of his position submitted to Portal on 25 October, he stated, in words that would have amazed Speer and Ganzenmüller, "I am not satisfied that . . . we are using our air power really effectively. The various types of operations should fit into one comprehensive pattern, whereas I feel that at present they are more like a patchwork quilt."[134] He then pinpointed the exposed nerve that Speer and Ganzenmüller were frantically trying to shield: "The one common factor in the whole German war effort, from the political control down to the supply of troops in the front line is communications. . . . In my opinion, our primary air objective should be the enemy's communications."[135]

He explained how the heavy bombers should focus their attention on railway centers, canals, and synthetic oil plants, especially in northwest Germany. These would be supported by fighter-bomber attacks on trains.[136] Unlike his opponents, he viewed the oil and transportation offensives as "complementary."[137] But the crucial distinguishing feature about transportation and the reason it was not a "panacea" target, was that the Germans could not substitute for it. Tedder contended that a concerted attack on the Ruhr and Frankfurt/Main–Mannheim areas would "create complete economic chaos."[138] He hoped thereby significantly to smooth the path forward of the Allied armies and simultaneously to ruin the German economy. The combined pressure of all the air forces concentrating on a conceptually and geographically coherent target system and the armies' continued attrition of the Wehrmacht would break Germany's war fighting power.

Tedder was successful. On 28 October, SHAEF adopted his plan and the combined chiefs ratified it.[139] The new directive was issued on 1 November. It placed oil first and transportation second on the priority list with the same proviso concerning weather as under the special priority.[140] The CSTC was ordered to develop a comprehensive plan to meet Tedder's goals. It interpreted them as providing assistance to the land armies and putting "the greatest possible pressure on the enemy's war production by interference with economic traffic."[141] The panel assumed that the war would conclude by the end of 1944. Opportunities for visual attack would be limited. Synergistic effects from other types of attacks such as oil raids and Hurricane would be factored into the target list. Repeat attacks would be necessary. Strikes on waterways would be coordinated with blows to marshalling yards. In selecting railway targets, centers combining marshalling and locomotive servicing would be given preference. Waterway targets would be chosen with an eye toward preventing long-distance haulage, thereby putting the maximum burden on the Reichsbahn. Germany was divided into nine transportation zones in descending order of importance. At the head of the list were the northeast approaches to the Ruhr followed by the Frankfurt-Mannheim area. Next came the Cologne-Koblenz region and then the Kassel area. These were followed by Karlsruhe-Stuttgart, Magdeburg-Leipzig, Upper Silesia, Vienna, and Bavaria. If this plan can be criticized, it can be faulted for the low priority given to the Magdeburg-Leipzig region, where RBD Halle was already quaking under the strain, and to Upper Silesia, where RBD Oppeln was weakening. The failure to emphasize these two regions allowed the ZVL to continue to use GBL-East as a reservoir to sustain the west. But under the circumstances prevailing in the Allied command, especially with the desire to render immediate assistance to the ground troops, little more could have been expected.[142] As it was, the first transportation plan represented a dire threat to the Reichsbahn and Speer's weakened production apparatus.

7 Spades against Bombs

One of the great imponderables in warfare, indeed in all human affairs, is time. Judgments of the influence of the time factor, how much was available and whom it favored, were at the heart of the issue between Tedder and Spaatz on the one hand and Speer and Ganzenmüller on the other. The German leaders had a better insight into the workings of time. They realized as early as June 1944 that it was moving against them, and they took appropriate steps. They consciously exploited elasticity of supply to stretch their resources over the looming crisis period with the hope that if they could surmount it then more time would become available which would allow them to take new measures. The Allies, Tedder excepted, consistently misjudged the play of time. They sought rapid results from their bombing effort, in large part because of their haste to end the war in Europe. The British in particular desired an early conclusion in order to spare their people additional casualties. In contrast, the Americans planned to transfer the bulk of their forces to the Pacific to help consummate the victory over Japan. This contributed heavily to their bad misjudgment of the length of time necessary for an air attack on transportation to reduce industrial output and supplies of weapons to the Wehrmacht. In part due to a dearth of air reconnaissance, they did not appreciate that the bombers were gradually winning their destructive race against the repair crews. They repeatedly pointed to the pipeline as a buffer between the transportation system, industry, and the enemy fighting formations. But weeks of air attacks on transportation, the pipeline itself, had shortened it and forced German industry to consume part of its reserves. With every passing day, the argument that stocks, the pipeline, and the recuperative powers of the transportation system would muffle the shocks of bombing lost validity. The struggle at this juncture resolved itself into a contest between the Allied air leaders and their consistency in the pursuit of their goal and the Germans' dogged efforts to repair bomb damage and improvise production arrangements. There can be no doubt that transportation bombing had disrupted the German economy. The key question now was whether the Allied air commanders could agree among themselves to continue the bombing and force its collapse.[1] The Luftwaffe was too weak to oppose them. But haste, lack of information, and bureaucratic infighting could still have granted Speer and Ganzenmüller the breathing space that they so desperately needed.

During November the Allied air forces redoubled their attacks on the Reich's transportation arteries. But on 5 December it appeared as if Speer's hopes might be realized. On that day a meeting of Allied commanders took place at SHAEF to decide air strategy for the near future. Tedder advocated the continuation of transportation attacks designed to weaken the German economy. He was supported by Spaatz and Lt. Gen. Hoyt S. Vandenberg, commander of the U.S. Ninth Air Force. But Gen. Omar Bradley, commander of the Twelfth Army Group, suggested that the heavy bombers be used to attack German defensive positions to ease the ground advance. In a crucial shift in the bureaucratic political situation, Eisenhower threw his support behind Bradley. The pressure from Washington for a quick end to the war was too great. Tedder lost the unstinting support of one of his major allies. The result was that oil retained first priority. Now carpet bombing to support the army moved into second place. Transportation attack was relegated to third. However, a significant proviso was attached to the new priority list. As before, oil targets would be hit only when visual conditions prevailed. To prevent a repetition of the tragedy that occurred in Normandy, where Allied troops were accidentally killed by heavy bombers, strikes supporting them also could be flown only during clear weather. Transportation raids could be flown under overcast conditions, using radar.[2]

Tedder did not suffer a complete defeat. Two factors continued to work in his favor. First, he continued to dominate the air commanders' conferences. Therefore, he could still exert heavy influence on target selection. Through this means, he ordered the CSTC to prepare a new transportation target priority list. It was completed on 8 December. First priority was given again to objectives such as marshalling yards and canals that would cause a long-term decline in transportation service. Second priority was accorded to yards and lines linking Hanover to Frankfurt/Main via Kassel, Giessen, Bebra, and Fulda. This new list pinpointed the gateways leading eastward and southward at their termini.[3] The second factor helping Tedder was the weather. Throughout November and the first half of December heavy cloud blanketed western and central Europe. The result was that the deluge of explosives falling on transportation targets intensified.

On 16 December 1944 the Wehrmacht crashed into the American lines in the Ardennes in a major counteroffensive. The Allies responded by redirecting their massive air forces to halt the German drive. The CSTC immediately prepared a new target list to guide the heavy bombers. It attempted to apply lessons that it learned from the bombing conducted prior to Overlord. First priority was given to bridges on six lines within an arc stretching from Cologne, east to Giessen, south to Hanau, south to Mannheim, and west to Saarbrücken. The purpose was to drive the Wehrmacht's railheads back at least across the Rhine. The second objective of the attacks was to destroy supplies in marshalling yards in and outside the bridge ring.[4] Clearly the lessons learned by the CSTC differed from those drawn by Tedder.

The consequence of these changes in strategic focus was that between 1 November and 15 December 1944, air attacks on transportation were scattered and target selection was inconsistent and did not fully exploit the geographical weaknesses of the Reichsbahn or the German economy. During the Ardennes phase, lasting from 16 December 1944 to the end of January 1945, it was more focused but still did not fully capitalize upon the geographical vulnerability of the transportation system. However, because of the sheer volume of explosives that was unleashed after weeks of severe bombing and the fact that the Reichsbahn was compelled to try to operate in the area most heavily attacked, the hail of blows was decisive. The onslaught unwittingly took advantage of the interdependence of the Reichsbahn system and overwhelmed it. Between the beginning of November 1944 and the end of January 1945 a total of 102,796 tons of bombs was dropped on transportation targets, primarily marshalling yards. The heaviest month was December 1944 when 45,818 tons smothered yards, lines, and bridges. The biggest contributor during the entire period was the Eighth Air Force, which accounted for 55 percent of the total.[5]

When the first transportation plan was implemented early in November, the inland waterway system was still reeling from the sledgehammer blows landed during September and October. The new wave of attacks that followed virtually eliminated it as a useful economic resource. The bombers were assisted by the onset of ice toward the end of December.

The Dortmund-Ems Canal at Ladbergen was attacked three times by Bomber Command. On 4 November the waterway was drained again along thirty-eight kilometers of its length and 299 vessels were backed up. The second raid, on 21 November, inflicted heavy damage just as it was about to be reopened. Ten kilometers of the canal were drained again. Finally, the Lancasters shut the waterway again on 1 January 1945. Vessels had been hurried through at night since 23 December and the canal drained during the day to fox Allied air intelligence. But ACIU saw through the ploy and the raid stopped all movement.[6]

Repairs were pressed with vigor. After the 4 November raid, the Reich Tugging Service attempted to coordinate countermeasures itself. But the disruption of telephone service caused by the attack prevented it from doing so. On the tenth, Speer burst onto the scene and took matters into his own hands by raising the priority for repair of the waterways to the same level as that of the Reichsbahn. He ordered a special draft of young waterway-construction specialists withdrawn from the OT to be thrown into the effort. He also ordered Pleiger personally to see to it that miners were sent to the scene as rapidly as possible to accelerate the work. The response to the 21 November raid was faster. Work began as soon as the bombs stopped falling. Over 1,000 OT laborers were committed. Pleiger brought in 3,000 miners. But cold that delayed the setting of concrete and lack of heavy earth-moving equipment delayed the work.[7]

The Inland Waterway Section in Berlin, along with Speer, also weighed in. Speer ordered that barge operators sail at night to avoid strafers. The Inland Waterway Section attempted to transfer boatmen from the Ruhr to the MLK east of Minden where they could help increase traffic on the Elbe. But the Reichsbahn could not carry them there, and the order to march the distance was not well received. Boatmen were also withdrawn from the army and sent back to their ships. But the military obstructed this initiative. Arrangements were made to use rail lines to shuttle coal from barges caught on one side of the break to vessels waiting on the other. On 19 December the RVM established new priorities for freight carriage on the waterways. Coal was given first place followed by food, armaments, and iron ore.[8] But all of these improvisations were nullified by the continued attacks. Overall, the Ladbergen passage was closed from 4 November to 23 December 1944 and from 1 January to 8 February 1945.

Aside from these setbacks, bad luck continued to dog the bargemen. On 20 November the Eighth Air Force struck a synthetic fuel plant at Gelsenkirchen. Some stray bombs dropped a nearby bridge into the Rhine-Herne Canal, blocking it and thereby severing access to the DEK from the Ruhr. Forty barges were trapped west of the cut. Incredibly, on 23 November during a similar raid, another bridge at Nordstern fell into the RHK blocking it again.[9] It took over a week to clear the wreckage of the two structures.

The result of these five attacks on the DEK system was a severe reduction in coal shipments out of the Ruhr to its dependencies in northern and central Germany. During December, coal movement past the Münster lock was 68 percent lower than the monthly average for the fourth quarter of 1943. In January it was fully 98 percent lower than the first quarter 1944 monthly average.[10]

Other attacks on the Mittelland Canal reduced coal supplies in central Germany even further. On 6 November the Eighth Air Force attempted to renew the break at Minden but missed. Movement here resumed on 9 November. The Eighth tried again on 6 December and failed.[11] Traffic east of Minden flowed freely until it was strangled by attacks at Gravenhorst near the junction with the DEK and ice. Bomber Command succeeded where the Eighth failed and shut the MLK at Gravenhorst on 21 November. It returned on 1 January 1945 and cut the canal again. About thirty kilometers of the waterway was drained on each occasion.[12] As a result, it was impassable from 21 November to 11 December 1944 and again from 1 January 1945 until the end of the war. As at Ladbergen, the Reich Tugging Service attempted to slip barges through at night when the waterway was open. But the results were puny compared to the dire need for coal in central Germany.[13] The RVM tried to use the Elbe as a substitute, hoping to employ the Reichsbahn to bring coal to the river and then to move it eastward by barge.[14] But the effort collapsed in confusion.[15] It continued to use the long detour over the Coastal Canal and the Weser. But over half of the vessels departing on this route never arrived at Minden. Some were lost to strafers, some had their loads confiscated, others were caught on the DEK. Ice on the eastern part of the MLK halted even this pitiful expedient in mid-December.[16]

The Ruhr's other waterway outlet, the Rhine, was also blocked for most of the period. Clearance work at the Cologne-Mülheimer Bridge continued but made little progress. During early November the autumn rains raised the river level, permitting barges to pass over the wreckage with reduced loads. But the combination of ice and the lowering of the river almost completely stopped this by 26 December.[17] Then bad luck again played havoc on the Rhine. In late December the Autobahn Bridge and the South Bridge south of the ruins of the Cologne-Mülheimer Bridge sagged close to the water due to air raid damage.[18] The result was an excruciating situation for the bargemen. When the water was high enough to pass over the Mülheimer Bridge it was too high to allow movement under the South and Autobahn bridges. When it was low enough there, it was too low at Mülheim. Then on 16 January 1945 the road bridge at Neuwied tumbled into the Rhine after an attack by the Ninth Air Force. All traffic ceased.[19]

As on the canals, attempts were made to bypass the Rhine bridge barriers using the Reichsbahn.[20] But by the end of December the RWKS was again distributing coal locally.[21] From 14 October to 31 December only 550,000 tons of coal passed Cologne, or only about 14 percent of normal traffic.[22] The impact of this drastic reduction can be gauged by examining coal shipments from Duisburg. Movement southward was so irregular that the coal loading target for the port was abandoned during the first week of December.[23] Compared to the monthly average for the fourth quarter of 1943, coal traffic from Duisburg fell by 73 percent in December and early January.[24]

Just nine attacks on western Germany's waterways prevented the Ruhr from shipping coal to its dependencies by water by mid-January 1945. All of the region's canal and river connections with central, southern, and northern Germany were severed.[25] One of the vital props of the division of labor had been knocked away. Only the Reichsbahn remained to support the regional interdependence of the Reich industries. But it too had been battered by the Allied air forces.

Prior to the Ardennes offensive, the coal gateways were not attacked systematically. The Hohenbudberg route was struck twice at Cologne and was strafed heavily by the Ninth Air Force. Wedau itself was bombed twice, and marshalling yards along its flow were hit, such as Duisburg, Düsseldorf-Derendorf, and, near the terminus, Mannheim and Ludwigshafen. The Soest gateway was struck twice at its source and twice at the Altenbecken Viaduct. The Geisecke gateway was bombed only once, at Kassel. An area raid disrupted operations at Vorhalle and Hagen, Giessen was pummeled three times, Frankfurt/Main twice, and Siegen once. The Hamm route was struck five times including twice at Hanover and twice at the Bielefeld Viaduct. Only seven raids were flown against the remaining gateway leading north through Münster: two at the source, three against Osnabrück, and one each against Wanne-Eickel and Essen, both of which sent coal along the route. Overall 150 transportation attacks were conducted during the six weeks following the promulgation of the first transportation plan, but only 59 fell on the gateways.

The intensity and focus of the attacks increased during the period of the Ardennes offensive. The Hohenbudberg flow was pounded eighteen times, the Wedau route eight times, Hamm twice, once at the great yard itself and once at Bielefeld. The Soest line was attacked only once, the Geisecke gateway twice, Münster not at all and the southward-leading Vorhalle line seven times. A clear pattern emerged. Attacks were concentrated in the area from Cologne south to Karlsruhe. This was the result of Tedder's desire simultaneously to weaken economic traffic and to support the armies. Given the predilections of the members of the CSTC, a slight but real preference was given to the second of Tedder's aims. Of equal importance was the fact that the air forces as often as not ignored the CSTC priority lists. From the beginning of November to the end of January only 53 percent of the total bomb tonnage dropped on transportation targets was directed against those recommended by the CSTC. Moreover, 96 percent was dropped using radar.[26]

Nevertheless, the impact on the Reichsbahn was shattering. The DR doggedly attempted to run trains south from the Ruhr to the Frankfurt/Main and Mannheim areas. It could not do otherwise. At all costs these regions had to be supplied with coal and components and their products distributed. It was also compelled to support the panzer divisions in the Eifel. For example, in December, RBD Cologne directly behind the area of the counterthrust devoted a quarter of its freight car space to moving Wehrmacht supplies. During the summer it had used only 12 percent for this purpose. The Vorhalle gateway was given over completely to Wehrmacht traffic: 1,400 trains were used to support the preparations for the drive alone.[27] The hinterland of the Bulge was like a siphon draining away the lifeblood of the Reichsbahn. But there was nothing that it could do to stanch the flow. The result of these two series of attacks was the debilitation of the entire system. There can be no doubt that a concerted, consistent assault on the gateways combined with attacks on RBD Halle and Oppeln would have precipitated the collapse of the Reichsbahn very quickly and brought the entire German economy tumbling down after it. But the campaign that was waged was sufficient to achieve almost the same result, albeit more slowly.

During the period from November 1944 to January 1945 the railway situation in the western pivot of the German economy, the Ruhr and RBD Essen, was chaotic. The disaster that befell the region spread like a black cancer to the areas dependent on it. Before briefly looking at events in those regions, it will be necessary to attempt to sort out the chaos that swept the Reich's industrial heart. The air attacks on RBD Essen struck two sensitive nerves: bridges and viaducts, and marshalling yards. The result was a catastrophic fall in coal car and general freight car placings, the disruption of telecommunications, and the slamming shut of the Ruhr gateways to the outside.

The loss of bridges added a new headache for the repair crews working under RBD Essen chief Lammertz. Throughout November and December an average of sixteen bridges were out of service in the region every day.[28] Traffic was never halted as a result, but the necessarily circuitous bypass routes caused delays that the DR and industry could ill afford.

More harmful were the attacks on two of the magnificent viaducts that supported the three coal gateways leading east. Sixty kilometers east of the great Hamm marshalling yard, on the high-density four-track line leading to Hanover and Berlin, was the 350-meter-long double viaduct at Bielefeld. In the event of an interruption there, the Reichsbahn planned to reroute traffic northwest at Lohne to Osnabrück and Rheine or south to Kassel. The Eighth Air Force severed this vital link for nine days with an attack on 2 November. On 29 November it slashed the artery again for eleven days. Attacks on 26 November 1944 and 17 January 1945 failed. RBD Hanover took energetic measures to restore service immediately after the first raid. The OT was brought in and the local Zublin construction firm was also contracted to accomplish some of the work. No permanent repairs were attempted—only temporary bridging of cuts. After the second successful raid, many of the piers settled, causing the track bed to buckle. Nevertheless, only the breaks were closed and traffic resumed. After the 29 November attack, a single track bypass line was begun. But difficulty in bringing up repair materials, disputes between Zublin and the OT, inadequate accommodations for the laborers, which led many to desert, and strafing by Allied fighters delayed the repair work and prevented completion of the bypass.[29]

The Altenbecken Viaduct near Paderborn was located on the double-tracked Soest-Halle gateway and bore a weight of freight traffic second only to that at Bielefeld. The sandstone and brick structure was 480 meters long and 33 meters high. The Reichsbahn rerouting plan provided for detours north to Hanover and the Hamm gateway at Lohne north of Bielefeld and south to Kassel and Giessen on the Vorhalle gateway. The Eighth Air Force landed a shattering blow to this artery on 26 November, completely halting traffic. The hammer fell again on 29 November. No train passed at Altenbecken until 11 February 1945. Six hundred foreigners were committed to the repair effort, and miners arrived from Hamm to assist. Day and night shifts were laid on. Here too a bypass was begun. But cold weather, confusion, and strafing greatly hindered the work, and it was never completed.[30]

Air attacks also rocked marshalling yards serving the coal gateways. By 7 November, Hamm, Bochum, Osnabrück, and Münster were shut. Three marshalling yards in Cologne were closed, as were two in Essen. Forty-six others operated at reduced levels.[31] Of twenty-nine major freight-loading yards in GBL-West, fourteen were shut, eight operated at reduced levels, and only seven functioned normally.[32] In early November all marshalling work at Hamm was abandoned.[33] More typical was the situation at Düsseldorf-Derendorf on the Wedau gateway. Repeated attacks gradually reduced the yard's marshalling capacity and finally rendered it almost useless. A raid on 2 November stopped all marshalling by damaging the sorting groups and switches. OT, Wehrmacht, and foreign contingents were thrown into the repair effort. On 29 November the hump and again the sorting groups were damaged. But the repair crews tenaciously fought back. Marshalling had been partially restored when, on 7 January 1945, the sorting group was shut down by twenty-five hits. Numerous other tracks were cut and the telephone system failed. A street bridge passing over the yard collapsed, halting all through traffic. An additional 1,300 laborers drawn from the Wehrmacht, private industry, and contractors were committed in a desperate effort to restore service. Operations resumed at a reduced level within a week. But the bombers were not finished. The Eighth Air Force blasted the yard again on 23 January. Marshalling continued but the capacity of the yard had been badly eroded.[34] During December, freight car placings were 80 percent below the fourth quarter 1943 monthly average. Contrary to Tedder's expectations, no locomotive shortage developed at Derendorf despite damage to the sheds. Indeed the yard had more locomotives available in December, fifty-seven, than at any time previously. In January the number of serviceable locomotives increased to sixty but car placings fell to a mere 10 percent of normal.[35]

The pattern that emerged at Hamm and Düsseldorf-Derendorf was repeated at the other marshalling yards serving the Ruhr. Through passages were rarely stopped. But sorting freight cars and forming trains became extremely difficult. Coordination among yards was ruined, and unless the damage could be made good, a drastic additional reduction in coal and general freight movement would result. At Hamm and Derendorf the repair crews lost this battle. Similar defeats were suffered at numerous yards throughout the Ruhr despite energetic, even desperate efforts by the Reichsbahn and the Speer ministry.

On 9 November, Speer committed the Organization Todt Regiment Speer and 50,000 forced laborers from Holland to the area.[36] Two days later he informed Hitler that he had thrown into the inferno 30,000 additional laborers from the armaments industry, and 4,500 skilled workers. A tenth of the Ruhr's coal miners were held ready to intervene, and the Gauleiters were empowered to commandeer industrial labor to help the Reichsbahn.[37] By 13 November, 95,000 people had been dragooned into the battle to reopen marshalling yards and bridges.[38] On 29 November, Hitler ordered that 150,000 laborers from elsewhere in the Reich be sent to the embattled Ruhr to lend their weight to the repair effort.[39] The Ruhr Staff collected 4,000 tractors to haul earth at work sites and to move freight around blockages.[40] On 30 November, 10,400 men were at work on the Hamm gateway line alone.[41] The Wehrmacht stepped in on the following day with 40,000 specialists in bridge, electrical, and telephone work.[42] In a move fraught with dangers in the internal political conflict, Ganzenmüller obtained Bormann's approval to shift civilian workers from building fortifications to repairing railways on 27 December.[43] But this colossal effort was nullified by disputes among the numerous agencies involved and the omnipresent Allied bombers. Repair materials and tools were repeatedly lost or delayed due to bureaucratic confusion or the disruption of marshalling by bombing.[44]

In addition to repairing damage, the Reichsbahn resorted to every conceivable improvisation to maintain the flow of freight. It built bypass lines around heavily bombed marshalling yards and transferred some traffic to secondary lines, although this made load and speed restrictions necessary. Even field railways and streetcars were used to bring freight to the edges of the area, where it could be reloaded on normal gauge cars.[45]

None of these desperate expedients sufficed to maintain the volume of freight space. Therefore the DR and the Speer ministry were compelled to take new steps to ensure that what car space remained was used most wisely and to reduce the demand for it. On 25 November the RVM ordered RBD Essen drastically to reduce car placings for general freight so as to release space for coal. Cuts would be made until a minimum of 11,000 units were placed for coal daily.[46] This was only half of the Ruhr's usual hard coal car target. The RWKS ordered all of its subsidiaries to strain every nerve to ensure that the Reichsbahn locomotives obtained sufficient coal.[47] On 29 November, Lammertz cut car placings for general freight by an additional 2,000 cars per day to free space. He warned Berlin that further cuts would cause a reduction in industrial activity by disrupting component deliveries.[48] Berlin attempted to help by slashing car placings for freight other than coal in Upper Silesia so that the eastern pivot could relieve the Ruhr of more of its burden.[49] RBD Oppeln was ordered to increase coal car placings to compensate for RBD Essen's setbacks.[50] Berlin also imposed severe embargoes on freight shipments to RBD Essen that excluded all but Wehrmacht goods and the most important semifinished products.[51] On 20 December each of the three GBLs was given a quota of cars that they could send to RBD Essen each day, bearing freight not on the priority list. In all, 810 cars were allowed under this dispensation in addition to the 143 trains scheduled to carry priority freight.[52] The Reichsbahn also arranged the exchange of trains on an individual basis between stations in RBD Essen and its neighbors.[53] It was hoped that this would reduce congestion in the region's marshalling yards.

The measures seemed to have a positive effect. On 1 January 1945, RBD Essen's daily coal target was raised to 15,000 units. First priority for coal was removed from the Reichsbahn and given to the armaments industry. But the respite was short lived. In part it had been due to the shift in focus of the Allied air attacks to the area behind the Bulge. In late January the bombers returned. In the east the Red Army burst into Upper Silesia. Immediately, locomotive coal was restored to first priority.[54]

Speer restricted the demand for coal by establishing consumption priorities. On 11 November, through Central Planning, he granted the Reichsbahn itself first priority, followed by shipping and gas plants. A month later the priorities were refined. Locomotives and ships shared first priority and were to get full supplies. Next came waterworks at full supplies and gasworks at 70 percent. In third place, receiving three-quarters of their usual consumption, were the electric utilities. Next, homes received half of their usual supplies. Finally, armaments plants that burned coal would be given enough only to complete weapons. On 25 January 1945 homes were denied all hard coal supplies in order to permit shipments to powder, liquid fuel, and munitions plants.[55]

The disruption of transportation in the Rhine-Ruhr area also forced the RMfRuK to impose revised restrictions on the supply of brown coal. In this case, dependencies of the RWKS that could no longer be supplied with hard coal were to be provided with an equivalent amount of brown coal first. Then utilities would receive 70 percent of their needs, followed by food processing plants, which would also obtain 70 percent of their requirements. Homes came next but were permitted only a quarter of their needs. Then came selected armaments plants with full supplies. All other industries would receive nothing.[56]

The RVM also attempted to simplify the control of traffic in the Ruhr. The various directorates and the RWKS had long chafed under the administration of Sarter and GBL-West. Both to satisfy the coal industry and to unify control of all transport assets in the region, Lammertz, chief of RBD Essen, was named by Ganzenmüller as General Plenipotentiary for the Regulation of Traffic Affairs for Armaments and War Production in the Rhenish-Westphalian Industrial Area. He was given full authority over all forms of transport at all levels within his directorate and also in RBDs Münster, Wuppertal, and Cologne.[57] On 10 November, the day before Lammertz assumed his new post, Dorpmüller visited the Ruhr to smooth relations with heavy industry. At RBD Essen headquarters he met with Schmidt of the RWKS and Sohl of VSt. Schmidt in particular voiced his concern that control of the distribution of coal was slipping from his group and was being assumed by the Reichsbahn and Speer. Dorpmüller assured him that nothing of the kind was contemplated. The aged railway chief then asked the industrial leaders for assistance in maintaining the flow of freight. He explained how plant and mine labor could be better utilized in repairing the Reichsbahn's bomb-battered facilities because, if the marshalling yards remained closed, their products could not be delivered anyway. Sohl and Schmidt heartily agreed to do everything in their power to help the beleaguered Reichsbahn, including providing labor. They decided to christen their program "Spades Against Bombs."[58]

None of this sufficed. On 19 January 1945, Dilli was forced to slash hundreds of trains from the schedule. He imposed a total embargo on all freight everywhere in the Reich. Only coal, the most necessary Wehrmacht shipments, and a few courier trains were retained. Even coal shipments were confined to areas adjacent to the mines.[59] Despite the massive infusion of labor and a drastic reduction both in traffic and demand, the Reichsbahn could no longer support the geographical division of labor. What had happened?

The first clue is the availability of the coal gateways. In the twenty-one days between 25 November and 15 December 1944, that is, before the Ardennes offensive, the Geisecke, Soest, and Vorhalle passages were closed to through traffic a third of the time. Hohenbudberg's route was blocked for only six days and Münster for only three. Passages at Hamm were impossible for only one day but here, as elsewhere, the capacity of the line was only about a third of normal. From the beginning of the Ardennes offensive on 16 December 1944 to the end of January 1945, Hohenbudberg was shut down for just four days. The Münster route was always open, and the Hamm gateway was passable most of the time to through traffic but nonetheless operated at greatly reduced capacity. Soest itself was closed just once but its route could be run only as far as Altenbecken. Geisecke was also closed only once. Vorhalle shut twice but its line was passable only as far as Siegen. Wedau was out of action for only five days; however, when it operated it confined itself almost entirely to slipping coal-laden unit trains to the Dynamit explosives plant at Troisdorf southeast of Cologne. Although the gateways were open on most days, hardly any coal was shipped to southern Germany.[60] The lines leading from RBD Essen were open, yet traffic plummeted. A look at the plight of the RWKS provides additional evidence as to why.

During December 1944 the overall amount of coal shipped by the Rhenish-Westphalian Coal Syndicate dropped 52 percent compared to September. Waterway dispatches fell by 68 percent and railway shipments by 47 percent.[61] The decline in waterborne dispatches can be easily explained by pointing to the cuts on the DEK and MLK and the block at Cologne. But the sharp drop in railway movement, especially since the gateways were frequently open, cannot be clarified so simply. In early November, instead of the usual 380 pairs of freight trains passing in and out of the Ruhr daily, only 140 moved.[62] At the end of December only 20 or 30 moved each day. The situation improved a bit by late January. Then about 90 train pairs could operate.[63] The volume of freight traffic, despite the Reichsbahn's corrective measures, was far less than half of normal for the entire three months from November 1944 through January 1945 despite the availability of lines. One possible cause for this can be seen by considering RBD Essen's supply of locomotives.

At first glance it might seem that RBD Essen had an abundance of motive power. Its supply of locomotives rose from 1,230 at the beginning of November to 1,308 at the end of December. The number in service increased also from 755 to 807.[64] But the number stored cold for lack of fuel jumped to 33 at the end of January 1945 compared to just one at the same time in 1944.[65] Locomotives were plentiful but coal to fire them was not. Stocks of locomotive coal in GBL-West were down to only five days as early as the end of November. But this did not harm RBD Essen as much as it did those directorates that were dependent upon the Ruhr for coal. During November, instead of the 20 service coal trains per day needed to supply these regions, an average of just 7 left RBD Essen.[66] Despite every effort the situation did not improve.[67] The Reichsbahn was driven to confiscating coal to keep its locomotives running.[68] This, combined with the disruption of marshalling in GBL-South, prevented them from sending empty cars back to the Ruhr to be used to ship coal. Here was a major component of the problem.

Lammertz recognized the difficulty. His lines were open but he could not use them. On 14 November he begged the ZVL for empty cars.[69] Even before Lammertz's appeal, Berlin attempted to relieve his plight. On 11 November, Dilli ordered that unit trains of empty open cars be formed in central Germany and Upper Silesia and rushed to the Ruhr. All locomotive reserves were to be thrown into the effort.[70] The surge occurred on 15 November.[71] On 29 November, Berlin ordered that the highest priority be given to sending open cars to the Ruhr.[72] Still RBD Essen lacked empty cars. The situation became so desperate that Lammertz ordered that freight simply be dumped from backed-up cars to free them to carry coal. Any semblance of orderly deliveries or notification of addressees was abandoned.[73] By any means the backlog simply had to be reduced. As of 29 December 1944, 450 trains were backlogged in GBL-West.[74] Many were coal trains. All tied up valuable cars and locomotives and clogged marshalling yards and even open lines. The critical difficulty, the other major component of the problem, was bringing open cars to RBD Essen from the areas of RBDs Frankfurt/Main, Mainz, Karlsruhe, and Stuttgart. These embattled regions in GBL-West and GBL-South were a sump drawing cars away from the Ruhr just as France had during the spring and summer of 1944. Bringing the cars to RBD Essen was just the beginning. Once there, they would have to be formed into trains. Using unit trains would ease matters only slightly because the region's marshalling yards had not recovered from the air attacks of September and October. Renewed attacks in January had depressed their capacity even further, as we have seen.

The result of the massive backlog in the south caused by the bombing of marshalling yards there and the disruption of marshalling at the Ruhr coal gateways was a disastrous fall in car placings. Throughout the period of the first transportation plan and the Ardennes offensive, overall freight car placings in RBD Essen were 60 percent below the level of the same period in the preceding year. Hard coal car placings were never more than half of normal. Brown coal car placings in RBD Cologne were almost 90 percent below normal by the end of January 1945.[75] In RBD Essen, even car placings for armaments were off by 90 percent in December.[76]

A major, irreparable disaster had been suffered by RBD Essen and the adjoining directorates. Damage to marshalling yards in the region and in the areas that it served was inflicted on such a massive and widespread scale and the disruption of telecommunications was so severe that the real capability to place cars in trains dropped precipitately and, moreover, the DR's ability to coordinate the activities of its numerous parts was ruined.[77] The Reichsbahn could no longer operate as a unit. Losses in one area could not be made good in others.[78] There was too much damage to too many important marshalling yards and too many telephone and telegraph lines were out. Added to these potentially fatal wounds were the bridge and viaduct cuts. The loss of the Bielefeld and Altenbecken viaducts simultaneously not only slashed two of the Ruhr's main railway arteries to the east, but also severely reduced the Reichsbahn's capacity to shift traffic to circumvent obstacles on either route. Nominally, the Ruhr's gateways remained open, but their ability to generate traffic and move it to the region's distant dependencies was fatally reduced by early January 1945.

The decline in rail service and the deterioration of the physical means of production increased the psychological friction under which the Reichsbahn and the Ruhr industrial leaders labored. The result was the disintegration of both the DR's and industry's administrative apparatus. Bitter disputes erupted between RBD Wuppertal and RBD Frankfurt/Main concerning the operation of the Wedau gateway.[79] Many companies, including the RWKS, expanded their private courier services to exchange information with their subsidiaries and to maintain at least tenuous contact with Berlin. None of them was coordinated with similar government activities and none could carry sufficient information quickly enough. As a result, not only were the physical links to the central authority loosened, but so were the psychological ones.[80] The RWKS in particular took energetic steps to adapt to the new circumstances. On 18 November, with the utmost reluctance, it abandoned all efforts to allocate car space to mines centrally and established three dispersed command centers on the edges of the Ruhr.[81] At the end of December it made arrangements independently from the government with the Upper Silesian Hard Coal Syndicate to direct coal relief trains from the east to the RWKS regional branches. The syndicate trading companies themselves were empowered to negotiate the scheduling of coal trains directly with the Upper Silesian syndicate.[82] This devolution of authority contributed to a loss of control. Reports increased in January 1945 that RWKS coal shipments were being pirated. In one case, a train destined for the Opel plant in Rüsselsheim was commandeered by the local Gauleiter.[83]

Friction also increased between the Reichsbahn and the steel industry. At a meeting in Essen held on 17 November, Rohland imperiously demanded more car space for his branch of industry. Ganzenmüller sharply rejected this and proceeded to lecture the steel leader on how his industry could use unit trains more effectively and conserve and store coal.[84]

The net result of the decline in both rail and waterway traffic and the disintegration of management cooperation was an industrial disaster in the Ruhr and a major economic calamity for the Reich as a whole. In the Ruhr itself, hard coal production in November and December 1944 was only half of the monthly average for the fourth quarter of the preceding year. In January 1945 output improved only marginally. Hard coal cut in Upper Silesia declined by about a fifth in November and December. Then it plummetted to less than half of normal in January due to the arrival of the Red Army. The result was an overall decline in Reich hard coal production of 40 percent in November and December 1944 and a massive 48 percent in January 1945. Overall production was 29.4 million tons lower than during the same three months of the preceding year. Only about a tenth of the decline can be attributed to the loss of territory such as Aachen and the Saar. Upper Silesia accounted for 15.6 percent of the total loss in coal production, virtually all sustained in January. Fully 53.8 percent of the hard coal production loss was suffered in the Ruhr. This came about solely through the disruption of transportation.[85]

Looked at from the perspective of actual deliveries, the enormity of the disaster comes into focus more clearly. Between August 1944 and January 1945, the Reichsbahn and the inland waterways delivered 36.5 million tons of hard coal less than during the same period in 1943.[86] The Reichsbahn alone accounted for 89 percent of the deficit. The equivalent of six weeks of production had been lost. Since factories rarely held more than four to six weeks' reserves, transportation bombing had eliminated the national stock of hard coal. Even if the mines had produced more coal it could not have been delivered. Here again an examination of the situation in the two main hard coal producing regions provides telling confirmation of the effectiveness of transportation bombing. In the Ruhr stocks of coal at the pit heads skyrocketed to 157.4 percent above normal in December 1944. Reich hard coal stocks, undelivered, still at the mines, were 110.7 percent above normal. Of the overall undelivered hard coal stock, 42 percent clogged the Ruhr mine yards.[87] Coal production was reduced because coal could not be delivered. The problem was most severe in the Ruhr where transportation bombing had been heaviest and most effective. Upper Silesia was unable to compensate because of the spread of confusion to it from the west and because of the advance of the Red Army.

The same phenomenon affected coke supplies. In this case, though, the implications were even more severe because of the Ruhr's heavy domination of the German coke market. Ruhr coke output by December 1944 was 55 percent of the fourth-quarter 1943 monthly average and in January 1945, 54 percent of the first-quarter 1944 monthly average. Reich coke production in the same months was 53 and 51 percent lower than usual.[88] Of the total loss of coke production to the Reich, 73 percent was sustained in the Ruhr, the equivalent of four and a half weeks of national output. Part of the cause was the damage to cokeries due to bombing.[89] But the overwhelming factor was the Reichsbahn's inability to ship their meager production. In December 1944, coke stocks in the Ruhr were 446.9 percent above normal. Indeed, at 2,649,000 tons they equalled over a month's normal production.[90] The hemorrhage in the Ruhr comprised 82 percent of the national total of unshipped coke. Again, transportation bombing, the disruption of marshalling in RBD Essen and associated directorates, and the cutting of the Ruhr's major waterways were decisive in preventing the Ruhr from shipping fuel to its dependencies. The losses sustained there far outweighed the the loss of Aachen, the Saar, and Upper Silesia. In the latter case, the damage was suffered too late to influence industrial production during the period from November 1944 to January 1945.

The only alternative energy source, brown coal, suffered a lesser though still severe decline. Here the greatest losses were sustained in the Rhenish area near Cologne, and the cause was the disruption of transport on the Rhine and the Reichsbahn. Brown coal production in the area was only a quarter of normal throughout the period. Reich output fell by about a quarter,[91] and 83 percent of the decline was sustained in the Rhenish region.

In the face of such crushing losses there was little that the government could do. Beyond the measures that it took to conserve energy, outlined above, it resorted to other anemic expedients. Central Planning granted factory workers an extended vacation from the day before Christmas to New Year's Day so that their factories could be closed to save coal. Pleiger drove the miners to work Sundays and holidays, not to cut coal, but to load it into freight cars.[92]

The enforced restructuring of the coal market was continued. Syndicates throughout Germany were again called upon to assist the RWKS by supplying its outlying customers. The leader was the Upper Silesian Hard Coal Syndicate. In November it sent 475,289 tons of coal to RWKS customers from Kiel to Mannheim.[93] In December it dispatched 520,000 tons. But this was only three-quarters of what it had been scheduled to ship.[94] In January, arrivals from Upper Silesia sank to only a third of target.[95] The failure of the Upper Silesian Hard Coal Syndicate's help to meet expectations triggered bitter recriminations against it from the RWKS. The Ruhr coal barons contended that the eastern syndicate was exploiting the situation to lure away its customers by providing coal on a preferential basis to consumers favorable to it.[96] Similar disputes arose between the RWKS and other syndicates.[97] Market considerations continued to be overriding even during a national crisis. These tensions reduced the efficiency of the German economy in ways that were real though unquantifiable.

To a very great extent, the RWKS's fears were unjustified. The Upper Silesian syndicate shipped what it could. But the Allied bombers intervened to veto its plans. The Reichsbahn was unable to move all of the trains that the eastern syndicate loaded because of snarls in marshalling yards in the west. For the same reason, the transfer of unuseable fuel from bomb-damaged facilities such as the Leuna synthetic fuel plant proved impossible. In this case, problems in RBD Halle nullified the RMfRuK's efforts.[98]

The implications of the breakdown in marshalling, the severing of the Ruhr's waterways, and the disintegration of telecommunications and interregional coordination were clear to Rüdiger Schmidt from his post in the Essen. Throughout November and December he reported to the RWKS board of directors that the source of the syndicate's problems was the decline in car placings and barge movements due to air raids. The collapse of telephone and telegraph service caused by the raids hindered coordination among the syndicate's mines and trading companies, with its customers and the Reichsbahn.[99] By the second week of November he already feared a collapse of industrial activity and considered the crisis the worst ever faced by the German mining industry. No scheduled distribution was possible and stocks could not be mobilized. In late November and early December he informed the board that stocks had been exhausted. Even the most important consumers could not be satisfied.[100] As he put it on 14 November, "It is in no way a production, rather only and exclusively a transportation problem."[101] For all of this he remained preoccupied with preserving the RWKS's dominant position in the hard coal industry. He understood that the key was to retain control of distribution, forcing consumers to rely entirely upon the syndicate. He had already subdued Pleiger. Now he perceived threats from the Reichsbahn and most importantly Speer and the Gauleiters.[102] The DR was the least dangerous adversary because it sought only sufficient coal to feed its locomotives. Beyond that, except in emergency situations when it was required to clear a yard, it was uninterested in who received the coal that it carried. More threatening in Schmidt's eyes were the RMfRuK and the Party. Speer and his organization were dynamic and espoused the concept of centralized control. A victory for them would, Schmidt feared, result in state capitalism, which was anathema to him and all of big business. The Party appeared wild and uncontrollable. It seemed to Schmidt and his colleagues that the triumph of the Party would lead to the end of capitalism itself. For these reasons, even as the bombs rained down, Schmidt devoted a tremendous amount of time and effort to defending the syndicate's prerogatives. All the while, he contributed to the disintegration of the unified management apparatus that Speer was still struggling to preserve.

In one very critical respect, Schmidt's forebodings were completely justified. The disruption of transportation and the resulting coal famine fatally weakened Ruhr industry. Coal and coke supplies to the region's gasworks fell sharply. In addition air attacks destroyed major plants at Duisburg, Hamborn, and Gelsenkirchen. The result of this combination of factors was the decline in gas output in the region by three-quarters by the end of January.[103] The electricity situation was somewhat better. Cuts in production of 30 percent were begun in early December to conserve coal, and demand had fallen by half due to bomb damage to factories.[104] Nevertheless, by the end of December three major generating plants, Reisholz, Werdohl, and Gevelsburg, had closed due to lack of coal.[105] Speer attempted to use the national grid to feed electricity into the Ruhr, but coal shortages at the generating plants in central Germany prevented it.[106]

The Ruhr's second major industry, iron and steel, was also badly hurt by the transportation offensive. In December, ore arrivals at the smelters were 80 percent lower than a year before. Even domestic ores were affected: arrivals were down 85 percent.[107] Ore stocks at the smelters fell by 44 percent in November.[108] As in the case of hard coal and coke production, the losses suffered in the Rhenish-Westphalian iron and steel industry marked the decisive break in Reich production of these commodities. By January 1945, Ruhr raw iron production was 64 percent lower than the monthly average for the same quarter during the previous year. Reich output was 73 percent lower. The Ruhr accounted for 42 percent of the loss, central Germany for 14 percent, and Upper Silesia for only 3 percent. The balance is accounted for by the loss of Saar production.[109] The same phenomenon appeared in steel making: by January 1945, as measured against the monthly average for the first quarter of 1944, Reich production had fallen by two-thirds. Ruhr output in January was 66 percent in arrears and accounted for 47 percent of the loss in steel production for the period November 1944 to January 1945.[110] Scrap supplies followed the same path.[111]

Yet with iron and steel, for reasons highlighted earlier, the causes of the decline in production were more complex than for coal. Many of the Ruhr steel plants had been damaged by bombing. In addition, the mill owners had intentionally restricted production to conserve raw materials for the postwar period. For these reasons a closer look at United Steel (see Table 7.1) may again prove rewarding. About a tenth of VSt's loss of iron and steel production can be attributed to direct damage to its Bochumer Verein subsidiary. Coke production fell due to the disruption by bombing of both the Reichsbahn and internal plant transportion, as shown by the decline in output and the massive increase in stocks at the coke ovens. The shrinkage of coal stocks at the mills can be attributed to the same factor. Since the company reduced iron and steel output in accordance with the availability of the least abundant resource, one may surmise that about half the production decline is attributable to coal, coke, and ore shortages due to transportation attacks. The remaining loss, about a third, was most likely caused by the drop in foreign ore supplies and direct damage to plants other than the Bochumer Verein, although repair of these facilities was also hampered by the transportation crisis.

These severe losses compelled the Planungsamt ruthlessly to slash steel allocations for the first half of 1945. Steel quotas for tank, aircraft, ammunition, and weapons programs were reduced by between 40 and 60 percent. Consumption of coal to produce this steel was to be half of the prior year's consumption for the larger programs.[112] This by itself is a clear indication that elasticity of supply had been exhausted at the level of capital goods production. But losses extended far beyond this sector.

In the Ruhr the failure of energy and component supplies caused a major loss of finished armaments production. Most programs failed to meet their targets. Completed items frequently sat in warehouses because the Reichsbahn could not take them away to the users.[113] In the Düsseldorf area, 20,000 freight cars were backed up at factory sidings, loaded with completed armaments.[114] Overall, 800,000 tons of iron and steel products rusted away in the Ruhr awaiting transport in mid-January 1945.[115] The Gau Economics Office in Düsseldorf concluded as early as 18 November 1944 that: "Under current transportation conditions it would be sensible to consider the ability to ship freight as the fundamental scale for the control of energy and labor utilization."[116] GBL-East considered the Ruhr isolated by early December.[117] On 17 January 1945, Schmidt moaned that all of the gateways and waterways leading from the Ruhr had been slammed shut by the bombers.[118] The Speer ministry, in a memorandum completed on the next day, concluded that the Ruhr existed as a traffic island isolated from its dependencies.[119] By late December 1944 or early January 1945 the Allied bombers had torn away the heart of the Reich division of labor. The result was a decisive drop in the nation's coal and steel production. The Ruhr itself suffered a major decline in armaments output. Losses among its dependencies and in Upper Silesia were no less catastrophic.

At Mannheim, coal arrivals on the Rhine virtually halted in November and were 77 percent below normal in January.[120] The

Table 7.1

United Steel's Situation, Fourth Quarter 1943–
Fourth Quarter 1944

Raw iron production	− 76.51%
Raw steel production	− 75.51%
Foreign ore stocks	− 55.18%
Coke production	− 55.17%
Plant's coal stocks	− 51.87%
GBAG coal production	− 36.76%
Plant's coke stocks	− 34.35%
Domestic ore stocks	− 27.22%
GBAG coal stocks	+ 831.32%
GBAG coke stocks	+ 1,308.34%

Sources: VSt, "Jahresbericht," Vertraulich, pp. 2–4; "Eildienst," December 1944,
p. 4, NA RG 243, 3(a)37.

Reichsbahn could not compensate. GBL-South had been thoroughly disorganized by bombing in its western areas. Car placings at the major marshalling yards at Stuttgart-Kornwestheim, Mannheim, and Karlsruhe sank drastically. The other GBLs frequently refused trains from GBL-South, contributing to congestion in its yards.[121] By mid-November a car surplus of enormous proportions had developed. By the first week of January 1945 all available space for storing cars was exhausted.[122] Air attacks had shut down Stuttgart-Kornwestheim and Mannheim a week before.[123] Telephone communications collapsed. GBL headquarters lost contact with the ports and its major marshalling yards along the Rhine and the locomotive sheds.[124] Headquarters itself was bombed out and forced to transfer from Munich to Freising. Scheduled, controlled movement was impossible.[125] The coal famine struck with devastating force. In early November, locomotive coal stocks stood at only nine and a half days. By mid-December they had disappeared.[126] Here again, the Reichsbahn began to confiscate coal to feed the fire boxes, this time from electrical plants.[127] With the virtual collapse of marshalling, the difficulty in running trains to other areas, and the chaotic telecommunications situation, the backlog in the region soared to 556 trains, aside from individual cars waiting to be marshalled.[128] In mid-December the Reichsbahn simply redirected trains backlogged in RBDs Stuttgart and Karlsruhe to recipients that it determined in the east.[129] Yet by mid-January 1945, the backlog in GBL-South had mounted to 606 trains.[130]

Under these circumstances orderly economic activity in the central Rhenish industrial region was impossible. A brutal coal famine depressed the economic life of the area. Coal supplies to industry were off by two-thirds. Electricity demand had fallen by three-quarters. Yet coal stocks at the generating plants were exhausted.[131] Of twenty-four firms on the left bank of the Rhine monitored by the Armaments Command Ludwigshafen, by January 1945 eight were badly short of coal and eight others were completely closed down due to lack of fuel.[132] In the same area the disruption of passenger train service, caused in part by the cancellation of runs to conserve locomotive coal, prevented workers from coming to the factories and caused some plants to shut down. Arrivals of components were rare and erratic. Some 7,991 tons of completed armaments clogged the warehouses and storage yards of the city's factories.[133] At the Giulini aluminum plant 4,700 tons of semifinished aluminum could not be shipped.[134] Across the Rhine in Mannheim, the Brown, Boveri et Cie. electrical equipment manufacturing company shipped 80 percent fewer transformers in January 1945 than it did monthly in the first quarter of 1944, despite still being able to produce them.[135] The transportation-induced paralysis spread farther afield. Both Opel in Rüsselsheim and BMW in Munich closed due to lack of coal.[136]

The situation was the same in central Germany. A major attempt was made to ship coal to the Reichswerke Hermann Göring by barge, using the Elbe and the long bypass around the Ladbergen and Gravenhorst obstacles.[137] But the effort on the Elbe was stultified both by confusion and by a lack of coal to propel the barges.[138] During December, coal shipments on the river declined.[139] Only a trickle slipped past Minden.[140] Unlike the Ruhr industries, the RWHG was completely under the control of the regime and therefore could not cut production to conserve coal. Pleiger drove his plant in an attempt to compensate for the setbacks suffered in the west. By early November, coal stocks had fallen by two-thirds to twelve days.[141] On 2 December, Pleiger deliberately subverted the government coal-rationing program and ordered the confiscation of eight barges bound for Berlin to feed his plant. He also ordered the Saxon Hard Coal Syndicate to step up its shipments to the RWHG.[142] But coal deliveries to Salzgitter continued to sink. In

November 1944 they were 42 percent below normal. Consumption was virtually unchanged. Deliveries remained dismal in December and January—41 percent lower than usual. In December coal stocks were 60 percent below the monthly average for the fourth quarter of 1943. That proved decisive, for in January consumption was finally slashed by 47 percent.[143] Pig iron production tumbled in the same month by 67 percent.[144] Semifinished steel output dropped by half.[145] Gas production fell 61 percent with dire consequences not only for the RWHG itself, but also for industries in the region dependent on it.[146] Electricity production fell sooner. In November it dropped to about half of usual and remained there or somewhat above through January. But sales to users outside the plant were cut by as much as 60 percent.[147] The combination of failing coal supplies, which forced reductions at the RWHG and other generating plants in central Germany, and cold weather, which restricted hydroelectric production, forced the Planning Office to order armaments firms to close one day each week to conserve electricity.[148]

An example of how transportation bombing reduced armaments final production in central Germany is provided by the Krupp-Gruson plant at Magdeburg. The failure of gas supplies from the RWHG, the collapse of coal deliveries to Gruson itself, and the disruption of components deliveries from Vomag and Nibelungen caused MK IV tank output to decline by 43 percent in January 1945 compared to the first quarter 1944 monthly average.[149]

Mediating between central Germany and its sources of energy and markets to the west and east was RBD Halle. This pivotal directorate struggled to maintain the flow of traffic. But the chaos in the west infected it. The inability to move trains to the bomb-ravaged areas, the disruption of communications, and confusion caused by air raids at the nearby synthetic fuel plants caused a decline in marshalling performance. During the period of the first transportation plan, RBD Halle actually increased car placings by 1.5 percent. But after 16 December they fell steadily. During the Ardennes offensive, which lasted until the end of January 1945, car placings in RBD Halle were 19.6 percent below the level of performance achieved during the same period of the preceding year.[150] The region, as we have seen, was used by the Speer ministry to substitute brown coal for the losses in hard coal supplies sustained in the Ruhr. Reflecting this, brown coal car placings in RBD Halle rose in November and December 1944 by 7.5 and 5.5 percent respectively compared to the monthly average attained during the fourth quarter of 1943. But in January 1945 they were 11.9 percent lower than the first quarter 1944 monthly average.[151] The disruption of marshalling denied the German economy even this inadequate substitute. RBD Halle's role as mediator between west, north, and east also declined. The number of freight trains passing through the region between the beginning of November and the end of January fell by 28.5 percent.[152] By mid-January, eighty-three trains were backed up in the area.[153]

Operations in the other great hard coal pivot, RBD Oppeln, also deteriorated, though for different reasons. Here the culprits were the spreading confusion from the west, incidental damage from air raids on synthetic fuel plants, the flood of refugees and the retreating Wehrmacht issuing from the east, and finally the Red Army. Overall freight car placings during the first transportation plan period were 17 percent below normal and during the Ardennes period 13 percent less than usual. In November, hard coal car placings were off by 22 percent, in December by 13 percent. But in January 1945 the roof fell in. The advance of the Red Army caused a 53.2 percent decline compared to the monthly average of the first quarter of 1944. By early January, car placings were insufficient for satisfying the Reichsbahn's own needs for locomotive coal. The phenomenon that occurred in the west repeated itself in Upper Silesia. Car placings plummeted, forcing the reduction in marshalling for freight other than coal. Yet they continued to fall until even the locomotives could not be satisfied, forcing additional reductions in traffic. The disease fed itself until the sufferer was completely debilitated. Traffic declined in RBD Oppeln due to the disruption of marshalling and the resultant coal shortage, not due to a shortage of cars, for here too they were being put aside by the thousands, and not due to a shortage of locomotives. As in RBD Essen, RBD Oppeln had more locomotives than at any time during the war and had a hefty reserve in the bargain.[154]

As in the west, the administrative structure in the east disintegrated. Companies looked only to their own interests. RBD Oppeln was deluged with requests for special allocations of car space. In mid-December it began simply to ignore them.[155] GBL-East, so long the calm preserve used to sustain the west, began to dissolve in confusion. Even the most vital shipments to the Ruhr were refused by intervening directorates, causing congestion at marshalling yards far to the east.[156] The Wustermark and Seddin yards in Berlin were bursting with immobilized trains refused by GBL-West.[157] Individual carload shipments virtually ceased in early December.[158] The effort to send empty cars to RBD Essen collapsed as the trains simply disappeared in the chaos reigning in the Rhineland. The system of shifting the burden of marshalling to RBD Posen and elsewhere collapsed.[159] The omnipresent telecommunications problem shrouded events in the west in a veil of rumor and speculation.[160] GBL-East took energetic measures to maintain operations in RBD Halle, dispatching locomotives to it and transferring some of its marshalling responsibilities east. It took over sections of RBD Hanover.[161] It also continued putting aside trains on a massive scale. Here as in the west, there was no car shortage. The problem was bringing cars to the places where they were needed. Nevertheless, by the end of December, 300 trains were in the GBL-East backlog.[162]

Bombing of marshalling yards in the west had weakened the Reichsbahn's intricate marshalling and traffic control system throughout the Reich. RBDs Halle and Oppeln had suffered even though they had not been subjected to transportation bombing. Yet so long as they could operate at levels approaching normal, both the Reichsbahn and the German economy could continue to resist, though at hopelessly inadequate levels. The coup de grace that lead to the cessation of railway and economic activity was administered by the Red Army. On 16 January 1945, after repeatedly painting the blackest pictures of Germany's industrial future due to the disaster in the Ruhr, Speer warned Hitler that the Red Army had knifed into Upper Silesia. The coal Magistrale was endangered. Germany's last hope of continuing even token resistance was slipping from its grasp. If the Magistrale were lost, Speer warned, the Reichsbahn would stop rolling in a few days, and German industry, such of it as was still operating, would grind to a halt.[163] However, even this was a problem for the future. Hitler was fighting the war with the barest economic expedients and he ignored Speer.

The combination of the disruption of transportation and the approach of the Soviets caused a serious decline in economic activity throughout eastern Germany. Over half of the coal miners in Upper Silesia were non-Germans. Hearing of the advance of the Red Army to the region's doorstep, they increasingly stayed away from their jobs, and when they did come, used every pretext to shirk. So not only did production decline, as seen earlier, but efficiency deteriorated markedly, and the quality of the coal cut worsened. Transportation problems caused hard coal stocks at Upper Silesian mines to rise in December to 159.6 percent above the fourth quarter 1943 monthly average. Coke stocks at the same time were an astronomical 974.3 percent above normal. As a direct result, gas production sank, enabling the works to satisfy only one-sixth of demand.[164]

Coal movements on the Oder in November and December were slightly below normal. But problems developed during December. Coordination between the mines, which worked irregular shifts, and the DR and barge operators was poor, causing cars and vessels to arrive for loading when the pits were closed. In January 1945 the Reichsbahn was unable to provide enough cars to transfer coal from the mines to the harbor at Gleiwitz. It cancelled passenger trains in an attempt to free locomotives and save fuel to support this traffic. But this prevented the already overworked stevedores from going to work. Finally, ice appeared on the Oder in early December and severely restricted traffic in January.[165]

The impact of these difficulties was felt in Berlin. Arrivals of coal-bearing barges from the Ruhr had virtually ceased. But into December, vessels appeared steadily from Upper Silesia.[166] Coal receipts by waterway were a fifth below target in November, entirely as a result of the DEK and MLK obstacles.[167] At the end of December, arrivals fell markedly and stopped on Christmas because of ice on the Oder.[168] Overall coal deliveries to Berlin in December were a third below normal.[169] As a result coal supplies at the city's gas works dropped to just sixteen days instead of the target of thirty-two.[170] At BEWAG the board of directors contemplated shutting their four least efficient plants to save coal. They feared that if coal supplies did not improve the utility would close entirely by mid-February 1945.[171] BEWAG received a tenth less coal in November and December than during the previous year, almost all of it from Upper Silesia. Due to government pressure and the declining quality of what it received, coal consumption actually rose in December by 7 percent. Stocks fell to a third below normal.[172] Electricity production held steady.[173] Clearly, however, the end was in sight.

The interdependence of the various components of the Reichsbahn and their coordination with the inland waterway system were the key factors in their successful support of the economic division of labor in Germany until the autumn of 1944. Each segment performed a specific function. The entire system was more powerful than the sum of the output of its individual constituents because of its flexibility and specialization. The disruption of these relationships fatally weakened the German economy's capacity to produce arms and other goods. Therefore, to put matters into perspective it might help to consider the overall performance of the Reichsbahn during the decisive period November 1944 to January 1945.

In so far as the ZVL was concerned, the crucial problem was its inability to bring empty cars to the places where they were needed. This situation was exacerbated by the collapse of barge traffic on the west German canals and the Rhine. It attempted to compensate by giving coal highest priority in receiving car space, even over food. Nevertheless, major declines occurred in car space available for moving coal and armaments. Emrich, at the meeting of 18 December 1944, emphasized how the combination of marshalling yard attacks, confusion in RBD Halle, and the inescapable need to support the Wehrmacht in the Ardennes was debilitating the Reichsbahn. The clearest indicator of this was the backlog of trains that mushroomed out of control in late December and in January.[174] Too many marshalling yards operated at reduced levels or not at all; too many lines, especially the two gateways passing over the viaducts, were out; too many telephone connections had collapsed.[175] The very system of controlling the movement of trains, the block signals, disintegrated in early January.[176] Ganzenmüller demanded more flak and fighter protection, an end to the conscription of his personnel into the Volkssturm, and a reduction in the demand for car space to the amount that the DR could provide.[177] But the Reichsbahn continued to sink, its heart, the marshalling yards in the Ruhr, beating ever more faintly, its ability to give them assistance evaporating under the merciless pummeling of the Allied bombers.

During the period of the first transportation plan, general freight car placings fell 22.8 percent below the level attained during the same period in 1943. They then dropped precipitately to 43.2 percent below the previous year's level during the Ardennes period.[178] Only a quarter of the daily target for open freight cars and a third of the target for box cars for armaments shipments, a total of just 4,000, was satisfied in the air-raid-ravaged areas during the last week of 1944.[179] In the other regions about 90 percent of combined demand was fulfilled.[180] Of decisive significance was the steady decline in coal car placings. By January 1945, hard coal car placings for the entire Reichsbahn were 55.8 percent below the previous year's first quarter monthly average. Brown coal car placings were 26.4 percent lower.[181] Movements of all types of coal on the inland waterways were 78.7 percent in arrears in December.[182] The vital supplement to the Reichsbahn, the barges, had been ripped away by the bombers.

The ZVL understood this and that there was no shortage of vehicles. Losses to strafing were trivial. At the end of December 1944 the Reichsbahn had more steam locomotives, 34,032, and a larger reserve of them, 6,114, than in July 1944. But 3,000 were idled by the lack of coal to fuel them. On 6 January 1945 the Reichsbahn turned to using brown coal to power its locomotives. This was risky. Brown coal fouled the fireboxes, emitted a cloud of heavy smoke filled with sparks that attracted Allied fighters, and could ignite flammable cargo. Fuel consumption tripled, and this necessitated the use of a second fireman and a larger tender.[183]

The crucial problem was that the Reichsbahn had lost control of its freight-car park due to the disruption of marshalling and telecommunications. In January, freight car turnaround time had skyrocketed to twenty days. The backlog soared to 1,994 trains on 18 January 1945. At least 100,000 cars, many bearing coal, were immobilized. We have observed how the ZVL used embargoes, redisposed marshalling, and put aside trains to combat this dread problem. But none of these measures sufficed. Control from Berlin loosened. The process of putting trains aside ran out of control. Yard crews sidetracked cars bearing even the highest priority code words. On 9 December 1944 the Reichsbahn took the desperate step of ordering that entire trains be derailed to relieve the glut of cars in vital marshalling yards and lines. On 28 January 1945 it set quotas totalling 125,000 cars to be derailed within a month. Every yard was to form crews to derail cars. Each directorate had to create twenty columns that were to derail ten cars each per day.[184] By late December 1944 and early January 1945, the Reichsbahn had disintegrated into segments operating semi-independently. Control had virtually collapsed. The transportation system ceased to play its role in the division of labor.

Throughout the events of 1944–1945, Speer and Kehrl fought to assist the Reichsbahn and to maintain a bare minimum of armaments production. In late November, Speer restricted the use of priority code words in hopes of reducing the demand for car space.[185] On 21 December he eliminated all transport space priorities except two, one for tank production and another for construction materials for transportation facility repair and the building of underground factories.[186] Wholesale regional electricity cutoffs were implemented in hopes of conserving coal.[187] But this only caused armaments factories and even air bases to be blacked out.[188] On 14 December, Kehrl issued a directive that established standards for the provision of car space based on the study of the economy's performance in 1943. Plenipotentiaries appointed by the RMfRuK would allocate car space to industry based on need and the amount available as determined by the DR.[189] It was still hoped that standards could be established centrally in Berlin and be applied locally by the plenipotentiaries. Speer and Kehrl were deliberately delegating their authority to local leaders, based on the realization that the confused transportation situation could not be grasped from Berlin. It also marked what was the final stage in their endeavor to centralize control of the economy in their own hands, for it constituted a component of their drive to extend their suzerainty over the Reichsbahn.

The latter part of 1944 and early 1945 witnessed the disintegration of Speer's delicate control apparatus. The physical means were wrenched from him by the bombers. The psychological pressure bearing upon him and the other leaders of the Reich economy was tremendous. Dorpmüller, Ganzenmüller, and Speer were constantly traveling to gather impressions, exhort, and resolve disputes. Emrich, Kehrl, and their staffs remained in Berlin. The pressure to get results amid the shrill complaints of Bormann and the Gauleiters, the lack of information, the squalid rooms, most windowless and unheated due to ceaseless bombings, and the growing reluctance of industry to heed their directives—all were insuperable. A general nervousness infected the bureaucrats. Most silently accepted that the war was lost. But they fought on. Hitler's hold over them and the dictates of patriotism would not permit them to capitulate.[190] It is this psychological factor that explains why Ganzenmüller, Speer, and the others continued to improvise, to prolong resistance despite the punishment Tedder meted out to the Reichsbahn. They understood the basic situation. As early as 8 November, Central Planning expressed its fear that elasticity was about to be exhausted.[191] Within a few days though, it proposed new ways to conserve raw materials and continue production.[192]

Speer, from his travels to the west, grasped the importance of the attacks on marshalling yards, especially those serving the Ruhr. On 11 November 1944 he described in a memorandum for Hitler how the disruption of marshalling and canal movement had unleashed a serious coal famine in the Ruhr that prevented it from supporting its dependencies. Yet he hoped that traffic could be restored by a massive repair effort. On 30 November he still considered stocks sufficient to maintain a high level of armaments output. In a speech given to his subordinates at Rechlin on 1 December, he again expressed his confidence in their ability to master the crisis. A few days later he called upon his organization and the Gauleiters fanatically to repair rail facilities in the Ruhr. Reopening a yard even one day sooner was important.[193]

But Speer's system buckled under the pressure. His very attempts to maintain control sparked opposition. On 30 January 1945 his own ministry began dispatching coal trains to relieve emergencies, thus sparking bitter opposition from the RWKS. This precipitated the final break between Schmidt and the syndicate and the RMfRuK. Vögler, of United Steel and the RVE, newly appointed as head of Speer's own Ruhr Staff, strongly opposed Kehrl's coal-transport space-allocation scheme and promised to ignore it on 22 December.[194]

The corrosive atmosphere of internal bureaucratic competition fostered by Hitler and the increase in the power of Martin Bormann, the head of his party chancellery, contributed to the further disintegration of Speer's system. The Party launched vitriolic attacks on the Reichsbahn, which the railway forcefully rejected. The SS also singled out the beleaguered railway for criticism. Dorpmüller took the extraordinary step of personally informing Kaltenbrunner of his refusal to countenance such attacks. Speer moved sharply to prohibit Gauleiters from confiscating coal from trains not intended for their region. But in January 1945 he arrogated the same powers to his own ministry.[195]

Speer had cooperated closely with the Reichsbahn since his appointment in 1942. He and Ganzenmüller in particular had developed a cordial professional relationship. But during November, Speer and Kehrl became increasingly dissatisfied with the Reichsbahn, suspecting that it suffered from inefficiencies similar to those that had afflicted it in 1942. At the end of the month they decided to incorporate it more fully into their bureaucratic domain. Kehrl negotiated with Dorpmüller and Ganzenmüller to create national and regional transport plenipotentiaries. On 5 December, in a letter to Kehrl that must have disappointed Speer, Ganzenmüller rejected the proposal. He argued that the ZVL and its regional organizations already adequately performed the task of distributing car and barge space. Acceptance of Kehrl's proposal would only compound the growing confusion. Speer and Kehrl overrode Ganzenmüller's objections and on the next day, 6 December, they named Dr. Fritz Rudorf as Plenipotentiary for Economic Transport. He and his subordinates were empowered to demand any information from all government and business institutions necessary to complete their tasks. Rudorf himself was to sit on the ZVL. Dorpmüller won a few concessions in subsequent negotiations. No plenipotentiaries were named at the GBL level and those appointed at the RBD level were prohibited from establishing their offices in a directorate's headquarters.[196] Dorpmüller had preserved the organizational independence of the Reichsbahn. But the close relationship between the RMfRuK and the DR that had prevailed before Speer's move would not be restored. The damage to Germany's economy stemming from this was incalculable.

The cancer of bureaucratic disintegration also infected Speer's own apparatus. On 15 November he reorganized his ministry. The Central Office, the Planning Office, and the Technical Office absorbed portions of the disbanded Armaments Supply Office. The rings and committees were juggled. The power of the regional armaments offices was undercut when Hitler granted confiscation powers to the Gauleiters in the Ruhr on 28 November. Supposedly they were to consult the Ruhr Staff before acting. But they took this as the signal to ignore it. We have already noted that Speer appointed Albert Vögler to head the Ruhr Staff. Vögler also assumed the title of General Plenipotentiary for the Rhine-Ruhr Area. He was empowered to take any initiative in Speer's name to override any other plenipotentiary. Not only did Bormann violently oppose the appointment, but Vögler used it to attempt to free Ruhr industry from Speer's control. Speer's frustration, both at the chaos caused by the bombers and the interminable bickering within his own apparatus and between it and the Party, prompted him to abolish all priorities in the allocation of resources on 14 December, effective 1 March 1945. He hoped to cut through the confusion to make the most flexible use of those resources that remained. He still thought that the war could be prolonged.[197]

The RVK also began to fall apart. Pleiger reorganized its board on 30 December and hoped thus to streamline it and reduce the influence of the SS. Many subordinate offices were also abolished.[198]

The severe losses suffered by the Reichsbahn, the coal and the steel industries finally broke the resolve to continue in January 1945. At a meeting of industrial leaders held at the RMfRuK, Rohland, other industrialists, and even members of the ministry refused to accept Saur's fanatical call for a final heedless effort.[199]

Speer was ambivalent. He was too intelligent not to perceive that the war was lost. But the Führer retained a hold over him too. In a report to his colleagues written on 27 January 1945, Speer went beyond praising their successes in maintaining armaments production. He clearly depicted the irreparable losses suffered in coal and steel production due to transportation bombing. He pointed to major failures to reach his goals for tank and aircraft output. But unlike Saur, he did not call for a fanatical effort to continue armaments production. Instead he ambiguously called upon them to make a final sacrifice to preserve the nation's basic economic structure so as to assure the continued existence of the German people.[200]

Just four days before, on 23 January 1945, he had issued his last and most desperate plan to sustain armaments production and continue the war. The "Emergency Program of the Führer" provided for the completion of as many weapons as possible from existing stocks of parts, using the barest minimum of energy. Labor-intensive processes would be used whenever possible. Simple weapons such as rifles, machine pistols, hand grenades, and anti-tank rockets were granted highest priority. In addition, antiaircraft guns and the new ME-262 jet and ME-163 rocket-propelled fighters would be produced. These simple but effective weapons would be used by the most highly motivated men and the Volkssturm to stop the advance of the Red Army and the punishment dealt out by the Allied bombers. Once Upper Silesia and the Ruhr had been freed of their respective tormentors, in May and June 1945, a new program would be introduced. It would make the most efficient use of the Reich's reduced sources of raw materials to produce a new generation of highly effective combat vehicles, small arms, and aircraft. These would throw back Germany's foes and permit a successful conclusion to the war.[201] It was a mad, hopeless scheme. How long Speer took it seriously cannot be determined. It is clear that Hitler and the likes of Saur and Bormann took it in earnest. The Emergency Program meant that the effort to resist would continue and justified the continued bombing of the Reich transportation net.

The bombing of the Reichsbahn and the inland waterways, which had been going on since September 1944, had exerted a fatal effect on the Reich economy by the end of December 1944 and early January 1945. Coal stocks among manufacturing industries dwindled from about three weeks' supply at the end of November to just a few days' by January 1945, among those plants permitted to use coal.[202] Gas plant stocks in many cases had been exhausted.[203] Approximately 450,000 kilowatts of electrical generating capacity had been lost to coal shortages alone.[204] Here too, coal stocks were down to just a few days inspite of the reduction in demand by a fifth.[205] Gas output by the municipal works had fallen 20 percent below the previous year's level in December. Cokery gas production was only half the 1944 level in January 1945.[206]

The decline in energy supplies due to transportation bombing and the disruption of component deliveries, more vulnerable since the dispersal of the spring of 1944, caused a major decline in armaments production. The fall was uneven, delayed in some sectors by the characteristics of materials, energy use and stocks in different industries, and Speer's system of priorities. But by January 1945, production, including that of the most important armaments, was on the retreat in every area. That favorite of early Allied strategic air planners, the ball-bearing industry, collapsed in December 1944 due to the failure of components deliveries. Despite the bombing of Germany's synthetic petroleum industry, stocks of lubricants remained at the required seven-day level in early January 1945. But they could not be distributed because of transportation snags.[207]

The bombers had worked their way down the pipeline during September and October, causing coal and raw materials shortages. In November and December, German industry consumed its stocks of these commodities and of parts and components. Finally in January

1945, production collapsed. The armaments production index spiraled down to 227.[208] This represented a 30 percent decline from the high point in July 1944. Arms output was depressed to the level of August 1943. The entire second armaments boom had been nullified. The standard laid down earlier in this account had been achieved. A one-third reduction in armaments production had occurred soon after similar or even greater losses had been sustained by basic industry. But more had been accomplished by transportation bombing. The actual supply of weapons to the Wehrmacht shrank. Acceptances of the K98 rifle were down from their November 1944 peak by 12 percent, and stocks were down by two-thirds to just three days in January 1945. In January, stocks of the 88mm antitank gun stood at just two weeks, a fall from the one-month stock held as recently as October 1944.[209] Stocks of shells and powder were also extremely low. But as the army quartermaster general made clear on 26 December 1944, the army stocks were out of reach due to the chaos that had swept the Reichsbahn.[210] Thousands of tons of powder waited at the factories to be taken to the Army Munitions Establishments.[211] Even the procedure of shipping weapons and munitions directly from the factory to the combat units had collapsed. By early January 1945 the bombing of marshalling yards and canals had caused a major weapons shortage in the Wehrmacht.[212]

The transportation offensive had both physical and psychological effects. On the one hand, the repeated bombing of marshalling yards, canals, and viaducts denied real resources to German industry and to the Wehrmacht. It prevented the distribution of coal, fatally disorganized the exchange of components, and compelled German industry to consume its reserves of both. The bombing also had the synergistic effect of reducing both the Reichsbahn's and industry's recuperative capacities. It created an emergency that exacerbated itself. On the other hand, the transportation offensive also created psychological pressures that gravely reduced the German industrial elite's capacity to react to emergencies. It magnified the tensions that the Nazi system either suppressed or, in the case of the Party and governmental structures, encouraged. The collapse of telecommunications, an unintended by-product of the attacks, made planning and coordination impossible. The results were a major coal famine with dire short-term effects on all of German industry, the disintegration of the division of labor, serious declines in armaments production, and a major reduction in supplies to the Wehrmacht. Yet in some places the disaster was not recognized. In early January 1945 neither in Hitler's headquarters nor in the majority of Allied air intelligence and command agencies was the collapse of the Reich economy perceived, though for different reasons.

8 The Wheels Stop Rolling

War is not simply a clash of the material assets mustered by the contenders. It is also a contest waged on the psychological plane. In a campaign such as the strategic air assault on the German transportation system, the psychological and intellectual factors were pronounced. Unlike those of a direct military confrontation, results were difficult to determine because they appeared only after some delay and because information about them could be assessed in very different ways. The ambiguous nature of economic data under the best of circumstances makes even short-term prognostications difficult. But when the object of analysis intentionally conceals as much of this information as possible, when efforts to obtain it are hindered by weather and bureaucratic obstructionism, then the task becomes infinitely more difficult. All of these impediments hindered the Allies in their attempt to peer across the Rhine to determine what had happened to the German economy as a result of their bombing.

The military officers and uniformed civilians engaged in judging the importance of economic intelligence repeatedly blundered. Poor weather reduced the volume of information that could be gleaned from photo reconnaissance. Equally important, stubborn bureaucratic opposition excluded some very revealing information gained by SIGINT. Consequently, while the German economy collapsed, the Allies groped for a strategy that would end the war. Only when the weather improved in January 1945, when it was realized that Ultra had unlocked important secrets, when Upper Silesia was overrun, and when Sir Arthur Tedder restored his authority—only then were the paralysis of the Reichsbahn and the coal famine perceived and a new consensus formed behind the transportation campaign. Ultimately, after much misunderstanding, segments of the Allied air intelligence community and all the Allied air commanders agreed to set bombing priorities in line with Tedder's conception. The consequence was a devastating new offensive against the

DR. But by then the Reichsbahn and the German economy with it were already grinding to a halt. The new wave of attacks crushed all hope of recovery among the more reasonable German leaders and abetted the final spasm of nihilistic destructiveness from Hitler and his followers.

Throughout November, doubts grew among Allied intelligence officers concerning the results of the first transportation plan. It seemed to them either to be taking too long or to be having no effect at all. The Ardennes offensive threw Allied air intelligence and command circles into despondency. After all, after four and a half years of bombing and many severe defeats on the battle fronts in the west and the east, Germany should not have been able to mount such a drive. From the high optimism of the summer and autumn, the Allies fell into deep pessimism. In USAAF circles it was predicted that the war would not end until the summer of 1945. The Combined Intelligence Committee of the CCS in Washington feared that Germany could prolong the war for a considerable time and discerned no deterioration in the Reich's ability to sustain combat. At Yalta the CCS informed the Soviets that they did not expect hostilities in Europe to cease until July or December 1945.[1] These dire predictions indicate how poorly the Allies understood the way the German economy functioned and how badly they misunderstood the effect of their bombing. For the most part they simply projected what they thought was the trend of the most recent events far into the future.

The apparent failure of the bomber offensive and the assault on the Reich transportation system in particular triggered another review of Allied air strategy. On 8 January 1945, General Arnold asked his staff to reevaluate the strategic bombing campaign, take a critical look at priorities and prepare a new set of proposals. Kuter responded for the air staff by admitting that severe mistakes had been made. But he could offer nothing radically new. He simply suggested focusing on short term goals and coordinating the transportation and oil offensives more effectively. He specifically rejected Zuckerman's concept of transportation bombing as too time-consuming, as if all the bombs that had fallen on marshalling yards and canals over the previous four months had never been dropped.[2]

Given what we know was happening in Germany while Kuter wrote his report, it might seem incredible that such mistakes could have been made. But Kuter and his colleagues in Washington and in London at the Air Ministry had fallen victim to the expansive claims made for air power and so expected results in an unreasonably short time. They believed their own myths and so were unable to see victory when it beckoned. Although accurate appraisals of the Reich's economic structure were available, they were ignored by most air strategists, especially among the Americans. It proved difficult for them to learn while engaged in operations. In this matter they reacted as most bureaucrats do. The responses that had been ingrained before the crisis and that had ensured promotion were difficult to cast off when they proved ineffective. This was especially difficult when the proliferation of intelligence agencies fostered bureaucratic egotism. These factors working against an accurate appreciation were reinforced by a serious lack of hard information. The gravest void stemmed from the dearth of photo intelligence.

ACIU was beset with two major obstacles—cloud cover and incorrect priorities. Throughout November, during most of December, and even through much of January 1945, heavy cloud prevented the reconnaissance aircraft from observing the German transportation system. Repeated sorties were necessary to monitor repair work, judge the state of marshalling, and gauge locomotive operations. But under the circumstances this proved impossible. The result was that photo interpreters and those reliant on them were forced to turn to conjecture. This opened the door for prejudice to govern appreciations. Since photo reconnaissance had played a predominant role in earlier intelligence assessments, its loss was especially important.[3]

Equally important was the poor application of what imagery they did obtain. The practice of allowing the user of intelligence to determine how collection assets were to be used exerted a harmful influence. The CSTC established the priorities for photo coverage and nominated lines likely to be carrying military traffic and sections of yards unrelated to economic movements. The result was that the coal gateways were not covered even when they were not blanketed by cloud. When photo interpreters did evaluate yards, they frequently failed to distinguish between passenger stations and marshalling yards, and they often emphasized damage to lines while ignoring the hump, switches, and locomotive sheds.[4] ACIU even had trouble assessing the situation at Bielefeld.[5] In contrast, because of the CSTC's support of canal attacks, coverage of the Ladbergen and Gravenhorst breaks was good.[6]

In light of these impediments it is not surprising that the overall level of intelligence assessment was low. MEW had repeatedly been disappointed in its predictions of the collapse of Speer's apparatus and now, reinforced by the Ardennes offensive, became extremely conservative in its estimates. In its review of the last six months of 1944, MEW concluded that no fall in armaments production could be anticipated in the near future. It discounted reports of a coal shortage and argued that the Reichbahn's biggest problem was a lack of personnel.[7]

EOU and the CSTC felt that their doubts about the transportation offensive had been confirmed. EOU crowed that "The bogey of strategic general attack on rail transport was almost, but not quite, laid."[8] The CSTC bemoaned the lack of photo reconnaissance and detailed statistical information.[9] It emphasized that through running had never been stopped and concluded that the attacks had not hindered troop deployment for the Ardennes drive, let alone hurt the economy. They stubbornly argued that territorial losses and the oil offensive were the causes of whatever declines in production had occurred.[10] Moreover, they asserted that the widespread disruption of transportation necessary to reduce significantly economic activity was unattainable.[11] As late as mid-January 1945, the CSTC argued that "no evidence has appeared of substantial interference with economic traffic such as the reduction in certain types of coal movements."[12] It also discounted the time factor. In doing so they were being quite consistent since in their estimation all the preceding transportation bombing, except the canal raids, had been ineffective and therefore the process of reducing Germany's stocks of materials and supplies was yet to begin. An effective form of transportation attack, which USSTAF representatives on the CSTC did not think could be found, would still have to wear down these resources, that is, overcome the Reich economy's elasticity of supply before it could reduce the combat power of the Wehrmacht.[13] The CSTC feared that another "eight months or a year" would pass before Tedder's concept would bear fruit.[14] Part of the committee's difficulty was that it was confused by Tedder's dual aim. Moreover, some of its members felt that the deputy supreme commander had tried to dupe them by calling for the heavy bombers to attack railway targets to support the army when he in fact hoped to to use these raids to pursue his economic goals.[15] But fundamentally the CSTC was wedded to oil and would consider other target systems only with the utmost reluctance.

Only Tedder's intelligence staff at SHAEF managed to put the puzzle together, although it lacked many important pieces. It was able to do so because it was receptive to the notion that transportation attacks could succeed and because it was closer to the combat zone and so received its information more quickly and directly. But especially in January, it experienced grave difficulty influencing the selection of targets because its chief was in eclipse. Tedder was among the greatest losers from the Ardennes surprise. His strategy seemed to have been decisively refuted by the panzer divisions. He had also come into conflict with some of the Allied ground commanders. A serious campaign was being waged for his ouster. Although his opponents lacked the power to achieve their highest aims, they did succeed in having him shunted off to Moscow on a trip lasting from 1 to 19 January.[16] SHAEF G-2 labored in the wilderness.

Nevertheless, SHAEF unwaveringly held to its position that attacks on marshalling yards supplemented by the canal raids were having serious and immediate economic consequences for Germany.[17] It gradually clarified the details of the situation in Germany. In early November it relied on prisoner of war reports indicating that the DR was satisfying only the bare minimum of economic demand. It suggested that the Reichsbahn still enjoyed a strong repair service that enabled it to overcome damage rapidly. It also credited the DR with being able to reroute traffic easily and to make more intense use of its locomotives. Nor did the Reichsbahn suffer from sabotage. But SHAEF went astray when it also perceived a sufficiency of locomotive coal and a smoothly functioning telecommunications system in the DR.[18] It also discovered the Reichsbahn's repair priorities based on agent and prisoner reports and photo reconnaissance. Line cuts were identified as having first priority. Marshalling yards came second, then passenger stations, freight loading areas, and finally locomotive sheds.[19] SHAEF did not draw the conclusion that the disruption of marshalling was much more important than damage to locomotive-servicing facilities. Instead it steadfastly insisted that there was a locomotive shortage. At the end of November it accepted a spurious report from Switzerland of an impending strike among Reichsbahn employees. At the same time, though, it placed an important piece of the puzzle. It noticed that a coal shortage had immobilized locomotives.[20] SHAEF continued to elaborate its picture of the German economy until, on 22 January 1945, it was able to conclude that economic activity in Germany had declined severely due to the disruption of transportation. The collapse of coal supplies, raw materials deliveries, and the exchange of components had badly dislocated production. "It would appear," SHAEF concluded, "that attacks on communications may have caused more far-reaching dislocation of production in this manner than has hitherto been thought to be the case."[21]

The slow process of coming to perceive the chaos reigning in Germany took an important step forward in February 1945. As part of the reevaluation of Allied air strategy set off by the Ardennes offensive, Sir Norman Bottomley, Deputy Chief of Air Staff of the RAF, ordered a complete review of Ultra, relating to the transportation offensive. The study demonstrated that for months the CSTC had been suppressing Enigma information on the Reichsbahn and the economy. Oliver L. Lawrence said that 20,000 commercial intercepts were made weekly but they were not analysed because they were not "likely to be particularly instructive."[22] The report resulting from Bottomley's investigation appeared on 28 February and yielded a cornucopia of startling information. One Ultra decrypt, dated 15 February 1945, read, "Although there are accumulations (commodities) such as coal in the places where they are produced, the inability to transport them is having an adverse effect on the production of various war supplies."[23] Another, which had lain unused since October 1944, stated, "On 20 October, Reich Minister for Equipment and War Production reported that, on account of destruction of traffic installations and lack of power, from 30 to 50 percent of all works in west Germany were at a standstill."[24] Other reports detailed the fall in coal stocks, the crippling of utility service, and the sharp decline in armaments production.[25]

This "new" information was insufficient to decide the bombing debate. Too many powerful individuals had strongly condemned the transportation offensive for there to be a quick reversal due simply to the appearance of new evidence. A "golden bridge" was necessary to salvage their reputations. That escape route was provided by the Red Army when it overran Upper Silesia. SHAEF G-2 was the first to sense the importance of the Red Army's success. On 5 February it stressed in its regular transportation report that the loss of Upper Silesia imposed an even heavier burden on the Ruhr and especially on the Reichsbahn's already weakened marshalling yards and arteries serving it.[26] This argument proved decisive. Yet it did not have an immediate effect on bombing priorities. The committee system used by the Allies to formulate strategy was slow. It produced flaccid compromises. Viewed in another light, it also prevented gross mistakes and it ensured that when a strategy was agreed it would be implemented by subordinate operational echelons. Moreover, the bureaucratic situation had been simplified by February. Tedder had returned from Moscow and reasserted his position. Now decision making centered on just two forums: the CSTC and the air commanders' conferences. Tedder retained his control of the latter and outmaneuvered the former.[27] The CSTC never fully accepted Tedder's strategy. It tolerated transportation attacks only in relation to what it considered an exceptional case—the Ruhr after the loss of Upper Silesia.[28]

Like a hunter closing in for the kill, SHAEF G-2 refined its arguments in favor of transportation bombing and pressed for a concerted effort to isolate the Ruhr. By mid-February it had accurately divined that armaments production in the Ruhr itself was declining and the region's ability to support its tributaries was waning. A final offensive against the Reichsbahn's network serving the region would end armaments production. SHAEF was in no doubt now about the root of the problem. A severe coal famine had erupted forcing the DR to burn brown coal in its locomotives. The bombing of marshalling yards before the loss of Upper Silesia had created a glut of freight cars forcing the Reichsbahn to derail them by the score.[29] In the space of a few weeks SHAEF had rapidly apprehended the situation. The CSTC, using the golden bridge, followed suit.

In mid-February, Lawrence, Wood, Bufton, and all the other members of the CSTC except the EOU representatives seized upon the loss of Upper Silesia as the crucial development that justified an air offensive to isolate the Rhenish-Westphalian industrial region.[30] By the end of the month it had completely adopted the SHAEF position. Its meeting of 28 February was dominated by discussion of the low level of Ruhr coal traffic and its vulnerability to bombing. A plan to isolate the region was proposed and tentatively accepted.[31] Tedder's dual aims were retained. In mid-February, Eisenhower and the SHAEF operations staff designated the Ruhr as the primary target for their planned ground offensive.[32] With the change in the CSTC outlook, air-reconnaissance coverage was shifted to the coal gateways and photo interpreters were ordered to observe marshalling and coal stocks at the locomotive sheds.[33]

Tedder had won a major victory which enabled him to steer priorities toward transportation. But the struggle remained difficult because a variety of powerful political factors heavily influenced target selection. The desire to end the war quickly by assisting the advancing armies, including the Soviets, and finally breaking the German people's will to resist caused frequent changes in target priorities. In mid-January, oil shared first priority with jet aircraft plants. Transportation targets, especially on routes serving the Ruhr, were next.[34] Then at the end of the month, the Berlin, Leipzig, and Dresden urban areas were raised to second position, transportation falling to third.[35] Churchill had decided that a final series of massive blows would push the German people to despair and to demand peace from their leaders. The attacks were conducted but the Germans struggled on grimly.[36] Tedder placed little importance on these operations and continued to work for greater concentration on transportation facilities serving the Ruhr.[37]

The nature of target selection changed during January. Because of the lack of consensus and the Ardennes crisis, priorities were set very broadly. The CSTC and the air commanders met weekly to choose objectives in light of the latest intelligence and the state of the internal debate. On 24 January the CSTC, at that stage still not reconciled to Tedder's view, proposed an interim plan to govern the transportation offensive. Its goal was to lay the groundwork for a definitive scheme, to exploit the chaos caused by the Ardennes bombings along the Rhine to prevent the withdrawal of German troops into reserve, and to reduce coal and general economic traffic. It placed the Mannheim–Frankfurt/Main–Mainz region at the head of its list, the Cologne-Bonn-Siegen-Dillenburg-Marburg area second, and the Ruhr arteries through Paderborn, Hamm, and Münster last.[38] Tedder realized that although the coal gateways figured prominently in these priorities, the crucial routes leading to the east were slighted. He resorted to behind-the-scenes maneuvering to have them lifted to first position.[39] A new feature of the attack, complementing the blows to marshalling yards, would be a major effort to cut viaducts and bridges along all of the coal gateways.

This "interim plan" was implemented from the end of January. However, bombing priorities remained a constant subject for debate in February.

Tedder continued to lobby for his plan and achieved a breakthrough when the CSTC visited SHAEF on 10 February.[40] It was agreed that the primary aim now should be the isolation of the Ruhr. On 14 February the CSTC began to prepare plans to achieve Tedder's goal.[41] The deputy supreme commander left nothing to chance. He had his staff at SHAEF formulate its own plan. It pinpointed the Hamm, Soest, and Münster gateways, incorporating the proposal to cut viaducts with a scheme to hit major marshalling yards within the Ruhr, not just along its periphery, in order to reduce the overall volume of traffic generated by the region.[42] This scheme was discussed at the air commanders' conference of 15 February. The air leaders recommended that marshalling yard, bridge and viaduct, and strafing attacks be coordinated closely to strangle the Ruhr.[43]

Tedder faced an additional threat. At the 1 February air commanders' meeting, Spaatz had proposed an attack on a large number of small railway facilities scattered throughout Germany. He hoped thereby to both weaken the Reichsbahn and to demonstrate Allied air superiority to the German people. He hoped that this would bring a rapid end to the fighting. Spaatz's proposal was not new. Similar schemes had been bruited about since the autumn. Tedder had opposed them as a dispersal of effort. The key to his conception was the concentration on transportation facilities that served the Ruhr and that played a major role in the functioning of the Reichsbahn. Clarion, as Spaatz's plan was dubbed, promised only dispersal of effort in terms of both geographical scope and impact on DR facilities. Tedder was unable or unwilling to prevent Clarion, possibly for fear of alienating Spaatz, who had been cooperating with him. Consequently, both the Eighth and Fifteenth Air Forces, flying at low altitude in clear weather on 22 February, struck stations, grade crossings, bridges, and marshalling yards across Germany, most of which had never been bombed before. Spaatz was so pleased with the apparent results that he ordered Clarion repeated on the next day. But the impact was slight. Dorpmüller stated after the war that the the attacks flown on the two days had been indistinguishable from any others.[44]

Meanwhile the CSTC had completed its plan to isolate the Ruhr.

The scheme was approved at the air commanders' conference held on 1 March. The Ruhr Plan, or Bugle as Tedder dubbed it, had two objectives. In order of importance, they were to cut off coal traffic from the region and to prevent reinforcement of the armies defending it against the planned Allied ground attack.[45] A bridge or viaduct would be cut on every line leading from the region in an arc stretching from Bremen to the Weser, to Bielefeld, and south to Koblenz. In all, eighteen bridges and viaducts were pinpointed, six of which were assigned to the heavy bombers. Within the arc every marshalling yard and locomotive-servicing facility was to be bombed heavily and repeatedly. These hammer blows would be complemented by strafing intended to cause local stoppages and create confusion.

Tedder had won another bureaucratic victory. However, it meant little for the outcome of the war. Even before the Ruhr Plan was implemented, the Rhenish-Westphalian region had ceased to play its role in the German economy's division of labor. The cascade of bombs that it unleashed, however, may have helped convince Germany's economic leaders that continued resistance was hopeless. Under the interim plan, 50,000 tons of bombs was dropped on transportation targets in February. In March the same amount was expended.[46] In both months the lion's share was contributed by the Eighth Air Force—35,141 tons in February, 28,563 tons in March.[47] Marshalling yards and other transportation targets sustained the most bombing, far ahead of oil targets and airfields, the next most heavily hit categories. Bomber Command kept the Dortmund-Ems and Mittelland canals closed with raids in February. A total of seventeen attacks was flown against the three main viaducts by the Eighth Air Force and Bomber Command. It was Bomber Command, using its heavy 12,000 and 22,000 pound weapons, that smashed each of them: Bielefeld on 14 March, Altenbecken on 19 March, and Arnsberg on 20 March. Overall, the Allied air forces flew forty-two major attacks against eighteen bridges and viaducts linking the Ruhr to its hinterland. Ten were completely destroyed, three were damaged and therefore impassable, and only one partly passable. Two came under artillery fire leaving only two operational.[48] The Luftwaffe attempted to ward off these attacks by concentrating flak along the coal gateways, near bridges and viaducts on the Hamm, Münster, and Soest routes and near important grade crossings on the Vorhalle line.[49] The effort was too weak and came too late.

The Reichsbahn, already reeling from months of repeated sledge-hammer blows, finally came to a halt. Although a few trains furtively made their way to Wehrmacht units carrying armaments or out of the Ruhr bearing a few tons of coal, for all practical purposes the wheels had stopped rolling. By the end of March, overall car placings were only 11 percent of normal.[50] In the Ruhr, coal car placings were a mere 10 percent of normal in February and by the end of March had ceased altogether. RBD Halle still placed cars for brown coal at three-quarters of the usual February level.[51] But this could not balance the losses suffered in the west and the east. Many of the trains simply sank into the backlog that soared to over 2,800.[52] Locomotive coal supplies were so scarce that some engineers desperately seeking fuel drove their engines to mine sidings.[53] The DR operated only 7,000 of its locomotives. About 23,000 were idled by lack of fuel and damage to repair facilities.[54] Cars continued to be derailed by the thousands. The DR even offered to give freight cars to companies so long as they would be removed from its rails.[55] Ganzenmüller admitted to Hitler in February that traffic in the south and west was paralyzed and that no real control was being exerted by Berlin in the remaining areas.[56]

While the Allies struggled to gain a reasonably accurate picture of events in the Reich, its economy sank deeper into the morass. In February hard coal production was a pitiful 30 percent of normal.[57] In the Ruhr coal production was off by 56 percent and coke output by two-thirds compared to the average monthly results for the first quarter of 1944.[58] But even this just piled up at the pit heads. Coal stocks left undeliverable at the mines were now 443.2 percent above the preceding year's level.[59] Brown coal production could provide no relief. Due to the loss of territory and reductions in the cut because the Reichsbahn could not move it, brown coal output was down by 44 percent.[60] Consequently, only 5 to 10 percent of the greatly reduced demand could be satisfied.[61] Both national and Ruhr steel output were just a quarter of normal.[62] The armaments production index collapsed to the level of late 1942. It fell fifty-two points in February alone.[63] The cessation of deliveries, not just of production, meant that a weapons and ammunition shortage debilitated the Wehrmacht for the last battles to defend the fatherland. The Stinder and Körner Works in Velbert in the Ruhr, west of Essen, ceased operations because 2,300 kilograms of high priority armaments goods choked its facilities. Some of them had been awaiting transport since October.[64] The OKW complained that instead of the forty-nine trains that it usually received each day carrying munitions, in February only eight or nine arrived per day.[65] Stocks of the Type 44 machine pistol and the K98 rifle dwindled to just three days, light field howitzers to two days, Panther tanks to one. Supplies of rifle bullets, 88mm antitank ammunition, and heavy field howitzer shells sank to just two weeks.[66] These stocks could not be distributed.[67] Nominally these and other weapons had been issued to the troops in higher numbers than ever before. But many had been lost in transit. Many units were without heavy weapons and had little ammunition.[68] Elasticity had been exhausted by months of transportation bombing. When the western Allies began their offensive across the Rhine in March and the Soviets steamrolled over the Oder in April, nothing faced them but an empty shell.

While production flickered out, the bureaucratic predators consumed each other in pointless struggle. Speer dissolved the remains of his production apparatus on 8 February. He divided the Reich into three areas, one in the west with headquarters at Heidelberg, one in the southeast based at Prague, and the other in the east with offices at Kopfenberg. Armaments plenipotentiaries who were empowered to make any decisions up to the limits of Speer's authority were named to head each area. They were to cooperate closely with business leaders, the Reichsbahn and the representatives of the rings and committees.[69]

Speer also moved to seize the Reichsbahn. On 14 February he discussed with Hitler his proposal to send Dorpmüller on leave due to the aged railwayman's illness, and to appoint himself commissar of the Reichsbahn. Hitler approved and signed Speer's draft of a decree creating a transportation staff in the RMfRuK chaired by Speer. The armaments minister acquired full power to allocate transport space. Members of the staff were to be named in agreement with the RVM.[70] At the moment of collapse Speer nearly absorbed one of the few entities in the economic sphere that had retained its independence since 1942. His motivations were ambiguous. He simultaneoulsy hoped to protect the DR from the fanatics in the Party and to increase his own power. Goebbels as Plenipotentiary for Total War attempted to divert its personel to trench digging or the Volkssturm. Bormann stuggled to radicalize and nazify it. In the face of all this, the Reichsbahn retained its separate identity and command structure to the end. Its heritage, its organization, were in tatters but still fuctioning, and the loyalty of its men to Dorpmüller and Ganzenmüller was too strong.

That defeat was at hand was apparent to all of the Reich's economic leaders. We have already seen that Ganzenmüller had warned Hitler that his railway was at the end of its tether. On 14 February, in a message to the remaining directorates, Dilli admitted that the Reichsbahn could no longer fulfill its responsibilities. He would attempt new palliatives to maintain a crude minimum of traffic to support the populace. But he had no faith in them. The game was up.[71]

On 7 March, Pleiger also admitted defeat. In a letter to Speer, he stated that the Ruhr had been isolated since 23 February. The combination of the isolation of the Ruhr and the loss of Upper Silesia meant the end of the coal economy. Coal could not be delivered to anyone, even the most important consumers. Collapse was unavoidable.[72]

Rüdiger Schmidt and the RWKS drew the same conclusion. For weeks, Schmidt had observed with horrible fascination the decline of RBD Essen and the starvation of the syndicate's dependents. At the board meeting of 28 March 1945 he painted the blackest picture to the syndicate's members. He also reported to them Gauleiter Terboven's order to shift the syndicate's operations east to Detmold. Terboven was one of the fanatics who harbored hopes for a change in fortune and who wanted to destroy all economic assets and evacuate the population before they fell into the hands of the advancing Allies. Hugo Stinnes, Jr., heir to one of the Ruhr's oldest coal fortunes, spoke up at this. He supported Schmidt's suggestion that Terboven's order be ignored and offered the convenient pretext that it was only a "recommendation." It was agreed to distribute one month's salary to everyone and to disperse. When conditions stablized after the end of the fighting they would gather again and resume operations.[73]

Possibly the most difficult capitulation was that of Speer. Contrary to the portrait painted in his memoirs, the young armaments minister battled on into 1945. Undoubtedly he fell prey to severe doubts about final victory as early as November 1944. But he continued to press for the restoration of transportation facilities and the continuation of armaments production. He took a hand in organizing the logistical support for the Ardennes offensive. Thereafter his confidence diminished. In January 1945 it is possible that he still hoped for a negotiated settlement or an armistice. But gradually, day by day, in January and February, he convinced himself not only that the war was lost but that it had to be ended as soon as possible.

In his report of 27 January, Speer stopped short of openly calling for capitulation. Instead, as we have seen, he wrote vaguely of fighting to preserve the German people and the preconditions for their existence.[74] This could easily have been interpreted to mean continued armed resistance since Hitler had claimed to be waging the war to protect the Volk from extinction. In his orders for the allocation of transport space after establishing the transportation staff in February, he accorded Wehrmacht movements highest priority. Significantly, however, he placed food second.[75] On 1 March he ordered a new, frantic effort to repair marshalling yards to maintain traffic; 800,000 people were to be thrown into the struggle.[76] Prisoners of war, concentration camp inmates, idled factory workers, and others from armaments plants were committed. But again the order emphasized that this was necessary for the successful continuation of the war.[77] On 14 March, Speer personally issued a set of transportation priorities that put troop trains in first place. But he stated this priority very narrowly. Only the most urgent movements necessary to maintain short-term resistance were to fall into this category. Food and repair materials for the Reichsbahn received next priority. Among bulk commodities food received highest priority, higher even than coal.[78] The Reichsbahn was given complete authority to refuse any freight that it deemed unworthy of transport.

These last orders indicate that by early March Speer had concluded that further resistance was futile. He arrived at this realization in part because of the damage caused by bombing to the transportation system and the synthetic fuel industry and in part because of his revulsion at Hitler's scorched-earth policy. The Führer had been moving since the autumn toward ordering the destruction of all economically valuable goods and structures. Speer had repeatedly put him off. In mid-March the young minister, reluctantly admitting that his accomplishments had been for naught and his organization shattered, collided with Hitler, who sought a last nihilistic wave of destruction. On 15 March 1945, Speer submitted a memorandum to Hitler that described the Reich's economic plight without reservations. Further resistance was hopeless, the people had done their duty. Now, he pleaded, the fighting should be stopped to preserve the bare existence of the German people. Three days later Hitler rejected Speer's appeal and ordered that Germany be laid waste before its enemies. This marked the final break between Speer and Hitler and the end of resistance by the most stubborn and capable of the economic elite. Speer persisted in subverting the scorched-earth order and in protecting the Reichsbahn from the order for its destruction issued on 29 March.[79]

By the end of March the British and the Americans had vaulted across the Rhine, and on 1 April their pincers snapped shut around the Ruhr. Three weeks later the Soviets encircled Berlin. After years of bombing, the physical occupation of much of Germany, and the crushing of its armed forces, resistance finally ended only after Hitler committed suicide on 29 April. The Americans had occupied the offices of the RWKS at Kettwig in early April. The United States Strategic Bombing Survey (USSBS) immediately began sifting the syndicate's documents for information. Dorpmüller had fled to Malente in Schleswig-Holstein, where segments of the Reich ministries had moved to administer the northern part of the country. Ganzenmüller went to Bavaria to oversee operations in the south. Both were taken into custody by the Americans and questioned by the USSBS in May.

Speer and Kehrl had agreed to separate. Speer would move south with the majority of the government and Kehrl would go north to supervise production there. But Speer hoped to be named economics minister in Dönitz's successor regime and to be allowed by the Allies to rebuild the German economy, so he too went north. On 23 May he was captured at Flensburg by the USSBS and interrogated extensively. His dreams proved unrealistic and he was imprisoned for twenty years by the Nuremberg Tribunal in 1946. Kehrl had reached Hamburg with a small band of associates. Once there he realized that the end was at hand and relieved his men of their responsibilities. He retired with his wife to a house on the Lüneburg Heath where he was found by John Kenneth Galbraith in June. It was fitting that the great adversary of Ganzenmüller and Speer, Sir Arthur Tedder, represented General Eisenhower at the formal surrender ceremony held in Berlin on 8 May 1945.[80]

9 Conclusions

Germany grew to become one of the world's leading industrial powers during the last third of the nineteenth century and the first third of the twentieth because it was able to exploit effectively a comparatively narrow resource base. Crucial to this development was the creation of a complex geographical division of labor predicated on the exchange of goods among regions specializing in particular facets of production. Basic commodities such as coal and steel produced in the Ruhr and Upper Silesia were exchanged for food from the east and finished manufactured goods from the southwestern and central areas. A balance developed that, because it encompassed the entire nation, was both resilient and adaptable.

The Nazis inherited this system in 1933, convinced that its primary limitation was its lack of strategic raw materials such as oil and iron ore necessary to compete militarily with large continental and imperial powers. Their acceptance of the stab-in-the-back myth caused them to fear that the German people would refuse to make the economic sacrifices necesssary to support the major wars of territorial expansion that they contemplated. Therefore the strategic flanks would be cleared in a series of short wars that would place relatively little burden upon the shaky populace because they would require only a modest level of economic effort compared to World War I. The culmination would be a short, violent campaign against the USSR, which would win for Germany the rich grain- and raw-material-producing regions of the Ukraine. Victory in these conflicts would assure Germany's resource and population bases and enable it to pursue Hitler's even more grandiose aims later. It was for these reasons that comparatively little was done to increase the capacity of the armaments industry before 1936. Then the Four Year Plan was introduced to rapidly increase output in a few crucial sectors such as liquid fuels, aircraft, and steel to make possible the initial campaigns. The pace was accelerated in 1938 when Hitler perceived an opportunity to achieve his goals sooner than he had expected. Throughout, the program was hobbled by administrative confusion and the attempt to shield the German public from the full burden of the effort. Nevertheless, it contrived to create a military force strong enough to subdue quickly Germany's comparatively unprepared initial opponents. By 1942, however, the scheme had collapsed, and new policies, designed to exploit available resources more fully, were required.

It was under these circumstances that Hitler called upon Albert Speer to manage the Third Reich's economy. Speer, reflecting commonly accepted ideas, appreciated what was politically feasible and recognized that decisions made prior to his entry into office had decisively limited his options. Therefore he embarked upon a program aimed at drastically increasing armaments production while making no additions to capital. In the factories he initiated a successful campaign for production efficiency that allowed the nation to produce weapons in quantities far exceeding previous expectations without significantly increasing raw material consumption. With difficulty, he also shifted assets from consumer to military production. However, the most important reallocations were made within manufacturing industry. Political opposition and the need to provide for the thousands suffering from area bombing necessitated a comparatively high level of consumer output until 1944.

Speer's efficiency drive was made possible by his marriage of regional executive mechanisms to his central policy-making bureaucracy. Throughout, he used young engineers and businessmen to manage their own branches of the economy. While reaping enormous advantages in terms of expertise, the policy also permitted the most powerful of them, notably the iron- and coal-industry leaders, to retain a degree of independence that enabled them to wield massive if indirect influence over economic policy. Because neither the Party nor Speer could replace them, Speer was forced to harness them through self-governing mechanisms—the rings and committees culminating in Central Planning—to steer the economy. The crucial link that enabled Speer to control the divergent elements of his system was the Planning Office under Hans Kehrl.

The other indispensable intermediary that physically united the entire system was the Deutsche Reichsbahn. It had matured with the economy both feeding upon and stimulating its growth. Aided by the inland waterway system, the Reichsbahn distributed the economy's life blood—coal. The coal/transport nexus was the very core of the division of labor. As long as it functioned, the mechanism could continue to produce. If it were severed, then the economy would necessarily, though not immediately, crash to the ground. The Reichsbahn was also the conduit for the exchange of semifinished for finished goods, of manufactured articles for food, and for the transport of military formations. The DR was indeed ubiquitous and of transcendent importance.

The Reichsbahn had not expanded its capital base during the 1930s. However a number of technical improvements, when added to its already sound management system, meant that when war erupted it was fully up to its task. Only when the short-war strategy failed was it overburdened. Then it too benefited from Speer's emphasis on efficiency. Albert Ganzenmüller brought fresh blood to the upper levels of management, and it mastered the new challenge. Unused reserves of strength were tapped and because movement of bulk commodities did not increase, the crucial marshalling yards were able to distribute successfully the mushrooming output of the armaments factories. The dispersal program, though ill planned and hurriedly carried out, brought the marshalling yards to the limit of their potential.

Thus by the spring of 1944 Speer had engineered armaments booms in 1942 and the first half of 1944 while staying within the psychological and technological parameters of the administrative and industrial systems. The organism was very finely balanced, with industry and the Reichsbahn both operating at or near maximum attainable efficiency. Speer and his cohorts had used their limited resources to adapt to an unexpected situation very well indeed.

The same cannot be said of the Allied air forces that sought to dismember Speer's system. Most importantly, with a few crucial exceptions and until it was quite late, they misunderstood the nature of the task facing them. Those segments of the Allied apparatus that did approach an accurate understanding were obstructed in translating it into an effective policy. In the end, the air forces succeeded because of the crushing superiority of power at their disposal and because of the successful bureaucratic game played by Sir Arthur Tedder.

The most fundamental mistakes were committed at the outset. MEW overestimated the degree of mobilization imposed upon the German economy and its overall level of efficiency. Consequently it exaggerated both its output and its susceptibility to external pressure. From the spring of 1943 MEW reversed the error, underestimating Germany's effort and output and pessimistically evaluating the potential for economic collapse. MEW was not alone in this. Every other agency engaged in the evaluation of intelligence on the German economy failed to question the universally accepted assumption concerning the Reich's allegedly high level of effort during the critical early years of the war. This was due to lack of preliminary study and, in the case of the Americans during the war, due to intellectual conformity, hasty analysis under deadlines set by command authorities, and mirror imaging. The upshot was that the air planners frequently received faulty advice for target selection.

Confusion concerning both the internal functions and the role of the Reichsbahn was even worse. Until the advent of Tedder and Zuckerman, only a few agencies understood the role of the Reichsbahn and marshalling yards, and they lacked the bureaucratic influence to make their views felt. Most of them, for a time including Zuckerman, confused locomotive strength with a railroad's capacity to move freight. Although Tedder and Zuckerman never fully rid themselves of this misconception, beginning in the summer of 1944 they did sense the importance of marshalling and its crucial relationship to coal as the primary energy source of the German economy, not only as locomotive fuel. No single intelligence organ fully understood the coal/transport nexus and the geographical division of labor though all the pieces of the puzzle had been found. This placed a premium on cooperation. But pooling information and insights proved very difficult under the prevailing atmosphere of interservice, interoffice, and inter-Allied conflict. This prevented the intelligence agencies that were well established in the ETO from putting the puzzle together. They were preoccupied with protecting their institutional turf and disputing prewar claims made for strategic bombing. It took the new group under Tedder and Zuckerman to take a fresh look at the information and formulate a new strategic compromise. They were able to do so precisely because at the outset they were uninvolved in these wrangles and because they stressed cooperation. Just as important, they had immediate access to the key decision makers: Eisenhower, Portal, Spaatz, and Harris.

The Allied intelligence apparatus controlled very powerful tools, which, if used properly and in concert, could have provided it with a sufficiently accurate picture of the disaster that gradually enveloped the German economy beginning in September 1944. But it did not use these tools effectively because it lacked the fundamental understanding of the German economy necessary to do so. Especially Ultra, but also photoreconnaissance and espionage offered information that, if properly exploited in a timely fashion and read in conjunction with the useful general appreciations that were lying on the shelf, could have exerted a beneficial influence over target selection. But errant preconceptions, the bias of bureaucratic politics, and the proliferation of bodies charged with the exploitation of intelligence prevented it. The Americans, EOU in particular, were guilty of mirror imaging and bureaucratic egotism of unusual dimensions in single-mindedly advocating the attack on oil and rejecting transportation out of hand as a viable target system. This is not to suggest that the oil offensive was misguided. Far from it. Rather it means that target selection was prevented from adapting to changing circumstances because of failings in the intelligence system itself. Oil was not crucial to German industry. Even if EOU's prescription had been fulfilled in its entirety, the assault on Germany's petroleum resources could not have harmed the Reich's basic industrial economy and, given the fanaticism of Nazi resistance, could not have ended the war alone. To a degree Sir Arthur Harris was correct in opposing the single-minded attack on narrowly defined target categories. So long as the Germans possessed the means to divert resources among various sectors of the economy they could thwart almost any such attack. The inability to comprehend how the relative importance of target systems changed over time was the greatest failing of Allied intelligence after its fundamental misappreciation of the German industrial effort. It prevented the Allies from formulating a more balanced and flexible air strategy by hindering the shifting of a greater portion of their bombing effort to transportation when it superseded synthetic fuel in importance in the autumn of 1944. Ironically, bad weather was as much the cause of the assault on the Reichsbahn as any decision made by the Allied air commanders. Flexibility of intelligence analysis and decision making was achieved only after the Ardennes offensive.

Misunderstandings of the influence of the time factor were pervasive, and most Allied intelligence analysts and air commanders never overcame them. Most underestimated the time needed for the oil offensive to become effective and overestimated the time in which the transportation offensive would. The majority never realized that the latter had begun to weaken Germany in September 1944.[1] Most importantly, all consistently misapprehended the time frame within which they were operating. Until the Ardennes offensive of December 1944, they repeatedly underestimated the prospective length of hostilities, and afterwards many overestimated it. They were especially prone to searching for rapid solutions that would redound to the prestige of their service. They failed to comprehend the capacity for resistance of a highly developed industrial economy. Only Sir Arthur Tedder sensed that a strategy of weakening the core of the enemy economy was necessary, that concentration need not be defined in narrow geographical terms, that results need not appear immediately, and that if consistently and ruthlessly applied, transportation bombing would paralyze the German economy in a surprisingly short time. Conceptually the transportation system was both sufficiently well defined to enable concentration of effort and functionally broad enough to strike at the root of the German economy while preventing it from shifting resources to counter losses. In this latter respect it was unique. It was this feature that bestowed upon it potentially decisive importance. Moreover, it would complement the oil offensive and perceptibly assist immediate ground operations.

Despite its weaknesses, the Allied air intelligence and command structure did fashion a workable compromise that enabled it to launch a successful offensive against Germany's transportation sector. The attack that was mounted was not perfect: it did not go according to plan. Target selection was not the best, and the enemy was allowed intervals for recuperation. Such is always the case in war. But ultimately the offensive did fulfill Tedder's promise.

Speer and Kehrl concluded from the Overlord transportation offensive that the Reichsbahn and the inland waterways of Germany would be subjected to an even fiercer assault soon after. With a keen appreciation of the working of the time factor, they consciously sought to exploit elasticity of supply to sustain the economy during the anticipated emergency. Beginning in June, basic goods production and non-essential output were cut back and final production of the most important armaments was pressed forward.

Stocks were ordered drawn down. Industry resisted but the gambit succeeded inasmuch as the weapons given priority continued to be turned out in increasing numbers.

The feared storm began in September as Tedder, using his influence with Spaatz and backed by Eisenhower, managed to have transportation raised to special priority. Significant cuts were made in the performance of both the Reichsbahn and the inland waterway system. But the repair crews limited the spread of the paralysis. Sharpened measures to focus on final arms production were implemented and stocks were reduced. The most serious losses in the last area were in coal where winter supplies could not be accumulated and existing caches shrank. The output of selected armaments continued to rise, although the overall armaments production index sank.

Beginning on 1 November the First Transportation Plan caused further reductions in the performance of the transportation system. A major effort by the repair crews and poor target selection allowed the Reichsbahn to rebound during mid-November. But its energies were fatally sapped in the effort. Production continued to rise in certain areas but at an ever slower rate. Speer applied additional managerial palliatives and appointed special deputies to assist him, but the situation was fast slipping from his grasp. The destruction was too great and his own apparatus was disintegrating.

The culmination was reached in late December 1944 and early January 1945. The Ardennes offensive threw the Allies into despair, and Tedder's influence waned. But they responded with an even more terrific pummeling of the Reichsbahn. The effort to support the offensive combined with the effects of three months of pounding from the air broke the DR's back. Coal distribution, with the alternative of water transport denied by bombing, was paralyzed. Car placings spiraled downward ever more rapidly. The hoped-for turn in the military situation did not occur, and Speer's gamble of relying on elasticity rebounded on Germany with a vengeance. Coal stocks were either exhausted or could not be redisposed. Components deliveries were hopelessly snarled. Finished goods could not be delivered. Telecommunications virtually collapsed, rendering centralized control impossible. Then the Red Army seized Silesia and pushed the system into complete collapse. The geographical division of labor was shattered. Production tumbled to levels far below the 33 percent decline set out earlier as a threshold, and it continued down to 1942 levels. Armaments reserves for the army ran perilously short and were virtually impossible to distribute.

The final waves of bombing in February and March only abetted the disintegration that had already set in. By February coherent economic activity had ceased. Speer continued to try to make do with an even more drastic Emergency Program. But the means for its implementation had been wrenched from his grasp by the bombers. The transportation system was in a shambles and telecommunications were in hopeless disarray. Elasticity had rebounded to the extent that, when the Allies finally burst through the military facade and raced across Germany in April 1945, they found the economy moribund. The decisive factor in bringing this about was the bombing of marshalling yards, not the destruction of rolling stock or even the paralysis of the inland waterway system. It was the disruption of marshalling that severed the coal/transport nexus, demolished the division of labor, and contributed heavily to the disorganization of Speer's administrative system.

Speer estimated that Germany could have resisted until early 1946 if the bombing had ceased in September 1944.[2] After that date transportation attacks were the largest component of the Allied bomber offensive as measured by tonnage and the overriding source of Germany's economic difficulties, far outweighing the loss of the occupied territories.[3] The transportation offensive severely weakened the German economy from October 1944 and induced its collapse in early January 1945. Allowing time for the consumption of the few meager reserves remaining with combat units, it can be claimed that the transportation campaign, imperfect as it was, gravely weakened the Wehrmacht from early January 1945 and would have compelled it to abandon organized armed resistance by May or June 1945. In light of Speer's estimate, it can be argued that transportation bombing placed a limit on how long the war could continue. Infighting among the Allied air commanders prevented the campaign from realizing its full potential, causing its fatal influence to be narrowly superseded by the advance of the ground forces. Indisputable and of real importance is the fact that transportation bombing weakened the Wehrmacht's ability to resist during the final six months of the war and ensured that once the Allies broke into Germany no coherent front could be formed against them again.

Transportation bombing did not achieve and could not have achieved victory unaided. Rather it formed a vital component of the strategic compromise that resulted in the ultimate triumph. The attack on Germany's synthetic petroleum industry led to crucial air battles that cemented Allied air superiority and caused a fuel shortage that virtually grounded the Luftwaffe and severely restricted the mobility of the army. Again, though, it must be stressed that the throttling of Germany's petroleum supplies was of military and not economic importance and could not have been decisive alone or even superseded transportation bombing in influence on the final outcome. The Red Army imposed on the German army that debilitating attrition which was the indispensable corollary to the dismemberment by transportation bombing of Germany's industrial organization from within. Of yet greater importance was the armies' occupation of territory. The loss of Upper Silesia was of inestimable economic significance, especially in conjunction with the isolation of the Saar. In contrast, direct damage to factories made little difference so long as Germany could redistribute resources to repair them and compensate for their temporary reduction in output. With the paralysis of the transportation system such substitution was no longer possible. But ultimately the decisive factor was psychological. The transportation offensive, coming hard on the heels of the devastating blows to the hydrogenation plants and at the same time as the Allied armies closed in on the Reich's borders, gravely weakened the morale of Germany's economic leaders. They continued to resist at lower levels of commitment because of a sense of patriotic duty and their inability to counter the last fanatical outpouring of Nazi hysteria. Only when Germany was overrun and when Hitler died did the will to resist finally flicker out. It was this combination of mutually reinforcing pressures that encompassed the demise of the Third Reich on 8 May 1945.

The history of the Deutsche Reichsbahn and the German economy under Albert Speer and their struggle against Allied bombing suggest a few observations of enduring significance. At the most basic level they make clear the importance of transportation to the operation of any modern industrial economy. More particularly, the Reichsbahn's experience illustrates how a sound organization that has prepared for difficulties in advance can resist massive external pressure for a prolonged period if its leaders do not tamper with it during a crisis. To the end, the Reichsbahn was inventive, flexible, and persistent in attempting to perform its economic tasks. It represented the best of traditional German civil service practice in that it loyally and efficiently made an unstinting effort to serve the state. It also embodied the worst of the old ideal of unquestioning submission to superior authority whatever its ends.

The crucial importance of mastering the flow of data is well illustrated by Speer's system. The improved exploitation of raw materials and labor and the better use of the Reichsbahn would have been impossible without the creation of the ZVL and the Planning Office. Speer's production success also demonstrates how enhanced efficiency can achieve rapid increases in industrial output. Germany's long resistance in the face of heavy odds demonstrates that complex modern industrial economies frequently possess unknown reserves of strength that can be tapped by creative managers acting energetically in peace or war. The greatest obstacles to their doing so are the political definitions of what is economically feasible and desirable. Moreover, this account clearly reinforces the notion that business may not subordinate the profit motive to the national interest even in times of direst crisis and that Nazism and big capitalism were only allies of convenience.

Looked at from the military perspective, it may be contended that strategic bombing can make a significant contribution to victory in war. But it is not a substitute for a balanced strategy encompassing every component of a nation's military power. It is peculiarly reliant on accurate intelligence, sensibly interpreted. Above all, strategic bombing is not a cheap, easy, or quick avenue to success. It involves a major investment of national resources to build a force powerful enough to be effective. To be successful, strategic bombing requires simultaneous and repeated strikes against a small number of indispensable sectors of the enemy economy after air superiority has been won.

Reconsideration of the assault on the Reichsbahn offers no more than these general guidelines. The slavish application of a similar strategy to another bombing offensive in the future would fail as abysmally as did the simplistic application of the oil and "interdiction" strategies to North Vietnam between 1965 and 1968. Each war presents new and unique problems for which the past provides no obvious solutions. Moreover there is no insurance against the bureaucratic egotism that caused both the Allies and the Nazis so much difficulty. Only the careful selection of responsible leaders

and the subordination of the military to a broadly based, democrati-
cally chosen government can mitigate their influence. It must also
be recalled that doggedness and resourcefulness can stymie a force
enjoying mere material superiority if that preponderance is not well
used. Ignorance of the Reichsbahn's stubborn struggle against overwhelming odds and the overriding importance of the psychological
and time factors in the final collapse of Nazi Germany help to explain the frustration of the American air effort over North Vietnam
between 1965 and 1968. This point assumes greater importance
when it is recalled that some of the same personalities who helped
the Eighth Air Force select targets and who obstructed the transportation offensive during 1944 played key roles in establishing the
strategy to bomb North Vietnam. Forty years after the events described here the concept of strategic bombing, albeit in new permutations, continues to be a source of heated debate. That is in large
part because the brave struggle of the Deutsche Reichsbahn related
here has been misunderstood.

Appendix

Table A.1

German Hard Coal Production (× 1,000 metric tons—lesser areas excluded)

Coal economy year	Reich With Protectorate	Without Protectorate	Ruhr	Upper Silesia	Saar
1937/38	—	188,067	129,823	25,410	13,733
1938/39	—	187,481	126,916	26,940	14,516
1939/40	214,581	204,797	129,451	44,569	11,858
1940/41	257,966	247,880	129,801	86,428	12,873
1941/42	257,697	248,260	129,239	83,688	17,092
1942/43	274,417	264,515	131,183	93,951	20,734
1943/44	278,118	268,297	125,356	101,512	22,878
Apr.	23,197	22,380	10,899	8,060	1,843
May	22,227	21,387	9,848	8,149	1,836
June	22,311	21,488	9,929	8,165	1,863
July	23,409	22,564	10,420	8,597	1,958
Aug.	22,584	21,776	9,964	8,367	1,895
Sept.	22,638	21,831	10,078	8,339	1,908
Oct.	23,124	22,311	10,357	8,480	1,920
Nov.	23,824	23,012	10,883	8,655	1,922
Dec.	23,685	22,877	10,893	8,545	1,892
Jan.	23,364	22,563	10,554	8,518	1,953
Feb.	23,065	22,276	10,482	8,432	1,880
Mar.	24,690	23,832	11,049	9,205	2,008
1944/45					
Apr.	22,478	21,706	10,037	8,412	1,865
May	23,736	22,917	10,705	8,789	1,919
June	23,169	22,379	10,339	8,726	1,865
July	22,629	21,854	10,143	8,450	1,829
Aug.	22,579	21,844	10,417	8,076	1,890
Sept.	18,797	18,140	9,381	7,074	708
Oct.	16,259	15,601	7,194	7,008	543
Nov.	14,188	13,518	5,228	6,744	642
Dec.	14,332	13,652	5,352	7,219	208
Jan.	11,344	—	5,740	4,127	211
Feb.	6,983	—	4,666	946	311
Mar.	—	—	2,015 ca.	—	—

Sources: RVK, Statistischer Bericht Nr. 13, p. 3, BBA 15/1103; RMfRuK, Planungs-amt, "Steinkohlenförderung und Kokserzeugung in regionaler Gliederung," Dr. Eb./Rg, Berlin, 16 March 1945, BA R3/1930, f. 553 for January and February 1945; GBL-West, "Wochenbericht GBL-West 17–23 März 1945," Geheim, Bad Wildungen, 23 March 1945, BA R5/111 for March 1945.

Table A.2

German Brown Coal Production (× 1,000 metric tons)

Coal economy year	Reich With Protectorate	Without Protectorate	East Elbia	Central Germany	Rhineland
1937/38	—	187,228	47,143	82,405	56,322
1938/39	—	199,564	52,153	86,998	58,934
1939/40	—	211,606	56,602	92,856	60,876
1940/41	227,493	226,753	61,402	100,572	63,531
1941/42	235,978	235,131	63,675	104,587	65,547
1942/43	249,783	248,850	66,357	111,148	70,097
1943/44	253,366	252,488	68,334	114,702	68,116
Apr.	20,852	20,781	5,517	9,321	5,833
May	24,505	21,429	5,747	9,619	5,968
June	20,735	20,665	5,643	9,302	5,641
July	21,321	21,252	5,950	9,784	5,433
Aug.	21,016	20,944	5,810	9,441	5,607
Sept.	20,898	20,830	5,694	9,435	5,618
Oct.	21,466	21,397	5,863	9,709	5,721
Nov.	20,819	20,740	5,613	9,625	5,361
Dec.	20,995	20,913	5,570	9,600	5,599
Jan.	21,281	21,207	5,615	9,660	5,794
Feb.	20,274	20,202	5,449	9,078	5,545
Mar.	22,204	22,128	5,863	10,128	5,996
1944/45					
Apr.	20,385	20,322	5,510	9,362	5,369
May	20,402	20,335	5,635	8,846	5,779
June	19,731	19,665	5,412	8,545	5,624
July	19,619	19,554	5,597	8,294	5,587
Aug.	19,360	19,292	5,656	8,110	5,431
Sept.	17,512	17,437	5,422	8,033	3,894
Oct.	16,944	16,873	5,660	8,560	2,556
Nov.	15,753	15,680	5,634	8,553	1,388
Dec.	15,250	15,181	5,759	7,846	1,488
Jan.	—	15,318	3,498	8,876	1,287
Feb.	—	11,901	2,674	7,565	1,000

Sources: RVK, Statistischer Bericht Nr. 13, p. 6, BBA 15/1103; RMfRuK, Planungs-amt, "Braun- u. Hartbraunkohlenförderung in regionaler Gliederung," Dr. Eb./Rg, Berlin, 16 March 1945, BA R3/1930, f. 554.

Table A.3

Reichsbahn Freight Car Placings

Coal economy year	Total freight cars	Hard coal	Brown coal
1940/41	48,373,843	16,755,046	7,021,224
1941/42	44,321,721	16,566,984	7,179,648
1942/43	47,947,837	17,704,156	7,872,571
1943/44	48,401,403	18,332,517	8,029,474
Apr.	4,212,504	1,543,563	724,882
May	4,314,253	1,510,917	737,670
June	4,244,053	1,542,558	719,569
July	4,425,408	1,587,478	727,545
Aug.	4,147,549	1,562,702	714,775
Sept.	4,053,384	1,549,386	692,166
Oct.	4,140,404	1,487,124	636,948
Nov.	3,814,007	1,426,495	572,132
Dec.	3,672,800	1,435,911	567,684
Jan.	3,773,474	1,567,836	640,645
Feb.	3,626,078	1,506,356	607,162
Mar.	3,977,489	1,612,191	688,296
1944/45			
Apr.	3,805,508	1,527,737	668,427
May	3,992,116	1,596,763	672,884
June	4,007,934	1,585,631	664,626
July	3,969,625	1,480,723	667,521
Aug.	3,940,944	1,393,692	666,957
Sept.	3,442,133	1,086,075	612,272
Oct.	3,241,506	883,443	568,058
Nov.	2,976,302	850,323	542,347
Dec.	2,570,707	888,779	508,235
Jan.	1,877,738	690,573	475,183
Feb.	1,069,322	—	—

Source: RZA, Blätter 90, 91, 92, NA RG 243, 200(a)95, 96, 97.

Table A.4

Reichsbahn Hard Coal Car Placings (in 10-ton units)

Year		Ruhr	Saar[a]	Upper Silesia	Total
1943	Jan.	630,253	141,749	622,208	1,524,162
	Feb.	572,756	140,144	630,613	1,462,673
	Mar.	645,983	156,855	719,774	1,659,237
	Apr.	607,103	150,487	655,464	1,543,563
	May	565,795	152,747	665,949	1,510,917
	June	565,214	158,574	691,447	1,542,558
	July	569,988	163,072	725,830	1,587,478
	Aug.	561,201	161,074	711,011	1,562,702
	Sept.	572,905	158,644	691,651	1,549,386
	Oct.	555,527	151,528	658,349	1,487,124
	Nov.	501,732	152,961	661,614	1,426,495
	Dec.	543,638	158,350	620,589	1,435,911
1944	Jan.	618,420	167,008	654,460	1,567,836
	Feb.	582,193	148,762	657,221	1,506,356
	Mar.	618,566	156,930	709,591	1,612,191
	Apr.	580,211	150,263	684,001	1,527,737
	May	591,430	149,682	734,392	1,596,763
	June	605,006	155,178	706,485	1,585,631
	July	586,117	146,640	633,170	1,480,723
	Aug.	565,143	135,470	582,330	1,393,692
	Sept.	436,246	52,068	524,222	1,086,075
	Oct.	252,595	35,967	532,562	883,443
	Nov.	232,210	49,890	503,741	850,323
	Dec.	253,330	9,024	558,198	888,779
1945	Jan.	299,632	10,509	315,175	690,573
	Feb.	215,368	15,835	65,773	318,542
	Mar.	66,129	15,197	72,570	368,753

Sources: RZA, Blatt 92, January 1943–January 1945; RVK, "Wagenstellung für Kohlen nach Revieren," BA R10 VIII/16, ff. 629, 631.

a. From November 1943 the Saar and Lorraine regions were combined by the Reichsbahn for the purpose of counting coal cars. The figures for the preceding months have been altered to facilitate comparison by adding together the figures for the two regions.

Table A.5
Inland Waterway Coal Movements, Hard and Brown Coal Combined
(× 1,000 metric tons)

Coal economy year	Total	Ruhr	Upper Silesia
1940/41	34,234	25,825	3,600
1941/42	34,920	27,561	3,444
1942/43	39,367	30,495	3,865
1943/44	30,182	23,071	2,880
Apr.	3,293	2,416	413
May	2,701	1,926	312
June	3,007	2,141	374
July	3,207	2,337	391
Aug.	2,659	2,080	248
Sept.	2,081	1,723	103
Oct.	2,309	1,898	126
Nov.	1,713	1,446	90
Dec.	1,934	1,587	118
Jan.	2,168	1,578	159
Feb.	2,345	1,804	217
Mar.	2,765	2,035	329
1944/45			
Apr.	2,672	2,001	315
May	3,112	2,207	446
June	3,059	2,207	421
July	3,131	2,352	317
Aug.	2,919	2,134	386
Sept.	2,283	1,752	227
Oct.	1,251	724	269
Nov.	979	433	379
Dec.	422	—	213

Source: RVK, Statistischer Bericht Nr. 13, p. 20, BBA 15/1103.

Table A.6

Estimated Hard Coal Deficit Caused by Shipping Difficulties (in million metric tons)[a]

| | | Reichsbahn | | Inland waterways | | |
		Shortfall	Cumulative	Shortfall	Cumulative	Total
1944	Aug.	1.7	1.7	—	—	1.7
	Sept.	4.8	6.5	0.25	0.25	6.8
	Oct.	5.7	12.2	0.89	1.1	13.3
	Nov.	5.9	18.2	0.96	2.1	20.3
	Dec.	5.6	23.8	0.73	2.8	26.6
1945	Jan.	8.7	32.5	1.2	3.9	36.5

Sources: Statistische Mitteilungen des Reichsbahn-Zentralamts Berlin, Blatt 92, January 1943–January 1945, "Wagenstellung für Kohlen, Koks und Brikette," NA RG 243, 200(a)96; RVK, Statistischer Bericht Nr. 13, pp. 15, 20, BBA 15/1103; Badisches Hafenamt, "Aufstellung über den Verkehr in den Mannheimer Häfen," NA RG 243, 200(a)165; "Durchgangs-Verkehr der Wichtigen Schleusen des Dortmund-Ems-Kanals," NA RG 243, 200(a)168.

a. The deficit was determined by comparing shipments in the coal economy year 1943/44 with those in 1944/45.

Table A.7
Reichsbahn Freight Car Placing Comparison

	Δ% I 1943–44	Δ% II 1943–44	Δ% III 1943–44	Δ% Special priority	Δ% First transportation plan	Δ% Ardennes offensive	Δ% CSTC interim	Δ% Ruhr plan
Reichsbahn	−1.83	−7.75	−4.22	−20.05	−22.84	−43.2	−70.44	−89.18%
RBD Essen	−0.94	−4.6	−9.67	−42.1	−59.96	−60.85	−66.71	
RBD Wuppertal	−1.81	−3.73	−5.7	−15.99	−37.37	−58.02	−66.13	
RBD Cologne	+7.59	−11.75	−9.05	−65.97	−78.46	−83.78	−86.00	
RBD Münster	+5.76	−4.59	−16.99	−36.39	−21.39	−31.02	−53.82	
RBD Saarbrücken	−1.35	−13.46	−34.41	−69.01	−75.46	−96.35	−89.27	
RBD Karlsruhe	−8.01	−11.84	−19.65	−22.83	−39.67	−72.41	−82.53	
RBD Stuttgart	−5.29	−3.54	−13.09	−27.51	−18.95	−52.00	−61.10	
RBD Kassel	−2.99	−3.07	−7.27	−25.86	−16.25	−45.30	−57.66	
RBD Hanover	+24.96	−8.63	−8.62	−14.09	−21.2	−29.93	−49.64	
RBD Berlin	−7.95	−19.46	−15.08	−8.84	+8.58	−15.99	−47.08	
RBD Halle	+3.94	−9.27	−6.14	−0.4	+1.49	−19.59	−44.16	
RBD Oppeln	+2.05	−1.09	−15.96	−17.35	−17.10	−13.16 ca.	−90.38 ca.	

Sources: RZA, Blatt 90, January 1943–January 1945, NA RG 243, 200(a)94, 95, 96, 116, 117; Wagenführ, *Deutsche Industrie*, p. 94; Wehde-Textor, "Dokumentarische Darstellung," p. 38, BA R5, Anh I/11; Wissenschaftliche Beratungsstelle, "Verkehrszahlen für die Besprechung," Pla 080/20-382/45g, 12.3, Geheim, Berlin, 12 March 1945, p. 1, BA R5/3699.

Table A.8

The GBLs and Their Directorates

GBL-West	GBL-South	GBL-East
RBD Essen	RBD Augsburg	RBD Berlin
Frankfurt/Main	Erfurt	Breslau
Hamburg	Karlsruhe	Danzig
Hanover	Munich	Dresden
Kassel	Nuremberg	Halle
Cologne	Linz	Hamburg (eastern part)
Mainz	Regensburg	Königsberg
Saarbrücken	Stuttgart	Oppeln
Wuppertal	Villach	Osten
		Posen
		Schwerin
		Stettin
		Vienna

Table A.9

Reichsbahn Coal Car Placing Targets, 24 May 1944

RBD	Units per day
Osten	60
Breslau	1,330
Oppeln	26,000
Hanover	930
Münster	370
Kassel	240
Halle	11,680
Dresden	6,580
Essen	20,850
Cologne	6,750
Saarbrücken	6,000
Frankfurt/Main	10
Erfurt	600
Augsburg	40
Munich	340
Regensburg	1,520
Vienna	950
Villach	300
Total	84,700

Source: Hauptwagenamt, WD 141 Vwbo 17, Berlin, 24 May 1944, BA R5/3181.

Table A.10
Germany's Coal Syndicates

Syndicate	Headquarters
Rhenish-Westphalian Coal Syndicate	Essen
Upper Silesian Hard Coal Syndicate	Berlin, Gleiwitz
Lower Silesian Hard Coal Syndicate	Waldenburg
Saxon Hard Coal Syndicate	Zwickau
Lower Saxon Coal Syndicate	Hanover
Coal Syndicate for Rhenish Bavaria	Munich
Ostmark Coal Syndicate	Vienna
Central German Brown Coal Syndicate	Leipzig
East Elbian Brown Coal Syndicate	Berlin
Rhenish Brown Coal Syndicate	Cologne
Sudeten Brown Coal Syndicate	Aussig
Gas Coke Syndicate	Berlin

Source: RWKS, "Entwicklung und derzeitiger Stand der kohlenwirtschaftlicher Gesetzgebung," G/Da., pp. 4–5, BBA 15/471 (1).

Table A.11
Syndicate Trading Companies of the RWKS

Kohlenkontor Hamburg
Handelsgesellschaft Bremen
Handelsgesellschaft Hannover, "Westfalia"
Handelsgesellschaft Dortmund
Westfälische Kohlen-& Koksverkaufgesellschaft, Magdeburg
Kohlenhandelsgesellschaft Hagen
Kohlenhandelsgesellschaft Köln
Kohlenhandelsgesellschaft Kassel, Hansa, Glückauf
Westfälische Kohlenverkaufsgesellschaft Berlin
Kohlenhandelsgesellschaft Westmark, Saarbrücken
Kohlenkontor Mannheim, Weyhenmeyer
Geschaftstelle Wien

Source: RWKS, "Entwicklung und derzeitiger Stand der kohlenwirtschaftlichen Gesetzgebung," G/Da, pp. 4–5, BBA 15/471 (1).

198

Figure A.1 *Armaments Production and Railroad Performance, 1943–1945*

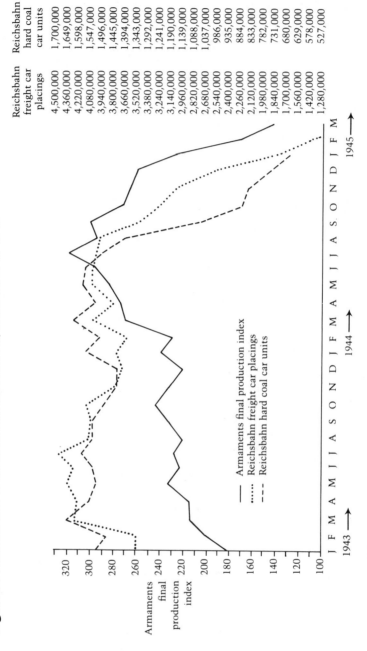

Sources: Wagenführ, *Deutsche Industrie*, pp. 66, 114, 178; RZA, Blätter 90, 91, 92, NA RG 243, 200(a)95, 96, 97.

Notes

Abbreviations

In addition to the abbreviations found in the text, the following abbreviations are used in the notes.

BA	Bundesarchiv (Federal Archives, Koblenz)
BA/MA	Bundesarchiv/Militärarchiv (Federal Archives, Military Branch, Freiburg-im-Breisgau)
BBA	Deutsches Bergbau-Archiv (German Mining Archive, Bochum)
BBSU	British Bombing Survey Unit
C&C	Wesley Frank Craven and James Lea Cate, *The Army Air Forces in World War II*
Coal Survey	USSBS, Records of the USSBS, "National Coal Statistics Office, Essen-Bredeney, Coal Deliveries, Coal Consumption, and Coal Stock Left from the Largest Industries," NA RG 243, 30(d), 30(e)
DRZWK	Wilhelm Deist, ed., *Das Deutsche Reich und der Zweite Weltkrieg*
EOU War Diary	Walt W. Rostow, "Economic Outpost with Economic Warfare Division, War Diary of the OSS London, Enemy Objectives Unit to April 30, 1945," 10 vols., NA RG 226
FIAT	Field Information Agency Technical
FO	Foreign Office (Great Britain)
Fwi Amt	Feldwirtschaftsamt (Field Economics Office in OKW)
Ic/Wi	Feindliche Lage/Wirtschaft (Enemy Intelligence, Economics Section of OKL)
GWK	Gauwirtschaftskammer (Gau Economic Chamber)
NA	National Archives, Washington, D.C.
Nachrichten	Nachrichten des Reichsministers für Rüstung und Kriegsproduktion (Newsletter of the Reich Minister of Armaments and War Production)
OKW/KTB	Percy Ernst Schramm, ed., *Kriegstagebuch des Oberkommandos der Wehrmacht* (Armed Forces High Command War Diary)
PRO	Public Record Office, Kew, London, Great Britain
Rü In	Rüstungsinspektion (Armaments Inspectorate)
Rü Kdo	Rüstungskommando (Armaments Command)
RWWAzK	Rheinisch-Westfälisches Wirtschaftsarchiv zu Köln (Rhenish-Westphalian Economics Archive in Cologne)

SSBzKP	Statistischer Schnellberichte zur Kriegsproduktion (Statistical Summary of War Production)
USAFHRC	United States Air Force Historical Research Center, Maxwell Air Force Base, Ala.
W&F	Sir Charles Webster and Noble Frankland, *The Strategic Air Offensive Against Germany*
WWi O	Wehrwirtschaftsoffizier (Defense Economics Officer)
Wk	Wehrkreis (Military District)
ZP	Zentrale Planung (Central Planning)

Preface

1. The most notable are Boelcke, *Wirtschaft;* Deist, *The Wehrmacht and German Rearmament;* DRZWK, vol. 1; Overy, *Goering,* "Heavy Industry and the State," "Hitler's War and the German Economy," and *The Nazi Economic Recovery.*

2. Kreidler, *Eisenbahnen.* While very informative, Kreidler's book gives only a skeletal account of the Reichsbahn's economic role and falls into the category of postwar West German histories that seek as much to exonerate their subjects for the defeat as to clarify the war years.

3. Only a very few merit mention, though even they are not fully reliable. Air Ministry, *Rise and Fall of the German Air Force;* Cooper, *German Air Force;* Murray, *Strategy for Defeat;* Freeman, *The Mighty Eighth;* Coffey, *Decision over Schweinfurt.*

4. W&F, 4 vols.; C&C, 7 vols. The USSBS issued 208 reports on the bombing of Germany from 1945 to 1947. See in this regard USSBS, *Summary Report (European War), Overall Report (European War),* and *German War Economy.* Useful secondary accounts include Hastings, *Bomber Command;* Frankland, *Bomber Offensive,* and *The Bombing Offensive Against Germany;* Verrier, *The Bomber Offensive;* Wagenführ, *Deutsche Industrie,* esp. pp. 91–129; Janssen, *Das Ministerium Speer,* esp. pp. 235–322; Weyres, "Die deutsche Rüstungswirtschaft," esp. pp. 107–8, 150–64; Milward, *War, Economy and Society.*

5. The most useful work in this very limited category is Golücke, *Schweinfurt und der strategische Luftkrieg.* This book is marred by its wholesale quotation in translation from English-language works. The best studies of particular industries remain the reports prepared by the USSBS. Only they escape the obsession with operations to the neglect of their consequences. Sweetman's *Operation Chastise* is also worth consulting.

6. See especially Rostow, *Pre-Invasion Bombing Strategy,* and Lytton, "Bombing Policy," pp. 53–58.

7. See Deist, *The Wehrmacht and German Rearmament;* DRZWK, vol. 1; Overy, *Goering,* "Heavy Industry and the State," "Hitler's War and the German Economy," and *The Nazi Economic Recovery.*

8. The transport of the Jews to the death camps was unimportant from the perspective of transport operations for three reasons. First, the camps

were situated on heavily traveled routes behind the Eastern Front and in
Silesia and therefore did not create diversionary flows. Second, they received low priority, as the delays reported by witnesses attest. They moved
more slowly than coal trains that weighed more than twice as much because they were pulled by older and weaker locomotives. Third, the overall
volume of cars and locomotives involved was minute. Using statistics developed by Raul Hilberg, it can be estimated that no more than 3,000 trains
were used to take Jews to the death camps between October 1941 and
October 1944. This equalled about 15 percent of the number of freight
trains run each day by the Reichsbahn. Clearly even if the estimate is doubled or tripled there would be no statistical difference. None of this is
intended to diminish the moral significance of this traffic. It is conceivable
that the death transports denied logistical support to the Wehrmacht on
the Eastern Front at critical junctures by diverting car space. See Hilberg,
"German Railroads/Jewish Souls," pp. 67, 70, and *Sonderzüge nach Auschwitz*, pp. 61, 63, 71, 78, 81, 89, 96; Lichtenstein, "Räder rollen für den
Mord," pp. 86–99, and *Mit der Reichsbahn in den Tod*, pp. 9, 34, 56, 96.

Chapter 1

1. Ganzenmüller, "Eisenbahner und Eisenbahnerinnen!," p. 1, BA R5
Anh II/45.

2. Schweitzer, *Big Business*, p. 334; Petzina, *Autarkiepolitik* (Petzina's
figures presented on p. 183, table 17, differ only slightly); Mitchell, *European Historical Statistics*, pp. 65, 68, table B2. The 1929 GNP of 90 billion
RM was first exceeded in 1937 when it reached 93 billion RM. The unemployment rate of 8.4 percent of 1928 was matched again only in 1936 with
a rate of 8.3 percent.

3. Petzina, *Autarkiepolitik*, pp. 50–51; Treue, "Hitlers Denkschrift,"
esp. pp. 195, 199, 208–9. Birkenfeld, *Synthetische Treibstoff*, pp. 84–93,
114; Riedel, *Eisen und Kohle*, pp. 90–96. USSBS, *Aircraft Industry*, pp. 15–
16; Heinkel, *Stormy Life*, pp. 148–49; Homze, *Arming the Luftwaffe*, pp.
46–220.

4. USSBS, *Oil Division Final Report*, p. 16; Birkenfeld, *Synthetische
Treibstoff*, pp. 102–7.

5. Riedel, *Eisen und Kohle*, p. 163; Overy, "Heavy Industry and the
State."

6. Riedel, *Eisen und Kohle*, p. 159. Göring ordered the formation of the
RWHG on July 1937.

7. Ibid., pp. 12–15, 21, 81.

8. Kube, *Pour le Mérite und Hakenkreuz*, p. 259. See also *DRZWK*,
1:497–98, 500, 530 for the confusion reigning among the military.

9. Riedel, *Eisen und Kohle*, p. 251. The first raw iron was smelted on 22
October 1939.

10. Boelcke, *Wirtschaft*, pp. 178, 185–87.

11. USSBS, *German War Economy*, pp. 73–74; Carroll, *Total War*, p. 158.

12. Schweitzer, *Big Business*, p. 336.

13. Petzina, *Autarkiepolitik*, p. 187, table 20; Schweitzer, *Big Business*, p. 334; Boelcke, "Kriegsfinanzierung," p. 56, Abbildung I. See also Boelcke's *Kosten*, p. 51, table 15. Using the statistics provided here, arms spending rose to 17 percent of GNP in 1938.

14. By 1917 defense spending accounted for about half of the Reich GNP and over nine-tenths of government spending. See Mitchell, *European Historical Statistics*, pp. 377, 411; Gerd Hardach, *The First World War*, p. 155, table 21; Karl Hardach, *Political Economy of Germany*, pp. 10, 224, table 21(A), 225, table 21(B). For a discussion of standards by which to evaluate national mobilization for war see Carroll, *Total War*, p. 189.

15. Petzina, *Autarkiepolitik*, p. 187, table 20; Milward, *War, Economy and Society*, p. 76.

16. On the haste of the Nazis' economic preparations see Volkmann, "NS-Wirtschaft," *DRZWK*, 1:248.

17. Based on statistics in Wagenführ, *Deutsche Industrie*, p. 17, and Boelcke, "Kriegsfinanzierung," p. 56, Abbildung I. This was the case whether one uses direct military spending or overall government expenditure. The later rose by about a fifth per year until 1938–39 when it jumped 58.2 percent and 1939–40 when it leaped by 81.6 percent. During the same years, Wehrmacht and armaments spending increased by 124.4 percent and 106.5 percent respectively after growth at an average annual rate of 52 percent. Even wartime increases did not approach these figures. These statistics are eloquent testimony to the haste and superficiality of the Nazi military preparations. In his latest work Boelcke provides somewhat different statistics. Using these, the largest percentage increase in arms spending including Mefo bills (87 percent) came in 1936. The largest real increase occurred in 1938 (RM 6.3 billion) but represented only a 57 percent rise compared to 1937. Nevertheless, Boelcke concludes that the most significant increase in economic activity due to arms spending occurred in 1938. See Boelcke, *Kosten*, p. 28, table 6, pp. 53–54.

18. Boelcke, *Kosten*, p. 54.

19. Barkai, *Wirtschaftssystem*, p. 15; Broszat, *Der Staat Hitlers*, pp. 219–20, and *The Hitler State*, p. 165. See also Schweitzer, *Big Business*, pp. 123–25, for the Schmitt-Hitler Agreement of July 1933.

20. Carroll, *Total War*, pp. 148–50.

21. Thomas, *Wehr- und Rüstungs Wirtschaft*, pp. 62–68.

22. Ibid., pp. 91–92, 98–104.

23. The Reichsstellen appeared in 1939 in the RWM as successors to the former exchange control boards. Some of the Economic Chambers and Chambers of Commerce and Industry were combined to form Gau Economic Chambers (Gauwirtschaftskammern) in April 1942. Essenwein-Rothe, *Wirtschaftsverbände*, p. 19. Neumann, *Behemoth*, pp. 241–47, 251; Boelcke, *Wirtschaft*, pp. 82–88; Broszat, *Der Staat Hitlers*, pp. 218–30 (pp. 164–72 in *The Hitler State*).

24. Petzina, *Autarkiepolitik*, pp. 50–51; Treue, "Hitlers Denkschrift," pp.

184–203, esp. pp. 195, 199. Kube, *Pour le Mérite und Hakenkreuz*, pp. 299, 303.

25. Barkai, "Sozialdarwinismus und Antiliberalismus," pp. 59–83.
26. Neumann, *Behemoth*, p. 80; Treue, "Hitlers Denkschrift," p. 199.
27. Herbst, *Totale Krieg*, pp. 92, 99.
28. Becker, "German War Economy under Speer," p. 49.
29. Picker et al., *Hitlers Tischgespräche*, p. 54; Hitler, *Mein Kampf*, pp. 239, 247.
30. Milward, *War, Economy and Society*, pp. 113–17; Herbst, *Totale Krieg*, pp. 78–81; Schoenbaum, *Hitler's Social Revolution*, pp. 86–90.
31. Ludwig, *Technik und Ingenieure*, pp. 44–58, 360–64.
32. See, for example, the Hossbach Memorandum in *Akten zur deutschen auswärtigen Politik 1918–1945*, series D, 1:25–26; Domarus, *Hitler: Reden und Proklamationen*, 2:1421; Cooper, *German Army*, p. 52, citing General von Weichs's notes on a talk given by Hitler on 28 February 1934.
33. Milward, *German Economy*, pp. 7–8, 11–12; Carroll, *Total War*, pp. 100–101. The military particularly favored the rapid, indeed constant, redisposition of weapons programs. Overy, *Goering*, pp. 86, 98, 107–8, 138–50, contends that Göring conducted a policy of broad capital expansion and deep rearmament that contradicted Hitler's plans and failed due to managerial ineptitude. His argument ignores the fact that Hitler never fully confided in anyone, including Göring. Hitler considered the Reichsmarschall as an instrument for the achievement of his own ends like all of his other subordinates. See Turner, *Hitler: Memoires of a Confidant*, p. 175.
34. On the armored warfare idea see Heinz-Ludger Borgert, "Grundzüge der Landkriegsführung," pp. 537–38, 546, 559, 561, 569; on Hitler's views relating to war preparations see Picker et al., *Hitlers Tischgespräche*, pp. 217, 351, 474. For Hitler's views on armored warfare see his article in the *Illustrierte Beobachter*, Heft 39 (1929): 490–92; on motorization and tanks, Picker et al., *Hitlers Tischgespräche*, pp. 207, 402, and Hitler, *Mein Kampf*, p. 958. Hitler's ideas on the form of the next war can be sampled in Rauschning, *Gespräche mit Hitler*, pp. 16–21. Consider also his statement concerning the invasion of Poland made on 22 August 1939: "Bei der Operationen sei Schnelligkeit in der Herbeiführung der Entscheidung von höchster Wichtigkeit," reprinted in *OKW/KTB*, 2:948. On the failure of the home front in World War I see Hitler, *Mein Kampf*, pp. 254–57, 265, 308–9, 313. Michael Salewski, "Die bewaffnete Macht im Dritten Reich," pp. 116–17, 143–44, along with the sources cited above relating to the concept of Blitzkrieg economics and Treue's discussion of the Four Year Plan memorandum are useful in relation to Hitler's timetable for rearmament.
35. Ludwig, *Technik und Ingenieure*, pp. 349–50; Carroll, *Total War*, p. 218; Milward, *German Economy*, p. 57; Seidler, *Todt*, p. 239.
36. Ludwig, *Technik und Ingenieure*, pp. 352, 354, 358; Thomas, *Wehr- und Rüstungs Wirtschaft*, pp. 231–32.
37. Ludwig, *Technik und Ingenieure*, pp. 382, 388–89, 393.
38. Cooper, *German Army*, pp. 333–37; Erickson, *Road to Stalingrad*, pp.

249–96. From June to December the army depots in the East sent only 348 MK.IV medium tanks to the front and received a mere 80 replacements. The picture was the same with the MK.III: 1,456 were dispatched while 385 were accepted. See *OKW/KTB*, 2:1104–21.

39. Wagenführ, *Deutsche Industrie*, p. 189.

40. RMfRuK, Planungsamt, "38. Wochenbericht des Planungsamtes" Pla 1401/29.9, Geheime Reichssache, Berlin, 29 September 1944, p. 11, BA R3/1957, f. 498.

41. Adolf Hitler, "Rüstung 1942," Nr. 1/42 g.K. OKW/WFSt/Org. = Wi-Rü Amt, Geheime Kommandosache, Führer Hauptquartier, 10 January 1942, in *OKW/KTB*, 2:1265–67, also in Thomas, *Wehr- und Rüstungs Wirtschaft*, appendix 2, document 16b, pp. 483–87.

42. Milward, *German Economy*, p. 68; Milward, *War, Economy and Society*, pp. 56–57.

43. Ludwig, *Technik und Ingenieure*, pp. 402–3; Müller, "Tod Dr. Fritz Todt," pp. 602–4; Hansen, "Fall Todt," pp. 604–5.

44. Milward, *German Economy*, p. 67; Thomas, *Wehr- und Rüstungs Wirtschaft*, pp. 153–56, 288, and appendix 2, documents 15 and 16; Carroll, *Total War*, pp. 86–91.

45. Boelcke, *Wirtschaft*, pp. 233, 244; Homze, *Foreign Labor*, p. 16, n. 31; Thomas, *Wehr- und Rüstungs Wirtschaft*, p. 155; for an overview of these affairs see Carroll, *Total War*, p. 232, and Seidler, *Todt*, pp. 252–65.

46. Schmidt, *Albert Speer*, pp. 77–81. Schmidt accepts Speer's account in its general import.

47. Speer, *Inside*, pp. 200–202.

48. Janssen, *Das Ministerium Speer*, p. 56.

49. Boelcke, *Deutschlands Rüstung*, pp. 28–29; Picker et al., *Hitlers Tischgespräche*, pp. 225–26.

50. Speer, *Inside*, pp. 218–19; Janssen, *Das Ministerium Speer*, pp. 60–61; Homze, *Foreign Labor*, pp. 105–6.

51. Becker, "German War Economy under Speer," pp. 118–19; Göring's order of 22 April 1942 for the creation of Central Planning can be found in BA R3/1562. A description of the body can be seen in "Nachrichten des Reichsministers für Bewaffnung und Munition," Nr. 2, 25 April 1942, p. 6, Item 5, cited in Weyres, "Die deutsche Rüstungswirtschaft," p. 8.

52. For an overview of these affairs see Carroll, *Total War*, p. 232.

53. Kehrl, *Krisenmanager*, p. 284. Kehrl was forty-two years old and owned a textile mill in Cottbus. He joined the NSDAP on 1 May 1933 and served in a variety of party and governmental advisory posts in Saxony and Berlin. An expert on synthetic fibers, Kehrl was noted for his energy, sharp intellect, and unbending advocacy of centralization. On his background see Turner, *German Big Business*, p. 202; International Military Tribunal, *Trials of War Criminals before the Nuernberg Military Tribunals*, vol. 13, pp. 677–85. On his relations with Pleiger see Kehrl, *Krisenmanager*, pp. 64, 75–76.

54. Kehrl, *Krisenmanager*, pp. 265–68, 284.

55. Thomas, *Wehr- und Rüstungs Wirtschaft*, pp. 310–15.

56. "Göring als Beauftragte für den Vierjahresplan," 3 March 1941, BA R10 VIII/14, ff. 108–9.

57. Becker, "German War Economy under Speer," p. 171; Janssen, *Das Ministerium Speer*, pp. 70–71.

58. Janssen, *Das Ministerium Speer*, p. 43.

59. Ludwig, *Technik und Ingenieure*, pp. 412–13. Ludwig's view is biased by his respect for Todt and resentment against Speer. The people raised by Todt were now given the power that he had been unable to gain for them.

60. Janssen, *Das Ministerium Speer*, pp. 44–45; Weyres, "Die deutsche Rüstungswirtschaft," p. 27; Wagenführ, *Deutsche Industrie*, p. 41; Kehrl, *Krisenmanager*, pp. 296–97; Milward, *German Economy*, p. 154.

61. Janssen, *Das Ministerium Speer*, p. 111; Salewski, *Die Deutsche Seekriegsleitung, 1935–1945*, 2:272–93.

62. Milward, *German Economy*, p. 136.

63. Janssen, *Das Ministerium Speer*, pp. 134–35; Becker, "German War Economy under Speer," pp. 128–36; Kehrl, *Krisenmanager*, p. 64.

64. Janssen, *Das Ministerium Speer*, p. 135; Becker, "German War Economy under Speer," p. 130.

65. Speer, *Inside*, pp. 284–86; Golücke, *Schweinfurt und die strategische Luftkrieg*, pp. 354–65; USSBS, *Anti-Friction Bearings Industry*, pp. 105–10.

66. Speer, *Inside*, p. 299; Boog, *Die deutsche Luftwaffenführung*, pp. 142–46; Galland, *The First and the Last*, pp. 169–70.

67. Janssen, *Das Ministerium Speer*, pp. 187–88.

68. USSBS, *German War Economy*, p. 60; Boelcke, *Deutschlands Rüstung*, p. 337, points 3–4, p. 338, points 5–16.

69. Speer, *Inside*, pp. 332–33; Janssen, *Das Ministerium Speer*, pp. 160–61, 163; Schmidt, *Albert Speer*, pp. 105–10.

70. Speer, *Inside*, pp. 327–29; Janssen, *Das Ministerium Speer*, pp. 164–68.

71. Speer, *Inside*, pp. 327–29; Janssen, *Das Ministerium Speer*, pp. 164–68; Lochner, *Goebbels Diaries*, pp. 292, 331–32, 383–84.

72. Speer, *The Slave State*, pp. 175–76; Höhne, *The Order of the Death's Head*, pp. 458–63; Georg, *Die wirtschaftlichen Unternehmungen der SS*, pp. 30–71.

73. Speer, *Inside*, pp. 28–30; Janssen, *Das Ministerium Speer*, pp. 157–64; Schmidt, *Albert Speer*, pp. 110–19.

74. Calculations based on Wagenführ, *Deutsche Industrie*, p. 66

75. Boelcke, "Kriegsfinanzierung," p. 56, Abbildung I.

76. Rolf Wagenführ, "Rohstoffproduktion und Industriebeschäftigung," Pla 451/16.11, Berlin, 16 November 1944, p. 1, BA R3/1966.

77. USSBS, *German War Economy*, p. 130, table 77. The index stood at 100 in 1939 and declined to 90.1 in 1941, 81.5 in 1942, and 72.8 in 1944.

78. USSBS, *German War Economy*, pp. 208–9, appendix, tables 7 and 8. The number of women employed in industry also did not change appreciably, increasing from 2.6 million on 31 July 1939 to 2.7 million on 31 May 1944.

79. Ibid., p. 214, appendix, table 12. The number rose from 4,512,000 to

5,586,000 on 31 December 1943 and 5,734,000 on 31 March 1944.

80. In light of this, and the superfluity of machine tools available, postwar assertions that the labor force was underutilized because it was working only one shift per day seem erroneous. RMfRuK, Planungsamt, "38. Wochenbericht des Planungsamtes," Pla 1401/29.9, Berlin, 29 September 1944, Geheime Reichssache, p. 11, BA R3/1957, f. 498.

81. Nachrichten, Nr. 38, 9 June 1944, p. 384, cited in Weyres, "Die deutsche Rüstungswirtschaft," p. 119.

82. Wagenführ, *Deutsche Industrie*, p. 55.

83. USSBS, *German War Economy*, p. 130, table 77.

84. Wagenführ, *Deutsche Industrie*, p. 125.

85. Ibid., pp. 39–42.

86. Welter, *Falsch und richtig Planen*, pp. 21–22.

87. For comments on the confusion that infected the Speer apparatus see Kehrl, *Krisenmanager*, p. 330, and Wagenführ, *Deutsche Industrie*, p. 42.

Chapter 2

1. On the growth of the Ruhr see Pounds, *The Ruhr*, pp. 61–95.

2. USSBS, *German War Economy*, p. 90. The crucial implication of this is that industry did not depend on petroleum for energy. See also n. 40 below.

3. Pleiger to Speer, draft letter, June 1942, p. 4, BA R10 VIII/20, f. 46.

4. Grainger and Gibson, *Coal Utilisation*, pp. 3–4, 15, table 1.5.

5. Gumz, *Die Kohle*, pp. 49–50, tables 15, 30.

6. Preussischen Ministers der öffentlichen Arbeiten, des Bayerischen Staatsministers für Verkehrsangelegenheiten, und der Eisenbahn Zentralbehörden anderer deutscher Bundesstaaten, *Das deutsche Eisenbahnwesen der Gegenwart*, 2:292; Regul, *Kohlenbergbau*, p. 33; Kroker and von Ragenfeld, *Rheinisch-Westfälisches Kohlen-Syndikat*, p. ix.

7. A form not substantial enough to be discussed in the text was briquettes. On their characteristics see Preussischen Ministers der öffentlichen Arbeiten, des Bayerischen Staatsministers für Verkehrsangelegenheiten, und der Eisenbahn Zentralbehörden anderer deutscher Bundesstaaten, *Das deutsche Eisenbahnwesen der Gegenwart*, 2:293; on where they were produced see Schultze-Rhonhof, *Verkehrsströme der Kohle*, p. 108. In the coal economy year 1943/44 total hard coal briquette production was 6,937,000 tons, with 59 percent stemming from the Ruhr: RVK, Statistischer Bericht Nr. 13, Die deutsche Kohlenwirtschaft in den Monaten April bis Dezember 1944. Geheim, Berlin, February 1945, p. 4, BBA 15/1103.

8. Grainger and Gibson, *Coal Utilisation*, p. 58; Pounds, *The Ruhr*, pp. 68–69, 99, 148–49.

9. RVK, Statistischer Bericht Nr. 13, pp. 3, 5.

10. Regul, *Kohlenbergbau*, p. 2.

11. Ibid.
12. Pounds, *The Ruhr*, p. 143; Regul, *Kohlenbergbau*, p. 13; RVK, Statistischer Bericht Nr. 13, pp. 3, 5.
13. Regul, *Kohlenbergbau*, p. 2.
14. RVK, Statistischer Bericht Nr. 13, p. 3.
15. Ibid., p. 5; 6,888,000 tons of coke were produced.
16. Regul, *Kohlenbergbau*, p. 2.
17. RVK, Statistischer Bericht Nr. 13, p. 5. Saar hard coal production was 22,878,000 tons and its coke output was 4,537,000 tons.
18. Dr. von Trotha, Planungsamt, "Vermerk zur Versorgungslage-Steinohle 15.10.44.," Pla 210/002/24.10, Geheim, Berlin, 24 October 1944, p. 2, BA R3/1930, f. 498; Dr. von Trotha, Planungsamt, "Vermerk zur Lage der Kohlenversorgung," Pla 210/009/2.11, Berlin, 2 November 1944, Anlage, BA R3/1854a, f. 387.
19. Regul, *Kohlenbergbau*, p. 21; Reichswirtschaftskammer, "Industriekohlenversorgung/Statistik," Tgb. Nr. VIII 1408/44, Berlin, 14 September 1944, RWWAzK 22/106.
20. Schultze-Rhonhof, *Verkehrsströme der Kohle*, p. 21; Regul, *Kohlenbergbau*, p. 21; USSBS, *Electric Utilities*, p. 20.
21. Total reserves accessible to strip mining were 16,663,000,000. The Rhenish region held 2,288,000,000 tons. Regul, *Kohlenbergbau*, p. 2.
22. Total brown coal production in the coal economy year 1943/44 was 253,366,000 tons. The Central German area accounted for 114,702,000 tons. Total brown coal briquette output was 61,568,000 tons, with the Central German area producing 28,257,000 tons. RVK, Statistischer Bericht Nr. 13, pp. 6–7.
23. USSBS, *Electric Utilities*, p. 6.
24. USSBS, *German War Economy*, p. 115; FO-MEW, *Economic Survey of Germany, Section D Fuel, Power and Public Utility Services*, Secret, London, December 1944, p. 45, NA RG 243, 3(a)77.
25. USSBS, *Electric Utilities*, pp. 5, 6, 10–11.
26. RMfRuK, "Statistische Schnellberichte zur Kriegsproduktion," Pla/4060–20.3.45, Geheime Reichssache, Berlin, 20 March 1945, p. 48, NA RG 243, 54(a)1; RMfRuK, "Statistische Schnellberichte zur Kriegsproduktion," Jahreshefte (Manuskript) 1938 bis 1944," Pla 4060, Geheime Reichssache, Berlin, January 1945, p. 48, NA RG 243, 3(a)68.
27. On Fischer's management apparatus see USSBS, *Electric Utilities*, pp. 14–18, and Reichslastverteiler, "Abschaltlisten 4," 24 May 1943, Geheim, BA R9 IV/3.
28. Becker, "German War Economy under Speer," p. 371.
29. USSBS, *Electric Utilities*, p. 35. The regions were as follows: I, East Prussia; II, Upper Silesia; III, Berlin; IV, Pomerania; V, Hanover-Hesse, Hamburg; VIa, Eastern Westphalia; VIb, Western Westphalia-Rhineland; VII, Central Germany; VIII, Saxony; IX, Bavaria; X, Baden, Württemberg; XI, Austria; XII, unknown; XII, Alsace-Lorraine.
30. USSBS, *German War Economy*, p. 118.

31. FO-MEW, *Economic Survey, Section D*, pp. 48–49.

32. Ibid., pp. 65–66. This entire section is very informative on all aspects of the gas industry.

33. Records of the USSBS, "Reference Material on Reichswerke Hermann Göring AG, Salzgitter," appendix IIA, NA RG 243, 66(a)4.

34. RMfRuK, SSBzKP, Jahreshefte, p. 48. The cokeries produced 1,869,000,000 m^3.

35. Ruhrgas AG, Thyssen'sche Gas- und Wasserwerke, "Die Ferngasverbundwirtschaft auf der Grundlage der Steinkohlenvorkommen an Ruhr, Wurm und Saar," Anlage 1 to Tgb.-Nr. 526/II, Geheime Reichssache, Düsseldorf, April 1936, p. 1, BA R4/279.

36. Bezirksgruppe Steinkohlenbergbau Ruhr der Wirtschaftsgruppe Bergbau, "Koksofengas-Abgabe nach Verbrauchern in Ruhrbezirk," (1943), BA R4/279.

37. RWKS, Abt. 2f, "Gaswerke im Absatzrevier der SHG Duisburg," Essen, 20 April 1945; RWKS, Abt. 2f, "Gaswerke im Absatzrevier der SHG Berlin," Essen, 21 April 1945, both in BBA 33/1437.

38. Coal Survey, sheets for Frankfurt/Main and Stuttgart. The "Coal Survey" is a series of large sheets contained in two bulging envelopes prepared for the USSBS by the RWKS in the summer of 1945. They are arranged by city. Forty-six are mentioned in all. They correspond with those served by the RWKS, and therefore some of the eastern cities are not mentioned. Some sheets for places in western Germany, such as Mannheim, are missing.

39. On this situation see Thomas, *Wehr- und Rüstungs Wirtschaft*, p. 246; USSBS, *Electric Utilities*, pp. 41–42; Reichslastverteiler, "Abschaltliste 5 bei Leistungsmangel im Energiebezirk VIb," Geheim, n.d., BA R8 IV/1.

40. The synthetic fuel plants consumed about 10 million tons of hard coal (4 percent of production) and about 50 million tons of brown coal (20 percent of production) in 1943. The chemical industry consumed 7,127,000 tons of hard coal (4.44 percent of production) in the coal economy year 1942–43. The fuel industry used 4,645,000 tons of hard coal (1.75 percent of production) during the same period. For example the hydrogenation plant at Leuna received in January 1944, a typical month, 2,487 tons of hard coal, all from the RWKS. It consumed 2,960 tons and held stocks of 4,338 tons. It also used 124,931 tons of coke, receiving 124,816 tons by rail, virtually all of it from the RWKS. It kept stocks of 119,478 tons. Leuna also consumed 874,657 tons of brown coal, all of which was obtained locally. Supplies were 877,736 and stocks 88,582. See USSBS, *German War Economy*, p. 76; "Verwendung von Steinkohle in der Industrie 1942/43," GRA 3, D.J.F.W. 43, BA R3/1930, f. 236; RVK, Statistischer Bericht Nr. 13, p. 23; Coal Survey, Merseburg. Note also that the Wehrmacht accounted for 68.3 percent of Germany's liquid fuel consumption during 1943: Wagenführ, *Deutsche Industrie*, p. 55.

41. RMfRuK, "Gliederung des Kohlenverbrauchs," Pla 4500/19.5.44, Geheim, Berlin, 19 May 1944, BBA 33/1080.

42. Reichbeauftragte für Kohle, "Kohlenbewirtschaftung Rundschreiben Nr. 15/41," 750/3 Pl/Schl, Vertraulich, Berlin, 17 April 1941, as Anlage to Arbeitsgemeinschaft der Industrie und Handelskammer in der RVM to all syndicates, Tgb. Nr. VII 5974/41, Vertraulich, Berlin, 17 April 1941, RWWAzK 22/42; Reichbeauftragte für Kohle, "Kohlensparmassnahmen/ Heizerprämien," Rst-A9177/42, Berlin, 1 August 1942, Anlage to RWM to Industrie und Handelskammer, VII 591/42, Berlin, 10 August 1942, RWW-AzK 22/1106; Abschrift of Pleiger Ordnung to RWKS and Oberschlesisches Steinkohlensyndikat, Ic 463/4.41, Berlin, 8 April 1941, BA R10 VIII/14, f. 35; Pounds, *The Ruhr*, p. 163.

43. Pounds, *The Ruhr*, p. 103; Kroker and von Ragenfeld, *Rheinisch-Westfälisches Kohlen-Syndikat*, p. viii; Gebhardt, *Ruhrbergbau*, pp. 29–31.

44. RWKS, "Entwicklung und der derzeitige Stand der kohlenwirtschaft-lichen Gesetzgebung," G/Da, pp. 6–7, BBA 15/471 (1).

45. Kroker and von Ragenfeld, *Rheinisch-Westfälisches Kohlen-Syndikat*, p. ix; Gebhardt, *Ruhrbergbau*, p. 52.

46. Rüdiger Schmidt was born in Siegburg on 17 March 1888. Before assuming his post at the RWKS he had been chairman of the board of the Harpener Bergbau AG in Dortmund and a member of supervisory boards of other transportation, machinery, and housing construction companies. *Wer Leitet?*, 3:786.

47. RWKS, Klonz, internal report, Essen, 2 May 1944, BBA 33/1052.

48. The following discussion of industrial and transportation zones is based on a study of product origination and shipment statistics provided in two publications of the Statistischen Reichsamt Berlin: *Statistik des deutschen Reichs*, vol. 593, *Die Seeschiffahrt im Jahre 1941*, sections 2 and 3, and *Statistik des deutschen Reichs*, vol. 596, *Die Güterbewegungen auf deutschen Eisenbahnen im Jahre 1942 (Emphang)*. Also used were the USSBS's discussion of traffic flows in USSBS, *German Transportation*, p. 5; Baumann, *Deutsches Verkehrsbuch*, pp. 100–143, 253–64, foldout map; Mellor, *German Railways*, map 29; Schultze-Rhonhof, *Verkehrsströme der Kohle*, for its discussion and its very illuminating maps and diagrams; Haufe, *Geographische Struktur des deutschen Eisenbahnverkehrs*; FO and MEW, *Economic Survey of South-Western Germany*; FO and MEW, *Germany Zone Handbook No. V*; Otto Wehde-Textor, "Dokumentarische Darstellung der Deutschen Eisenbahnen in Zweiten Weltkrieg, Teil 4. Der Verkehr," BA R5 Anh I/11, pp. 4, 9–12, 23–25; and a list of industries by city compiled from MEW, *Bomber's Baedeker*, 2d ed., May 1944, NA RG 243, 53(c)35, 53(c)36.

49. RVE, "Zugang an Erzen sowie sonstigen eisenhaltigen Rohstoffen bei den Hochofen-Stahlwerken und den mit ihnen verbundenen Gießereien nach Herkunft Bezirke 1 bis 11," BA R13 I/534, f. 131.

50. RVE, "Bestand am Letzten an Erzen sowie eisenhaltigen Rohstoffen bei den Hochofen-Stahlwerken und den mit ihnen ortlich verbundenen Gießereien nach Metallgruppen," BA R13 I/534, f. 140 (Bezirke 1–11), f. 141 (Bezirk 1 Northwest).

51. RVE, "Die gesamte Roheisen-Erzeugung nach Bezirken," Eil 1, Ge-

heim, Berlin-Wilmersdorf, 7 March 1945, BA R13 I/537, f. 21; RVE, "Die gesamte Rohstahl-Erzeugung (Rohblöcke, Schweisstahl u. Stahlformguß) nach Bezirken," Eil 2, Geheim, Berlin-Wilmersdorf, 22 January 1945, BA R13 I/549, f. 26. A significant constituent of the charge of an open hearth is scrap. It has not been included as a key indicator because it played a supplementary role and because of its low demand for transport space. In late 1944 the DR allocated 1,308 units per day to scrap movement or only about 1 percent of total freight car placings. The 10,246,000 tons moved in 1943 constituted only 1.7 percent of total freight carried by the Reichsbahn. For the role of scrap in steel making see Pounds, *The Ruhr*, pp. 178–79. For traffic statistics see RZA, "Statistische Mitteilungen des Reichsbahn Zentralamts Berlin, Güterwagenstellung," Blatt 91, Berlin, October 1944, NA RG 243, 200(a)97; Deutsche Schrott-Vereinigung to Schelp, Berlin, 5 October 1944, BA R5/3177; USSBS, *German Transportation*, p. 9, exhibit 8.

52. RVE, Zugang Erzen, Nordwest.

53. RVE, Bestand Erzen, Nordwest.

54. RVE, Roheisen-Erzeugung.

55. RVE, Rohstahl-Erzeugung.

56. On the origins and structure of VSt see Seebold, *Ein Stahlkonzern im Dritten Reich*, 1981, pp. 21–32, 52–63.

57. VSt, Hauptstatistik, "Eildienst," Geheim, Düsseldorf, December 1944, pp. 2, 4, NA RG 243, 3(a)37; VSt, Hauptstatistik, "Zugang, Verkauf, Abgabe, Verbrauch und Bestand an Brennstoffen (Steinkohle)," Düsseldorf, 25 October 1944, NA RG 243, 200(a)129; VSt, Hauptstatistik, "Jahresübersicht," Vertraulich, Düsseldorf, n.d., p. 4, NA RG 243, 3(a)37.

58. VSt, Hauptstatistik, "Jahresübersicht," p. 3.

59. RVE, Roheisen-Erzeugung.

60. USSBS, Heavy Industry Branch, *Reichswerke Hermann Goering*, exhibits A, C, and H.

61. USSBS, Motor Vehicles and Tanks Branch, *Friedrich Krupp Grusonwerke*, p. 4; Weir, "Imperial Naval Office," pp. 62–63.

62. USSBS, Motor Vehicles and Tanks Branch, *Friedrich Krupp Grusonwerke*, pp. 3, 10; USSBS, Ordnance Branch, *Friedrich Krupp Grusonwerke*, exhibits I and J.

63. Coal Survey, Magdeburg, 1943.

64. USSBS, Motor Vehicles and Tanks Branch, *Friedrich Krupp Grusonwerke*, exhibit B; USSBS, Ordnance Branch, *Friedrich Krupp Grusonwerke*, exhibit A.

65. USSBS, *Gebrueder Giulini*, p. 1.

66. Records of the USSBS, "Giulini, Ludwigshafen, Receipts of Raw Materials," NA RG 243, 24(b).

67. RVE, Roheisen-Erzeugung.

68. BEWAG, "Technische Monatsberichte Erzeugung," January 1943–December 1943; BEWAG, Technischer Büro, "Monatsberichte der Abt. Kraftwerksleitung," January 1943–December 1943," BEWAG-Archiv, o/60.

Chapter 3

1. Pleiger to Speer, draft, 17 June 1942, pp. 1–2, BA R10 VIII/20, ff. 46–47.

2. RVK, "Die Kohlenlage," Aufstellung I 401a/42g, Geheim, Berlin, 28 May 1942, BA R10 VIII/20, f. 33.

3. RVK, "Wagenstellung in den Revieren," Aufstellung IV, 401a/42g, Geheime Reichssache, BA R10 VIII/20, ff. 36, 39.

4. RVK, "Die Kohlenlage," 401a/42g, Geheim, Berlin, 28 May 1942, BA R10 VIII/20, f. 38.

5. ZP, "Ergebnisse der 23. Sitzung der Zentralen Planung am 3.11.1942," ZP 12, Geheime Reichssache, Berlin, 4 November 1942, p. 1, NA T-83, R-76, FR 3447842.

6. Becker, "German War Economy under Speer," pp. 215–16, based on FIAT Report no. 89, part 2, "The Achievements and Difficulties of the Reichsvereinigung Eisen and the Iron Industry," by Hans Sohl, p. 12, available in the Imperial War Musuem.

7. Kehrl, *Krisenmanager*, p. 278.

8. Wagenführ, *Deutsche Industrie*, pp. 98, 101.

9. Kreidler, *Eisenbahnen*, p. 336, table 3.2. The Reichsbahn carried 675.1 million tons of freight; inland waterways 82 million tons; and private railways, narrow-gauge railroads, and street cars 123.3 million tons.

10. Meinberg, "Der Verkehr im Kohlenwirtschaftsjahr 1943/44," T942/44, Geheim, Berlin, 16 June 1944, pp. 4, 5, BA R5/57; RVK, Statistischer Bericht Nr. 13, pp. 16, 20.

11. Records of the USSBS, "Operating Characteristics of the German Railroad," p. 2, NA RG 243, 200(a)52; Schymanietz, *Organisation der deutschen Eisenbahnen*, pp. 20, 25, 27, 31. On the history of German railroading see the following: Klee, *Preussische Eisenbahngeschichte*; Fremdling, *Eisenbahnen und deutsches Wirtschaftswachstum*; Germany, RVM, *Hundert Jahre Deutsche Eisenbahnen*; O'Brien, *Railways in Western Europe*; Mellor, *German Railways*; Kleinmann, "Dr.-Ing. Julius Dorpmüller," pp. 721–23.

12. See the organizational charts in BA R5/125; USSBS, *German Transportation*, p. 9, exhibit 9; Kreidler, *Eisenbahnen*, p. 323, and the discussion on pp. 201–7.

13. Kreidler, *Eisenbahnen*, pp. 202–4. For a list of the districts controlled by the respective GBLs see Table A.8.

14. Ibid., p. 242; Baumann, *Deutsches Verkehrsbuch*, p. 253; Wehde-Textor, "Leistungen," p. 14; Records of the USSBS, Railroad Administration and Interrogations, "Interrogation of Dorpmüller," 29 May 1945, pp. 8–9, NA RG 243, 200(a)127.

15. A. Dobmaier, *Das Fernmeldewesen der Reichsbahn*, p. 15, BA R5 Anh II/46.

16. Hans Quarck, "Bericht VIIId, Fernmeldewesen," Trier, 1957, p. 9, BA R5 Anh I/19.

17. Records of the USSBS, Railroad Administration and Interrogations,

"Reichsbahn Methods of Communications," pp. 3, 4, NA RG 243, 200(a)
127; USSBS, *German Transportation,* p. 78.

18. Quarck, "Bericht VIIId, Fernmeldewesen," pp. 10, 11, 13.

19. Dobmaier, *Das Fernmeldewesen der Reichsbahn,* p. 1.

20. Ibid., pp. 1–2. See also R. Euler, "Erfahrungsbericht," Frankfurt/Main,
n.d. [postwar], p. 1, BA R5 Anh I/38.

21. Euler, "Erfahrungsbericht," pp. 2–3; Quarck, "Bericht VIIId, Fern-
meldwesen," p. 2.

22. SHAEF, G-2, "Transportation Intelligence Bulletin No. 2," Restricted,
27 May 1945, "Interrogation of Dorpmüller," p. 9, NA RG 243, 200(a)58.
Also available in USAFHRC R-A5179, 506.611A.

23. Quarck, "Bericht VIIId, Fernmeldewesen," p. 12.

24. DR, "Auszug aus der Dienstvorschrift für den Reichsbahn-Fern-
schreibdienst," 476a, effective 1 August 1942, pp. 3, 10, 22, BA R5/13.

25. RVM, Abt. L, "Anlage to R/L. W12.1820/38g, Geheim," p. 7; DR,
"Niederschrift über die Fernspruch-Präsidentenkonferenz am 24 Juli 1944,"
Anlage to 2 Aasp 83, Geheim, August 1944, p. 9. Abteilung L was responsi-
ble for relations between the DR and the Wehrmacht and concealed the DR
Abwehr office. See Abt. L, "R/L. W6, Nr. 1323/35," 28 November 1935, BA
R5/30.

26. Hampe, *Zivile Luftschutz,* pp. 86–89, 314–15, 488–92; Records of the
USSBS, "Dilli Interrogation," 18 June 1945, p. 2; "Ganzenmüller Interrogation," 30 May 1945, p. 8, both in NA RG 243, 200(a)127; Kreidler, *Eisenbahnen,* pp. 251–52; USSBS, *German Transportation,* p. 52.

27. Kreidler, *Eisenbahnen,* pp. 219–20.

28. Ibid., p. 28.

29. Ibid., p. 258; USSBS, *German Transportation,* p. 51.

30. Kreidler, *Eisenbahnen,* p. 252; USSBS, *German Transportation,* p. 51;
Hampe, *Zivile Luftschutz,* pp. 398–99.

31. Kreidler, *Eisenbahnen,* pp. 250–51; USSBS, *German Transportation,*
p. 78.

32. USSBS, *German Transportation,* p. 51; Records of the USSBS, "Interrogation of Eckhard Burger," 1 April 1945, p. 2, NA RG 243, 200(a)127.

33. RZA, "Fahrdienstvorschriften," Berlin, effective 1 April 1944, pp. 39,
63, 70, 139; Dr. Zissel, "GBL-West," n.d. [postwar], pp. 11, 12, BA R5 Anh
I/27; DR, GBL-West, "Anlage 1 zum Bericht GBL-West," B21 Baü, 19 November 1942, BA R5/2086; DR, GBL-West, "Niederschrift über die Arbeiten zur Vorbereitung der Umladestellen Duisburg und Wanne-Eickel
vom 19–22.4.1943 in Düsseldorf," VII 71, Vgbwf, Essen, 24 April 1943, NA
RG 243, 200(a)62.

34. See, for example, DR, "Niederschrift über die 74. Präsidentenkonferenz am 13 Januar 1940," BA R5 Anh I/69.

35. DR, "Niederschrift über die 85. Präsidentenkonferenz am 31. März
1942," Beilage b, "Vortrag des Herrn Ministerialdirektors Treibe über die
Verkehrslage," Geheim, pp. 1–2, BA R5 Anh I/69, ff. 295–96. In March 1942
the Reichsbahn placed an average of 130,000 cars per day. Demand was for
220,000 per day. The RVK set a target of 82,000 coal units per day. In Janu-

ary the DR placed an average of 73,000 per day and in March, 77,000 per day.

36. RMfRuK, Speerchronik, 1942, 13 May, p. 35, BA R3/1736, f. 14; Speer, *Inside*, pp. 222–23; Kreidler, *Eisenbahnen*, p. 205.

37. RMfRuK, Speerchronik, 1942, 23 May, p. 38, BA R3/1736, f. 44; DR, *Verzeichnis der oberen Reichsbahnbeämter*, p. 10; VRB, Information, "Gustav Dilli," *Die Bundesbahn*, Nr. 14, p. 5.

38. RVM, *Grossdeutscher Verkehr*, 1942, p. 259, BA R5 Anh I/49; *Das Reich*, Nr. 44, 31 October 1942, p. 1; *Das Reich*, Nr. 47, 22 November 1942, p. 10.

39. Some additions were also made to sidings and yard facilities. See Kreidler, *Eisenbahnen*, pp. 242, 248. On increased locomotive production see Gottwaldt, *Deutsche Kriegslokomotiven*, and *Deutsche Eisenbahnen*, pp. 94–107, 114–25; Piekalkiewicz, *Deutsche Reichsbahn*, pp. 80–83.

40. Thomas, *Wehr- und Rüstungs Wirtschaft*, p. 361; Kreidler, *Eisenbahnen*, pp. 196–97.

41. RMfRuK, Speerchronik, 1942, 24 June, p. 44, BA R3/1736, f. 51.

42. Kreidler, *Eisenbahnen*, pp. 194–95, 206; Speer, *Inside*, pp. 223–25.

43. Kehrl, *Krisenmanager*, pp. 274–75, 460, n. 20.

44. Kreidler, *Eisenbahnen*, p. 229; Kehrl, *Krisenmanager*, p. 275; see also as an example of how the program was publicized in Rüstungs-Inspektion VII to Rüstungs-Kommando Munich, and Rüstungs-Kommando Augsburg, "Transportwesen," Nr. 58092/42, Z. Abt. Gr. Ib, Munich, 18 August 1942, NA T-73, R-112, FR 3271602–54, esp. FR 3271611, 3271612–18, and 3271650.

45. Simon, "Verkehrsausweitung, Verkehrslenkung und Transportentflechtung," pp. 419–41.

46. DR, *Verzeichnis der oberen Reichsbahnbeämten*, p. 38.

47. Kreidler, *Eisenbahnen*, pp. 234–35; Wehde-Textor, "Leistungen," p. 15; ZVL, "Verteilung der Massengüter auf das ganze Jahr entsprechend der Leistungsfähigkeit der Verkehrsträger," Pr(Z) 81 Val 5, Berlin, 31 May 1944, 5 Anlagen, BA R5 Anh II/38, also in BA R5/3173.

48. RVK, "Aktennotiz," Berlin, 30 April 1943, p. 1, NA T-83, R-76, FR 3447847.

49. Kreidler, *Eisenbahnen*, pp. 269–70; USSBS, *German War Economy*, pp. 46, 206, appendix, table 5.

50. Kreidler, *Eisenbahnen*, p. 337, table 3.3; Records of the USSBS, "Operating Characteristics of the German Railroad," pp. 2–3, 7–8, NA RG 243, 200(a)52.

51. RZA, "Statistischer Monatsübersicht Nr. 7, Juli 1944," Berlin, October 1944, p. 17, NA RG 243, 200(a)88.

52. DR, *Verzeichnis der Maschinenämter*, p. 67. There were also 83 car repair works (Bahnbetriebswagenwerke, Bww).

53. DR, *Verzeichnis der Maschinenämter*, pp. 21, 29. An example was Halle with 1,240 men in the locomotive shed (Bw) and 570 men in the car shed (Bww).

54. RVK, Statistischer Bericht Nr. 13, p. 30; RZA, "Statistischer Monats-

übersicht, Nr. 7, Juli 1944," Berlin, October 1944, p. 20, NA RG 243, 200(a)88.

55. Kreidler, *Eisenbahnen*, pp. 264–65.

56. Baumann, *Deutsches Verkehrsbuch*, pp. 298–99.

57. RWKS, Abt. 2f, "Deutsche Reichsbahn," 20 April 1945, BBA 33/1040. The DR obtained 13,373,900 tons of hard coal in calendar year 1943 from the RWKS. On the shares of the various syndicates in overall DR coal supplies see RWKS, "Reichsbahndienstkohlenlieferungen (einschl. Werkskohlen) nach Revieren," n.d., BBA 33/1040. The latter is a chart giving information for January and February 1944.

58. Kreidler, *Eisenbahnen*, pp. 230, 337, table 3.3, 339, table 3.7.

59. Records of the USSBS, "Dilli Interrogation," 18 June 1944, p. 4, NA RG 243, 200(a)127; RMfRuK, "Nachrichten des Reichministers für Rüstung- und Kriegsproduktion," Nr. 45, Vertraulich, Berlin, 15 September 1944, p. 470, NA RG 243, 101(a)10; Wehde-Textor, "Dokumentarische Darstellung," pp. 39–40.

60. Baumann, *Deutsches Verkehrsbuch*, p. 253.

61. DR, "Niederschrift über die 83. Präsidentenkonferenz am 31. März 1942, Beilage a, Vortrag des Min. Dir. Leibbrand, Betreibslage," Geheim, Berlin, n.d., pp. 2, 7–8, BA R5 Anh I/69, ff. 285, 290–91.

62. Baumann, *Deutsches Verkehrsbuch*, p. 252.

63. Wehde-Textor, "Dokumentarische Darstellung," p. 21; Wehner, "Einsatz der Eisenbahnen," p. 113.

64. Wehner, "Einsatz der Eisenbahnen," p. 37.

65. Records of the USSBS, "Dilli Interrogation," 18 June 1945, p. 1, NA RG 243, 200(a)127; Kreidler, *Eisenbahnen*, p. 245; Records of the USSBS, "Ganzenmüller Interrogation," 30 May 1945, p. 11; Records of the USSBS, "Dorpmüller Interrogation," 29 May 1945, p. 7, NA RG 243, 200(a)127.

66. The description of marshalling yard operations is based on the discussion in Preussischen Ministers der öffentlichen Arbeiten, des Bayerischen Staatsministers für Verkehrsangelegenheiten, und der Eisenbahn Zentralbehörden anderer deutscher Bundesstaaten, *Das deutsche Eisenbahnwesen der Gegenwart*, 1:93–96; Obermayer, *Taschenbuch der Eisenbahn*, 2:179–87; Baumann, *Deutsches Verkehrsbuch*, pp. 275–77; Droege, *Freight Terminals and Trains*, pp. 60–100.

67. Wehde-Textor, "Dokumentarische Darstellung," p. 23.

68. RZA, "Statistische Mitteilungen des Reichsbahn-Zentralamts Berlin, Güterwagenstellung, Blatt 91, January–December 1943, NA RG 243, 200(a) 95. The USSBS records contain a complete set of these monthly statistical reports for the period January 1937–January 1945; USSBS, *German Transportation*, p. 50; "RBD Essen," n.d. [postwar], pp. 11, 12. For information on the capacity of marshalling yards see OSS, R&A, No. 799, "Railway Resources of Axis Europe," Secret, Washington, D.C., n.d. [probably 1943], appendix i, part 2, pp. 80–84. This report is available from three sources: the Library of Congress; NA RG 59, Department of State; USAFHRC R-A5395, 512.611A, FR 695–97; see also DR, Zentralamt Berlin, *Amtliches*

Bahnhofs Verzeichnis; Rüdiger Schmidt, "Tagesberichte," Geheim, 25 November 1944–27 March 1945, BBA 33/1061.

69. USSBS, *German Transportation,* pp. 54–55; Records of the USSBS, "Marshalling Yards, Locomotive Shops, and Bridges over the Lippe Canal and River at Hamm," 19 October 1945, p. 3, NA RG 243, Physical Damage Division Report No. 67.

70. USSBS, *German Transportation,* p. 5.

71. Riedel, *Eisen und Kohle,* p. 351.

72. RZA, Blatt 91, January–December 1943.

73. Ibid.

74. "Sammlung von Material über die Leistungen der Deutschen Eisenbahnen im letzten Kriege; hier: Direktionsbezirk Halle (Saale)," Mainz, 1 June 1953, BA R5 Anh I/41.

75. Ibid., pp. 246–47, 250; Albrecht Zahn, "Dokumentarische Darstellung der Eisenbahnen im Zweiten Weltkrieg," Stuttgart, 1957, pp. 66–67, BA R5 Anh I/9.

76. USSBS, *German Transportation,* p. 7; Wehde-Textor, "Dokumentarische Darstellung," pp. 22–24; GBL-Ost, ZVL, "Verteilung der Massengütertransporte auf das ganze Jahr entsprechend der Leistungsfähigkeit der Verkehrsträger," Pr(Z)81 Val 5, Berlin, 31 May 1944, esp. Anlagen 1, 3 and 5, BA R5 Anh II/38 and R5/3173; Meinberg, "Der Verkehr im Kohlenwirtschaftsjahr 1943/44," T942/44, Berlin-Halensee, 16 June 1944, pp. 3, 7, BA R5/57.

77. Records of the USSBS, "Ganzenmüller Interrogation," 30 May 1945, p. 2, NA RG 243, 200(a)127.

78. RZA, Blatt 91, January–December 1943.

79. GBL-Ost, ZVL, "Niederschrift 41. Sitzung der ZVL," Pr(Z)81 Val, Geheim, Berlin, 12 August 1944, Anlage f, BA 5/37.

80. RZA, "Statistische Mitteilungen des Reichsbahn-Zentralamts Berlin, Wagenstellung für Kohlen, Koks und Brikette, Blatt 92, Nur für den Dienstgebrauch, January–December 1943, NA RG 243, 200(a)96. The files of the USSBS contain a set of these statistical compilations for every month from January 1937 to January 1945.

81. DR, "Statistische Angaben 1944, III Kohlenverkehr," p. 120, NA RG 243, 200(a)124. In 1943 the Reichsbahn moved 160,758,121 tons of hard coal, hard coal briquettes, and coke; 82,911,557 tons of brown coal and its derivatives; and 48,546,555 tons of service coal for a total of 292,216,233 tons.

82. RZA, Blatt 92, November 1943.

83. Wehde-Textor, "Dokumentarische Darstellung," p. 36; Telegrammbrief, DRB 10 Vwb 198 to Hwa, 5 May 1942, BA R5/3180; ZP, "Niederschrift über die 6. Besprechung der Zentralen Planung am 28. Mai 1942," Geheim, Berlin, 29 May 1942, p. 2, NA T-83, R-76, FR 3447777; Telegrammbrief, DRB 10 Vwb to Hwa, No. 206, Berlin, 17 August 1942, BA R5/3180.

84. USSBS, *German Transportation,* p. 57, exhibit, 52.

85. Wehde-Textor, "Dokumentarische Darstellung," pp. 43–44; DR, "Niederschrift über die 91. Präsidentenkonferenz am 6 Dezember 1943," 2 Aasp 81, Geheim, Berlin, 5 January 1944, Anlage, p. 12, BA R5 Anh I/69.

86. GBL-West, "Dienstkohle," 11 August 1945, p. 3, NA RG 243, 200(a)130.

87. RWKS, "Dienstkohlen der Deutschen Reichsbahn," BBA 33/1040; DR, "Niederschrift über die Fernspruch-Präsidentenkonferenz am 24 Juli 1944," Anlage to 2 Aasp, Geheim, Berlin, August 1944, p. 22, BA R5 Anh I/69.

88. RMfRuK, Planungsamt, "50. Wochenbericht des Planungsamts," Pla 1401 g. Rs./21.12, Geheime Reichssache, Berlin, 21 December 1944, p. 3, BA R3/1957, f. 653. The entire set of these reports is available in this file.

89. Dr. Karl Ottmann, "Wochenbericht Referat II 3/4," 15 May 1944, NA T-77, R-200, FR 936035. This roll contains a complete set of Ottmann's reports, which contain preliminary daily freight car and coal car placing statistics and comments on the transportation situation.

90. Computed from RZA, "Statistische Mitteilungen des Reichsbahn-Zentralamts Berlin, Güterwagenstellung bei der Deutschen Reichsbahn, Blatt 90," weeks 1–52, 1943, NA RG 243, 200(a)94, 95, 96, 116. The USSBS holdings include all of these weekly statistical compilations from 1942 through week 9 (25 February–3 March) of 1945. See also Kreidler, *Eisenbahnen*, p. 338, table 3.6.

91. GBL-Ost, ZVL, "Verkehrsplan 1944," Pr(Z)81 Val 5, Berlin, 31 May 1945, Anlage 5, p. 1, BA R5 Anh II/38, BA R5/3173.

92. Kreidler, *Eisenbahnen*, p. 227; Wehde-Textor, "Leistungen," p. 13; Records of the USSBS, "Dorpmüller Interrogation," 29 May 1945, p. 3, NA RG 243, 200(a)127; Records of the USSBS, "Ganzenmüller Interrogation," 30 May 1945, pp. 3–4; For examples of dispersal by individual firms see the list compiled by the RMfRuK in NA T-73, R-14, RMfRuK/z 359, FR 1061084–1187 and USSBS, *Aircraft Industry*, pp. 23–26, figures II-1, II-2, II-3, II-7, VII-1, VII-2.

93. Wehde-Textor, "Leistungen," pp. 3, 5, 10, 23; Wehde-Textor, "Dokumentarische Darstellung," p. 38; Thomas, *Wehr- und Rüstungs Wirtschaft*, pp. 96, 147; Carroll, *Total War*, p. 197; Kreidler, *Eisenbahnen*, pp. 31–32, 36–37, 46–47.

94. Petzina, *Autarkiepolitik*, p. 130. See also U.S. Chief Counsel for the Prosecution of Axis Criminality, *Nazi Conspiracy and Aggression*, 6:729, "Second Meeting of the Reich Defense Council, 23 June 1939," 3787-PS, and 3:901, "Conference at the General Field Marshal Goering's at 1000, 14 Oct. 1938, in the Air Ministry," Top Secret, 1301-PS.

95. Wehner, "Einsatz der Eisenbahnen," p. 30.

96. Ibid., pp. 35–38.

97. Kreidler, *Eisenbahnen*, pp. 242, 248.

98. Baumann, *Deutsches Verkehrsbuch*, pp. 276–77.

99. Wehner, "Einsatz der Eisenbahnen," p. 38.

100. Kreidler, *Eisenbahnen*, p. 336, table 3.2. Total freight tonnage car-

ried by the inland waterway peaked at 126.9 million tons in 1939 and stood at 82 million tons in 1943. Its share of Ruhr coal movements fell from 32 percent (29.6 million tons) in 1941 to 27 percent (24.4 million tons) in 1943. See Leiter der BVL-West, "Anlage: Ruhrkohlen-Förderung und -Abfuhr auf den Bahn- und Wasserwege 1941–1944," BA R5 Anh I/11. Total movement by inland waterway of all types of coal fell from 34.2 million tons in the coal economy year 1940/41 to 30.2 million tons in the coal economy year 1943/44. See RVK, Statistischer Bericht Nr. 13, p. 20.

101. DR, *Verzeichnis der oberen Reichsbahnbeämter*, p. 10.

102. Becker, "German War Economy under Speer," p. 408.

103. OSS, R&A, *German Inland Waterways*, appendix, pp. 15, 18–20.

104. Ibid., pp. 12, 14.

105. RVM, Abt. B, Berlin, 18 August 1944, II Schiffsraumbestand 1943.

106. Kreidler, *Eisenbahnen*, p. 336, table 3.2.

107. Meinberg, "Der Verkehr im Kohlenwirtschaftsjahr 1943/44," T942/44, Berlin-Halensee, 16 June 1944, pp. 4, 6, BA R5/57. A total of 30,981,522 tons of coal of all types was carried in calendar year 1943.

108. Wehde-Textor, "Dokumentarische Darstellung," p. 23; Kreidler, *Eisenbahnen*, p. 228.

109. RVM, "Einsatzfähiger Binnenschiffahrtsbestand Herbst 1944 nach Meldungen der Schiffahrtstellen," B898444, Berlin, 9 December 1944, 7a Rheinstromgebiet 1 August 1944, BA R5/82.

110. Records of the USSBS, "Work Sheets for Transportation Division Final Report," Chart No. 13, planned for exhibit 27, actually appeared as exhibit 26; see also Schultze-Rhonhof, *Verkehrsströme der Kohle*, pp. 28–29. Duisburg suffered a substantial decline in traffic during the war due to the loss of its oceangoing trade.

111. Schultze-Rhonhof, *Verkehrsströme der Kohle*, pp. 103, 105.

112. Badisches Hafenamt Mannheim 5/S, "Aufstellung über den monatlichen Umschlag in den Mannheimer Häfen," NA RG 243, 220(a)165. This report was also prepared postwar for the USSBS. See also, FO-MEW, *Economic Survey of Germany, Section E Transport and Communication*, Restricted, London, December 1944, pp. 42, 45, NA RG 243, 3(a)74.

113. FO-MEW, *Economic Survey, Section E*, p. 17, NA RG 243, 3(a)74; Engineer Research Office, North Atlantic Division, Corps of Engineers, Military Intelligence Division, *Navigable Waterways of Germany*, 4:13-2.

114. RVM, "Einsatzfähiger Binnenschiffahrtsbestand," 6 Kanalgebiet, BA R5/82.

115. Schultze-Rhonhof, *Verkehrsströme der Kohle*, p. 29.

116. "Durchgangs-Verkehr der Wichtigen Schleusen des Dortmund-Ems-Kanals nach Schiffzahl, Tragfähigkeit und Ladungstonnen und nach Güterarten von 1938 bis . . . ," VI sec. 73, p. 6, NA RG 243, 200(a)168. This is a logbook with daily entries for passages through the Münster lock, most likely kept by the Reichsschleppbetrieb in the Wasserstrassen Direktion Münster.

117. Corps of Engineers, *Navigable Waterways of Germany*, 4:15-4.

118. Schultze-Rhonhof, *Verkehrsströme der Kohle*, pp. 29–30.
119. Records of the USSBS, "Effects of Air Attacks on Canal Traffic: Rothensee Shiplift," No. 11, NA RG 243, 200(a)2. Total traffic was 4,584,157 tons.
120. RVM, "Einsatzfähiger Binnenschiffahrtsbestand," 3. Oder, BA R5/82.
121. FO-MEW, *Economic Survey, Section E*, p. 47, NA RG 243, 3(a)74.
122. Franzius, Oberpräsident der Provinz Niederschlesien, Wasserstrassendirektion, "Oderschiffahrt im Monat November 1944," 5c S 3375, Breslau, 20 December 1944, p. 1, BA R5/80, f. 58. Similarly, this statistic should be regarded as an estimate. Actual coal shipments were probably somewhat lower. For 1938 statistics see FO-MEW, *Economic Survey, Section E*, p. 48. In 1938 tonnage overall was 3,860,000.
123. Meinberg, "Der Verkehr im Kohlenwirtschaftsjahr 1943/44," T942/44, Berlin-Halensee, 16 June 1944, pp. 3, 5, BA R5/57. Movements in coal economy year 1940/41 totaled 34.2 million tons; in 1942/43, 39.4 million tons; and in 1943/44, 30.2 million tons.
124. Telegramm, Pleiger to Göring, Tel 977831-Nr. 9501-4.4.44-136/133w, Berlin, 4 April 1944, BA R10 VIII/19; see also RVK, Statistischer Bericht Nr. 13, p. 3; for the coal target see ZP, "Ergebnisse der 36. Sitzung der Zentrale Planung am 22.4.1943," ZP 61, Geheime Reichssache, Berlin, 26 April 1943, p. 5, NA T-83, R-46, FR 3447853.
125. Emrich, ZVL, "Ergebnisse der Untersuchung betr. Verkehrsplanung 1944," Anlage 5 to Pr(Z)81 Val 5, Berlin, 31 May 1944, p. 1, BA R5/3173 and BA R5 Anh II/38; Meinberg, "Der Verkehr im Kohlenwirtschaftsjahr 1943/44," p. 3.
126. Meinberg, "Der Verkehr im Kohlenwirtschaftsjahr 1943/44," p. 7.
127. ZP, "Stenographischer Bericht über die 58. Sitzung der Zentralen Planung am 25.5.44," Geheim, Berlin, May 1944, pp. 2, 5, 20, 36–37, 46, 47, 49–55, BA R3/1736, ff. 5, 8, 23, 39–40, 51, 53, 55 and appendix 9.
128. See especially the statements by Steinbrink of the RVK in ZP, "58. Sitzung," pp. 21–24, ff. 24–27; Rosenkrantz of the RVK, pp. 40–41, ff. 43–44, 64; Rohland of the RVE, pp. 48, 67, 68, ff. 54, 67, 68.
129. Ibid., pp. 48, 67, 68, ff. 54, 67, 68.
130. Ibid., pp. 25–28, 47–48, 68, 73, ff. 28–31, 47–48, 68, 73.

Chapter 4

1. Douhet, *Command of the Air*, pp. 5, 19, 49, 58–60.
2. W&F, 1:64–65, 103, 342–43; Harris, *Bomber Offensive*, p. 15.
3. For a very informative discussion of the development of concepts of strategic air power in the United States before World War II see Sherry, *Rise of American Air Power*, pp. 47–75. Also worth consulting is Schaffer, *Wings of Judgment*, pp. 20–30.
4. C&C, 2:300, 305.
5. Milward, *New Order and the French Economy*, p. 265, table 2.

6. Creveld, *Fighting Power*; Dupuy, *Numbers, Predictions and War*, pp. 103–10, 163–65.

7. Calculated by comparing German tank and aircraft output with full British and Soviet production and four-fifths of American output.

8. See Ergebnisse, 59, ZP, 10 June 1944, p. 1, BA R3/1960, f. 117. The pipeline for steel plate from receipt of an order to delivery to the plant where it would be installed was six to twelve weeks. See also Speer Interrogation, 30 May 1945, W&F, 4:376–77, appendix 37. Speer estimated that the length of time for crude steel to appear in finished form was as follows: as ball-bearings, three to four months; as motor, six months; and as tank, four to five months.

9. W&F, 3:3; on the Lancaster see Robertson, *Lancaster*, p. 126.

10. Hansell, *Air Plan*, p. 281, appendix, charts 21, 22.

11. Green, *Famous Bombers*, 1:33, 96.

12. Hansell, *Air Plan*, pp. 281–82, appendix, charts 21, 22.

13. Calculated by assuming an 80 percent availability rate with the entire force operating twice each week. The rate of operation is purposely low to account for unfavorable weather. Both forces actually operated more often. By 1945, tonnages far in excess of the baseline offered in the text were being delivered regularly. The point is that ample bomber capacity existed to attack the targets envisaged by both sides in the bombing debate from mid-1944 onward.

14. C&C, 2:748, 3:6–7; W&F, 2:4–5, 3:18–19; Pogue, *The Supreme Command*, pp. 124–25.

15. Tedder, *With Prejudice*, pp. 510–11.

16. Middlebrook, *The Nuremberg Raid*.

17. Stanley, *World War II Photo Intelligence*, pp. 40–43, 57–58.

18. W&F, 1:473; Hinsley, *British Intelligence*, 3 (1):466.

19. USAAF, *Ultra*, p. xvi.

20. Hinsley, *British Intelligence*, 1:357, 2:668.

21. War Department, Military Intelligence Service, "History of the Special Branch, MIS, War Department 1942–1944," SRH-035, pp. 28, 30, 88–89, NA RG 427.

22. Maj. Gen. J. A. Ulio to Commanding Generals of U.S. Forces, ETO, USSTAF, "Security of Signal Intelligence Within European, North African and Middle Eastern Theaters of Operations," AG 312.1, 11 March 1944, SRH-045, pp. 51–52, 62, NA RG 427.

23. Hinsley, *British Intelligence*, 2:29; Lewin, *Ultra Goes to War*, p. 127.

24. Hinsley, *British Intelligence*, 2:23, 25–27.

25. W&F, 1:261–62; Hinsley, *British Intelligence*, 2:3–5.

26. USSBS, *Physical Damage Division Report*, p. 107; W&F, 1:261–62, 264–67; Hinsley, *British Intelligence*, 1:225–26, 2:141, 654; Medlicott, *Economic Blockade*, 2:385–86.

27. W&F, 3:208–9.

28. W&F, 1:266.

29. Roosevelt, *War Report of the OSS*, 1:11, 106, 174.

30. EOU War Diary, 1:47, 5:16.

31. Rostow, *Pre-Invasion Bombing Strategy*, p. 21. This book is a reprint of vol. 5 of the EOU War Diary, though not designated as such; there are a number of crucial omissions from the original.

32. Copp, *Forged in Fire*, pp. 104–5.

33. Hansell, *Air Plan*, pp. 12–48, 61–71.

34. Perera, *Leaves*, pp. 69–71.

35. W&F, 1:7, 13–14.

36. EOU War Diary, 5:49.

37. Perera, *Leaves*, pp. 72–73.

38. W&F, 1:281, 2:252–53, 3:302; Hinsley, *British Intelligence*, 1:232–33, 238–39, 240, 310–11, 2:140–41; Medlicott, *Economic Blockade*, 2:6–7, 8–10; Hansell, *Air Plan*, p. 74; Perera, *Leaves*, pp. 76–77.

39. Hinsley, *British Intelligence*, 1:154–55, 2:159.

40. W&F, 2:249.

41. Hinsley, *British Intelligence*, 2:150–52; Medlicott, *Economic Blockade*, 2:399–400.

42. OSS, R&A, "Speer's Appointment as Dictator of the German Economy," No. 1194, 13 September 1943, Restricted, p. 3, NA RG 226.

43. OSS, R&A, "Economic Controls in Nazi Germany," No. 1156, 10 December 1943, Restricted, pp. viii, 6, 8, NA RG 226.

44. OSS, R&A, "Speer's Appointment as Dictator," p. 10.

45. Hinsley, *British Intelligence*, 1:306, 2:132, 3 (1):56–57.

46. Hinsley, *British Intelligence*, 1:307; USSBS, *German War Economy*, p. 44.

47. USSBS, *Aircraft Industry*, p. 74, table 5.7.

48. Hinsley, *British Intelligence*, 3 (1):492.

49. Hansell, *Air Plan*, pp. 82–83; C&C, 2:352; Guido Perera, "History of the Organization and Operations of the Committee of Operations Analysts 16 November 1942–10 October 1944," 2 vols., 1:18, USAFHRC, R-1000, 118.01, FR 26.

50. Ballard to MacDonald, "Evaluation of German Transport as a Strategic Target System," 27 December 1943, Secret, USAFHRC, R-A5686, 519.425-3, FR 1383–85.

51. USSBS, "An Appraisal of Pre and Post Raid Intelligence," Special Paper No. 5, Confidential, 20 August 1945, p. 45, NA RG 243, 134(a)26.

52. EOU War Diary, 5:90.

53. AAF-Evaluation Board, MTO, "The Relative Effectiveness of Strategic Air Force Attack against Transportation," n.d., Restricted, pp. 2, 11, 13, 17, USAFHRC, R-A1177, 138.5-3, vol. 2, part 2, FR 51, 60, 62, 66.

54. FO-MEW, *Economic Survey of Germany, Section E, Transport and Communications*, Restricted, December 1944, NA RG 243, 3(a)74 among others.

55. Hinsley, *British Intelligence*, 2:153.

56. RRS, "Railways: The Importance of Marshalling Yards. Paper 2," November 1940, USAFHRC, R-A5393, 512.611C, FR 896–903.

57. E. D. Brant, "Locomotives and Locomotive Depots as Air Targets. Paper 3," 2 November 1940, USAFHRC, R-A5393, 512.611C, FR 903–6.

58. C. E. R. Sherrington, "German Communications," 23 March 1941, USAFHRC, R-A5393, 512.6111C, FR 951–94.

59. War Office, TN.1(c), MI.8, "The Ruhr (Germany) Railway Handbook," November 1943, pp. 37, NA RG 243, 200(a)140.

60. OSS, R&A, "Railway Resources in Axis Europe," No. 799, n.d., Secret, pp. vi, 16, 18, 22, 25–26, 56; OSS, R&A, "German Strategic Survey—Railroads," No. 788, Para. 38a, 17 February 1943, Confidential, pp. 61, 63, 67, 72, 76–77, 81–82, NA RG 59.

61. OSS, R&A, "Covering Report on Higher Personnel of the German Railways," No. 1938, March 1944, Confidential, pp. 2, 6, 8, NA RG 59.

62. Tedder, *With Prejudice*, pp. 502–4, 509, 529, 537, 540; Zuckerman, *From Apes to Warlords*, pp. 222, 232–33, 289–90.

63. Zuckerman, *From Apes to Warlords*, p. 210; Zuckerman, "Air Attacks on Rail and Road Communications: An Analysis of Operations Carried out in Sicily and S. Italy," 28 December 1943, pp. ii–vi, 41, USAFHRC R-A5686, 519.425-1, FR 1211–12, 1272.

64. EOU War Diary, 5:86–89.

65. Ibid., p. 79.

66. Ibid., p. 71.

67. Ibid., p. 80.

68. Ibid., p. 78.

69. Rostow, *Pre-Invasion Bombing Strategy*, p. 144.

70. W&F, 3:27.

71. USSTAF, "Minutes of 25 March 1944 Meeting on Overlord Bombing Plan," pp. 4–8, USAFHRC, R-A5617, 519.3171-8, FR 1127–32.

72. Zuckerman, *From Apes to Warlords*, p. 236; Pogue, *The Supreme Command*, p. 127; Hamilton, *Master of the Battlefield*, p. 287.

73. Copp, *Forged in Fire*, pp. 457–58; Rostow, *Pre-Invasion Bombing Strategy*, p. 45.

74. Pogue, *The Supreme Command*, p. 130.

75. Ibid., p. 132; Tedder, *With Prejudice*, p. 532.

76. W&F, 3:46–47.

77. Ibid., 3:35–36.

78. Tedder, *With Prejudice*, p. 601.

79. Ibid., p. 537.

Chapter 5

1. BBSU, *The Effects of Air Attack on Inland Communications*, p. 58, appendix 3, table 1, USAFHRC R-A5346, 512.552-5, FR 765.

2. USSBS, *German Transportation*, p. 12.

3. Air Ministry, *Rise and Fall of the German Air Force*, p. 354.

4. Ibid., pp. 355–56.

5. Koch, *Flak*, p. 259.

6. RVM, Waterway Summary, July, August, September, 1943–44, BA R5/45.

7. Bezirksgruppe Steinkohlenbergbau, "Lagebericht Wirtschaftsgruppe Bergbau August 1944," G239, Geheim, Essen, 12 September 1944, p. 3, BA R10 VIII/7.

8. Ernst Freeden to Ref B 19, "Bericht über den Probleme der Binnenschiffahrt nach eine Reise an der Rheinhäfen 11–24 July 1944," B 21/36558 44, Blankensee, 5 August 1944, pp. 10–11. Freeden was a member of the Kontrolstab Binnenschiffahrt, under Dr. Ebhardt, B 19 in the RVM.

9. Saur, "Stichwörte für die Rüstungskartei," 30 June 1944, BA R5/1989.

10. ZVL, "45. Sitzung, 5.10.1944," Pr(z)81, Geheim, Berlin, 9 October 1944, p. 2, BA R5/57, f. 61.

11. Dr. Sarter, GVL-West, to RVM, B21 R1 2273/44g, Geheim, 29 June 1944, p. 4, BA R5/57.

12. ZVL, "41. Sitzung, 10. August 1944," Pr(z)81 Val, Geheim, Berlin, 12 August 1944, pp. 1–2, 4, BA R5/37, ff. 31–32, 34.

13. ZVL, "42. Sitzung, 23. August 1944," Pr(z)81 Val, Geheim, Berlin, 29 August 1944, pp. 1–3, 5–7, BA R5/37, ff. 36–38, 40–42. It should be noted that ammunition still had to be sent to the Heeres Munitionsanstalten (army munitions establishments) to be filled with powder and explosive.

14. Boelcke, *Deutschlands Rüstung*, p. 379, point 1; "Soforthilfe für die Reichsbahn," 3 July 1944 in Rü In Wiesbaden, "Kriegstagebuch Rü In XIIIa Wiesbaden, Nr. 20, 1.7–30.9.44," Nr. 2330/44g, Z.Abt./Ib, Anlage 2, BA/MA RW 20-12/29.

15. ZVL, "43. Sitzung, 6. September 1944," Pr(z)81, Geheim, Berlin, 9 September 1944, p. 5, BA R5/37, f. 53.

16. DR, "Vermerk," 10 Vwb 1261, Berlin, 9 September 1944, BA R5/3173; RVM, "Aktenvermerk über die Besprechung vom 2 Juni 1944 in Essen betr: Prämienverfahren für Brennstoffsendungen in geschlossenen Zügen von den westlichen Kohlenrevieren," Tge 1268, p. 3, BA R5/3002.

17. DR, Ref 13 to Ref 10, "Minettetransporte von dem Brieyer Raum nach dem Ruhrgebiet," 13 Tge 1839, Berlin, 22 August 1944, BA R5/2987.

18. GVL-West, "Abwicklung des Transportprogramms für inlandischen Eisenerze. Monat August 1944," 20 September 1944, BA R5/3177.

19. RZA, Blatt 91, March–August 1943, 1944; RZA, Blatt 92, March–August 1943, 1944.

20. Ibid.

21. RVK, Statistischer Bericht Nr. 13, pp. 3, 15.

22. RBD Saarbücken, "Übersicht über die Betriebslage (Stand vom 20.5.1944), p. 1; "Überblick über die Betriebslage," 10 June 1944, pp. 1–3, and 17 June 1944, pp. 1–2, BA R5 Anh I/81.

23. RZA, Blatt 91, Blatt 92, March–August 1943, 1944.

24. RVE, Zugang Erzen, Südwest.

25. RVE, Roheisen-Erzeugung, Rohstahl-Erzeugung.

26. RVE, Zugang Erzen, Reich.

27. RVE, Bestand Erzen, Nordwest.

28. RVE, Roheisen-Erzeugung.

29. VSt, Hauptstatistik, "Jahresübersicht," Vertraulich, Düsseldorf, pp. 3, 4; VSt, Hauptstatistik, "Eildienst," Vertraulich, Stat. N 0600/44, pp. 4–5.

30. Herbst, *Totale Krieg*, pp. 304, 334.

31. Klöckner-Werke, "Anlage I zum Fragebogen der USSBS . . . ," NA RG 243, 34(b)2; LWA Düsseldorf, "Die Kohlenversorgung der Industrie in SK und SKK ab April 1943," NA RG 243, 34(a)6.

32. GBL-Süd, "Wochenbericht, 2.9 bis 8.9.44," Munich, 9 September 1944, pp. 1–2, 4–6, NA RG 243, 200(a)55.

33. Rü In XIIb [a running list of firms giving their coal stocks by type from 1 April to 1 November 1944], BA/MA RW 21-40/11, also in NA T-84, R-46.

34. Badisches Hafenamt Mannheim 5/S, "Aufstellung über den monatlichen Umschlag in den Mannheimer Häfen, NA RG 243, 200(a)165.

35. Rü Kdo Mannheim, Z1-Gruppe, "Monatsbericht für die Zeit vom 1–30 September 1944," Ha/Gi, 27 September 1944; Rü Kdo Mannheim, "Monatsbericht 1–31.9.1944," H/U, 22 September 1944, BA/MA RW 20-5/31.

36. "Durchgangs-Verkehr der Wichtigen Schleusen des Dortmund-Ems-Kanals," p. 73, NA RG 243, 200(a)168; RVK, Statistischer Bericht Nr. 13, p. 6; RZA, Blatt 92, April–September 1943, 1944; RVE, Roheisen-Erzeugung; Rü In XIa Hannover, "KTB 1 Juli–30 September 1944," Nr. 273/44gK, Geheime Kommandosache, 13 December 1944, pp. 3–4, BA/MA RW 20-11/33.

37. Schäfer to Söhngen, Fs PRD 69, Essen, 3 September 1944, BBA 33/1442; RWKS, Abt. 2e, 2f, "Auswertung der Meldebogen," 17 October 1944, BBA 33/1436; RWKS, "Gesamtversand auf Bahn u. Wasser Monatsdurchschnitt," [two bar charts]; Fernschreiben, Schmidt to Sogemeier, Fs BRD 531, Essen, 19 July 1944, BBA 33/1032.

38. GBL-Ost, "Wochenbericht 2.9–8.9.1944," Vertraulich, Berlin, 9 September 1944, pp. 1–2, BA R5 Anh I/41.

39. GBL-Ost, "Wochenbericht 9.9–15.9.1944," Vertraulich, Berlin, 16 September 1944, pp. 1–2, 4, BA R5 Anh II/41.

40. RZA, Blatt 90, April–September 1943, 1944.

41. RVM, Waterway Summary, July, August 1944, BA R5/45.

42. RVK, Statistischer Bericht. Nr 13, p. 3.

43. RVE, Roheisen-Erzeugung.

44. Rü In VIIa, "Übersicht 1.7–30.9.1944," Wi/IF 5.959, Geheim, Breslau, pp. 30, 35, BA/MA RW 20-8/29.

45. RVM, Waterway Summary, August 1944, BA R5/45; G. H. Teetzmann to Pleiger and Meinberg, Ludwigslust, 24 October 1944, BA R10 VIII/61; Wasserstrassendirektion Potsdam, "Leistungsplan nach Güterarten für den Monat August 1944," Anlage to WS 5241/44, BA R5/108, f. 3.

46. BEWAG, "Niederschrift über die Vorstandssitzung am 14 September 1944," 11/44, BEWAG-Archiv.

47. Rü Kdo I, "KTB 1.7–30.9.1944," Berlin, September 1944, pp. 8, 13, BA/MA RW 21-2/9, also in NA T-73, R-20.

48. RVK, Statistischer Bericht Nr. 13, pp. 3, 5, 6.

49. Dr. von Trotha, Pla, "Wochenmeldung Nr. 36/44, 28.8–2.9.1944," Pla 210/009/8.9, Berlin, 8 September 1944, BA R3/1930, f. 460.

50. RVK, Statistischer Bericht Nr. 13, p. 15.

51. RVE, Bestand Erzen.

52. RMfRuK, SSBzKP, February 1945, pp. 2, 6.

53. RVE, "Verbrauch an Erzen sowie sonstigen eisenhältigen Rohstoffen bei den Hochofen-Stahlwerken und den mit ihnen ortlich verbundenen Giessereien nach Metallgruppen," BA R13 I/534, f. 134.

54. RMfRuK, SSBzKP, February 1945, p. 6.

55. Wagenführ, *Deutsche Industrie*, pp. 66, 178. The rate of growth was calculated from the indices presented here and depicted in Figure 1.1.

56. RMfRuK, "Ausstoss-Übersicht 1940–44 Waffen Geräte, Munition," Geheime Reichssache, 6 February 1945, BA R3/1729.

57. Kehrl, *Krisenmanager*, p. 394.

58. "Erlass des Führers über die Konzentration der Rüstung und Kriegsproduktion," 19 June 1944, reprinted in Nachrichten, Nr. 41, Vertraulich, Berlin, 3 August 1944, pp. 429–33, NA RG 243, 101(a)8; Speer, *The Slave State*, p. 144.

59. Reichstellen Eisen und Stahl, "Anordnung E I der Reichsstellen Eisen und Stahl (Neuordnung der Eisenbewirtschaftung)," 26 June 1944 in Nachrichten, Nr. 40, p. 469, NA RG 243, 101(a)10.

60. Weyres, "Die deutsche Rüstungswirtschaft," pp. 158–59.

61. Saur, "Stichwörte für die Rüstungskartei," 13 July 1944, BA R3/1989.

62. Boelcke, *Deutschlands Rüstung*, p. 400, point 2.

63. Saur, "Stichwörte für die Rüstungskartei," 1 August 1944, BA R3/1989.

64. RMfRuK, "Schaffung von Rüstungskommissionen," ZA/Org-200-Gew-208/44, Berlin, 1 August 1944, BA R5/3173; NSDAP, Partei-Kanzlei, Martin Bormann, "Verstärkter Einsatz der Gauleiter für die Rüstung und Kriegsproduktion," Lg/Tr., Nr. 320, Munich, 1 August 1944, BA R5/3173; RMfRuK, Speerchronik, 1944 II, 6 September 1944, pp. 252, 254–55, BA R3/1740, ff. 103, 105–6.

65. Nachrichten, Nr. 46, 29 September 1944, pp. 474–75, NA RG 243, 101(a)10.

66. Speer, *The Slave State*, p. 243; Speer Interrogation, 20 May 1945, Flensburg, p. 14, NA RG 243, 40(b)26.

67. RMfRuK, Speerchronik, 1944 II, p. 255a, BA R3/1740, f. 107.

68. RWKS, "Niederschrift. Sitzung SHG," Essen, 30 August 1944, pp. 5–6, BBA 33/340; RWKS to all mines, "Landabsatz," Tgb.-Nr. 2555, Essen, 5 September 1944, BBA 33/1442.

69. Rü Kdo Frankfurt/Main, copy of "Rüstungsbefehl," 9 September 1944 in Rü Kdo XIIa, "KTB 1.7–30.9.1944," Anlage 5, Wi/IF 5.3102, NA T-77, R-401, FR 1254660.

70. RMfRuK, "Erlaß betr. Kohlesparaktion," RLA-ER-HF, Nr. 10260/44, Berlin, 20 September 1944, BA R3/1854a, ff. 400–402, and in BA R13 XX/138.

71. Kehrl, *Krisenmanager*, pp. 409–10; Söhngen to various sections, Ludwigslust, 13 May 1944, BBA 33/1466; RWKS, Abt. R, to member mines, "Nachrichtenübermittlung," Geheim, Essen, 12 September 1944, BBA 33/1044.

72. Bennett, *Ultra in the West*, pp. 63–64, citing Ultra decrypts KV 5446, KV 8562, KV 8818, KV 3015; Hinsley, *British Intelligence*, 3 (1):54.

73. EOU, "The Use of Allied Air Forces After the Establishment of the Bridgehead," 27 May 1944, reprinted in EOU War Diary, 5:99.

74. C&C, 3:281.

75. MEW, "Intelligence Weekly. Survey of Economic Developments in German Europe in the Six Months ending 30 June 1944," Rep. No. 134, L.1/3/6Z, 31 August 1944, pp. 30–32, 61, NA RG 243, IV 22 k.

76. Capt. C. P. Kindelberger to Lt. Col. A. A. Part, "Interim Report on the Rail Movement of German Reserves," 16 June 1944, reprinted in Rostow, *Pre-Invasion Bombing Strategy*, pp. 134–35.

77. Zuckerman, *From Apes to Warlords*, pp. 300–302; the chart is reproduced in Tedder, *With Prejudice*, facing p. 541.

78. BBSU, *Inland Communications*, p. 61, USAFHRC R-A5346, 512. 552–5, FR 767.

79. Ibid., p. 69, FR 775.

80. Tedder, *With Prejudice*, p. 579.

81. Ibid., p. 534.

82. Ibid., p. 583.

83. EOU, "The Employment of Heavy Bombers Against Germany from the Present to V-Day," July 1944, reprinted in EOU War Diary, 5:105–6.

84. W&F, 3:53–55, 99.

85. USSTAF HQ, "Target Priorities," Secret, 1 September 1944, USAFHRC R-A5223, 509.425A, FR 1185–86.

86. W&F, 3:51, 58–59.

87. SHAEF, "96th Allied Air Commanders Conference, 12 September 1944," Top Secret, 14 September 1944, p. 4, USAFHRC R-A5087, 505.25-8, FR 572.

88. Portal and Arnold to Spaatz and Bottomley, Octagon 29, 14 September 1944, PRO AIR 37/1013.

89. W&F, 3:63.

90. SHAEF, "98th Allied Air Commanders Conference," Top Secret, 19 September 1944, p. 2, USAFHRC R-A5087, 505.25-8, FR 566.

Chapter 6

1. USSBS, *German Transportation*, p. 13.

2. Ibid., p. 41, table 10.

3. USSBS, *Rate of Operation*, p. 36, table 6.

4. BBSU, *Strategic Air War against Germany*, p. 123, USAFHRC R-A5346, 512.552–11, FR 1404.

5. W&F, 4:174–76, appendix 8, no. 42.

6. DR, "Niederschrift über die Besprechung der Dezernenten 21 am 20/21 October 1944 in Fischerhütte," Anlage 1 to 34 Bubl 35, 28 October 1944, BA R5/2088.

7. "Oberpräsident," Wasserstrassendirektion, Abt. Reichsschleppbe-

trieb, "39. Wochenbericht des RSB vom 22.9 bis 28.9.1944," Geheim, Münster, 30 September 1944, p. 1. NA RG 243, 200(a)190.

8. RMfRuK, Planungsamt, "40. Wochenbericht," Pla 1401 g. Rs./12.10, Geheime Reichssache, Berlin, 12 October 1944, p. 5, BA R5/1957, f. 524.

9. Meier, "Aktenvermerk," Tgb. Nr. 612, Geheim, Düsseldorf, 27 October 1944, NA RG 243, 200(a)190.

10. USSBS, *German Transportation*, p. 18, exhibit 12A.

11. ZVL, "46. Sitzung, 19.10.1944," Berlin, 10 October 1944, Geheim, p. 7, BA R5/37, f. 75.

12. RVM, Waterway Summary, September and October 1944, BA R5/45, ff. 44–46, 57–59; "Durchgangs-Verkehr der Wichtigen Schleusen des Dortmund-Ems-Kanals," NA RG 243, 200(a)168.

13. USSBS, *German Transportation*, p. 26, exhibit 13, figure 1.

14. RMfRuK, Speerchronik 1944 II, 28 October 1944, p. 281, BA R3/1740, f. 133.

15. Bahndienstfernschreiben, DRB 10 Vwb to Abt. B in RVM, RBD Hannover and Münster, 24 October 1944, BA R5/3173.

16. Telegramm, Kohlenwache Ludwigslust to Kohlenhandel Bremen, 27 October 1944, BA R10 VIII/65.

17. Bahndienstfernschreiben, Kohlenwache Berlin to Schiffahrtsstelle Dortmund, Nr. 56, RVM B22 B8616/44, 28 October 1944, BA R10 VIII/65.

18. *Deutsche Rheinbrücken*, p. 13a; USSBS, *German Transportation*, p. 18.

19. ZVL, "46. Sitzung, 19.10.1944," Geheim, Berlin, 24 October 1944, p. 2, BA R5/37, f. 72; "Oberpräsident," Wasserstrassendirektion, Abt. Reichsschleppbetrieb, "42. Wochenbericht, 13.10 bis 19.10.1944," 2208/44g, Streng Vertraulich, Münster, 21 October 1944, NA RG 243, 200(a)190; Duisburg harbor operations calculation based on Records of the USSBS, Work Sheets for the Transportation Division Final Report, "Waterway Traffic, Charts 7, 8, 8a, 11, 13," NA RG 243, 200(a)2; RVM, Waterway Summary, September and October 1944, BA R5/45, ff. 47–49, 56–59.

20. Reichsgruppe Industrie to GWK, 2 8500/44 (2800/1), Berlin, 29 September 1944, BA R10 8/61; RVM to Schiffahrtsstellen Duisburg, Dortmund, Hamburg, Berlin, Breslau, Danzig, Wien, Königsberg, "Dringlichleit der Transporte in der Binnenschiffahrt," B21 B7702/44, Berlin, 26 October 1944, BA R5/97.

21. RWKS, "Übersicht über die Benutzung der Leitungsweg seit Beginn der Sperre Westbezirk," n.d., BBA 33/1106.

22. Schmidt to Pleiger, 18 October 1944, BBA 33/1032.

23. Referat in ZP, "Kohlenversorgungslage Anfang November 1944," 8 November 1944, BA R10 8/19, f. 115.

24. Kehrl, *Krisenmanager*, p. 43; RMfRuK, Speerchronik 1944 II, 27 October 1944, p. 280, BA R3/1740, f. 132.

25. Boelcke, *Deutschlands Rüstung*, pp. 426–27.

26. RMfRuK, Planungsamt, "41. Wochenbericht," Pla 1401 g. Rs./20.10, Berlin, 20 October 1944, p. 1, BA R3/1957, f. 540.

27. Janssen, *Das Ministerium Speer*, p. 261; H. Reuter, Ruhrstab, to RBD Essen, "Sicherung des Verkehrs, Aufstellung von Eisenbahn-Eingreiftrupps," 2012/44c, Geheim, Kettwig, 4 October 1944, NA RG 243, 3(b)15; OKL, Ic/Wi, "Zum Luftkrieg gegen Bahn . . . 21–31.10.44," 2 November 1944, p. 1, BA R5/3699.

28. Dez 6 to Dez 7, GWK Düsseldorf, "Zulaufssperre für das linksrheinische Gebiet," 22 September 1944, RWWAzK, 22/246/681; RMfRuK, Planungsamt, "41. Wochenbericht," Pla 1401 g. Rs./20.10, Berlin, 20 October 1944, p. 5, BA R3/1957, f. 544; Dr. Pelzer, Dez 7, GWK Düsseldorf, to other interested sections in house, "Sperre bei der Reichsbahn," P/L, 26 October 1944, RWWAzK 22/246/681.

29. DR, "Sondermassnahmen West," 23 Bfg 144, Berlin, 19 September 1944, pp. 2–3, BA R5 Anh II/45; Bahndienstfernschreiben, DRB 26 Bau to GBLs, Berlin, 22 September 1944, BA R5/2089.

30. RVM, "Aktenvermerk über die Besprechung am 2 Oktober 1944 15 Uhr in Berlin über Güterzugfahrplanmassnahmen zur Bedienung des rheinisch-westfälisches Industriegebietes," Anlage 1 to 23 Bfg 144, Berlin, 19 October 1944, pp. 1–2, BA R5 Anh II/45. See also RVK to Schmidt, "Aktenvermerk, 'Besprechung im RVM, 2.10.1944, 15 Uhr, Güterzugfahrplanmassnahmen . . . ,'" 9 October 1944, BBA 33/1032.

31. RMfRuK, "Zustellung von Gütern an Notempfänger," Rü A/Ag. Verk (E) Nr. 11814/44, Vertraulich, 11 October 1944, in Nachrichten, Nr. 50, pp. 517–18, NA RG 243, 100(a)9.

32. Ministerialrat Dr. Ottmann, "Wochenbericht Referat II 3/4," Berlin, 26 October 1944, Wi/If 5.974, NA T-77, R-200, FR 936011.

33. Telegrammbrief, RVM Abteilung I, Schelp to RBDs, 10 Vwb 1348, Berlin, 7 October 1944, BA R5/2092.

34. ZVL, "44. Sitzung, 21.9.1944," Geheim, Berlin, 25 September 1944, p. 8, BA R5/37, f. 59.

35. ZVL, "46. Sitzung, 19.10.1944," Geheim, Berlin, 24 October 1944, p. 4, BA R5/37, f. 73.

36. Bahndienstfernschreiben, Schelp to all RBDs and Hwa, "Wagenstellung für Rüben, Kohlen und Kali," B-Nr. 697, Berlin, 20 October 1944, BA R5/3173.

37. Bahndienstfernschreiben, DRB 10 Vwb (Kohlen) 204 to RBDs Dresden, Essen, Köln, Regensburg, Hwa, 21 October 1944; RVK to Schelp, Berlin, 13 October 1944, BA R5/3181; Pla, "42. Wochenbericht, 16–21.10. 1944," Pla 1401 g. Rs./24.10, Geheime Reichssache, Berlin 24 October 1944, p. 5, BA R3/1957, f. 557.

38. ZVL, "44. Sitzung, 21.9.1944," Berlin, 25 September 1944, Anlage; ZVL, "46. Sitzung, 19.10.1944," Berlin, 24 October 1944, Anlage 4, BA R5/37, ff. 60–78.

39. Dr. von Trotha, Pla, "Vermerk zur Lage der Kohlenversorgung," Pla 210/009/2.11, Berlin, 2 November 1944, pp. 1–2, BA R3/1854a, ff. 382–83, R3/1930, ff. 523–24; Pleiger to Kohlenverteilungsstellen, LWA, Beauftragten der Gauleiter für Kohlenfragen, Bezirksbeauftragten für den Kohlen-

handel, "Richtlinien für die Versanddringlichkeit," Rst C 617/44, Vertraulich, Berlin, 14 October 1944, BBA 33/1106, and NA T-73, R-175, FR 3346507–8.

40. Maintenance Section 128, "List of Air Attacks on Hamm," Hamm, 4 May 1945, pp. 1–2, NA RG 243, 200(a)46.

41. Bahndienstfernschreiben, Essen to Berlin, Nr. 805, 11 October 1944, BA R5/3173.

42. RMfRuK, Planungsamt, "42. Wochenbericht, 16–21.10.1944," Pla 1401 g. Rs., Geheime Reichssache, Berlin, 24 October 1944, p. 5, BA R3/1957, f. 557.

43. GBL-Ost, "Wochenbericht 14.10–20.10.1944," Vertraulich, Berlin, 21 October 1944, p. 3, BA R5 Anh II/41.

44. RMfRuK, Planungsamt, "42. Wochenbericht, 16–21.10.1944," Pla 1401 g. Rs., Geheime Reichssache, Berlin, 24 October 1944, p. 3, BA R3/1957, f. 555.

45. Dr. Kritzler, RWKS, to Meinberg, Essen, 8 January 1945, BA R10 VIII/65; RWKS, Abt. 2c, 2f, "Auswertung der Meldebogen," BBA 33/1436; Referat in ZP, "Kohlenversorgungslage Anfang November 1944," Berlin, 8 November 1944, p. 7, BA R10 VIII/19, f. 117.

46. RMfRuK, Planungsamt, "40. Wochenbericht," Pla 1401 g. Rs., Geheime Reichssache, Berlin, 12 October 1944, pp. 3–4, BA R3/1957, ff. 522–23; RWKS, Rixfähren, "Aushilfslieferungen O.S.," 23 October 1944, BBA 33/1030.

47. Rüdiger Schmidt, "Niederschrift der Beiratssitzung," Essen, 19 September 1944, p. 5, BBA 33/329; Rüdiger Schmidt, "Niederschrift der Beiratssitzung," Essen, 18 October 1944, p. 7, BBA 33/329; Reichsstelle für Kohle to LWA, Rst Ia 724/44 Pt/en, Nur für den Dienstgebrauch, Ludwigslust, 12 October 1944, NA T-73, R-175, FR 3346505; Rüdiger Schmidt, "Niederschrift der Beiratssitzung," Essen, 18 October 1944, p. 7, BBA 33/329.

48. Rüdiger Schmidt, Rundschreiben to all mines, "Versandlenkung," Abt. 7a/2710, Essen, 7 October 1944, pp. 1–2, BBA 33/1442; Rüdiger Schmidt, Rundschreiben to all mines, "Versandlenkung," Abt. 7a/Nr. 2740, Essen, 28 October 1944, BBA 33/1442; RWKS, "Aktenvermerk," 19 October 1944, pp. 2–3, BBA 33/1040.

49. RZA, Blatt 92, September, October 1943, 1944.

50. RVK, Statistischer Bericht Nr. 13, pp. 3, 5, 15.

51. Speer to Pleiger, 61615, 31 October 1944, BA R10 VIII/5; RMfRuK, Planungsamt, "43. Wochenbericht, 23–28.10.1944," Pla 1401 g. Rs./1.11, Geheime Reichssache, Berlin, 1 November 1944, pp. 2–3, BA R3/1957, ff. 564–65.

52. Dr. von Trotha, Planungsamt, "Wochenmeldung Nr.44/44, vom 31.10–4.11.1944," Pla 210/009/11.11, Geheim, Berlin, 11 November 1944, pp. 2–3, BA R3/1930, ff. 435–36; USSBS, *21 Rheinische-Westfälische Elektrizitätswerke AG*, pp. nn. 8–9; WWi O, Wk VI, "Monatsbericht über die 'Allgemeine wehrwirtschaftliche Lage' nach dem Stände vom 31.10 und

30.11.44," Nr. 5379/44g, Geheim, Münster, 4 December 1944, p. 3, NA T-77, R-353. Wi/IF 5.2299, FR 1192543.

53. RZA, Blatt 92, September, October 1943, 1944.

54. RVK, Statistischer Bericht Nr. 13, p. 6.

55. Rohland to Ganzenmüller, Düsseldorf, 30 September 1944; Telegramm, Stab-Rohland, VSt, Düsseldorf, to Rohland, Nr. 818, Berlin, 26 September 1944; Rohland to Ganzenmüller, Düsseldorf, 30 September 1944, BA R5/3177.

56. ZVL, "45. Sitzung, 5.10.1944," Berlin, 9 October 1944, pp. 4–6, BA R5/57, ff. 62–63.

57. Sohl, Stab Rohland, VSt, Düsseldorf, to Transleit, Ruhrunion, Berlin, to be forwarded to Schelp, FS Nr. 650/0, 10 October 1944, BA R5/3177.

58. RVM, 10 Vwb to GBLs ZVL, Hwa, 1350, Berlin, 10 October 1944; RVM, C81 Vgbm to GBLs West, Süd, RBDs Berlin, Dresden, Halle, Essen, Wuppertal, Berlin, 14 October 1944, BA R5/3177.

59. DRB 10 Vwb (Erze) 60 to Sohl, Ver. Stahl, BA R5/3177.

60. RMfRuK, Planungsamt, "39. Wochenbericht," Pla 1401 g. Rs./9.10, Geheime Reichssache, Berlin, October 1944, p. 11, BA R3/1957, f. 510.

61. RMfRuK, Planungsamt, "41. Wochenbericht," Pla 1401 g. Rs./20.10, Geheime Reichssache, Berlin, 20 October 1944, pp. 5–6, BA R3/1957, ff. 544–45.

62. RMfRuK, "Anordnung Nr. 12 des Reichsbeauftragten für Eisen und Metall ... Begrenzung der Eindeckung und Beschlagnahme von Lagerbeständen an Erzeugnissen aus Eisen und Stahl, 31 Oktober 1944," in Nachrichten, Nr. 49, Vertraulich, 20 November 1944, Anlage 1, p. 505, NA RG 243, 101(a)10.

63. Dilli to GBLs, RBDs, 26 Bau 270, Berlin, 21 October 1944, BA R5/3181.

64. Sohl to Schmidt, Düsseldorf, 28 October 1944, BBA 33/1106.

65. Herbst, *Totale Krieg*, pp. 346, 404, 406–7.

66. RVE, Roheisen-Erzeugung, Rohstahl-Erzeugung.

67. RVE, Bestand Erzen, Nordwest.

68. RVE, Zugang Erzen, Nordwest; Bestand Erzen, Nordwest; Roheisen-Erzeugung; Rohstahl-Erzeugung.

69. VSt, Hauptstatistik, "Eildienst," No600/44, Düsseldorf, pp. 2, 4, NA RG 243, 3(a)37.

70. Speerchronik, 1944 II, 27 October 1944, p. 280, BA R3/1740, f. 132; RMfRuK, "Querschnittsbesprechung am 26.10.1944," RLA/KE/Ia/Dr. Bl/Pi, Berlin, 31 October 1944, p. 2, BA R3/1969, f. 142; Wwi O, Wk VI, "Monatsbericht über die 'Allegemeine wehrwirtschaftliche Lage nach dem Stande vom 31.10 und 30.11.44,'" Nr. 5379/44g, Geheim, Münster, 4 December 1944, p. 10, NA T-77, R-353, Wi/IF 5.2299, FR 1192550; Records of the USSBS, Klöckner-Werke AG, "Anlage 1 zum Fragebogen der USSBS," NA RG 243, 34(b)2; Fritz Hulvershorn, Fertigungsbericht, Bocholt, Westfalen, Geheim, BA/MA RW 21-51/19, also in NA T-85, R-44, EAP 66-b-10/14.

71. RWKS, "Von den Zechen fertiggestellte Kohlen- und Kokszüge Verteilungspläne . . . ," BBA 33/1044; RMfRuK, Planungsamt, "43. Wochenbericht, 23–28.10.1944," Pla 1401 g. Rs./1.11, Geheime Reichssache, Berlin, 1 November 1944, p. 2, BA R3/1957, f. 564; Dr. von Trotha, Planungsamt, "Vermerk zur Lage der Kohlenversorgung," Pla 210/009/2.11, Berlin, 2 November 1944, p. 5, BA R3/1854a, f. 386; Kelchner, "Aktenvermerk zur Besprechung beim Chef des Zentralamtes Oberbürgermeister P. Liebel," K/GZ, Saarbrücken, 31 October 1944, BA R5/3177.

72. GBL-Süd, Wochenberichte, 9–15, 16–22, 23–29 September, 30 September–6 October, 7–13, 14–20 October, 28 October–3 November 1944, Vertraulich, NA RG 243, 200(a)55.

73. RVM, Waterway Summary, September and October 1944, BA R5/45, ff. 45–49, 60–61; Badisches Hafenamt Mannheim, "Aufstellung über den monatlichen Umschlag in den Mannheimer Häfen," n.d., NA RG 243, 200(a)165.

74. RVK to Schelp, Berlin, 18 October 1944, BA R5/3181.

75. ZVL, "45. Sitzung, 5.10.1944," Berlin, 9 October 1944, p. 6, BA R5/57, f. 64.

76. Kugler to Stütz, Söhngen, Rosenkranz, Teetzmann, "Aushilfslieferungen für Mannheim," Dr K/HG, Berlin, 26 October 1944, BBA 33/1589.

77. GWK Schwaben to Kohlenkontor Weyhenmeyer & Co., Roe/Lp., 9 November 1944, NA T-73, R-175, FR 3346498.

78. Rü Kdo Mannheim, "Monatsbericht, 1–30.9.1944," H/U, 22 September 1944; Rü Kdo Mannheim, Zi-Gruppe, "Monatsbericht 1–30 September 1944," 27 September 1944, BA/MA RW 20-5/31.

79. RVK, "Niederschrift über die Sitzung in Hannover am 17.10.1944 . . . ," DR R/VO, Berlin, 18 October 1944, pp. 1–2, BA R10 8/28.

80. Dr. von Trotha, Planungsamt, "Wochenmeldung Nr. 44/44, 31.10–4.11.1944," Pla 210/009/11.11., Geheim, Berlin, 11 November 1944, p. 1, BA R3/1930, f. 435.

81. USSBS, Heavy Industry Branch, *Reichswerke Hermann Goering*, exhibit A, p. 2, exhibit B, exhibit C, p. 1, exhibit H, exhibit J, exhibit K.

82. RVE, Roheisen-Erzeugung.

83. GBL-Ost, Wochenberichte, 24.9–29.9., 30.9–6.10, 7.10–13.10, 14–20.10., 21–27.10., 28.10–3.11.1944, BA R5 Anh II/41.

84. Dr. Ottmann, "Wochenbericht Referat 2 3/4," Berlin, 26 October 1944, NA T-77, R-200, Wi/IF 5.474, FR 935011.

85. GBL-Ost, Wochenberichte 9–15.9, 16–23.9, 24–29.9, 30.9–6.10, 7–13.10, 14–20.10, 21–27.10, 28.10–3.11, 1944, BA R5 Anh II/41.

86. RZA, Blatt 90, weeks 38–43, 1943, 1944; RZA, Blatt 92, October 1943, 1944.

87. RZA, Blatt W 15.1, October 1944.

88. RVK, Statistischer Bericht Nr. 13, p. 6.

89. Söhngen to Rixfähren and Stütz, So/B, Ludwigslust, 13 October 1944, BBA 33/1589.

90. RZA, Blatt 90, weeks 38–43, 1943, 1944; Blatt 92, October 1943,

1944; Blatt W 15.1, 1944.

91. Calculated from RVK, Statistischer Bericht Nr. 13, pp. 3, 5, 15.

92. RMfRuK, Planungsamt, "39. Wochenbericht," Pla 1401 g. Rs./9.10, Geheime Reichssache, Berlin, 9 October 1944, p. 4, BA R3/1957, f. 503.

93. RVE, Roheisen-Erzeugung.

94. Fernspruch, Abt. Präs. Thomas to Krüger, RMfRuK, Oppeln, 25 September 1944, BA R5/3173.

95. RVM, Waterway Summary, September and October 1944, BA R5/45, ff. 44–45, 55–56.

96. GBL-Ost, "Wochenbericht, 14–20.10.44," Vertraulich, Berlin, 21 October 1944, p. 1, BA R5 Anh II/41.

97. Oberpräsident Wasserstrassendirektion, "Monatsbericht . . . September 1944," W.S. 5698/44/15 A, Potsdam, 3 November 1944, pp. 1–2, BA R5/80, f. 27; Wasserstrassendirektion Potsdam, "Leistungsplan nach *Güterarten* . . . September 1944," W.S. 5642/44/Tt 15A, Potsdam, BA R5/108, f. 1.

98. Wasserstrassendirektion Potsdam, "Leistungsplan nach *Güterarten* . . . Oktober 1944," Potsdam, BA R5/107, f. 195.

99. RWKS, Abt. 2b, 2f, "Auswertung der Meldebogen," BBA 33/1436.

100. BEWAG-Archiv.

101. BEWAG, "Niederschrift über die Vorstandssitzung am 13 Oktober 1944," 12/44. BEWAG-Archiv, o/12.

102. BEWAG-Archiv.

103. RZA, Blatt 90, weeks 38–43, 1943, 1944 for freight cars, and Blatt 92, October 1943, 1944 for coal cars.

104. RMfRuK, Planungsamt, "50. Wochenbericht 10–16.12.1944," Pla 1401 g. Rs./21.12, Geheime Reichssache, Berlin, 21 December 1944, p. 3, BA R3/1957, f. 653.

105. OKL, Ic/Wi, "Einwirkungen des feindlichen Luftkreiges auf der Eisenbahnverkehr im Oktober 1944," Geheim, 25, October 1944, p. 4, BA R5/3699.

106. USSBS, *German Transportation*, pp. 74–75, exhibit 72; ZVL, "45. Sitzung, 5.10.1944," Geheim, Berlin, 9 October 1944, p. 2, BA R5/57, f. 62.

107. RZA, "Stand der Güterwagenausbesserung," Blatt W 12, Woche 15.10–21.10.1944, Nur für den Dienstgebrauch, NA RG 243, 200(a)113.

108. RZA, Blatt W 15.1, October 1944.

109. Dr. von Trotha, Planungsamt, "Vermerk zur Lage der Kohlenversorgung," Pla 210/009/2.11, Berlin, 2 November 1944, p. 4, BA R3/1854a, f. 386.

110. Ibid., p. 1, f. 383.

111. Wagenführ, *Deutsche Industrie*, pp. 66, 178.

112. RVK, Statistischer Bericht Nr. 13, p. 3.

113. Wagenführ, *Deutsche Industrie*, p. 179.

114. RMfRuK, Ausstoss-Übersicht, p. 5, BA R3/1729, f. 7.

115. Rüstungslieferungsamt, Amtsgruppe G, "Informationsdienst für die Mittelinstanz," Sch. Geheim, Berlin, 30 October 1944, BA R3/1969, f. 33.

116. Chef des Heeresrüstung und Befehlshaber des Ersatzheeres, "Über-

blick über den Rüstungsstand des Heeres," Stab Rüst IIIc, Nr. 574d/44 g. Kdos., Geheime Kommandosache, 15 November 1944, BA/MA RH 8/v. 1104.

117. See, for example, SHAEF, "Enemy Communications Summary, No. 9," 5 October 1944, p. 7, USAFHRC R-A5178, FR 1732.

118. A case in point is RRS, Report No. 265, Secret, 27 September 1944, p. 1, USAFHRC, R-A5111, FR 292.

119. SHAEF, "Enemy Communications Summary No. 12," Secret, 9 November 1944, p. 1, USAFHRC, R-A5178, FR 1783; C. E. R. Sherrington, RRS, Report No. 270, Secret, 1 November 1944, p. 3, USAFHRC, R-A511, FR 1785.

120. C. E. R. Sherrington, RRS, Report No. 269, Secret, 25 October 1944, p. 1, USAFHRC, R-A5111, FR 288; MEW, Intelligence Weekly, Report No. 143, 2 November 1944, p. 3, NA RG 243, 4 22b.

121. OSS, London, No. SQ-2069, 27 October 1944, USAFHRC, R-A5717, FR 1736; SHAEF, "Enemy Communications Summary No. 11, Secret, 30 October 1944, p. 2, USAFHRC, R-A5178, FR 1760.

122. See for example the belated and garbled report on Speer's speech at Posen in the Japanese Military Attaché's report, transmitted 24 October 1944, D7599, NA RG 427, SRA 13011; compare to the account in Speer, *Inside*, p. 393.

123. OSS London, No. SQ-1931, 30 September 1944, USAFHRC, R-A5717, FR 1309.

124. SHAEF, "Enemy Communications Summary No. 9," Secret, 9 October 1944, p. 2, USAFHRC, R-A5178, FR 1726.

125. Lt. Col. W. F. R. Ballard, Chief of Analysis Section, MAAF, "Recommendations on Program for Heavy Bombardment, MAAF/s 6662/INT, 28 September 1944, USAFHRC, R-A5686, FR 1330–32; Target Section, USS-TAF, "Suggested Plans for Attack on German Transportation System," 14 September 1944, USAFHRC, R-A5616, FR 477, 479, 481.

126. Arnold to Kuter, "Priority Targets, Europe," 19 October 1944, USAFHRC, R-A1378, FR 49.

127. Paraphrase of cipher message from Joint Chiefs of Staff to British Chiefs of Staff, J.S.M. 312, Top Secret, 21 October 1944, PRO AIR 37/1005.

128. DD.B. Ops. (1), AI(3)E, "Air Attack on Transportation Targets Germany," Top Secret, 30 September 1944, USAFHRC, R-A5686, FR 1376–77.

129. Herrington, *Air Power*, p. 313.

130. AC/AS Plans, "Proposed Target Priorities," Secret, October 1944, USAFHRC, R-A1377, FR 833–35.

131. Air Staff, "Combined Strategic Targets Committee," C.M.S., Top Secret, 13 October 1944, PRO AIR 37/1013.

132. The CSTC was simply the Joint Oil Targets Committee with a new name. See the following for some of the substance behind Tedder's fears. CSTC, "Minutes of a Meeting Held at the Air Ministry, Whitehall, on October 24, 1944 . . . ," Secret, USAFHRC, R-A5090, FR 171–74. At the second meeting of the CSTC, Lawrence said that the oil offensive, if pressed with the utmost vigor, could end the war in sixty days. CSTC, "Minutes of the

2nd Meeting of the CSTC, 25 October 1944," Top Secret, p. 3, PRO AIR 40/1269.

133. Tedder to Bottomley, S.65388, Secret, SHAEF Main, 4 November 1944, PRO AIR 37/1013. See also letter to Derek Wood, Top Secret, 30 October 1944, PRO FO 837/385.

134. Tedder, "Notes on Air Policy to Be Adopted with a View to Rapid Defeat of Germany," DSC/TS.100d/d, Top Secret, 25 October 1944, p. 1, PRO AIR 37/1013. This is reprinted in W&F, vol. 4, appendix 25.

135. Ibid., p. 5.

136. Ibid., p. 2.

137. Ibid., p. 1.

138. For evidence supporting Tedder's conclusion see CSTC, "Review of the Operations of the the CSTC Working Committee (Communications), 'Summary of the Further Statement by Mr. Brant on 26 October 1944, at the Air Ministry, Whitehall,'" Top Secret, 26 October 1944, USAFHRC, R-A5223, FR 859.

139. This came after the plan was apparently agreed to at a dinner attended by Portal, Bottomley, Spaatz, and Tedder on 27 October 1944. SHAEF, D/COS (Air), Historical Record, October 1944, p. 5, PRO AIR 37/1060.

140. W&F, 3:73, vol. 4, appendix 8 XLIIIb, pp. 178–79.

141. CSTC, "Review," appendix 3, "Plan for Attack on German Transportation System," 7 November 1944, p. 1, USAFHRC R-A5223, FR 814.

142. Ibid., pp. 2–3, FR 862–63. It is astonishing to note that Oliver Lawrence, head of the Working Committee (Communications) was simultaneously head of the Working Committee (Oil). He doubted the workability of the transportation plan that he himself had drawn up. CSTC, "Minutes of the Third Weekly Meeting," Top Secret, 1 November 1944, p. 4, PRO AIR 40/1269.

Chapter 7

1. This should be seen in light of the following statement made by Speer to his subordinates: "You must not think that the enemy, during half or three-quarters of a year, will obstinately attack the same target again and again. It is quite possible that he will change his targets." "Speech by Reich Minister Speer at Rechlin on the situation in the Ruhr, 1 December 1944," reprinted in W&F, vol. 4, appendix 36, p. 359.

2. C&C, 3:655–56.

3. CTSC, Working Committee (Communications), to Bufton, 8 December 1944, USAFHRC, R-A5223, 509.425B, FR 1047.

4. CSTC, "Review," p. 9, USAFHRC, R-A5223, 509.425B, FR 821.

5. USSBS, *Rate of Operation*, pp. 36, 49, tables 6, 23; CSTC, "Review," appendix 9, table B, USAFHRC, R-A5223, 509.425B, FR 944.

6. Oberpräsident, Wasserstrassendirektion, Wasserstrassenbevollmächtigter to RVM, "Luftangriff auf den Dortmund-Ems-Kanal am 4.11.1944,"

WEV Nr. 2300/44g, Geheim, Münster, 6 November 1944, NA RG 243, 200(a)190; Oberpräsident, Wasserstrassendirektion, Abt. Reichsschleppbetrieb, "44–46. Wochenbericht des Reichsschleppbetriebes vom 27.10–16. 11.1944," Tgb. Nr. 2254/44g,- Geheim, Bergeshövede, 18 November 1944, NA RG 243, 200(a)190; Oberpräsident, Wasserstrassendirektion, Abt. RSB, "47. Wochenbericht des RSB vom 17. bis 23.11.44.," Geheim, Bergeshövede, 25 November 1944, pp. 1–2, NA RG 243, 200(a)190; RSB to RVM, "Angriff auf den Dortmund-Ems-Kanal," Bergeshövede, 2 January 1945, pp. 1–2, BA R5/98.

7. Meier, Schiffahrtsstelle Duisburg, "Aktenvermerk, ME/R Tgb. Nr. 901g, Geheim, Duisburg, 7 November 1944, NA RG 243, 200(a)190; Speer to Pleiger, 364/44, Berlin, 10 November 1944, BA R10 VIII/5; Wasserstrassenbevollmächtigte, Oberpräsident der Provinz Hannover, "Pendelverkehr," Nr. WBV. 450a.2443XVg, Geheim, Hannover, 25 November 1944, NA RG 243, 200(a)190; Speer to Pleiger, Berlin, 29 November 1944, BA R10 VIII/5; Beirat to Schmidt, 28 November 1944, pp. 3–4, BBA 33/1032.

8. Speer to Hettlage, Geheim, Berlin, 27 November 1944; Nachrichten, Nr. 50, 14 December 1944, p. 516, NA RG 243, 100(a)9; RVM, Orr. Müller to Schiffahrtsstelle Duisberg, B 26 RL 5000/44g, Geheim, Berlin, 12 January 1945, BA R5/7; Teetz to Teetzmann, Berlin, 14 December 1944, BA R10 VIII/61; Speer to Oberpräsident der Rheinprovinz Westfalen, EN 44200/44, Berlin, 21 November 1944, BA R10 8/65; Schiffahrtsstelle Duisburg to all offices in the Rhine area, "Verkehrsleitende Anordnung über Genehmigungspflicht der Transport innerhalb des Rheinstromgebietes," Düsseldorf, 19 December 1944, BA R5/97.

9. Oberpräsident, Wasserstrassendirektion, Abt. RSB, "47. Wochenbericht des RSB vom 17. bis 23. 11.44," Geheim, Bergeshövede, 25 November 1944, p. 1, NA RG 243, 200(a)190.

10. "Durchgangs-Verkehr der Wichtigen Schleusen des Dortmund-Ems-Kanals," NA RG 243, 200(a)168.

11. RVK, "Mitteilung vom RVM, Berlin," BBA 33/1032.

12. Oberpräsident, Wasserstrassendirektion, Wasserstrassenbevollmächtigter to RVM, "Luftangriff auf den Dortmund-Ems-Kanal am 4.11.1944," WEV Nr. 2300/44g, Geheim, Münster, 6 November 1944; Oberpräsident, Wasserstrassendirektion, Abt. Reichsschleppbetrieb, "44–46. Wochenbericht des Reichsschleppbetriebes vom 27.10–16.11.1944," Tgb. Nr. 2254/ 44g, Geheim, Bergeshövede, 18 November 1944; Oberpräsident, Wasserstrassendirektion, Abt. RSB, "47. Wochenbericht des RSB vom 17. bis 23.11.44.," Geheim, Bergeshövede, 25 November 1944, pp. 1–2, NA RG 243, 200(a)190.

13. Records of the USSBS, "Coal through Minden East. Chart 10a," NA RG 243, 200(a)2.

14. Fernschreiben, Baur, RVM, to Elbe ports, B19 B375/45, Berlin, 19 January 1945, BA R10 8/62.

15. Speditions und Elbeschiffahrt-Konter Gebrüder Wanckel to Baur, RVM, Schonebeck, 25 January 1945, BA R10 VIII/62.

16. USSBS, *German Transportation*, p. 23; RVM, Waterway Summary, November, December 1944, BA R5/45, ff. 27, 37–39.

17. RWKS, Schmidt, situation reports, Geheim, 23–26 December 1944, BBA 33/1061.

18. RVK, "Wochenbericht vom 28 Januar bis 3/4 Februar 1945," Geheim, p. 6, BA R10 VIII/69.

19. RWKS, Schmidt, situation report, Geheim, 16 January 1945, BBA 33/1061.

20. Schiffahrtsstelle Duisburg, "Aktenvermerk-Kohlentransporte," Tgb. Nr. 1553g, Geheim, Duisburg, 28 November 1944, BA R5/57.

21. RWKS, Schmidt, situation report, Geheim, 29 December 1944, BBA 33/1061.

22. "Die Binnenschiffahrt im Dezember 1944," 19 January 1945, BA R5/80, f. 78.

23. Schiffahrstelle Duisburg, "Leistungsplan nach Verkehren," 1 November–20 December 1944, BA R5/107, ff. 38–47.

24. Schiffahrtstelle Duisburg, "Leistungsplan nach Verkehren, Dekade 21.12.44 bis 31.12.44," Düsseldorf, 4 January 1945; "Leistungsplan nach Verkehren, Dekade 1.1.45 bis 10.1.45," Düsseldorf, 14 January 1945, BA R5/107, ff. 32, 36.

25. RMfRuK, Planungsamt, "Die Verkehrslage in Grossdeutschland," (Stichtage 18.1.1945.), p. 2, BA R3/1957, f. 728.

26. CSTC, "Review," appendix 9, table A, USAFHRC, R-A5223, 509. 425B, FR 644.

27. BBSU, *Inland Communications*, p. 192, appendix 20, USAFHRC R-5346, 512.552–5, FR 1016; Fwi Amt, Fachabteilung T u V, "Aktennotiz über die 49. ZVL-Sitzung am 1.12.1944," Nr. 3012/44geh, Geheim, Berlin, 2 December 1944, p. 1, NA T-77, R-13, Wi/IF 5.105, FR 723692; Zahn, "Dokumentarische Darstellung," p. 23, BA R5 Anh I/9.

28. USSBS, *German Transportation*, pp. 56, 60.

29. USSBS, *Railway Viaduct at Bielefeld*, pp. 1, 3, 9, 13, NA RG 243, 200(a)181.

30. USSBS, *Railway Viaduct at Altenbecken*, pp. 1–3, NA RG 243, 200(a)190; B. O. R. Bartsch, "Bahnhof Altenbecken in den Kriegsjahren 1944–1945," BA R5 Anh I/46.

31. RMfRuK, Planungsamt, "44. Wochenbericht," Pla 1401 g. Rs./11. 11.44, Geheime Reichssache, Berlin, 11 November 1944, p. 6, BA R3/1957, f. 579; Sts. Fischböck, Planungsamt, "Folgen der Feindeinwirkung im Ruhrgebiet," Pla 210/009/7.11, Geheim, Berlin, 7 November 1944, p. 1, BA R3/1854a, f. 393.

32. Münzer, History of GBL-West written for the USSBS, 10 June 1945, p. 6, NA RG 243, 200(a)40. Münzer was Sarter's successor.

33. Maintennance Section 138, Hamm (Westfalen), "List of Air Attacks on Hamm," 4 May 1945, pp. 1–2, NA RG 243, 200(a)46. This is a USSBS translation of a document prepared by the RAW at Hamm. The original has been lost.

34. "Bericht . . . RBD Wuppertal," Geheim, 3 November 1944, document 207; 29 November 1944, document 221; 7 January 1945, document 230; 8 January 1945, document 232; 24 January 1945, document 237, BA R5 Anh I/87.

35. Verkehrskontrolle II, RBD Wuppertal, 25 May 1945, NA RG 243, 34(d)2.

36. RVM E-Abt. (L-4), "Die Einwirkungen des Luftkrieges auf der Bahn . . . 1–8 November 1944," Geheime Reichssache, Berlin, 9 November 1944, p. 3, BA R5/3699.

37. Speer to Hitler, 11 November 1944, reprinted in W&F, vol. 4, appendix 35, p. 350.

38. RVM/E-Abt. (L-4), "Die Einwirkung des Luftkrieges . . . 1–12 November 1944," Berlin, 13 November 1944, p. 5, BA R5/3699.

39. Boelcke, *Deutschlands Rüstung*, p. 444.

40. Dr. G. A. Pilz, Vertrauensmann des Rüstungsobmann VIb des RMfRuK den Arbeitsamtbezirk Velbert, "Rundschreiben an alle Industriefirmen des Kreises Niederberg, Material- und Transportschwierigkeiten," 22 November 1944, RWWAzK, 22/42.

41. Ganzenmüller, 9 December 1944, p. 6, BA R5/3699. A translation is available in NA RG 243, 200(a)137.

42. Hampe, "Technische Wehrmachthilfe: Ihre geschichtliche und Ihre Aktuelle Bedeutung," pp. 280–86; Fwi Amt, Fachabteilung T u. V, "Einsatz der Wehrmacht zur Aufrechterhaltung bezw. Wiederinbetriebnahme des Eisenbahnverkehrs und der Binnenschiffahrt," B. Nr. 4071/44 geh, Geheim, Berlin, 1 December 1944, NA T-77, R-13, Wi/IF 5.105, FR 723691.

43. Bahndienstfernschreiben, RVM to RBDs Saarbrücken and Köln, Nr. 660, 27 December 1944, BA R5 Anh II/52.

44. Bahndienstfernschreiben, RBD Köln to Beauftragter des RVM beim Ruhrstab Hoesel, Nr. 61, Köln, 1 December 1944, BA R5/3181.

45. Münzer, History of GBL-West, p. 10, NA RG 243, 200(a)40; Ganzenmüller, 9 December 1944, pp. 1–2, BA R5/3699.

46. Bahndienstfernschreiben, DRB, 10 VWB (Kohlen) to RBDs Essen, Köln, Hwa, "Wagenstellung für Kohlen im Ruhrgebiet," Nr. 240, Berlin, 25 November 1944, BA R5/3181.

47. RWKS, Schmidt, Rundschreiben to all mines, Tgb. Nr. 2972, Essen, 28 November 1944, BBA 33/1442.

48. Bahndienstfernschreiben, Lammertz to Hwa, GBL-West, ZVL (Emich personally), "Wagenstellung fuer Brennstoffe im Ruhrgebiet," Nr. 702, 29 November 1944, BA R5/3181.

49. Bahndienstfernschreiben, DRB, 10 Vwb (Kohlen) to RBD Oppeln, Nr. 243, Berlin, 4 December 1944, BA R5/3181.

50. Bahndienstfernschreiben, DRB 10 Vwb (Kohlen) to RBDs, Hwa, "Verbesserung der Wagenstellung für Kohlen," Nr. 242, Berlin, 4 November 1944, BA R5/3181.

51. RMfRuK, "Anlage, Sammelbericht," 11 December 1944, BA R 3/300; Fwi Amt, Fachabteilung T u V, "Aktennotiz über die 49. ZVL-Sitzung am

1.12.1944," Nr. 3012/44 geh, Geheim, Berlin, 2 December 1944, pp. 1–2, NA T-77, R-13, Wi/IF 5.105, FR 723692.

52. Telegrammbrief, 10 A Vusg to all GBLs, RBDs, Hwa, Nr. 2810, 20 December 1944, BA R5/3167.

53. Bahndienstfernschreiben, DR, 26 Bau to all GBLs, RBDs, Berlin, 9 December 1944, BA R5/2088.

54. RWKS, Schmidt, situation report, Geheim, 1–2 January 1945, BBA 33/1061; RWKS to all mines, "Dienstkohlen für die Deutsche Reichsbahn," Tgb. Nr. 128, Essen, 24 January 1945, BBA 33/1442.

55. Dr. von Trotha, Planungsamt, "Wochenmeldung Nr. 44/44 vom 31.10–4.11.1944," Pla 210/009/11.11. Berlin, 11 November 1944, pp. 1–2, BA R3/1930, ff. 435–36; Kehrl, "Vorläufige Richtlinien für die Kohlenversorgung," Pla 00/210/003/3.12, Geheim, Berlin, 3 December 1944, pp. 1–2. BA R3/1854a, ff. 352–53, also in BA R3/1916, ff. 150–51; Pleiger to LWA and Kohlenverteilungsstellen, Rst I 398/45g, 25 January 1945, BBA 33/1106.

56. Dr. von Trotha, Planungsamt, "Wochenmeldung Nr. 49/44 vom 27.11–3.12.44," Pla 210/090/10.12, Geheim, 10 December 1944, p. 1, BA R3/1930, f. 427.

57. Fernschreiben, Ganzenmüller to Lammertz, Berlin, 7 November 1944, BA R5/3173; Speer to Hitler, 11 November 1944, p. 1, reprinted in W&F, vol. 4, appendix 35, p. 349. See also NA T-73, R-182, RMfRuK/1840, FR 3394854.

58. Schmidt, "Aktenvermerk," 10 November 1944, BBA 33/1032.

59. DR, "Aktenvermerk über die Besprechung am 19 Januar im RVM über eisenbahnbetriebliche Massnahmen zur Einsparung von Kohle," 23 g. Rs./Bmba 59, Geheime Reichssache, Berlin, 26 January 1945, BA R5/54.

60. Compiled from the Tagesberichte kept by Rüdiger Schmidt in his personal files, BBA 33/1061.

61. RWKS to Meinberg, Essen, 20 November 1944; letter, RWKS to Meinberg, Essen, 8 February 1945, BA R10/ 8/65.

62. RVM/E-Abt. (L-4), "Die Einwirkungen des Luftkrieges . . . 1–12 November 1944," Berlin, 13 November 1944, p. 2, BA R5/3699.

63. Records of the USSBS, "Ganzenmüller Interrogation," 30 May 1945, pp. 4, 8–9; "Dilli Interrogation," 18 June 1945, p. 2, NA RG 243, 200(a)127.

64. RZA, Blatt W 15.1, November, December 1944.

65. English translation of RBD Essen document dated 2 July 1945, NA RG 243, 200(a)1. The original has been lost.

66. Bahndienstfernschreiben, GBL-West to Mineis 36, Nr. 11, 1 December 1944, BA R5/3181.

67. RWKS, Abt. 2f, to Schmidt, 16 January 1945, BBA 33/1040.

68. Bahndienstfernschreiben, RVM to RKA Essen and Gleiwitz, and RWKS, Berlin, 8 November 1944; Fernschreiben, RWKS to Kohlenwache Berlin/Ludwigslust, Essen, 9 November 1944, BBA 33/1032.

69. Bahndienstfernschreiben, RBD Essen to RBDs, OZL u. WG. Hannover, Münster, Hamburg, Wuppertal, Kassel, Frankfurt/Main, Hwa, Mi-

neis 10, 23, Nr. 661, 14 November 1944, BA R5/3173.

70. Bahndienstfernschreiben, DRB 26 Bau to GBLs, RBDs Hamburg, Hannover, Berlin, Halle, Erfurt, Kassel, Hwa, Berlin, 11 November 1944, BA R5/2089.

71. Bahndienstfernschreiben, DRB 23 Bfg to RBDs Breslau, Oppeln, Osten, Posen, Stettin, GBL-Ost, "Sonderaktion West-Ost," Berlin, 15 November 1944, BA R5/2089.

72. Bahndienstfernschreiben, DR 10 Vwb (Kohlen), Nr. 243, Berlin, 29 November 1944, BA R5/3181.

73. RBD Wuppertal 7 Vgba to Verkehrsbeauftragten für die Wirtschaft, Dr. Peltzer, GWK Düsseldorf, Zweigstelle Wuppertal, "Bahnhofräumung," Wuppertal, 16 December 1944, RWWAzK, 22/246/681.

74. Fwi Amt, Fachabteilung T u V, "Aktennotiz über die 51. ZVL-Sitzung am 29.12.44," Nr.3210/45geh, Geheim, Berlin, 2 January 1945, p. 1, NA T-77, R-13, Wi/IF 5.105, FR 723682.

75. RZA, Blatt 90, weeks 45–52, 1943, 1–4, 45–53, 1944, 1–4, 1945; Blatt 92, November, December 1943, 1944, January 1944, 1945.

76. Fwi Amt, Fachabteilung T u V, "Aktennotiz über die 51. ZVL-Sitzung am 29.12.44," Nr. 3210geh, Geheim, Berlin, 2 January 1945, pp, 3–4, NA T-77, R 13, Wi/IF 5.105, FR 723684–5.

77. GBL-Ost, "Wochenbericht 4–10.11.1944," Berlin, 11 November 1944, p. 3, BA R5 Anh II/41; note in Schmidt files dated 11 November 1944, BBA 33/1054; DRB 26 Bau to GBLs and RBDs, Nr. 250, Berlin, 27 November 1944, BA R5/2088.

78. RMfRuK, Planungsamt, "44. Wochenbericht, 30.10–4.11.44," Pla 1401 g. Rs./11.11.44, Geheime Reichssache, Berlin, 11 November 1944, p. 6, BA R3/1957, f. 579.

79. Telegramm, 26 Baü to RBDs Frankfurt/Main and Wuppertal, Nr. 280, 19 December 1944, BA R5/2089.

80. For example see RWKS to participants in its courier system, "Sicherung der Nachrichtenübermittlung/Kurierverbindungen 4. Ergänzungsrundschreiben," Essen, 15 December 1944, BBA 33/1044; W. Müllenhagen to W. M. Buchwald internally at Ford-Köln-Niehl, 30 November 1944, NA RG 243, I 3b(15); Dr. Peltzer, Rundschreiben, "Postverkehr," P/L, Vertraulich, 15 January 1945, RWWAzK, 22/42.

81. RWKS, Abt. 7a, to member mines in the Ruhr, 2756, Essen, 18 November 1944, BBA 33/1106.

82. Hortmann, Oberschlesisches Steinkohlensyndikat, to RWKS, "Aushilfslieferungen/Direktgeschäfte," IVc/5013, H/Gi, Berlin, 23 December 1944; RWKS to SHGs, "Aushilfslieferungen von O/S. Direktgeschäfte," DR.E./STR. 2f, 30 December 1944, BBA 33/589.

83. RVK, "Aktenvermerk," DR. Pi/Scho-A2182, Berlin, 8 January 1945, BA R10 VIII/5.

84. Schmidt, "Aktenvermerk," Chârlottenhof, 17 November 1944, BBA 33/1032.

85. RVK, Statistischer Bericht Nr. 13, p. 3; Seebauer, Produktionsamt,

5167/45-S/K, 30 January 1945, BA R3/1560, f. 69.

86. Calculated from RVK, Statistischer Bericht Nr. 13, pp. 16, 18, BBA 15/1103; RZA, Blatt 92, August–December 1943, 1944; Badisches Hafenamt, "Aufstellung über den Verkehr in den Manheimer Häfen," NA RG 243, 200(a)165; "Durchgangs-Verkehr der Wichtigen Schleusen der Dortmund-Ems-Kanals," NA RG 243, 200(a)168. The deficit was determined by comparing shipments during the period under discussion with those of the previous year.

87. RVK, Statistischer Bericht Nr. 13, p. 15.

88. Ibid., p. 5.

89. Dr. von Trotha, Planungsamt, "Wochenmeldung Nr. 49/44, 27.11– 3.12.1944," Pla 210/090/10.12, Geheim, 10 December 1944, p. 2, BA R3/1930, f. 428.

90. RVK, Statistischer Bericht Nr. 13, p. 15.

91. Ibid., p. 6.

92. RMfRuK, Planungsamt, "50. Wochenbericht 10. bis 16.12.1944," Pla 1401 g. Rs./21.12, Geheime Reichssache, Berlin, 21 December 1944, p. 1, BA R3/1957, f. 651; Liebel, "Kohlenfereien," Pla 00/210/009/13.11, Berlin, 13 November 1944, BA R3/1854a; RVK to RVM, EA, Ludwigslust, 28 November 1944; RVK to RVM, EA, Ludwigslust, 6 January 1945, BA R5/3181.

93. Dr. Kugler, "OS. Ruhraushilfe November 1944," Berlin, 13 December 1944, BBA 33/1589.

94. Söhngen to Sogemeier, Berlin, 12 January 1945, BBA 33/1589.

95. Schmidt, "Vermerk," February 1945, BBA 33/1106.

96. RWKS, Sekretariat R, to Söhngen, "Aushilfen," Essen, 27 November 1944, BBA 33/1589.

97. Schmidt to Sogemeier, 4 January 1945, BBA 33/1030.

98. Söhngen, "Besprechung bei der Generalbetriebsleitung Ost am 14.12. 44/Kohlenlieferungen," Ludwigslust, 16 December 1944; Oberschlesisches Steinkohlensyndikat to KK Weyhenmeyer, "Aushilfslieferungen," 10 January 1945; Sogemeier to Söhngen, "Leuna-Koks," Ludwigslust, 8 December 1944, BBA 33/1589.

99. RWKS, "Beiratssitzung, 14 November 1944," p. 7, BBA 33/329; Schmidt to Pleiger, 2 December 1944, BBA 33/1106.

100. RWKS, "Beiratssitzung," 28 November 1944, pp. 6–7; RWKS, "Beiratssitzung," 12 December 1944, p. 4. BBA 33/329.

101. RWKS, "Beiratssitzung," 14 November 1944, p. 8, BBA 33/329.

102. Schmidt, "Aktenvermerk," 10 November 1944, BBA 33/1032, RWKS, "Beiratssitzung," 28 November 1944, p. 6, BBA 33/329.

103. Dr. Grünberg, Planungsamt, "Wochenmeldung Nr. 4/45 vom 22– 27.1.45.," Pla 210/09/27.1, Geheim, Berlin, 27 January 1945, p. 2, BA R3/1854a, f. 294.

104. Dr. von Trotha, Planungsamt, "Wochenmeldung Nr. 49/44 vom 27.11–3.12.44," Pla 210/090/10.12, Geheim, Berlin, 10 December 1944, p. 2, BA R3/1930, f. 428.

105. RWKS, "Beiratssitzung," 27 December 1944, p. 8, BBA 33/329.

106. Dr. Baudisch, Planungsamt, "Wochenmeldung Nr. 3/45 vom 15–20.1.45," Geheim, Berlin, 20 January 1945, pp. 3–4, BA R3/1854a, ff. 314–15.

107. RVE, Zugang Erzen, Nordwest. Domestic ore production was down by 64.25 percent in January 1945 compared to the 1/1944 average. RMfRuK, SSBzKP February 1945, p. 2. The cause was a shortage of coke at the mines due to transportation difficulties. RMfRuK, Planungsamt, "50. Wochenbericht 10 bis 16.12.1944," Pla 1401 g. Rs./21.12., Geheime Reichssache, Berlin 21 December 1944, p. 5, BA R3/1957, f. 654.

108. RVE, Bestand Erzen, Nordwest.

109. RVE, Roheisen-Erzeugung.

110. RVE, Rohstahl-Erzeugung.

111. RMfRuK, SSBzKP, February 1945, p. 6.

112. RMfRuK, Planungsamt, "Vermerk, Eisen- und Stahlverbrauch," Pla 200/0/11.1, Geheime Reichssache, Berlin, 11 January 1945, pp. 1–2, BA R3/1842.

113. Oberstleutnant Böhm, WWi O, Wk 6, "Monatsbericht über die Allgemeine wehrwirtschaftlichelage nach dem Stande vom 31.10 und 30.11. 1944," Nr. 5379/44g, Geheim, Münster, 4 December 1944, pp. 2–3, 10, NA T-77, R-353, Wi/IF 5.2299, FR 1192542, 1192543, 1192550; Oberstleutnant Böhm, WWi O, Wk 6, "Monatsbericht über die Allgemeine wehrwirtschaftlichelage nach dem Stande vom 31.12.44," Nr.5553/44g, Geheim, Münster, 5 January 1945, pp. 13, 17–18, NA T-77, R353, Wi/IF 5.2299, FR 1192553, 1192557, 1192558.

114. Dez 7, GWK Düsseldorf, Düsseldorf, 4 January 1944, RWWAzK, 22/246/681.

115. RWM, "Versorgung- und Produktionsprobleme," Geheim, 18 January 1945, pp. 4–5, NA T-77, R-34, RWM/5/10, FR 428595–96.

116. Dez 6 to Dez 7, GWK Düsseldorf, "Energie- und Versorgunslage im Gau Düsseldorf," 3099g, Geheim, 18 November 1944, p. 3, RWWAzK, 22/42.

117. GBL-Ost, "Wochenbericht 2–8.12.1944," Berlin, 9 December 1944, p. 4, BA R5 Anh II/41.

118. RWKS, "Beiratssitzung," 17 January 1945, p. 4, BBA 33/329.

119. RMfRuK, "Die Verkehrslage in Grossdeutschland, (Stichtag 18.1. 1945)," Geheim, p. 1, BA R3/1957, f. 727.

120. Badisches Häfenamt Mannheim, "Aufstellung über den monatlichen Umschlag in den Mannheimer Häfen," NA RG 243, 200(a)165.

121. GBL-Süd, "Wochenbericht 4.11 bis 10.11.1944," Vertraulich, Munich, 11 November 1944, p. 1, NA RG 243, 200(a)55.

122. GBL-Süd, "Wochenbericht 30.12.44 bis 5.1.1945," Vertraulich, Freising, 6 January 1945, p. 1, NA RG 243, 200(a)55.

123. GBL-Süd, "Wochenbericht 16.12 bis 22.12.44," Vertraulich, Freising, 26 December 1944, p. 3, NA RG 243, 200(a)55.

124. GBL-Süd, Wochenberichte, 25 November 1944, p. 6, 16 December 1944, p. 2, 30 December 1944, p. 7, NA RG 243, 200(a)55.

125. GBL-Süd, "Wochenbericht 18.11 bis 24.11.44," Vertraulich, Munich, 25 November 1944, p. 7, NA RG 243, 200(a)55.

126. See GBL-Süd, Wochenberichte 11 November, 18 November, 25 November, 9 December, 16 December 1944, NA RG 243, 200(a)55.

127. GBL-Süd, "Wochenbericht 9.12 bis 15.12.44," Vertraulich, Munich, 16 December 1944, p. 11, NA RG 243, 299(a)55.

128. Ibid., p. 4.

129. Fernschreiben, Dilli to GBL-Süd, GBL-West, RBDs Augsburg, Essen, Erfurt, Kassel, Nürnberg, Stuttgart, Wuppertal, "Bewegung Westwind Süd," Berlin, 16 December 1944, BA R5/2088.

130. GBL-Süd, "Wochenbericht 13.1.45 bis 19.1.45," Vertraulich, Munich, 20 January 1945, p. 4, NA RG 243, 299(a)55.

131. Rü Kdo Ludwigshafen/Rhein, "Bericht über die Lage der Betriebe im Raum Ludwigshafen am Rhein in Januar 1945," Vertraulich, Ludwigshafen, 28 January 1945, Anlage 3, pp. 1–3, BA/MA RW 21-51/19. Also in NA T-84, R-44, EAP 66-b-10/14.

132. Rü Kdo Ludwigshafen, "Verzeichnis über Stillegungen infolge Brennstoffmangel," BA/MA RW 21-40/11. Also in NA T-84, R-46.

133. Rü Kdo Ludwigshafen/Rhein, "Bericht über die Lage der Betriebe im Raum Ludwigshafen am Rhein in Januar 1945," Vertraulich, Ludwigshafen, 28 January 1945, p. 2, BA/MA RW 21-40/12. (This copy has no Anlagen but is undamaged; the copy in BA/MA RW 21-51/19 has the Anlagen, but the text is incomplete.) Also in NA T-84, R-44, EAP 66-b-10/14.

134. Ibid., Anlage 2, 3, p. 1, BA/MA RW 21–51/19.

135. USSBS, *Brown, Boveri & Cie, Mannheim, Käfertal*, pp. 2, 23, 33.

136. Dr. von Trotha, Planungsamt, "Wochenmeldung Nr.2/45," Pla 210/09/13.1, Geheim, Berlin, 13 January 1945, p. 1, BA R3/1854a, f. 308.

137. RVM, "Fernspruch aus Hannover," B 22B, 236 45, Berlin, 12 January 1945, BA R5/98.

138. Schnellbrief, Baur, RVM, to RVK, B 19 B 9449/44, Berlin, 30 November 1944, BA R10 VIII/64.

139. Dr. Ebhardt, RVM, to Teetzmann and Teetz, B 19 B 9821/44, Berlin, 13 December 1944, BA R10 VIII/62.

140. Records of the USSBS, "Work Sheet, Coal Through Minden, Chart 10a," NA RG 243, 200(a)2.

141. St.-Sek. Fischböck, Planungsamt, "Folgen der Feindeinwirkung im Ruhrgebiet," Pla 210/009/7.11, Geheim, Berlin, 7 November 1944, p. 2, BA R3/1854a, f. 394.

142. Ruhrkohle Berlin to Kohlenwache Ludwigslust, "Bericht aus Hannover," Nr. 212/d, Berlin, 9 January 1945, BA R10 8/65; RWKS, "Vermerk: Ruhraushilfe des Sächsischen Steinkohle-Syndikat für Hütte Watenstedt," Berlin, 2 December 1944, BBA 33/1589.

143. USSBS, *German Transportation*, p. 89, exhibit 97.

144. USSBS, Heavy Industry Branch, *Reichswerke Hermann Goering*, exhibit H.

145. Ibid., exhibit K.

146. Ibid., exhibit M.

147. Ibid., exhibit N.

148. RMfRuK, Planungsamt, "51. Wochenbericht 18–29.12.44," Pla 1401 g. Rs./5.1.45, Geheime Reichssache, Berlin, 5 January 1945, p. 4, BA R3/1957, f. 656.

149. USSBS, Ordnance Branch, *Friedrich Krupp Grusonwerke*, p. 7; Motor Vehicles and Tanks Branch, *Friedrich Krupp Grusonwerke*, pp. 3–4, 21–22.

150. RZA, Blatt 90, weeks 45–52, 1943, 45–53, 1944, 1–4, 1944, 1945.

151. RZA, Blatt 92, November, December 1943, 1944, January 1944, 1945.

152. Zugleitung Bf Halle, "Gefahrene Züge auf den Zahlstrecken Halle-Grosskorbetha und Halle-Eisleben," 26 May 1945, NA RG 243, 200(a)42.

153. RBD Halle, "Rückstau an Güterzugen für den Bezirke der RBD Halle bei den 7 Nachbardirektionen, NA RG 243, 200(a)153.

154. RZA, Blatt 90, weeks 45–52, 1943, 45–53, 1944, 1–4, 1944, 1945; Blatt 92, November, December 1943, 1944, January 1944, 1945. RVM, Abt. 3 to Abt. 1 erg, Berlin, 5 January 1945, BA R5/3181; RZA, Blatt W 15, November, December 1944.

155. RBD Oppeln to Eisenbahnabteilung DR, III 7 Wg Vwb, Oppeln, 16 December 1944, BA R5/3173.

156. GBL-Ost, "Wochenbericht 4–10.11.1944," Vertraulich, Berlin, 11 November 1944, p. 2, BA R5 Anh II/41.

157. GBL-Ost, "Wochenbericht 25.11–1.12.1944," Vertraulich, Berlin, 2 December 1944, pp. 2–3, BA R5 Anh II/41.

158. GBL-Ost, "Wochenbericht 2–8.12.1944," Vertraulich, Berlin, 9 December 1944, p. 4, BA R5 Anh II/41.

159. GBL-Ost, "Wochenbericht 9–15.12.1944," Vertraulich, Berlin, 16 December 1944, p. 3, BA R5 Anh II/41.

160. GBL-Ost, "Wochenbericht 16–22.12.1944," Vertraulich, Berlin, 23 December 1944, p. 6, BA R5 Anh II/41.

161. GBL-Ost, "Wochenbericht 11–17.11.1944," Vertraulich, Berlin, 18 November 1944, p. 5, BA R5 Anh II/41.

162. FWi Amt, Fachabteilung T u V, "Aktennotiz über die 51. ZVL-Sitzung am 29.12.44," Nr. 3210/45 geh, Geheim, Berlin, 2 January 1945, p. 1, NA T-77, R-13, Wi/IF 5.105, FR 723682.

163. Speer to Hitler, Berlin, 16 January 1945, BA R3/1532.

164. RVK, Statistischer Bericht Nr. 13, pp. 11, 15; Dr. Frisch, Planungsamt, "Wochenmeldung Nr. 3/45," Pla 210/09/20.1, Geheim, Berlin, 20 January 1945, p. 3, BA R3/1854a, f. 314.

165. Oberpräsident der Provinz Niederschlesien, Wasserstrassendirektion, "Oderschiffahrt im Monat November 1944," OP II. 5c S3375, Berlin, 20 December 1944, p. 1, BA R5/80, f. 58; RVM, Waterway Summary, November, December 1944, BA R5/45, ff. 24–25, 34; RVM, Abt. B, "Vermerk," B 21 B 9692/44, Berlin, 4 December 1944, BA R5/100; FWi Amt, Fachabteilung T u V, to Min. Rat Twiehaus in RVM, "Oder Verkehr," B Nr. 562/45, Breslau, 8 January 1945, BA R5/100; RVK to Meinberg, Berlin, 16 January

1945, BA R10 VIII/62; RVM, Waterway Survey, December 1944, BA R5/45, ff. 24–25.

166. RVM, Waterway Summary, December 1944, BA R5/45, ff. 24–25.

167. Oberpräsident Wasserstrassendirektion, "Monatsbericht über die Verkehrslage der Markischen und der Stettiner Binnenschiffahrt im November 1944," W.S. 6534/44/T22, Potsdam, 20 December 1944, pp. 1–2, BA R5/80; Wasserstrassendirektion Potsdam, "Leistungplan nach *Güterarten* für den Monat November 1944, " BA R5/107, f. 194.

168. Wasserstrassendirektion Potsdam, "Leistungsplan nach Verkehr für Dekade 11 bis 20 Dezember 1944," W.S. 6655; "Leistungsplan nach Verkehr für Dekade 21 bis 31 Dezember 1944," Anlage to WS 60, BA R5/108.

169. USSBS, *Effects of Area Bombing on Berlin*, p. 14.

170. Wirtschaftgruppe Gas- und Wasserversorgung, "Übersicht über die Kohlenlage der Rangfolgewerke nach dem Stande von etwa dem 18.1.1945," Geheim, 24 January 1945, BA R13 XVII/45.

171. Dr. Nain, BEWAG, "Niederschrift über die Vorstandssitzung am 18.1.1945," 2/45, 3 February 1945, BEWAG-Archiv o/12.

172. BEWAG, "Monatsbericht der Abt. Kraftwerkleitung," BEWAG-Archiv o/60.

173. BEWAG, "Technische Monatsberichte-Erzeugung," BEWAG-Archiv, o/60.

174. FWi Amt, Fachabteilung T u V, "Aktennotiz über die 49. ZVL-Sitzung am 1.12.1944," Geheim, Nr. 3012/44 geh, Berlin, 2 December 1944; "Aktennotiz über die 50. ZVL-Sitzung am 15.12.1944," B. Nr. 3074/44geh, Geheim, Berlin, 18 December 1944, p. 1; "Aktennotiz über die 51. ZVL Sitzung am 29.12.44," Nr. 3210/45 geh, Geheim, Berlin, 2 January 1945, NA T-77, R-13, Wi/IF 5.105, FR 723692, 723686, 723682.

175. Ganzenmüller, "Verkehrslage," Berlin, 9 December 1944, p. 4, BA R5/3699.

176. RBD München, "Richtlinien für das Fahren auf Sicht," IV 32 B 3 Bauf, Freising, 26 January 1945, as Anlage to RVM order Bauf 536 of 2 January 1945, BA R5 Anh II/45.

177. RVM/E-Abt. (L-4) to OKL Ic, "Die Auswirkungen des verscharften Luftkrieges auf die Betriebsfuhrung der DRB," 4 December 1944, p. 2, BA R5/3699. Also in NA RG 243, 200(a)47. Ganzenmüller, 9 December 1944, p. 8, BA R5/3699 and in NA RG 243, 200(a)137.

178. RZA, Blatt 90, weeks 45–52, 1943, 45–53, 1944, 1–4, 1944, 1945.

179. Fwi Amt, Fachabteilung T u V, "Wochenbericht 24–30.12.1944," B. Nr. 43/45, Geheim, Berlin, 3 January 1945, p. 1, NA R-13, Wi/IF 5.105, FR 723621.

180. FWi Amt, Fachabteilung T u V, "Aktennotiz über die 51. ZVL-Sitzung am 29.12.44," Nr. 3210/45 geh, Geheim, Berlin, 2 January 1945, p. 1, NA T-77, R-13, Wi/IF 5.105, FR 723682.

181. RZA, Blatt 92, November, December 1943, 1944, January 1944, 1945.

182. RVK, Statistischer Bericht Nr. 13, p. 20.

183. RZA, Blatt W 15.1, December 1944; Dr. Ing. Schleip, GWK Würt-

temberg-Hohenzollern, dis-be-240g, Geheim, Stuttgart, 30 January 1945, p. 2, BA R3/300; RZA to all RBDs, "Braunkohlen als Lokfeuerung," BKo B lst 11/44, Berlin, 6 January 1945; RZA, "Vorläufige Richtlinien für die Beimischung von Braunkohlen und Braunkohlenbrikette zur Lokomotivefeuerung," Berlin, January 1945, NA RG 243, 200(a)130.

184. Records of the USSBS, Dilli Interrogation, 18 June 1945, p. 4, NA RG 243, 200(a)127; RMfRuK, "Die Verkehrslage in Grossdeutschland (Stichtag 18.1.1945)," Geheim, p. 1, BA R3/1957, f. 727; Ganzenmüller, "Verkehrslage," 9 December 1944, p. 4, BA R5/3699; Dr. Ing. Schleip, GWK Württemberg-Hohenzollern, dis-be-240g, Geheim, Stuttgart, 30 January 1945, p. 2, BA R3/300; Fernschreiben, RVM, 10 Vgb to all RBDs, Berlin, 22 December 1944, BA R5/2089; Bahndienstfernschreiben, DRB 26 Bau to all RBDs, "Rückstausondermassnahmen," 9 December 1944, BA R5/2088; Fernschreiben, Regierungsrat Rossmüller to all RBDs, 28 January 1945, BA R5/2089.

185. Speer, Rü A/AG, Verkehr, Nr. 19861/44g, Geheim, Berlin, 21 November 1944, BA R10 3/81.

186. Janssen, *Das Ministerium Speer*, p. 261.

187. (B)ewag hptv Berlin RLV to Bezirkslastverteiler des Mitteldeutsches Frequenzblocks, "Gebietsweise Stromsperren," Fs 2751/44, Geheim, Berlin, 18 December 1944, BA R8 IV/1.

188. Fischer, Reichslastbln to Bezirkslastverteiler, Fs 2868/45, Geheim, Berlin, 5 January 1945, BA R8/4/1.

189. Kehrl, "Erlass über eine Kontingentierung von Wirtschaftstransporte," Pla 200 220/18.12, B/Zi, Berlin, 14 December 1944, Anlage to 10 Val 209, Berlin, 4 January 1945, BA R5/95.

190. Kehrl, *Krisenmanager*, pp. 413–14.

191. ZP, Referat, Dr. Rgl/Gr, "Kohlenversorgunglage Anfang November 1944," 8 November 1944, p. 7, BA R10 VIII/19.

192. Wagenführ, "Wochenbericht für die Zeit vom 13 bis 18.11.1944," Pla 404/17.11, Berlin, 17 November 1944, p. 1. BA R3/1966.

193. Speer to Hitler, 11 November 1944, reprinted in W&F, vol. 4, appendix 35, pp. 349, 354, 356; Speer, "Informationsdienst Nr. 2," Pla 140 71g/30.11, Geheim, Berlin, 30 November 1944, BA R3/1558; "Speech of Reichsminister Speer at Rechlin on the situation in the Ruhr, 1 December 1944," in W&F, vol. 4, appendix 36, p. 370; Speer, "Informationsdienst Nr. 2," Pla 140 71g/12.12, Berlin, 12 December 1944, pp. 1–3, BA R3/1558.

194. RMfRuK to WiGr. Bergbau, "Einrichtung von Kohlennotstandzügen, RoA 1/630/30.11, Berlin, 30 January 1945, BBA 15/278; Telegramm, Söhngen to Schmidt, Ludwigslust, 15 January 1945, BBA 33/1466; RWKS, "Beiratssitzung," 17 January 1945, pp. 13–14, BBA 33/329; Weyres, "Die deutsche Rüstungs Wirtschaft," p. 157; Vögler to Kehrl, Dortmund, 22 December 1944, BBA 33/1084.

195. Fernschreiben, Parteikanzlei to Schelp, FS. NR 15542, Munich, 8 November 1944, BA R5/3181; Robe, RBD Wuppertal, to NSDAP Gauleitung Düsseldorf, "Neue Massnahmen im Berufsverkehr," RWWAzK, 22/246/681; Chef der Sicherheitspolizei und der SD, "Klagen über die Deut-

sche Reichsbahn," II D 2 Az 11878/44, Berlin, 2 January 1945; Dr. Wendler, 10 Vwb to Chef der Sicherheitspolizei und der SD, Berlin, 19 January 1945, BA R5/3174; Speer to Reichsverteidigungskommissare, Berlin, 20 December 1944, BBA 33/1106; Schnellbrief, RMfRuK, Zentralstelle für Rüstungsverkehr und Transportordnung, Amtsgruppe Verkehr (zbV), E 261, Berlin, 29 January 1945, BBA 15/278.

196. Ganzenmüller to Kehrl, "Bevollmächtigten für Wirtschaftstransporte," 5 December 1944, BA R5/95; RMfRuK, "Anordnung über Massnahmen zur Sicherung kriegswirtschaftlischen Transporte auf Grund der Verordnung zur Durchführung des Vierjahresplans Vom 6 Dezember 1944," reprinted in "Nachrichten Nr. 50," Vertraulich, 14 December 1944, p. 515, NA RG 243, 100(a)9; Dorpmüller to RBDs, Hwa, "Bestellung von Bevollmächtigten für Wirtschaftstransporte," 10 Val 209, Berlin, 4 January 1945, BA R5/95.

197. Speer, "Vereinfachung der Organisation des Reichministeriums für Rüstung und Kriegsproduktion durch Auflösung und Zusammenlegung von Ämtern," Berlin, 15 November 1944, reprinted in Nachrichten, Nr. 49, 20 November 1944, pp. 500–502, NA RG 243, 100(a)10; Boelcke, *Deutschlands Rüstung*, p. 446, point 13; Speer, ZA/Org. 206-145/44, Berlin, 6 December 1944, BA R10 8/5; Speer, "Aufhebung aller Dringlichkeitsregelungen," Berlin, 14 December 1944, reprinted in Nachrichten, Nr. 51, 10 January 1945, pp. 524–28, NA RG 243, 100(a)9.

198. Sogemeier to Alfred Krupp, Vertraulich, Ludwigslust, 30 December 1944, BA R10 VIII/3.

199. RWM, "Versorgung- und Produktionsprobleme," Geheim, pp. 8–13, 16, 19, NA T-71, R-34, RWM/5/10, FR 428599, 428606, 428607, 428610.

200. Speer, "Rechenschaftsbericht," Nr. M 1362/45, g. Rs., Berlin, 27 January 1945, pp. 1, 2, 21–22, 24, NA RG 243, 54(a)1. A copy of a draft may be found in BA R3/1560.

201. Wagenführ, *Deutsche Industrie*, p. 117; RMfRuK, "Notprogram der Rüstungsendfertigung," Anlage to Führerbefehl, 31 January 1945, BA R10 III/93.

202. GWK Düsseldorf, "Amtliche Meldebogen," January, February 1945, Records of the USSBS, NA RG 243, 34(f)1, 34(c)3; RVK, "Die Kohlenwirtschaft im Dezember 1944," 364/45, Geheim, Berlin 5 January 1945, p. 3, BA R10 VIII/5.

203. Dr. Grünberg, Planungsamt, "Wochenmeldung Nr. 4/45 vom 22–27.1.45," Pla 210/09/27.1, Geheim, Berlin, 27 January 1945, p. 3, BA R3/1854a, f. 295.

204. Speer, "Rechenschaftsbericht," p. 11.

205. Dr. Grünberg, Planungsamt, "Wochenmeldung Nr. 4/45 vom 22–27.1.45," Pla 210/09/27.1, Geheim, Berlin, 27 January 1945, Anlage, BA R3/1854a, f. 296.

206. RMfRuK, SSBzKP, February 1945, p. 48.

207. USSBS, *Anti-Friction Bearings Industry*, p. 61; RMfRuK, Planungsamt, "51. Wochenbericht, 18–29.12.44," Pla 1401 g. Rs./5.1.45, Geheime Reichssache, Berlin, 5 January 1945, p. 6, BA R3/1957, f. 678.

208. Wagenführ, *Deutsche Industrie*, p. 179.

209. Heereswaffenamt, "Überblick über den Rüstungsstand des Heeres, Teil Waffen," Nr. 601/45/45 g. Kdos., Geheime Kommandosache, Zossen, 15 March 1945, Blatt 3, 30, BA/MA RH 8/v. 1861, ff. 18, 43.

210. OKH, Gen. St. d. H./Gen Qu, "Vortragsnotiz über die Munitionslage Stand 1.12.1944," AZ. 2300 Abt. I/Gr. Mun. Nr. 19272/44 g. Kdos., BA/MA RH 8/v. 1019.

211. DR, "Vermerk," Berlin, 27 December 1944, BA R5/3174.

212. Von Mellenthin, *Panzer Battles*, p. 323.

Chapter 8

1. USAAF, *Ultra*, pp. xii, 172; Combined Intelligence Committee, "Estimate of the Enemy Situation: Europe," CIC 47/13, JIC (45) 38, Secret, 30 January 1945, p. 2, USAFHRC R-A5109, 505.42-22, FR 397; Erickson, *Road to Berlin*, p. 485.

2. Arnold to Maj. Gen. Clayton Bissell, Top Secret, 8 January 1945; Kuter to Arnold, Top Secret, 13 January 1945, USAFHRC, R-A1378, 145. 1–162, FR 97, 103–5; Kuter to Spaatz, 7 January 1945, Secret, USAFHRC R-A5534, 519.161-9, FR 1782.

3. ACIU, "Summary of Damage to Selected Railway Centers for the Week Ending 6 December 1944, Intelligence Report No. FD 3," HNJ/PD, Secret, 7 December 1944, USAFHRC R-A5111, 505.43-20, FR 568; USSTAF, "Air Intelligence Summary No. 62," 16 January 1945, pp. 18–19, NA RG 243, 5q(3) Env. 36c.

4. USSBS, *Kassel Marshalling Yards*, p. 60.

5. USSBS, *Railway Viaduct at Bielefeld*, p. 8.

6. ACIU, "Summary of Damage to Selected Railway Centers for the Week Ending 30 December 1944, Intelligence Report No. FD 6," Secret. 30 December 1944, pp. 1–2; "Summary of Damage to Selected Railway Centers for the Week Ending 11 March 1945, Intelligence Report No. FD 16," Secret, 12 March 1945, pp. 1–2, USAFHRC R-A5111, 505.43-20, FR 522–23, 563.

7. FO-MEW, "Six-Monthly Report," No. 1, Secret, London, 28 February 1945, pp. 2–4, 16–17, 51–52, USAFHRC, 512.609Q, FR 1139–41, 1149–50, 1184–85.

8. EOU War Diary, 5:10.

9. CSTC, "Review," p. 6.

10. W&F, 3:245, 249; CSTC, "Minutes of the 7th Meeting of the CSTC at the Air Ministry," Secret, 29 November 1944, p. 3, USAFHRC, R-A5110, 505.43-6, FR 1380; "Minutes of the 14th Meeting of the CSTC at the Air Ministry, Secret, 17 January 1945, pp. 1–2, USAFHRC R-A5110, 505.43-6, FR 136–37; "The Locomotive Position of German Europe," Secret, 14 January 1945, reprinted as appendix 4 in "Review," USAFHRC R-A5223, 509. 25B, FR 872–73; Working Committee (Communications), Bulletin No. 5,

Top Secret, 10 January 1945, pp. 1–5, USAFHRC R-A5111, 505.43-23, FR 1319–23.

11. CSTC, "Review," p. 11.

12. CSTC, "The Current German Rail Situation and the Problem of Air Attack, 10 January 1945, reprinted in "Review," p. 13, USAFHRC R-A5223, 509.425B, FR 825.

13. USSTAF, "Railway Targets in a Limited Area," January 1945, p. 3, Top Secret, USAFHRC R-A5617, 519.323-12, FR 238.

14. CSTC, "The Current German Rail Situation and the Problem of Air Attack," 10 January 1945, reprinted in "Review," USAFHRC R-A5223, 509. 25B, FR 826.

15. CSTC, "Minutes of the 10th Meeting," Top Secret, 22 December 1944, p. 3, PRO AIR 40/1269. Bottomley had similar suspicions. SHAEF, D/CoS (Air), Historical Record, December 1944, p. 16, PRO AIR 40/1060.

16. When asked on 15 January 1945 by his headquarters if his journey had been worthwhile, Tedder responded tersely, "No." SHAEF, D/CoS (Air), Historical Record, January 1945, p. 10, PRO AIR 37/1060.

17. ACOS G-2, SHAEF, "Notes on the German Railway Situation, Secret, 15 December 1944, reprinted in "Review," Appendix 4, USAFHRC R-A5223, 509.425B, FR 880–84.

18. SHAEF G-2, "Enemy Communications Summary No. 12," 9 November 1944, p. 3, USAFHRC R-A5178, 506.6111, FR 1785.

19. SHAEF G-2, "Enemy Communications Summary No. 13," 18 November 1944, p. 1, USAFHRC R-A5178, 506.6111, FR 1804.

20. SHAEF G-2, "Enemy Communications Summary No. 14," 27 November 1944, p. 1, USAFHRC R-A5178, 506.6111, FR 1837.

21. SHAEF G-2, "Enemy Communications Summary No. 22," 22 January 1945, p. 1, USAFHRC R-A5178, 506.6111, FR 659.

22. CSTC, "Minutes of the 10th Meeting," Top Secret, 22 December 1944, p. 7, PRO AIR 40/1269. GC and CS had made major progress since the spring of 1944. It had solved the key of Wehrkreis VI, which encompassed the Ruhr, in November 1944. In August 1944 it solved its first western Reichsbahn key, "Blunderbuss," and in October a second DR key, "Culverin." Hinsley, *British Intelligence*, 3 (2):527, 847, 856–57.

23. USAAF, *Allied Strategic Air Force Target Planning*, SRH-017, p. 52, NA RG 457; Hinsley, *British Intelligence*, 3 (2):607 citing BAY/BT 65.

24. Ibid., p. 53; Hinsley, *British Intelligence*, 3 (2):526 citing Ultra decrypt HP 4397. Hinsley notes that this message was decrypted on 24 October 1944. It is certain that this and other decrypts from late 1944 were ignored by the CSTC until the end of February 1945.

25. Bennett, *Ultra in the West*, pp. 202–8. See also pp. 209–10 for reports on the failure of supplies to the Wehrmacht due to transportation problems.

26. SHAEF G-2, "Enemy Communications and Supply Summary No. 24," 5 February 1945, pp. 1–2, USAFHRC R-A5178, 506.6111, FR 726–27.

27. Tedder to Bottomley and Spaatz, FWD-18890, Top Secret, 10 April 1945, PRO AIR 37/1036. In this letter, Tedder reaffirmed that the CSTC was to function in conformity with aims established by him and his fellow commanders.

28. CSTC, "Minutes of the 25th Meeting," Top Secret, 4 April 1945, p. 7, PRO AIR 40/1269.

29. SHAEF, "Army Intelligence Review of Current Strategic Bombing Priorities," Secret, 19 February 1945, p. 1, USAFHRC R-A5110, 505.43-6, FR 1334; SHAEF G-2, "Enemy Communications and Supply Summary No. 27," 26 February 1945, pp. 1–2, USAFHRC R-A5178, 506.6111, FR 810–11.

30. CSTC, "Minutes of the 19th Meeting of the CSTC at the Air Ministry," Secret, 21 February 1945, p. 2, USAFHRC R-A5110, 505.43-6, FR 1350. JIC had shared SHAEF's view on the effectiveness of transportation bombing in Germany since August 1944. Hinsley, *British Intelligence*, 3 (2):526, 605, 607.

31. CSTC, Working Committee (Communications), Bulletin No. 12, Top Secret, 28 February 1945, pp. 1–6, USAFHRC R-A5111, 505.43-23, FR 1242–48.

32. Weigley, *Eisenhower's Lieutenants*, pp. 623–24.

33. MEW, "Intelligence Weekly, Report No. 162," Secret, 15 March 1945, p. 4, NA RG 243, 4 22k; ACIU, "Intelligence Report No. FD 18, USAFHRC R-A5111, 505.43-20, FR 518–21.

34. W&F, 3:97; C&C, 3:721.

35. W&F, 3:104.

36. On the Dresden raid the best work is Bergander, *Dresden im Luftkrieg*.

37. Tedder, *With Prejudice*, p. 660.

38. CSTC, Working Committee (Communications), Bulletin No. 7, Top Secret, 24 January 1945, pp. 1–8, USAFHRC R-A5111, 505.43-23, FR 1298–1306.

39. Tedder, *With Prejudice*, p. 660; Derek Wood, CSTC, memorandum, Top Secret, 29 January 1945, USAFHRC R-A5223, 509.425B, FR 1098.

40. SHAEF, "Allied Air Commanders Conference," Top Secret, 6 February 1945, pp. 2, 6, USAFHRC R-A5087, 505.25-8, FR 800, 804; D/CoS (Air), SHAEF, Historical Record, February 1945, p. 5, PRO AIR 37/1060.

41. CSTC, "Minutes of Meeting," Secret, 14 February 1945, pp. 3–4, USAFHRC R-A5110, 505.43-6, FR 1340–41.

42. SHAEF, "Isolation of the Ruhr," SHAEF(M) Air/S.35102/A-3, Top Secret, 17 February 1945, USAFHRC R-A5165, 506.454C, FR 758.

43. SHAEF, "Allied Air Commanders Conference," Top Secret, 15 February 1945, p. 2, USAFHRC R-A5087, 505.25-8, FR 793.

44. SHAEF, "Allied Air Commanders Conference," Top Secret, 1 February 1945, pp. 3–4, USAFHRC R-A5087, 505.25-8, FR 810–11; C&C, 3:732–34; Records of the USSBS, Dorpmüller Interrogation, 29 May 1945, pp. 7–8, NA RG 243, 200(a)127.

45. SHAEF, "Allied Air Commanders Conference," Top Secret, 1 March

1945, p. 5, USAFHRC R-A5087, 505.25-8, FR 782; USSBS, *German Transportation*, pp. 14–15; SHAEF, D/CoS (Air), Historical Record, February 1945, p. 5, PRO AIR 37/1060.

46. BBSU, *Strategic Air War against Germany*, p. 123.

47. USSBS, *Rate of Operation*, p. 36, table 6.

48. Tedder, *With Prejudice*, p. 671.

49. OKL, Lwfst, Ic/Wi, "Objektschutz von Verkehrsanlagen," 16 February 1945, BA R5/3699.

50. RZA, Blatt 90, weeks 4–9, 1944; Wagenführ, *Deutsche Industrie*, p. 48;, Wehde-Textor, "Dokumentarische Darstellung," p. 38, BA R5 Anh I/11.

51. RVK, "Wagenstellung für Kohlen nach Revieren," BA R10 VIII/16, ff. 629, 631.

52. RVM, E-Abt. (L 4), "Lagebericht-Reichsbahn," Geheime Reichssache, Berlin, p. 3, BA R5/3699.

53. RWKS, "Beiratssitzung," Zeche Carl Funke, 13 March 1945, p. 6, BBA 33/329.

54. Dr. Ing. Schleip, Gauwirtschaftskammer Württemberg-Hohenzollern, Abt. Industrie, Stuttgart, 16 February, p. 1, BA R3/300.

55. Dr. Stellwaag, Hauptring Metalle, Hauptring Metallhalbzeug, "Rundschreiben," Berlin, 14 March 1945, BA R13 24/23.

56. RVM, E-Abt. (L-4), "Lagebericht-Reichsbahn," Geheime Reichssache, p. 3, BA R5/3699.

57. RVK, Statistischer Bericht Nr. 13, p. 3; RMfRuK, "Steinkohlenförderung und Kokserzeugung in regionaler Gliederung," Berlin, 16 March 1945, BA R3/1930, f. 553.

58. RVK, Statistischer Bericht Nr. 13, p. 3; RMfRuK, "Steinkohlenförderung und Kokserzeugung in regionaler Gliederung," Berlin, 16 March 1945, BA R3/1930, f. 553.

59. RVK, Statistischer Bericht Nr. 13, p. 15; RWKS, "Beiratssitzung," Zeche Carl Funke, 27 February 1945, p. 4, BBA 33/329.

60. RVK, Statistischer Bericht Nr. 13, p. 6; RMfRuK, "Braun.- u. Hartbraunkohlenförderung in regionaler Gliederung," Berlin, 16 March 1945, BA R3/1930, f. 554.

61. Dr. Böhm, RVE, "Vermerk über die Sitzung der Zentralverkehrsleitstelle am 9 Febr. 1945," Streng Vertraulich, 12 February 1945, p. 1, BA R10 III/95, f. 1.

62. RVE, Rohstahl-Erzeugung.

63. Wagenführ, *Deutsche Industrie*, pp. 66, 114, 178. In January 1945 the armaments production index stood at 227.

64. Stinder und Körner to Verkehrsbeauftragten für die Wirtschaft, "Abtransport von Rüstungsgütern durch geschlossene Züge," Velbert, 2 February 1945, RWWAzK, 22/246/681.

65. *OKW/KTB*, 7:22.

66. Heereswaffenamt, "Überblick über den Rüstungsstand des Heeres, Teil Waffen," p. 17 for Sturmgewehr 44, p. 18 for Schusswaffen 98, p. 72 for

leFH 15, BA/MA RH 8 v. 1861; Teil Kfz, p. 108 for the Panther, BA/MA RH 8 v. 1861; Teil Munition, p. 14 for bullets, p. 57 for 8.8 Spr. Patr., p. 101 for s.FH Mun, BA/MA RH 8 v. 1927.

67. BBSU, *Strategic Air War against Germany*, p. 133.

68. Speer, *Inside*, p. 435; von Mellenthin, *Panzer Battles*, p. 363.

69. Copy of RMfRuK order ZA/Org 206–192/45, "Einsatz von Rüstungs-bevollmächtigten," Berlin, 14 February 1945, BBA 33/1106; copy of RMf-Ruk order ZA Org 206-188/45, "Rüstungsbevollmächtigten," Berlin, 8 February 1945, BBA 33/1106.

70. Saur, "Stichwörte für die Rüstungskartei," 14 February 1945, BA R3/989; RMfRuK, "Führererlass über die Bildung eines Verkehrsstabes vom 18.2.1945," Anlage zum SB 24.2.45, BA R3/300.

71. Dilli to RBDs, "Reichs- und Rüstungszüge," Berlin, 14 February 1945, BA R5/ Anh II/45.

72. Schnellbrief, Pleiger to Speer, "Kohlenwirtschaftliche Lage," Rst S-4087/45, Geheime Reichssache, Berlin, 7 March 1945, BA R10 VIII/20, also in NA T-73, R-4, RMfRuK/73, FR 1049353–54.

73. RWKS, "Beiratssitzung," Zeche Carl Funke, 28 March 1945, p. 5, BBA 33/329.

74. Speer, draft of "Rechenschaftbericht," Berlin, 27 January 1945, pp. 1–2, 24, BA R3/1560, ff. 4–5, 15. Also in NA RG 243, 54(a)1.

75. Speer, M4185/45, Geheim, Berlin, 19 February 1945, NA RG 243, 200(a)130.

76. Speer, Verkehrsstab, "Einsatz von Arbeitskräften zur Schadensbeseitigung bei Verkehrsanlagen," 1 5/45g, Geheim, Berlin, 1 March 1945, NA RG 243, 200(a)130.

77. RMfRuK to Rü Kdo, Rü In, "Vervielfachung der Arbeitskräfte für die Wiederinstandsetzung der Verkehrsanlagen," ZA Arb E u. Arb L V/1a-570, Geheim, Berlin, 6 March 1945, NA RG 243, 200(a)130; Speer to Rü Kdo's, ZA Arb E u. L 7-731–414/45g, Geheim, Berlin, 12 March 1945, NA T-73, RMfRuK/538, FR 3157423.

78. Speer, Verkehrsstab, "Richtlinien für Wagenstellung," Berlin, 14 March 1945, BA R3/129, f. 42; Kehrl to Rüstungsbevollmächtigte, Rü Kdo, Hauptausschüsse, Hauptringe, Produktionsausschüsse, Pla 200 220/17.3. Dr. B/Zi, Berlin, 17 March 1945, BA R3/129, f. 41. Also in BA R5/103 and BBA 15/278.

79. Speer to Hitler, "Wirtschaftslage März–April 1945 und Folgerungen," Berlin, 15 March 1945, BA R3/1536. Also in NA T-73, R-180, RMfRuK/679, FR 3392527–30; Janssen, *Das Ministerium Speer*, pp. 311–12, 315–16; Speer, *Inside*, p. 453.

80. Janssen, *Das Ministerium Speer*, p. 321; Kehrl, *Krisenmanager*, p. 433; Tedder, *With Prejudice*, pp. 683–86.

Chapter 9

1. The Army Air Forces' classified history of Ultra's role in target planning reached the following damning conclusion: "Now that the full returns are coming in (autumn 1945), it seems probable that Allied intelligence officers did not at the time have a full appreciation of what railway bombing was doing to the German economy." USAAF, *Target Planning*, p. 29. Parentheses in the original.

2. "Interrogation of Albert Speer, former Reich Minister of Armaments and War Production. (6th Session, 15:00–17:00 hours, 30 May 1945)," W&F, 4:373, appendix 37, para. 4; see also p. 376, para. 12. The determining factor in Speer's 1946 limit was chrome. See Speer, "Supplies (imports) from Abroad," FIAT, Report No. 55, Part 3, 8 August 1945, pp. 12–13, available in the Imperial War Museum, cited in Becker, "German War Economy under Speer," pp. 275–76.

3. Between 16 September 1944 and the end of the war, transportation targets received 35.5 percent of all bomb tonnage delivered by the strategic air forces. BBSU, *Strategic Air War against Germany*, pp. 56–58, tables 7, 8, 9. See also USSBS, *Rate of Operation*, pp. 28–60.

Bibliography

Bibliographies, Archival Guides, and Other Reference Works

Daniels, Gordon, ed. *A Guide to the Reports of the United States Strategic Bombing Survey*. London: Royal Historical Society, 1981.
Eyll, Klara van, et al. *Deutsche Wirtschaftsarchive*. Wiesbaden: Steiner, 1978.
Granier, Gerhard, et al. *Das Bundesarchiv und seine Bestände*. 3d ed. Boppard am Rhein: Boldt, 1977.
Guptil, Marilla B., and John Mendelsohn. *Records of the United States Strategic Bombing Survey. Inventory of Record Group 243*. Washington, D.C.: National Archives and Records Service, 1975.
Kroker, Evelyn. *Das Bergbauarchiv und Seine Bestände*. Bochum: Deutsches Bergbau-Museum, 1977.
Kroker, Evelyn, and Norma von Ragenfeld. *Rheinisch-Westfälisches Kohlen-Syndikat 1893–1945. Findbuch zum Bestand 33*. Bochum: Deutsches Bergbau-Museum, 1980.
Mayer, Sidney L., and William L. Kolney. *The Two World Wars: A Guide to Manuscript Collections in the United Kingdom*. London: Bowker, 1976.
Minerva Handbuch. *Archive im deutschsprachigen Raum*. 2 vols. Berlin: Walter de Gruyter, 1974.
United States. American Historical Association and National Archives and Records Service. *Guides to Captured German Documents Microfilmed at Alexandria, Virginia*. No. 1, Reichswirtschaftsministerium; No. 4, Organisation Todt; No. 5, Miscellaneous Records; No. 7, Oberkommando der Wehrmacht, Part 1; No. 5, Miscellaneous Records; No. 10, Reichsministerium für Rüstung- und Kriegsproduktion; No. 32, Reichsführer SS und Chef der Deutschen Polizei, Part 1. Washington, D.C.: National Archives and Records Service, 1958– .
United States. National Archives. *Guide to the National Archives of the United States*. Washington, D.C.: U.S. Government Printing Office, 1974.
United States. United States Strategic Bombing Survey. *Index to the Records of the United States Strategic Bombing Survey*. Washington, D.C.: United States Strategic Bombing Survey, June 1947.
Verein deutscher Archivare. *Archive und Archivare in der Bundesrepublik Deutschland, Österreich und der Schweiz*. Darmstadt: Selbstverlag des Vereins deutscher Archivare, 1982.
Volkmann, Hans-Erich. *Wirtschaft im Dritten Reich. Teil 1: 1933–1939. Eine Bibliographie*. Munich: Bernard & Graefe, 1980.
———. *Wirtschaft im Dritten Reich. Teil 2: 1939–1945. Eine Bibliographie*. Koblenz: Bernard & Graefe, 1984.

Wer Leitet? Die Männer der Wirtschaft und der einschlägigen Verwaltung,
1940. 3 vols. Berlin: Hoppenstedt, 1940.
Werrell, Kenneth P. *Eighth Air Force Bibliography: An Extended Essay*
and Listing of Published and Unpublished Materials. Manhattan,
Kans.: Military Affairs/Aerospace Historian Publishing, 1981.

Archival Collections

Bergbau-Archiv, Bochum.
  Bergbaugruppe Ruhr. 13/829, 830, 833, 834, 836, 838, 839.
  Wirtschaftsvereinigung Bergbau e.V. 15/471(1), 471(2).
  Rheinisch-Westfälisches Kohlen-Syndikat. 33/320–1, 320–2, 329, 340–
    41, 380, 421, 571, 583, 644, 904, 1030, 1032, 1036, 1040, 1044, 1046,
    1048, 1051, 1052, 1054, 1056, 1059, 1061, 1078, 1080, 1082, 1084,
    1099, 1105, 1106, 1205, 1213, 1214, 1215, 1220, 1422, 1423, 1235,
    1237, 1351, 1412, 1422, 1423, 1425, 1433, 1435, 1436, 1437, 1442,
    1454, 1461, 1465, 1466, 1589, 1614, 1638.
BEWAG-Archiv, Berlin.
Bundesarchiv, Koblenz.
  Reichsministerium für Rüstung- und Kriegsproduktion. R 3/74, 75, 129,
    300, 1532, 1536, 1558, 1559, 1560, 1561, 1658, 1661, 1690, 1704,
    1726, 1727, 1729, 1730, 1736, 1740, 1789, 1842, 1845a, 1861, 1916,
    1927, 1930, 1948, 1957, 1959, 1961, 1966, 1969, 1989, 3006, 3007.
  Generalinspekteur für Wasser und Energie. R 4/94, 276, 277, 278, 299.
  Reichsverkehrsministerium. R 5/6, 7, 8, 13, 25, 26, 30, 37, 39, 43, 44,
    45, 47, 51, 54, 55, 57, 59, 64, 71, 73, 79, 80, 82, 85, 86, 87, 93, 94, 95,
    97, 98, 100, 103, 125, 107, 108, 109, 110, 111, 113, 116, 117, 122, 589,
    2073, 2083, 2086, 2092, 2418, 2419, 2420, 2421, 2422, 2423, 2424,
    2430, 2431, 2433, 2432, 2456, 2978, 2980, 2986, 2987, 2988, 3002,
    3003, 3005, 3007, 3008, 3015, 3016, 3017, 3026, 3029, 3040, 3109,
    3110, 3167, 3172, 3173, 3174, 3177, 3179, 3180, 3181, 3182, 3183,
    3184, 3204, 3640, 3641, 3642, 3649, 3666, 3680, 3699, 3743, RD
    98/64–1944, 72.
  Sammlung Sarter, R 5 Anh I/9, 11, 18, 19, 21, 26, 27, 28, 30, 31, 32, 35,
    36, 37, 38, 39, 41, 42, 43, 44, 45, 46, 47, 50, 56, 69, 71, 72, 74, 77, 80,
    81, 82, 83, 86, 96, 100, 118, 124, 132.
  Sammlung Kreidler, R 5 Anh II/29, 34, 38, 39, 40, 41, 45, 46, 49, 51.
  Reichslastverteiler, R 8 IV/1, 3, 12.
  Reichsvereinigung Eisen, R 10 III/81, 87, 89, 90, 93, 94, 95, 111, 114.
  Reichsvereinigung Kohle, R 10 VIII/2, 3, 4, 5, 7, 10, 14, 16, 18, 19, 20,
    fol.1, 21, 22, 24, 27, 28, 47.
  Reichswirtschaftskammer, R 11/75, 76.
  Wirtschaftsgruppe Eisenschaffende Industrie, R 13 I/531, 532, 534, 537,
    543, 544, 549, 550, 552, 573.
  Wirtschaftsgruppe Gas und Wasser Versorgung, R 13 XVII/45, 46, 48.
  Wirtschaftsgruppe Metallindustrie, R 13 XXIV/13, 16, 17, 23.

Bundesarchiv-Militärarchiv, Freiburg-im-Breisgau.
Heer, RH 8/v. 1018, 1019, 1025, 1032a, 1032b, 1042, 1043a, 1043b, 1086, 1087a, 1087b, 1087c, 1103, 1103b, 1104, 1126, 1364, 1861, 1927, 2598.
Rüstungsamt, RW 19-40/11, 19/69, 209.
Rüstungsamt, RW 20-4/20, 26, 20-5/31, 20-7/15, 20-8/29, 35, 20-10/22, 23, 20-11/33, 40, 20-12/16, 29, 37, 20-13/7, 20-17/8.
Rüstungsamt, RW 21-2/9, 21-3/11, 21-4/19, 21-5/5, 21-6/7, 21-7/18b, 21-8/13, 21-10/9, 21-11/20, 21-17/17, 21-19/20, 21-22/20, 21-27/8, 9, 21-30/18, 21-36/20, 21-40/12, 21-48/9, 21-51/19, 21-52/3, 21-64/3.
Rüstungsamt, RW 46/433 Teil I, 433 Teil II, 427, 434, 444, 455, 456, 458, 462, 466.
Wehrwirtschafts- und Rüstungsamt, Wi/IF 5/993, 996, 997, 998, 1848, 3197.
Wehrwirtschafts- und Rüstungsamt, Wi/IF VI 174.
National Archives, Washington, D.C.
Department of State. Record Group 26.
Office of Strategic Services, Research and Analysis Reports 410, 674, 788, 799, 975, 1156, 1194, 1323, 1450, 1514, 1628.2, 1760.1, 1760.2, 1933, 1938, 2106, 2306, 2470, 2539, 2566, 2712, 2935.
Records of the Office of Strategic Services. Record Group 226.
Enemy Objectives Unit–Economic Warfare Division. War Diary, Research and Analysis Branch, Office of Strategic Services, London, England. 10 vols. 1 February 1946.
Records of the United States Strategic Bombing Survey. Record Group 243.
Reference Library. 3 (a) 3, 4, 21, 24, 33, 36, 37, 50, 51, 52, 68, 74, 77, (b) 4, 7, 13, 14, 15; (c) 45. 4(e)1–3, 6, 15. 24,(a, b). 30 (a) 13. 31 (d), (e), (i). 33 (d) 1–6, (f)2, (j)3, 5, 7–10, (r). 34 (b), 1, 3–5, (c)1–10, (d)2–11, (f). 35 (b)3, (f)2, (i)2, (m)1. 36 (j)1, 3, (l)1, 3. 37 (b)1–2, (c)1–2, (e)2, 4, 6,(f)1 -2. 39 (b)4, 12, 16, (c)7, (d)4, 9, (f)4, (h)3, 7–8, (k)8, 10, 16, 17, 19, 20. 40 (b), 20, 23–24, 26–28, 30–31. 50 (b)53, 56, 59, 61, 65. 53 (c)35–37. 54 (a)1, 10. 66 (a)4. 67 (a)14. 68 (a)1–2. 71 (a)6. 76(g)1, 4, 8, 15–16, 19, 21. 91 (a)1, 5. 92 (a)7. 101 (a)8–10, 12. 106 (a). 110 (b)17, (d)36, 135. 134 (a)26, 28–29, 54–57, (b)15–21, 26, 28, 30, 47, 59. 174 (a)1. 181(a)1. 190 (a). 191 (a). 198 (a). 200 (a)1–8, 28–29, 34, 36–38, 40, 41, 42, 44, 46, 47, 48, 50, 52, 58, 59, 62, 82–88, 91–130, 137–38, 140–41, 143, 147–48, 153, 157, 167, 174, 178, 190.
European Intelligence Library. 5 (b)2, (j)8, (q)3, (w)22. 13 (q)3, (u), (w). 17 (a) (Env. No. 95), 6 (Env. 395), (c) (Env. 395), (e)4 (Env. No. 135). 22 (k) (Env. No. 1), (o) (Env. No. 135). 41 (b) (Env. No. 134). 62 (e)5 (Env. No. 393), (o) (Env. No. 431). 64 (i) (Env. No. 450).
European Target Intelligence. 2 (o)1(k); 2 (o)20(a), (b).
Records of the National Security Agency, Record Group 457. SRQ-02, SRH-013, -015, -017, -033, -035, -041, -044, -062, -099, -116, -117, -132, -141, -146, -153, -185, -228.
Japanese Diplomatic Messages—Magic. Boxes 17, 18, 20, 21, 85, 94, 99, 100, 101, 102, 104, 105.

Captured German Documents Microfilmed at Alexandria, Virginia.
Reichswirtschaftsministerium, T-71, Roll 74.
Reichsministerium für Rüstung- und Kriegsproduktion, T-73, Rolls 1,
    3, 4, 13–14, 19–23, 29, 105, 110, 112–13, 132, 173–74, 179–82.
Oberkommando der Wehrmacht, T-77, Rolls 13, 163, 188–89, 200,
    202, 206, 209, 215, 286, 288–89, 299, 303, 305, 313, 315, 326, 340,
    353–54, 364–66, 370, 375, 382, 397, 401–2, 420–22, 435, 748, 750.
Miscellaneous German Records Collection, T-84, Rolls 46, 52.
Reichsführer SS und Chef der deutschen Polizei, T-175, Roll 68.
Records of Private Austrian, Dutch, and German Enterprises, T-83,
    Rolls 42, 69, 70, 76.
Office of Air Force History, Washington, D.C.
Microfilmed document rolls A 1005–9, 1176–77, 1239–40, 1260, 1248,
    1256, 1260, 1270–72, 1298, 1377–78, 1380, 5087–88, 5110–13, 5165–
    66, 5169–70, 5178–79, 5223A, 5224, 5248, 5346, 5615–7, 5719, 5719A,
    5724, 5358–59, 5378, 5387, 5534, 5686–87, 5867, B5047–48, 5063,
    5065.
Rheinisch-Westfälisches Wirtschaftsarchiv zu Köln e.V.
Gauwirtschaftskammer Wuppertal, Abteilung 22: 38; 42; 106; 232/640,
    641, 642; 233/643, 644; 236, 237/654, 655, 656; 238; 245/682, 683,
    684; 246/678, 681, 685; 253/707, 708.
Public Record Office, Kew, London, Great Britain.
Air Ministry (AIR). 14/281, 902, 1197, 1207, 1228, 1229, 1230, 2427;
    22/81, 82, 436, 502, 503; 37/1005, 1009, 1013, 1014, 1034, 1036, 1037,
    1042, 1043, 1044, 1052, 1060, 1106, 1126; 40/1146, 1147, 1189, 1263,
    1264, 1265, 1266, 1269, 1270, 1272, 1467, 1514, 1954, 2059, 2060,
    2070, 2071, 2161.
Cabinet (CAB). 84/67, 68; 101/27.
Foreign Office (FO). 837/30, 31, 122, 123, 385, 1146, 1147, 1189, 1263,
    1264.

Published Documents

Akten zur deutschen auswärtigen Politik 1918–1945. Series D, 1937–1941.
    Vol. 1. Baden-Baden: Imprimerie Nationale, 1950.
Bernsee, Hubert, and Gustav Röhr, eds. *Die Dienststellen der Deutschen
    Reichsbahn einschliesslich der ehemaligen Österreichischen Bundes-
    bahn, Protektoratsbahnen Böhmen und Mähren, Polnische Staats-
    bahnen (Ostbahn), Elsass-Lothringen sowie Dienstellen der Privat und
    Kleinbahnen Stand 1944.* Krefeld, Bochum: Privately published, 1974.
    Reprint of the original published by the Deutsche Reichsbahn in 1944.
Boelcke, Willi A., ed. *Deutschlands Rüstung im zweiten Weltkrieg. Hit-
    lers Konferenzen mit Albert Speer 1942–1945.* Frankfurt/Main: Aka-
    demische Verlagsgesellschaft, Athenaion, 1969.
Bundesbahndirektion Mainz. *Verzeichnis der Knotenbahnhöfe mit den*

zugehörigen Nichtknotenbahnhöfe im Gebiet der Bundesrepublik Deutschland. Mainz: Oscar Schneider, 1959.

Deutsche Reichsbahn Gesellschaft. *Deutsche Reichsbahn Geschäftsberichte 1927–1935.* Berlin: Reichsdruckerei, 1928–1936.

————. *Güterkursbuch, Sommer 1930.* Berlin: Reichsdruckerei, 1922. Reprint. Landsberg/Lech: Ritzau KG Verlag für Eisenbahn-Geschichte, 1970.

Dobmaier, A. *Das Fernmeldewesen der Reichsbahn.* Berlin: Tetzlaff, 1942. Available in BA R5 Anh II/46.

Domarus, Max, ed. *Hitler: Reden und Proklamationen, 1932–1945.* 2 vols. Neustadt a. d. Aisch: Verlagsdruckerei Schmidt, 1962.

Frank-Auschuss für Energiewirtschaft im Ruhrgebiet. "Zechenwirtschaft und offentliche Elektrizitätsversorgung." Essen: October 1950.

Germany. Deutsche Reichsbahn. *Statistische Angaben über die Deutsche Reichsbahn im Geschäftsjahr 1943.* Berlin: Reichsdruckerei, 1944. Available in National Archives, Record Group 243, 200(a)124.

————. *Verzeichnis der Maschinenämter, Bahnbetriebswerke, Bahnbetriebswagenwerke, Lokomotivbahnhöfe, Bahnhofsschlossereien und Hilfszüge.* Vienna, Staatsdruckerei, 1941. Reprint. Freiburg: Eisenbahn-Kurier, 1976.

————. *Verzeichnis der oberen Reichsbahnbeämter 1943.* Leipzig: Verkehrswissenschaftliche Lehrmittel-Gesellschaft, Rheinhold Rudolf, 1943. Available in Library of Congress.

————. Kursbuchbüro. *Deutsches Kursbuch. Jahresfahrplan 1944/45.* Berlin: Generalbetriebsleitung Ost, 3 July 1944. Available in Library of Congress.

————. Zentralamt Berlin. *Amtliches Bahnhofs Verzeichnis der Deutschen Reichsbahn 1938.* Berlin: Deutsche Reichsbahn, 1938.

Germany. Reichsverkehrsministrium. Kartographisches Büro. *Sammlung von Übersichtsplänen von wichtiger abzweigungs Bahnhöfe der Reichsbahn.* Berlin: Reichsdruckerei, n.d. Reprint. Inzlingen: Ferrovia-Verlag, 1976.

Germany. Statistisches Reichsamt. *Statistik des deutschen Reichs. Band 593. Die Seeschiffahrt im Jahre 1941.* Berlin: Verlag für Sozialpolitik, Wirtschaft und Statistik, Paul Schmidt, 1943. Reprint. Osnabrück: Otto Zeller, 1979.

————. *Statistik des deutschen Reichs. Band 596, Hlbd. 1. Die Güterbewegung auf deutschen Eisenbahnen im Jahre 1942.* Berlin: Verlag für Sozialpolitik, Wirtschaft und Statistik, Paul Schmidt, 1943. Reprint. Osnabrück: Otto Zeller, 1979.

————. *Statistik des deutschen Reichs. Band 596, Hlbd. 2 Die Güterbewegung auf deutschen Eisenbahnen im Jahre 1942.* Berlin: Verlag für Sozialpolitik, Wirtschaft und Statistik, Paul Schmidt, 1944. Reprint. Osnabrück: Otto Zeller, 1979.

————. *Statistisches Jarhbuch für das Deutsche Reich. Band 59, 1941/42.* Berlin: Statischen Reichsamt, 1942.

Geschäftsführung, Reichsgruppe Industrie. *Gliederung der Reichsgruppe Industrie.* Leipzig: Lühe-Verlag, 1941.

Great Britain. Air Ministry Intelligence. *The Rise and Fall of the German Air Force.* London: Air Ministry, 1948. Reprint. New York: St. Martin's, 1983.

Great Britain. Foreign Office and Ministry of Economic Warfare, Economic Advisory Branch. *Economic Survey of South-Western Germany, Zone 7. Württemberg, Baden, the Saar and Bavarian Palatinate.* Restricted. London: January 1945. Available in Library of Congress.

———. *Germany Zone Handbook No. 5 West (Rhine Province, Westphalia, Lippe, Schaumburg-Lippe) Part 2, Economic Survey.* Restricted. London: July 1944, April 1945. Available in Library of Congress.

———. Interservice Topographical Department. *Plans and Photographs of German Railway Facilities.* London: Inter-Service Topographical Department, 1944. Available in Library of Congress.

Heiber, Helmut, ed. *Hitlers Lagebesprechungen: Die Protokollfragmente seiner militärischen Konferenzen, 1942–1945.* Stuttgart: Deutsche Verlags-Anstalt, 1962.

International Military Tribunal. *Trials of the Major War Criminals.* 42 vols. English edition. Nuremberg: n.p., 1946–48.

———. *Trials of War Criminals before the Nuernberg Military Tribunals.* 15 vols. Washington: U.S. Government Printing Office, 1949.

Länderrat des Amerikanischen Besatzungsgebiets. *Statistisches Handbuch von Deutschland 1928–1944.* Munich: Franz Ehrenwirth-Verlag, 1949.

MacIsaac, David, ed. *The United States Strategic Bombing Survey.* Vols. 1–6. New York: Garland, 1976. This is a reprint of twenty reports concerning the strategic bombing of Germany.

Picker, Henry, et al., eds. *Hitlers Tischgespräche im Führerhauptquartier 1941–1942.* Stuttgart: Seewald, 1965.

Schramm, Percy Ernst, ed. *Kriegstagebuch des Oberkommandos der Wehrmacht.* 4 vols. Frankfurt/Main: Bernard & Graefe, 1961–79; Herrsching: Pawlak, 1982.

United States. Chief Counsel for the Prosecution of Axis Criminality. *Nazi Conspiracy and Aggression.* 8 vols. Washington, D.C.: U.S. Government Printing Office, 1946–48.

United States. Department of Commerce. *Statistical Abstract of the United States.* Washington, D.C.: U.S. Government Printing Office, 1970.

———. Bureau of the Census. *Historical Statistics of the United States.* 2 vols. Washington, D.C.: U.S. Government Printing Office, 1975.

United States. Engineer Research Office, North Atlantic Division, Corps of Engineers, Military Intelligence Division. *Navigable Waterways of Germany.* 9 vols. Washington, D.C.: Office, Chief of Engineers, U.S. Army, August 1944. Available in National Archives, Record Group 243, 200(a)183, and in Library of Congress.

United States. United States Army Air Force. *Ultra and the History of the*

United States Strategic Air Force in Europe vs. the German Air Force. SRH-13. Reprint. Frederick, Md.: University Publications of America, 1980.

United States. United States Strategic Bombing Survey. *Adam Opel A.G., Rüsselsheim, Germany.* Washington, D.C.: U.S. Government Printing Office, January 1947.

_____. *Aircraft Division Industry Report.* Washington, D.C.: U.S. Government Printing Office, January 1947.

_____. *Air Force Rate of Operation.* Washington, D.C.: U.S. Government Printing Office, January 1947.

_____. *August Thyssen Hütte A.G.* Washington, D.C.: U.S. Government Printing Office, January 1947.

_____. *A Brief Study of the Effects of Area Bombing on Berlin, Augsburg, Bochum, Leipzig, Hagen, Dortmund, Oberhausen, Schweinfurt, and Berlin.* Washington, D.C.: U.S. Government Printing Office, January 1947.

_____. *A Brief Study of the Effects of Area Bombing on Wuppertal.* Washington, D.C.: U.S. Government Printing Office, January 1947.

_____. *Brown, Boveri and Cie, Mannheim Käfertal.* Washington, D.C.: U.S. Government Printing Office, January 1947.

_____. *Daimler-Benz A.G. (Untertürkheim).* Washington, D.C.: U.S. Government Printing Office, January 1947.

_____. *The Defeat of the German Air Force.* Washington, D.C.: U.S. Government Printing Office, January 1947.

_____. *Dortmund-Hoerder Huttenverein AG.* Washington, D.C.: U.S. Government Printing Office, January, 1947.

_____. *The Effects of Strategic Bombing on German Transportation.* Washington, D.C.: U.S. Government Printing Office, June 1947.

_____. *The Effects of Strategic Bombing on the German War Economy.* Washington, D.C.: U.S. Government Printing Office, 31 October 1945.

_____. *Electrical Generating Station, Mannheim, Germany.* Washington, D.C.: U.S. Government Printing Office, April 1947.

_____. *Gebrueder Giulini Gmbh., Ludwigshafen.* Washington, D.C.: U.S. Government Printing Office, October 1945.

_____. *The German Anti-Friction Bearings Industry.* Washington, D.C.: U.S. Government Printing Office, January 1947.

_____. *German Electric Utilities Industry Report.* Washington, D.C.: U.S. Government Printing Office, January 1947.

_____. *Hoesch A.G. Hüttenwerk, Dortmund, Germany.* Washington, D.C.: U.S. Government Printing Office, January 1947.

_____. *Kassel Marshalling Yards, Kassel, Germany.* Washington, D.C.: U.S. Government Printing Office, October 1945.

_____. *Ludwigshafen-Oppau Works of I.G. Farbenindustrie, Ludwigshafen.* Washington, D.C.: U.S. Government Printing Office, January 1947.

_____. *Maschinenfabrik Augsburg-Nurnberg.* Washington, D.C.: U.S.

Government Printing Office, January 1947.
_____. *Oil Division Final Report*. Washington, D.C.: U.S. Government Printing Office, January 1947.
_____. *Overall Report (European War)*. Washington, D.C.: U.S. Government Printing Office, 30 September 1945.
_____. *Physical Damage Division Report (ETO)*. Washington, D.C.: U.S. Government Printing Office, April 1947.
_____. *Railway Viaduct at Altenbecken, Germany*. Washington, D.C.: U.S. Government Printing Office, 18 October 1945.
_____. *Railway Viaduct at Bielefeld, Germany*. Washington, D.C.: U.S. Government Printing Office, 19 October 1945.
_____. *Summary Report (European War)*. Washington, D.C.: U.S. Government Printing Office, 30 September 1945.
_____. *21 Rheinische-Westfalische Elektrizitaetswerke AG*. Washington, D.C.: U.S. Government Printing Office, April 1947.
_____. Heavy Industry Branch. *Friedrich-Alfred Huette Rheinhausen, Germany*. Washington, D.C.: U.S. Government Printing Office, January 1947.
_____. *Reichswerke Hermann Goering A.G., Salzgitter*. Washington, D.C.: U.S. Government Printing Office, January 1947.
_____. Motor Vehicles and Tanks Branch. *Friedrich Krupp Grusonwerke, Magdeburg, Germany*. Washington, D.C.: U.S. Government Printing Office, January 1947.
_____. *Friedrich Krupp A G, Borbeck Plant Essen, Germany*. Washington, D.C.: U.S. Government Printing Office, January 1947.
_____. Ordnance Branch. *Friedrich Krupp Grusonwerke A.G., Magdeburg, Germany*. Washington, D.C.: U.S. Government Printing Office, January 1947.
United States. War Department. Office of Strategic Services. Research and Analysis Branch. *Civil Affairs Guide. Administration of German Railroads*. No. 31–144. Confidential. Washington, D.C.: War Department, 22 July 1944. In Library of Congress.
_____. *Civil Affairs Guide. German Inland Waterways under Military Government*. No. 17060.1. Confidential. Washington, D.C.: War Department, 22 July 1944. Available in National Archives, Record Group 26, and Library of Congress.
_____. *Export Surpluses, Import Requirements and Rail and Water Traffic of South Germany*. Washington, D.C.: War Department, 1944. Confidential. Available in Library of Congress.

Secondary Works

Andrews, Allan. *The Air Marshals—Arnold, Dowding, Portal, Tedder, Goering—in World War II*. New York: Morrow, 1970.
Arnold, Henry H. *Global Mission*. New York: Harper, 1949.

Babington-Smith, Constance. *Air Spy: The Story of Photo Intelligence in World War II.* New York: Harper, 1957.

Bagel-Bohlan, Anja E. *Hitlers Industrielle Kriegsvorbereitungen 1936–1939.* Koblenz: Wehr & Wissen, 1975.

Barkai, Avraham. "Sozialdarwinismus und Antiliberalismus in Hitlers Wirtschaftskonzept, zu Henry A. Turner Jr. 'Hitlers Einstellung zu Wirtschaft und Gesellschaft vor 1933.'" *Geschichte und Gesellschaft* 3 (1977): 406–17.

———. *Das Wirtschaftssystem des Nationalsozialismus.* Cologne: Verlag Wissenschaft und Politik, 1977.

Baumann, Hans. ed. *Deutsches Verkehrsbuch.* Berlin: Deutsche Verlagsgesellschaft, 1931.

Baumgart, Winfried. "Eisenbahnen und Kriegführung in der Geschichte." *Technikgeschichte* 38 (1971): 191–219.

Becker, Peter W. "The Basis of the German War Economy under Albert Speer, 1942–1944." Ph.D. dissertation, Stanford University, 1971.

Bell, Ernest L. *An Initial View of Ultra as an American Weapon.* Keene, N.H.: TSU, 1977.

Below, Nicolaus von. *Als Hitlers Adjutant.* Mainz: von Hase & Koehler, 1981.

Bennett, Ralph. *Ultra in the West: The Normandy Campaign 1944–45.* London: Hutchinson, 1979.

Bergander, Götz. *Dresden im Luftkrieg. Vorgeschichte-Zerstörung-Folgen.* Köln: Böhlau, 1977. Munich: Heyne, 1979.

Bernhardt, Wolfgang. *Die deutsche Aufrüstung 1934–39. Militärische und Politische Konzeptionen und ihre Einschätzung durch die Allierten.* Frankfurt/Main: Bernard & Graefe, 1969.

Birkenfeld, Wolfgang. *Der Synthetische Treibstoff 1933–1945.* Göttingen: Musterschmidt, 1964.

Block, Herbert. *German Transportation Policy During the War.* New York: New School for Social Research, [1944].

Boelcke, Willi A. *Die Deutsche Wirtschaft 1930–1945. Interna des Reichswirtschaftsministeriums.* Düsseldorf: Droste, 1983.

———. *Die Kosten von Hitlers Krieg.* Paderborn: Schöningh, 1985.

———. "Kriegsfinanzierung in internationalen Vergleich." In *Kriegswirtschaft und Rüstung 1939–1945,* edited by Friedrich Forstmeier and Hans-Erich Volkmann, pp. 14–69. Düsseldorf: Droste, 1977.

Boog, Horst. *Die deutsche Luftwaffenführung 1935–1945. Generalausbildung, Führungsprobleme, Spitzengliederung.* Stuttgart: Deutsche Verlags-Anstalt, 1982.

Borgert, Heinz-Ludger. "Grundzüge der Landkriegführung von Schlieffen bis Guderian." In *Deutsche Militärgeschichte,* edited by Militärgeschichtliches Forschungsamt, 6:427–584. Munich: Bernard & Graefe, 1983; Herrsching: Pawlak, 1983.

Boyle, Andrew. *Trenchard: Man of Vision.* London: Collins, 1962.

Boyne, Walter J. *Messerschmitt Me-262: Arrow to the Future.* Washington,

D.C.: Smithsonian, 1980.

Bracher, Karl-Dietrich. *The German Dictatorship: The Origins, Structure and Effects of National Socialism*. Translated by Jean Steinberg. New York: Praeger, 1970.

Brandt, Karl. "Germany's Vulnerable Spot: Transportation." *Foreign Affairs* 21, no. 2 (January 1943): 221–38.

Brauer, Karl. "Die Deutsche Kohlenwirtschaft im Kriege." *Jahrbücher für Nationalökonomie und Statistik* 153 (1941): 81–88, 203–5.

Brehmer, G. "Grundzüge der staatlichen Lenkung der Industrieproduktion in der deutschen Kriegswirtschaft von 1939 bis 1945 (unter besonderer Berücksichtigung der Verhältnisse in der elektronischen Industrie)." Ph.D. dissertation, University of Bonn, 1968.

Broszat, Martin. *Der Staat Hitlers*. Munich: Deutsche Taschenbuch Verlag, 1969.

———. *The Hitler State*. Translated by John Hiden. London: Longmans, 1983.

Carroll, Berenice. *Design for Total War: Arms and Economics in the Third Reich*. The Hague: Mouton, 1968.

Carter, Ernest F. *Railways in Wartime*. London: F. Muller, 1964.

Clark, J. Maurice, ed. *Readings in the Economics of War*. Chicago: University of Chicago Press, 1918.

Clayton, Aileen. *The Enemy Is Listening*. London: Hutchinson, 1980.

Coffey, Thomas M. *Decision over Schweinfurt: The U.S. Eighth Air Force Battle for Daylight Bombing*. New York: David McKay, 1977.

Cooke, Ronald C., and Roy Conyers Nesbit. *Target, Hitler's Oil: Allied Attacks on German Oil Supplies 1939–45*. London: Kimber, 1985.

Cooper, Matthew. *The German Air Force 1933–1945: An Anatomy of Failure*. London: Jane's, 1981.

———. *The German Army 1933–1945: Its Political and Military Failure*. New York: Stein and Day, 1978.

Copp, DeWitt S. *A Few Great Captains: The Men and Events That Shaped the Development of U.S. Air Power*. Garden City: Doubleday, 1980.

———. *Forged in Fire: Strategy and Decisions in the Airwar over Europe 1940–1945*. New York: Doubleday, 1982.

Craven, Wesley Frank, and James Lea Cate. *The Army Air Forces in World War II*. 7 vols. Chicago: University of Chicago Press, 1947–58.

Creveld, Martin Van. *Fighting Power: German and U.S. Army Performance 1939–1945*. Westport, Conn.: Greenwood Press, 1982.

Dalton, Hugh. *The Fateful Years: Memoirs 1931–1945*. London: Muller, 1957.

Davidson, Eugene. "Albert Speer and the Nazi War Plants." *Modern Age* 4 (1966): 383–98.

Davies, W. J. *Continental Railway Handbook: West Germany*. London: Ian Allen, 1971.

Deist, Wilhelm. *The Wehrmacht and German Rearmament*. Toronto: University of Toronto Press, 1981.

_____, ed. *Das Deutsche Reich und der Zweite Weltkrieg.* Vols. 1–4. Stuttgart: Deutsche Verlags-Anstalt, 1979–83.

Demps, Laurens. "Zum weiteren Ausbau des staatmonopolitischen Apparates der faschistischen Kriegswirtschaft in den Jahren 1943 bis 1945 und zur Rolle der SS und der Konzentrationslager im Rahmen der Rüstungsproduktion." Ph.D. dissertation, Humboldt-Universität zu Berlin, 1970.

Deutsche Kohlenbergbau-Leitung. *Die Kohle in der Elektrizitätswirtschaft.* Essen: Verlag Glückauf, 1952.

Deutsche Reichsbahn Gesellschaft. *Die Deutschen Eisenbahnen in ihrer Entwicklung 1835–1935.* Berlin: E. S. Mittler and Sohn, 1935.

Die Deutschen Rheinbrücken. Cologne: Stahlbau-Verlag, 1956.

Donat, Gerhard. "Die Leistungen der deutschen Rüstungsindustrie im 2. Weltkrieg." *Wehrwissenschaftliche Rundschau* 17 (1967): 329–39.

Dorman, James R., Jr. "Hitlers Economic Mobilization." *Military Review* 28 (November 1953): 46–57.

Douhet, Giulio. *The Command of the Air.* Translated by Dino Ferrari. New York: Coward-McCann, 1942. Reprint. Washington, D.C.: U.S. Government Printing Office, 1984.

Droege, John A. *Freight Terminals and Trains.* New York: McGraw-Hill, 1912.

Dupuy, Trevor N. *Numbers, Predictions and War: Using History to Evaluate Combat Factors and Predict the Outcome of Battles.* Indianapolis: Bobbs-Merrill, 1979.

Eicholz, Dietrich. *Geschichte der deutschen Kriegswirtschaft 1939–1945.* Vol. 1, *1939–1941.* Berlin (East): Akadamie-Verlag, 1969.

_____. "Das Minette-Revier und die deutsche Montanindustrie: Zur Strategie der deutschen Monopole im zweiten Weltkrieg (1941–1942)." *Zeitschrift für Geschichtswissenschaft* 25 (1977): 816–38.

Erbé, René. *Die nationalsozialistische Wirtschaftspolitik im Lichte der modernen Theorie.* Zurich: Polygraphischer Verlag, 1958.

Erickson, John. *The Road to Berlin.* Boulder: Westview, 1983.

_____. *The Road to Stalingrad.* London: Weidenfeld and Nicolson, 1975. Reprint. Boulder: Westview, 1984.

Esenwein-Rothe, Ingeborg. *Die Wirtschaftsverbande von 1933 bis 1945.* Berlin: Duncker & Humblot, 1965.

Eucken, Walter. "On the Theory of the Centrally Administered Economy: An Analysis of the German Experiment." *Economica,* n.s. 15, pt. 1 (May 1948): 79–100.

Fabyanic, Thomas A. *Strategic Air Attack in the United States Air Force: A Case Study.* Manhattan, Kans.: Military Affairs/Aerospace Historian Publishing, 1976.

Facius, Friedrich. *Wirtschaft und Staat. Die Entwicklung der staatlichen Wirtschaftsverwaltung in Deutschland.* Boppard am Rhein: Boldt, 1959.

Ferrero, Guglielmo. *Peace and War.* Translated by B. Pritchard. New York: Macmillan, 1933.

Feuchter, Georg W. *Geschichte des Luftkrieges: Entwicklung und Zu-*

kunft. Bonn: Athenäum, 1954.

Fischer, Wolfram. *WASAG: Die Geschichte eines Unternehmens 1891–1966*. Berlin: Duncker & Humblot, 1966.

———. *Die Wirtschaftspolitik des Nationalsozialismus*. Hanover: Nidersächsische Landeszentrale für Politische Bildung, 1961.

Fisher, Irving. *The Making of Index Numbers*. Boston: Houghton, Mifflin, 1922.

Forstmeier, Friedrich, and Hans-Erich Volkmann, eds. *Kriegswirtschaft und Rüstung 1939–1945*. Düsseldorf: Droste, 1976.

Frankland, Noble. *Bomber Offensive: The Devastation of Europe*. New York: Ballantine, 1971.

———. *The Bombing Offensive Against Germany: Outlines and Perspectives*. London: Faber and Faber, 1965.

Freeman, Roger A. *The Mighty Eighth: A History of the U.S. Eighth Army Air Force*. Garden City: Doubleday, 1970.

———. *Mighty Eighth War Diary*. London: Jane's, 1981.

———. *Mighty Eighth War Manual*. London: Jane's, 1984.

Fremdling, Rainer. *Eisenbahnen und deutsches Wirtschaftswachstum, 1840–1879: Ein Beitrag zur Entwicklungstheorie und zur Theorie der Infrastruktur*. Dortmund: Gesellschaft für Westfälische Wirtschaftsgeschichte, 1975.

Friedensburg, Ferdinand. *Die Bergwirtschaft der Erde: Bodenschätze, Bergbau, Mineralversorgung der Einzelnen Länder*. Stuttgart: Ferdinand Enke, 1938.

———. *Die mineralischen Bodenschätze als weltpolitische und militärische Machtfaktoren*. Stuttgart: Ferdinand Enke, 1936.

Galland, Adolf. *The First and the Last*. Translated by Mervyn Savill. New York: Ballantine, 1968.

Ganzenmüller, Albert. "Eisenbahner und Eisenbahnerinnen!" *Die Reichsbahn*, Jahrgang 1945 (January), p. 1. Available in BA R5 Anh II/45.

Garlinski, Josef. *The Enigma War*. New York: Scribner's, 1980.

Gebhardt, Gerhard. *Ruhrbergbau. Geschichte, Aufbau, und Verflechtung seiner Gesellschaften und Organisationen*. Essen: Verlag Glückauf, 1957.

Geer, Johann S. *Der Markt der geschlossenen Nachfrage: Eine morphologische Studie über die Eisenkontingentierung in Deutschland 1937–1945*. Berlin: Duncker & Humblot, 1961.

Georg, Enno. *Die wirtschaftlichen Unternehmungen der SS*. Stuttgart: Deutsche Verlags-Anstalt, 1963.

Germany. Preussischen Ministers der Offentlichen Arbeiten, des Bayerischen Staatsministers für Verkehrsangelegenheiten, und der Eisenbahn-Zentralbehörden anderer Deutscher Bundesstaaten. *Das deutsche Eisenbahnwesen der Gegenwart*. 2 vols. Berlin: Reimar Hobbing, 1911.

Germany. Reichsverkehrministerium. "Albert Ganzenmüller." *Grossdeutscher Verkehr*, Jahrgang 1942, p. 259. Available in Bundesarchiv R5 Anh I/49.

_____. *Hundert Jahre Deutsche Eisenbahnen*. Leipzig: Verkehrswissen-schaftliche Lehrmittelgesellschaft, 1935.

Geyer, Michael. *Aufrüstung oder Sicherheit: Die Reichswehr in der Krise der Machtpolitik 1924–1936*. Wiesbaden: Steiner, 1980.

_____. *Deutsche Rüstungspolitik 1860–1980*. Frankfurt/Main: Suhrkamp, 1984.

Gillingham, John R. *Industry and Politics in the Third Reich: Ruhr Coal, Hitler and Europe*. New York: Columbia University Press, 1985.

Girbig, Werner. *1000 Tage über Deutschland: Die 8. Amerikanische Luft-flotte im 2. Weltkrieg*. Munich: Lehmans, 1964.

Goldsmith, R. W. "The Power of Victory: Munitions Output in World War II." *Military Affairs* 10 (1946): 69–72.

Golücke, Friedhelm. *Schweinfurt und der strategische Luftkrieg 1943*. Paderborn: Schöningh, 1980.

Gordon, David L., and Royden Dangerfield. *The Hidden Weapon: The Story of Economic Warfare*. New York: Harper, 1947.

Gottwaldt, Alfred B. *Deutsche Eisenbahnen im zweiten Weltkrieg: Rü-stung, Krieg und Eisenbahn*. Stuttgart: Franckh, 1983.

_____. *Deutsche Kriegslokomotiven 1939–45: Lokomotiven, Wagen, Panzerzüge und Geschütze*. Stuttgart: Franckh, 1973.

Gräfe, S. "Die Eisenbahn und das Militärwesen." *Eisenbahn-Jahrbuch* 10 (1972): 58–65.

Grainger, Leslie, and Joseph J. Gibson. *Coal Utilisation: Technology, Economics and Policy*. New York: Halstead, 1981.

Green, William. *Famous Bombers of the Second World War*. Vol. 1. New York: Doubleday, 1967.

Greenfield, Kent Roberts. *American Strategy in World War II: A Reconsid-eration*. Baltimore: Johns Hopkins University Press, 1970.

Gritzbach, Erich. *Herman Goering: The Man and His Work*. London: Hurst and Blackett, 1939. Reprint. New York: AMS Press, 1973.

Grunberger, Richard. *The Twelve Year Reich: A Social History of Nazi Germany 1933–1945*. New York: Holt, Rinehart, Winston, 1971.

Gumz, Wilhelm. *Die Kohle. Warenkunde für den Kohlenkaufmann*. Ber-lin: Verlag Deutsche Kohlenzeitung Wilhelm Ohst, 1943. Available in Bundesarchiv R 3/1930.

Hamilton, Nigel. *Master of the Battlefield: Monty's War Years 1942–1944*. New York: McGraw-Hill, 1983.

Hampe, Erich. "Luftschutztruppen Einst, Jetzt und in Zukunft." *Wehr-wissenschaftliche Rundschau*, Jahrgang 1959, pp. 455–65.

_____. "Technische Wehrmachthilfe: Ihre geschichtliche und ihre aktuelle Bedeutung." *Wehrwissenschaftliche Rundschau*, 1963, pp. 280–86.

_____. *Der Zivile Luftschutz im zweiten Weltkrieg: Dokumentation und Erfahrungsbericht über Aufbau und Einsatz*. Frankfurt/Main: Bernard & Graefe, 1963.

Hampe, Erich, and Dermot Bradley. *Die Unbekannte Armee: Die Tech-nischen Truppen im zweiten Weltkrieg*. Osnabrück: Biblio, 1979.

Hamsher, William. *Albert Speer: Victim of Nuremberg?* London: Frewin, 1970.

Hansell, Haywood S., Jr., *The Air Plan That Defeated Hitler.* Atlanta: Higgins-McArthur/Longino and Porter, 1972.

Hansen, Reimer. "Albert Speers Konflikt mit Hitler." *Geschichte in Wissenschaft und Unterricht* 17, no. 10 (October 1966): 596–621.

———. "Der Ungeklärte Fall Todt." *Geschichte in Wissenschaft und Unterricht* 181 (1967): 604–5.

Hardach, Gerd. *The First World War 1914–1918.* Berkeley: University of California Press, 1977.

Hardach, Karl. *The Political Economy of Germany in the Twentieth Century.* Berkeley: University of California Press, 1980.

Haufe, Helmut. *Die Geographische Struktur des deutschen Eisenbahnverkehrs.* Langensalza: Verlag von Julius Belz, 1931.

Harris, Arthur T. *Bomber Offensive.* London: Collins, 1947.

Hastings, Max. *Bomber Command.* New York: James Wade/Dial Press, 1979.

Heiman, Grover. *Aerial Photography: The Story of Aerial Mapping and Reconnaisance.* New York: Macmillan, 1972.

Heinkel, Ernst. *Stormy Life.* Translated by Jürgen Thorwald. New York: E. P. Dutton, 1956.

Henke, Ernst. *Das RWE nach seinen Geschäftberichten 1898–1948.* Essen: Girardet, 1948.

Herbst, Ludolf. *Der Totale Krieg und die Ordnung der Wirtschaft: Die Kriegswirtschaft im Spannungsfeld von Politik, Ideologie und Propaganda 1939–1945.* Stuttgart: Deutsche Verlags-Anstalt, 1982.

Herington, John A. *Air Power Over Europe, 1944–1945.* Canberra: Australian War Memorial, 1963.

———. *The Air War Against Germany and Italy, 1939–43.* Canberra: Australian War Memorial, 1954.

Heyl, John D. "Hitler's Economic Thought: A Reappraisal." *Central European History* 6, no. 1 (March 1973): 83–96.

Hilberg, Raul. "German Railroads/Jewish Souls." *Society* 14, no. 1 (November–December 1976): 60–74.

———. *Sonderzüge nach Auschwitz.* Mainz: Dumjahn, 1981.

Hinsley, Frances H. *British Intelligence in the Second World War.* 3 vols. London: Her Majesty's Stationery Office, 1979–1988.

Hitler, Adolf. *Illustrierte Beobachter,* Heft 39 (1929), pp. 490–92.

———. *Mein Kampf.* Translated by Ralph Mannheim. Boston: Houghton Mifflin, 1943.

Höhne, Heinz. *The Order of the Death's Head: The Story of Hitler's SS.* Translated by Richard Barry. New York: Ballantine, 1971.

Holley, Irving B., Jr. *Buying Aircraft: Material Procurement for the Army Air Forces.* Washington, D.C.: U.S. Government Printing Office, 1964.

Homze, Edward L. *Arming the Luftwaffe: The Reich Air Ministry and the German Aircraft Industry 1919–1939.* Lincoln, Nebraska: University of Nebraska Press, 1976.

_____. *Foreign Labor in Nazi Germany.* Princeton: Princeton University Press, 1967.

Huber, Ernst R. *Selbstverwaltung der Wirtschaft.* Stuttgart: W. Kohlhammer, 1958.

Hunke, Heinrich. *Grundzüge der deutschen Volks- und Wehrwirtschaft.* Berlin: Haude and Spener, 1943.

Hüttenberger, Peter. "Nationalsozialistische Polykratie." *Geschichte und Gesellschaft* 2 (1976): 417–42.

Hyde, H. Montgomery. *British Air Policy Between the Wars 1918–1939.* London: Heinemann, 1976.

Iklé, Fred Charles. *The Social Impact of Bomb Destruction.* Norman: University of Oklahoma Press, 1958.

Infield, Glen B. *Unarmed and Unafraid.* New York: Macmillan, 1970.

Irving, David. *The Rise and Fall of the Luftwaffe.* Boston: Little Brown, 1973.

Jäckel, Eberhard. *Hitlers Weltanschauung.* Translated by Herbert Arnold. Cambridge: Harvard University Press, 1981.

Jäger, Jorg-Johannes. *Die wirtschaftliche Abhängigkeit des Dritten Reiches vom Ausland dargestellt am Beispiel der Stahlindustrie.* Berlin: Berlin Verlag, 1969.

_____. "Sweden's Iron Ore Exports to Germany 1933–1944. A Reply to Rolf Karlbom's Article on the Same Subject." *Scandinavian Economic History Review* 15, nos. 1–2 (1967): 139–47.

Janis, Irving L. *Air War and Emotional Stress: Psychological Studies of Bombing and Civilian Defense.* New York: McGraw-Hill, 1957. Produced under the auspices of the Rand Corporation.

Janssen, Gregor. *Das Ministerium Speer: Deutschlands Rüstung im Krieg.* Frankfurt/Main: Ullstein, 1968.

Joachimsthaler, Anton. *Die Breitspurbahn Hitlers. Eine Dokumentation über die geplante transkontinentale 3-Meter-Breitspur-Eisenbahn der Jahre 1942–1945.* Freiburg: Eisenbahn-Kurier, 1981.

Johnson, Brian. *The Secret War.* New York: Methuen, 1978.

Jones, Reginald V. *The Wizard War: British Scientific Intelligence 1939–1945.* New York: Coward, McCann and Geohagen, 1978.

Jung, Hermann. *Die Ardennen-Offensive 1944–1945. Ein Beispiel für die Kriegsführung Hitlers.* Göttingen: Musterschmidt, 1971.

Kaldor, Nicholas. "The German War Economy." *Review of Economic Studies* 13 (1), no. 23 (1945–46): 33–52.

Karlbom, Rolf. "Sweden's Iron Ore Exports to Germany, 1933–1944." *Scandinavian Economic History Review* 15, nos. 1–2 (1967): 65–73.

Kehrl, Hans. *Krisenmanager im Dritten Reich: 6 Jahre Frieden-6 Jahre Krieg.* Düsseldorf: Droste, 1973.

Kindelberger, Charles P. "World War II Strategy." *Encounter* 51, no. 5 (November 1978): 39–42.

Kingston-McCloughry, Edgar J. *The Direction of War.* London: Jonathan Cape, 1955.

_____. *War in Three Dimensions.* London: Jonathan Cape, 1949.

Klass, Gerd von. *Albert Vögler*. Tübingen: Rainer Wunderlich Verlag, 1957.

Klee, Wolfgang. *Preussische Eisenbahngeschichte*. Stuttgart: Kohlhammer, 1982.

Kleinmann, Wilhelm. "Dr.-Ing. Julius Dorpmüller." *Die Reichsbahn* 29–30 (19–26 July 1939): 721–23.

Knorr, Klaus. *The War Potential of Nations*. Princeton: Princeton University Press, 1956.

Koch, Horst-Adalbert. *Flak. Die Geschichte der deutschen Flakartillerie und der Einsatz der Luftwaffenhelfer*. Bad Nauheim: Podzun, 1965.

Krauskopf, Robert W. "The Army and the Strategic Bomber." *Military Affairs* 22, no. 2 (Summer 1958): 85–94.

Kreidler, Eugen. *Die Eisenbahnen im Machtbereich der Achsenmächte während des zweiten Weltkrieges*. Göttingen: Musterschmidt, 1975.

Krüger, Peter. "Zu Hitlers Nationalsozialistischen Wirtschaftskentnissen." *Geschichte und Gesellschaft* 6 (1980): 263–83.

Kube, Alfred. *Pour le Mérite und Hakenkreuz: Hermann Göring im Dritten Reich*. Munich: Oldenbourg, 1986.

Kurowski, Franz. *Der Luftkrieg über Deutschland*. Düsseldorf: Econ, 1977.

Lee, Asher. *Goering: Air Leader*. London: Duckworth, 1972.

Lewin, Ronald. *Ultra Goes to War*. New York: Pocket Books, 1980.

Lichtenstein, Heiner. *Mit der Reichsbahn in den Tod: Massentransporte in den Holocaust*. Cologne: Bund-Verlag, 1985.

———. "Räder rollen für den Mord: Die Deutsche Reichsbahn und der Holocaust." *Tribune* 21, no. 82 (1982): 86–99.

Liebl, Toni, et al. *Offizieller Jubilaumsband der Deutschen Bundesbahn: 150 Jahre deutschen Eisenbahnen*. Munich: Eisenbahn-Lehrbuch Verlagsgesellschaft, 1985.

Lochner, Louis P., ed. and trans. *The Goebbels Diaries 1942–1943*. New York: Doubleday, 1948.

Longmate, Norman. *The Bombers: The RAF Offensive Against Germany 1939–1945*. London: Hutchinson, 1983.

Ludwig, Karl-Heinz. "Die deutsche Kriegs- und Rüstungswirtschaft 1939–1945: Ein Bericht über den Forschungsstand." *Militärgeschichtliche Mitteilungen* 2 (1968): 135–55.

———. *Technik und Ingenieure im Dritten Reich*. Düsseldorf: Athenäum-Droste, 1979.

Lumer, Hyman. *War, Economy and Crises*. New York: International, 1954.

Lüthgen, Helmut. *Das Rheinisch-Westfälische Kohlensyndikat in der Vorkriegs-, Kriegs- und Nachkriegszeit und seine Hauptprobleme*. Leipzig: A. Deichert, 1926.

Lutz, Walther. *Verkehrs Entwicklung in Deutschland*. Leipzig: A. G. Teubner, 1910.

Lytton, Henry D. "Bombing Policy in the Rome and Pre-Normandy Invasion Aerial Campaigns of World War II: Bridge-Bombing Strategy Vindicated and Railyard Bombing Strategy Invalidated." *Military Affairs* 47 (April 1983): 53–58.

Macdonald, Charles. *A Time for Trumpets.* New York: Morrow, 1984.

MacIsaac, David. "Reflections on Air Power in World War II." *Air Force* 13, no. 9 (September 1980) 128–39.

———. *Strategic Bombing in World War II: The Story of the Strategic Bombing Survey.* New York: Garland, 1976.

———. "Voices from the Central Blue." In *Makers of Modern Strategy from Machiavelli to the Nuclear Age*, edited by Peter Paret, pp. 624–47. Princeton: Princeton University Press, 1986.

Manvell, Roger, and Heinrich Fraenkel. *Goering.* New York: Simon and Schuster, 1962.

Markmann, Fritz, ed. *Die deutschen Wasserstrassen.* Heidelberg: Vowinckel, 1938.

Medlicott, William N. *The Economic Blockade.* 2 vols. London: Her Majesty's Stationery Office, 1952, 1959. Reprint. Nendeln, Liechtenstein: Kraus, 1978.

Meinck, Gerhard. *Hitler und die deutsche Aufrüstung 1933–1937.* Wiesbaden: F. Steiner, 1959.

Mellenthin, Friedrich W. von. *Panzer Battles.* Translated by H. Betzler. Norman: University of Oklahoma Press, 1956.

Mellor, Roy E. H. *German Railways: A Study in Historical Geography of Transport.* Aberdeen: Department of Geography, University of Aberdeen, 1979.

Mendershausen, Horst. *The Economics of War.* New York: Prentice-Hall, 1941.

Messenger, Charles. *Bomber Harris and the Strategic Bombing Offensive, 1939–1945.* London: Arms and Armour Press, 1984.

Messerschmidt, Wolfgang. *Taschenbuch Deutsche Lokomotivfabriken.* Stuttgart: Franckh, 1977.

Middlebrook, Martin. *The Nuremberg Raid: The Worst Night of the War, 31 March 1944.* New York: Morrow, 1974.

Militärgeschichtliches Forschungsamt. *Deutsche Militärgeschichte.* 6 vols. Munich: Bernard & Graefe, 1983; Herrsching: Pawlak, 1983.

Milward, Alan S. "Could Sweden Have Stopped the Second World War?" *Scandinavian Economic History Review* 15, no. 15 (1967): 127–38.

———. *The German Economy at War.* London: Athlone Press, 1965.

———. *The New Order and the French Economy.* London: Oxford University Press, 1970.

———. *War, Economy and Society 1939–1945.* Berkeley: University of California Press, 1979.

Mitchell, Brian R. *European Historical Statistics 1750–1970.* New York: Columbia University Press, 1975.

Moscow Institut Marksizma-Leninizma. *Geschichte des Grossen Vaterländischen Krieges der Sovjetunion.* 6 vols. Berlin: Deutscher Militärverlag, 1968.

Mosley, Leonard. *The Reich Marshal: A Biography of Hermann Goering*. Garden City: Doubleday, 1974.

Müller, Max, "Der plötzliche und mysteriöse Tod Dr. Fritz Todt." *Geschichte in Wissenschaft und Unterrricht* 18 (1967): 602–4.

Murray, Williamson. *Strategy for Defeat: The Luftwaffe 1933–1945*. Maxwell Air Force Base, Ala.: Air University Press, 1983.

Musgrove, Gordon. *Pathfinder Force: A History of 8 Group*. London: Macdonald and Jane's, 1976.

Nathan, Otto. *The Nazi Economic System: Germany's Mobilization for War*. Durham, N.C.: Duke University Press, 1944.

Neal, Alfred C. ed. *Introduction to War Economics*. Chicago: Irwin, 1942.

Neumann, Franz. *Behemoth: The Structure and Practice of National Socialism 1933–1944*. Rev. ed. New York: Oxford University Press, 1944.

Obermayer, Horst J. *Taschenbuch der Eisenbahn*. Vol. 1, *Fahrzeuge und Bahntechnik*. Vol. 2, *Bahnanlagen und Fahrdienst*. Stuttgart: Franckh, 1975, 1977.

O'Brien, Patrick K. *The New Economic History of Railways*. New York: St. Martin's, 1977.

———. *Railways in the Economic Development of Western Europe 1830–1914*. New York: St. Martin's, 1983.

Orlow, Dietrich. *History of the Nazi Party*. 2 vols. Pittsburgh: University of Pittsburgh Press, 1969.

Ostendorf, Rolf. *Eisenbahn Knotenpunkt Ruhrgebiet*. Stuttgart: Motorbuch, 1979.

Ottmann, Karl, and Hans Joachim Ritzau. *Deutsche Eisenbahn-Geschichte*. Landsberg: Pürgen, 1975.

Overy, Richard James. *The Air War, 1939–1945*. London: Europa, 1980.

———. *Goering: The "Iron Man."* London: Routledge and Kegan Paul, 1984.

———. "Heavy Industry and the State in Nazi Germany: The Reichswerke Crisis." *European History Quarterly* 15 (1985): 313–40.

———. "Hitler's War and the German Economy: A Reinterpretation." *Economic History Review* 35 (1982): 272–91.

———. *The Nazi Economic Recovery 1932–1938*. London: The Macmillan Press, 1982.

Pahl, Walther. *Weltkampf um Rohstoffe*. Leipzig: Wilhelm Goldmann, 1939.

Perera, Guido R. *Leaves from My Book of Life*. Vol. 2, *The Washington and War Years*. Boston: Stinehour Press, 1975.

Persico, Joseph E. *Piercing the Reich. The Penetration of Nazi Germany by American Secret Agents during World War II*. New York: Viking, 1979.

Petzina, Dietmar. *Autarkiepolitik im Dritten Reich. Der Nationalsozialistischen Vierjahresplan*. Stuttgart: Deutsche Verlags-Anstalt, 1968.

———. "Hauptprobleme der deutschen Wirtschaftspolitik 1932–1933." *Vierteljahrshefte für Zeitgeschichte* 15, no. 1 (January 1967): 18–55.

———. "Hitler und die Deutsche Industrie. Ein kommentierter Literatur-

und Forschungsbericht." *Geschichte in Wissenschaft und Unterricht* 17 (1966): 482–91.

————. "Die Mobilisierung deutscher Arbeitskräfte vor und während des zweiten Weltkrieges." *Vierteljahrshefte für Zeitgeschichte* 18, no. 4 (October 1970): 443–55.

Piekalkiewicz, Janusz. *Die Deutsche Reichsbahn im Zweiten Weltkrieg.* Stuttgart: Motorbuch, 1979.

Pigou, Arthur C. *The Political Economy of War.* London: Macmillan, 1921, 1940.

Pogue, Forest C. *The Supreme Command.* Washington, D.C.: U.S. Government Printing Office, 1954.

Postan, Michael M. *British War Production.* London: Her Majesty's Stationery Office, 1953. Reprint. Liechtenstein: Kraus, 1975.

Pounds, Norman J. G. *The Ruhr: A Study in Historical and Economic Geography.* Bloomington: Indiana University Press, 1952. Reprint. Westport, Conn.: Greenwood Press, 1968.

Pounds, Norman J. G., and William N. Parker. *Coal and Steel in Western Europe: The Influence of Resources and Techniques on Production.* Bloomington: Indiana University Press, 1957.

Powys-Lybbe, Ursula. *The Eye of Intelligence.* London: Kimber, 1983.

Prest, Alan R. *War Economics of Primary Producing Countries.* Cambridge: Cambridge University Press, 1948.

Price, Alfred. *Instruments of Darkness: The History of Electronic Warfare.* London: Macdonald and Jane's, 1978.

Rauschning, Hermann. *Gespräche mit Hitler.* New York: Europa, 1940.

Regul, Rudolf. *Der Kohlenbergbau des vereinigten Wirtschaftsgebietes.* Essen: Verlag Glückauf, 1949.

Rehbein, Elfried, et al. *Deutsche Eisenbahnen 1835–1985.* Berlin: Transpress, 1985.

Das Reich. Nr. 44, 31 October 1942, p. 1; Nr. 47, 22 November 1942, p. 10.

Richards, Denis. *Portal of Hungerford.* London: Heinemann, 1977.

Richardson, Helen R. *Railroads in Defense and War.* Washington, D.C.: Association of American Railroads, 1953.

Riedel, Matthias. *Eisen und Kohle für das Dritte Reich: Paul Pleigers Stellung in der NS-Wirtschaft.* Göttingen: Musterschmidt, 1973.

————. "Die Eisenerzversorgung der deutschen Hüttenindustrie zu Beginn des Zweiten Weltkrieges." *Vierteljahresschrift für Sozial- und Wirtschaftgeschichte* 58, no. 4 (Fourth Quarter 1971): 482–96.

Ritzau, Hans J., and Werner Mertl. *Das Kursbuch- und Fahrplanwesen der deutschen Eisenbahnen.* Landsberg/Lech: Ritzau KG Verlag für Eisenbahngeschichte, 1978.

Robbins, Michael. "The Third Reich and Its Railways." *Journal of Transport History* 2, no. 2 (1979): 83–90.

Robertson, Bruce. *Lancaster—The Story of a Famous Bomber.* Hertfordshire: Harleyford, 1964.

Robertson, Esmond M. *Hitler's Pre-War Policy and Military Plans 1933–1939.* New York: Citadel Press, 1967.

Rohland, Walter. *Bewegte Zeiten: Erinnerungen eines Eisenhüttenmannes.* Stuttgart: Seewald, 1978.

Roosevelt, Kermit. *War Report of the OSS (Office of Strategic Services).* Vol. 1. New York: Walker, 1976.

———. *The Overseas Targets: War Report of the OSS.* Vol. 2. New York: Walker, 1976.

Rostow, Walt W. *Pre-Invasion Bombing Strategy: General Eisenhower's Decision of March 25, 1944.* Austin: University of Texas Press, 1981.

Rumpf, Hans. *The Bombing of Germany.* Translated by Edward Fitzgerald. New York: Holt, Rinehart and Winston, 1963.

Rust, Kenn C. *Eighth Air Force Story.* Temple City, Calif.: Historical Aviation Album, 1978.

———. *Fifteenth Air Force Story.* Temple City, Calif.: Historical Aviation Album, 1976.

Salweski, Michael. "Die bewaffnete Macht im Dritten Reich 1933–1939." In *Deutsche Militärgeschichte,* edited by Militärgeschichtliches Forschungsamt, 4:13–286. Munich: Bernard & Graefe, 1983; Herrsching: Pawlak, 1983.

———. *Die Deutsche Seekriegsleitung, 1933–1945.* Vol. 2, *1942–1945.* Munich: Bernard & Graefe, 1975.

Sarter, Adolf. *Die Deutschen Eisenbahnen im Kriege.* Stuttgart, Deutsche Verlags-Anstalt, 1930.

———. *Landesverteidigung und Eisenbahn.* Bad Hersfeld: Gerstenberg, 1955.

Saward, Dudley. *"Bomber" Harris: The Authorised Biography.* London: Cassell, 1984.

Schaffer, Ronald. *Wings of Judgment: American Bombing in World War II.* New York: Oxford, 1985.

Schausberger, Norbert. *Rüstung in Österreich 1938–1945.* Vienna: Hollinek, 1970.

Schmidt, Mathias. *Albert Speer: Das Ende eines Mythos.* Munich: Goldmann, 1983.

———. *Albert Speer: The End of a Myth.* Translated by Joachim Neugroschel. New York: St. Martin's, 1984.

Schnatz, Helmut. *Der Luftkrieg im Raum Koblenz 1944–1945: Eine Darstellung seines Verlaufs, seiner Auswirkungen und Hintergründe.* Boppard: Harald Boldt, 1981.

Schoenbaum, David. *Hitler's Social Revolution.* New York: Norton, 1980.

Schultze-Rhonhof, Friedrich C. *Die Verkehrsströme der Kohle im Raum der Bundesrepublik Deutschland 1913–1957.* Bad Godesberg: Bundesanstalt für Landeskunde und Raumforschung, 1964.

Schweitzer, Arthur. *Big Business in The Third Reich.* Bloomington: Indiana University Press, 1964.

Schymanietz, Peter A. *Die Organisation der deutschen Eisenbahnen*

1835–1975. Freiburg: Eisenbahn-Kurier, 1977.

Scotland, R. "Rückwirkungen der Kriegszerstörungen und Betriebsein-schränkungen auf den Verkehr der Deutschen Reichsbahn in den Jahren 1945–1946." Ph.D. dissertation, Technische Hochschule Hannover, 1949.

Seebold, Gustav-Hermann. *Ein Stahlkonzern im Dritten Reich: Der Bochumer Verein 1927–1945.* Wuppertal: Hammer, 1981.

Seidler, Franz W. *Fritz Todt: Baumeister des Dritten Reiches.* Munich: Herbig, 1986.

Sherry, Michael S. *The Rise of American Air Power: The Creation of Armageddon.* New Haven: Yale University Press, 1987.

75 Jahre Dortmunder Hafen 1899–1974. Dortmund: Dortmunder Hafen und Eisenbahn AG, 1974.

Simon, Gerhard. "Verkehrsausweitung, Verkehrslenkung und Transportentflechtung in der deutschen Kriegswirtschaft des zweiten Weltkriegs." *Jahrbuch für Sozialwissenschaft* 20 (1969): 419–41.

Slessor, Sir John. *The Central Blue.* New York: Praeger, 1957.

Smith, Malcom. *British Air Strategy Between the Wars.* London: Oxford University Press, 1984.

Smith, Richard H. *OSS: The Secret History of America's First Central Intelligence Agency.* Berkeley: University of California Press, 1972.

Speer, Albert. *Inside the Third Reich.* Translated by Richard and Clara Winston. New York: Macmillan, 1970.

———. *The Slave State: Heinrich Himmler's Masterplan for SS Supremacy.* Translated by Joachim Neugroschel. London: Weidenfeld and Nicolson, 1981.

———. *Spandau: The Secret Diaries.* Translated by Richard and Clara Winston. New York: Macmillan, 1976.

———. *Technik und Macht.* Edited by Adelbert Reif. Esslingen: Bechtle, 1979.

Spiegel, Henry William. *The Economics of Total War.* New York: Appleton-Century, 1942.

Stanley, Roy M. *World War II Photo Intelligence.* New York: Scribner's, 1981.

Steller, Paul. *Führende Männer des Rheinisch-Westfälischen Wirtschaftslebens.* Berlin: R. Hobbing, 1930.

Stieler, Karl. *Aus meinem Leben: Ein Stuck deutscher Eisenbahngeschichte.* Cologne: Röhrig-Verlag, 1950.

Stolper, Gustav, Karl Hauser, and Knut Borchart. *The German Economy: 1870 to the Present.* Translated by Toni Stolper. New York: Harcourt, Brace and World, 1967.

Streetly, Martin. *Confound and Destroy: 100 Group and the Bomber Support Campaign.* London: Macdonald and Jane's, 1978.

Strössenreuther, Hugo, ed. *Eisenbahnen und Eisenbahner zwischen 1941 und 1945.* Vols. 3, 4, 5. Frankfurt/Main: Redactor, 1973.

Stumpf, Berthold. *Geschichte der deutschen Eisenbahnen.* Mainz: Verlagsanstalt Huhig and Dreyer, 1960.

Sweetman, John. *The Dams Raid: Epic or Myth. Operation Chastise.* London: Jane's, 1982.

———. *Schweinfurt: Disaster in the Skies.* New York, Ballantine, 1971.

Syrett, David. "The Secret War and the Historians." *Armed Forces and Society* 9, no. 2 (Winter 1983): 293–328.

Sywotek, Jutta. *Mobilmachung für den Totalen Krieg.* Opladen: West Deutscher Verlag, 1976.

Tedder, Lord. *With Prejudice.* London: Cassell, 1966.

Terraine, John. *A Time for Courage: The Royal Air Force in the European War, 1939–1945.* New York: Macmillan, 1985.

Thomas, George. *Geschichte der deutschen Wehr- und Rüstungs Wirtschaft (1919–1944/45).* Edited by Wolfgang Birkenfeld. Boppard: Boldt, 1966.

Thompson, Harry C., and Lida Mayo. *The Ordnance Department: Procurement and Supply.* Washington, D.C.: U.S. Government Printing Office, 1960.

Tipton, Frank B., Jr. *Regional Variations in the Economic Development of Germany During the Nineteenth Century.* Middletown, Conn.: Wesleyan University Press, 1976.

Treue, Wilhelm. *Die Feuer Verlöschen Nie: August Thyssen Hütte 1926–1966.* Düsseldorf: Econ, 1969.

———. *Die Geschichte der Ilseder Hütte.* Munich: Bruchmann, 1961.

———. "Hitlers Denkschrift zum Vierjahresplan 1936." *Vierteljahresheft für Zeitgeschichte* 3 (1955): 184–210.

———. "Politische Kohle im ersten und zweiten Weltkrieg." *Welt als Geschichte* 11 (1951): Heft 4, 185–202.

———. Gunther Frede. *Wirtschaft und Politik 1933–1945.* Brunswick: 1953.

Turner, Henry Ashby, Jr. "Fascism and Modernization." *World Politics* 24, no. 4 (July 1972): 547–64.

———. *German Big Business and the Rise of Hitler.* New York: Oxford University Press, 1985.

———, ed. *Hitler: Memoires of a Confidant.* Translated by Ruth Hein. New Haven: Yale University Press, 1985.

———. "Hitler's Secret Pamphlet for Industrialists." *Journal of Modern History* 40, no. 3 (September 1968): 348–74.

Ulrich, Johann. *Der Luftkrieg über Österreich 1939–1945.* Vienna: Österreichischer Bundesverlag, 1967.

Verein Deutscher Eisenhüttenleute. *100 Jahre VDE, 1860–1960.* Düsseldorf, Stahleisen, 1960.

Verrier, Anthony. *The Bomber Offensive.* New York: Macmillan, 1969.

Volkmann, Hans-Erich. "L'importance économique de la Lorraine pour le IIIe Reich." *Revue d'histoire de la Deuxième Guerre Mondiale* 120, no. 198 (1980): 69–93.

———. "Die NS-Wirtschaft in Vorbereitung des Krieges." In *Das Deutsche*

Reich und der Zweite Weltkrieg, edited by Wilhelm Deist, 1:177–368. Stuttgart: Deutsche Verlags-Anstalt, 1979.

———. "Zur Interdependenz von Politik, Wirtschaft und Rüstung in NS-Staat." *Militärgeschichtliche Mitteilungen* 1 (1974): 161–72.

VRB, Information. "Gustav Dilli." *Die Bundesbahn,* no. 14 (December 1971): 5.

Wagenführ, Rolf. *Die Deutsche Industrie im Kriege 1939–45.* Berlin: Duncker & Humblot, 1954.

Wagner, Alfred. "Die Rüstung im 'Dritten Reich' unter Albert Speer." *Technikgeschichte* 33 (1966): 205–27.

Walz, Werner. *Deutschlands Eisenbahnen 1835–1985.* Stuttgart: Motorbuch, 1985.

Weber, Hans-Adolf. *Betriebsdienst der Deutschen Reichsbahn.* Berlin: Verlag Beamtenpresse, 1944.

Webster, Sir Charles, and Noble Frankland. *The Strategic Air Offensive Against Germany 1939–1945.* 4 vols. London: Her Majesty's Stationery Office, 1961.

Wehde-Textor, Otto. "Die Leistungen der Deutschen Reichsbahn im zweiten Weltkrieg." *Archiv für Eisenbahnwesen,* no. 71 (1961): 1–47.

Wehner, Heinz. "Der Einsatz der Eisenbahnen für die verbrecherischen Ziele des faschistischen deutschen Imperialismus im 2. Weltkrieg." Ph.D. dissertation, Hochschule für Verkehrswesen, Dresden, 1961.

Weigley, Russell F. *Eisenhower's Lieutenants: The Campaigns of France and Germany, 1944–1945.* Bloomington: Indiana University Press, 1981.

Weir, Gary E. "The Imperial Naval Office and the Problem of Armor Prices in Germany, 1897–1914." *Military Affairs* 48, no. 2 (April 1984): 62–65.

Welter, Erich. *Falsch und richtig Planen: Eine kritische Studie über die deutsche Wirtschaftslenkung im zweiten Weltkrieg.* Heidelberg: Quelle and Mezer, 1954.

Westwood, John N. *Railways at War.* San Diego: Howell-North, 1981.

Weyres von Levetzow, Hans-Joachim. "Die deutsche Rüstungswirtschaft von 1942 bis zum Ende des Krieges." Ph.D. dissertation, University of Munich, 1975.

Wiedenfeld, Kurt. *Die Eisenbahn im Wirtschaftsleben.* Berlin: Springer, 1938.

Winterbotham, Frederick W. *The Ultra Secret.* New York: Dell, 1975.

Wisotzky, Klaus. *Der Ruhrbergbau im Dritten Reich: Studien zur Sozialpolitik im Ruhrbergbau und zum sozialen Verhalten der Bergleute in den Jahren 1933 bis 1939.* Düsseldorf: Schwann, 1983.

Wittekind, Kurt. "Aus 20 Jahren deutscher Wehrwirtschaft 1925–1945." *Wehrkunde* 6 (1957): 495–504.

Wolf, Werner. *Luftangriffe auf die deutsche Industrie 1942–1945.* Munich: Universitas, 1985.

Woolf, Stuart J. *The Nature of Fascism.* London: 1968.

Woolston, Maxine B. (Sweezy). *The Structure of the Nazi Economy.* New

York: Russell and Russell, 1968.

Zilbert, Edward R. *Albert Speer and the Nazi Ministry of Arms: Economic Institutions and Industrial Production in the German War Economy.* Rutherford, N.J.: Fairleigh Dickinson University Press, 1981.

Zuckerman, Solly. *From Apes to Warlords.* New York: Harper and Row, 1978.

Zumpe, Lotte, and Helga Nussbaum, eds. *Wirtschaft und Staat in Deutschland 1933 bis 1945.* Berlin: Akademie-Verlag, 1979.

Index